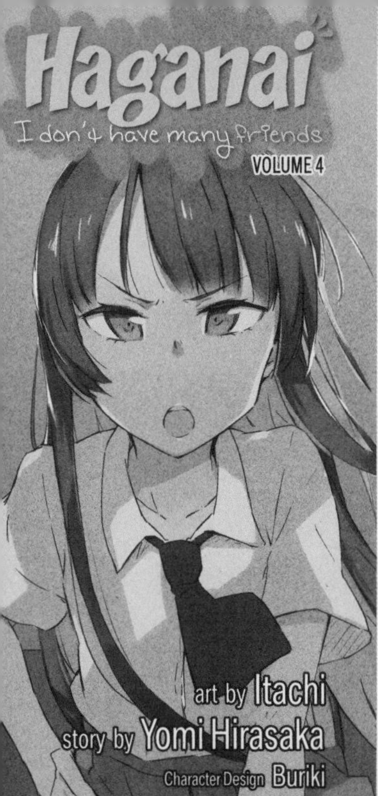
Haganai
I don't have many friends
VOLUME 4
art by Itachi
story by Yomi Hirasaka
Character Design Buriki

STAFF CREDITS

translation Ryan Peterson
adaptation Ysabet Reinhardt MacFarlane
lettering Roland Amago
layout Bambi Eloriaga-Amago
cover design Nicky Lim
copy editor Shanti Whitesides
editor Adam Arnold

publisher Jason DeAngelis
Seven Seas Entertainment

HAGANAI: I DON'T HAVE MANY FRIENDS VOL. 4

READING DIRECTIONS

This book reads from *right to left*, Japanese style. If this is your first time reading manga, you start reading from the top right panel on each page and take it from there. If you get lost, just follow the numbered diagram here. It may seem backwards at first, but you'll get the hang of it! Have fun!!

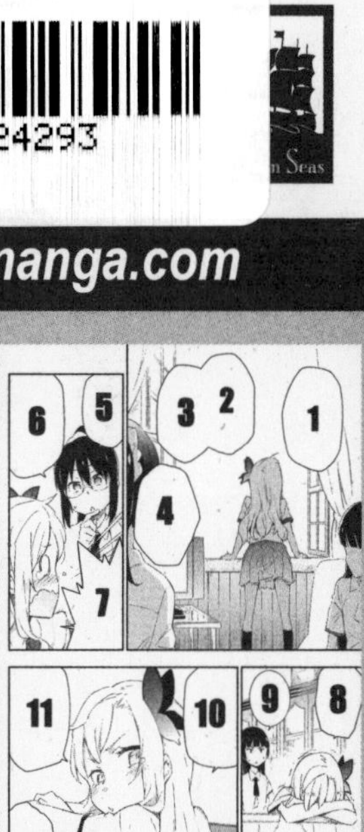
1
2
3
4
5
6
7
8
9
10
11
12

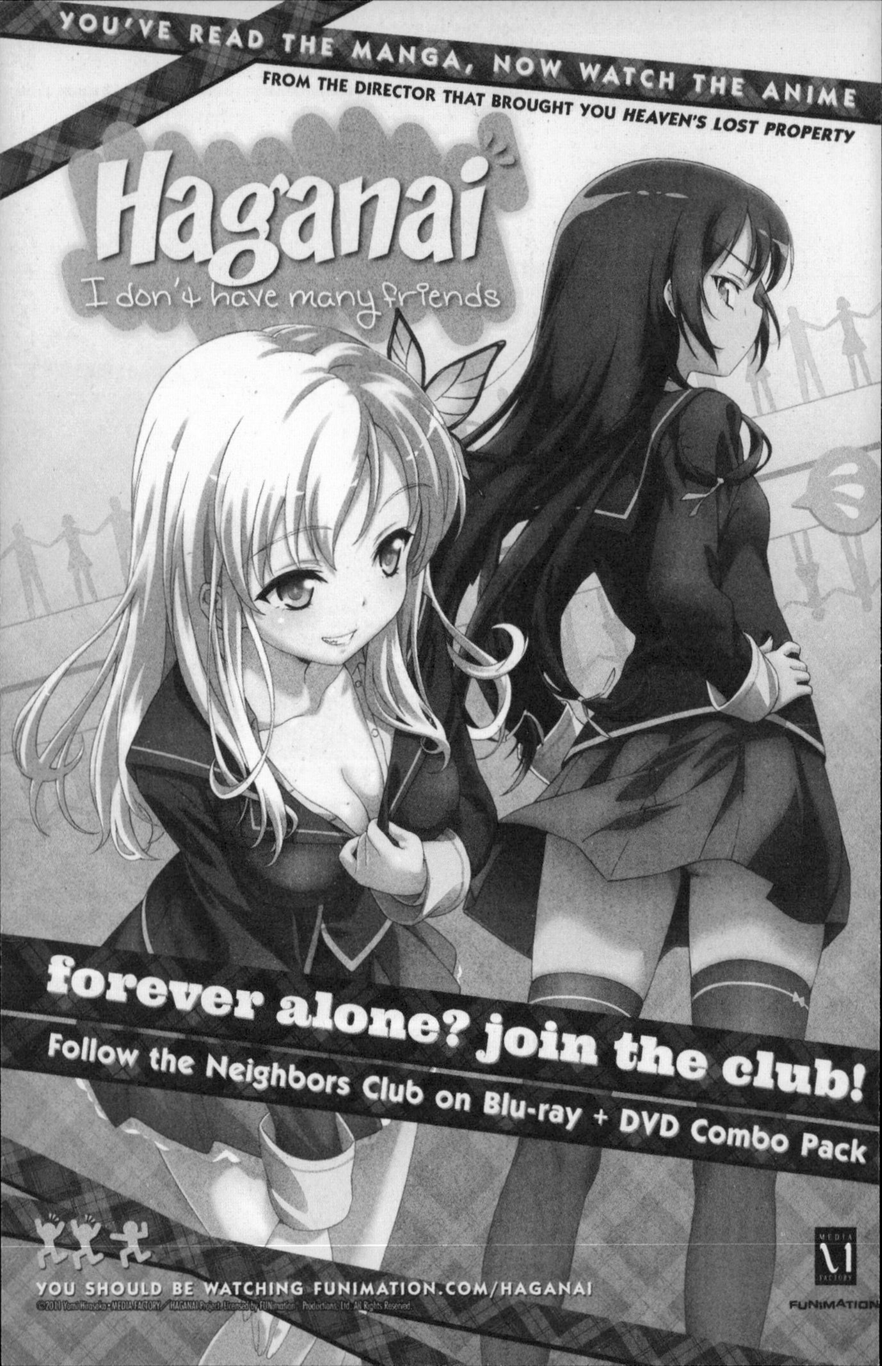
YOU'VE READ THE MANGA, NOW WATCH THE ANIME
FROM THE DIRECTOR THAT BROUGHT YOU HEAVEN'S LOST PROPERTY
Haganai
I don't have many friends
forever alone? join the club!
Follow the Neighbors Club on Blu-ray + DVD Combo Pack
YOU SHOULD BE WATCHING FUNIMATION.COM/HAGANAI
©2011 Yomi Hirasaka • MEDIA FACTORY / HAGANAI Project. Licensed by FUNimation Productions, Ltd. All Rights Reserved.
MEDIA FACTORY
FUNIMATION

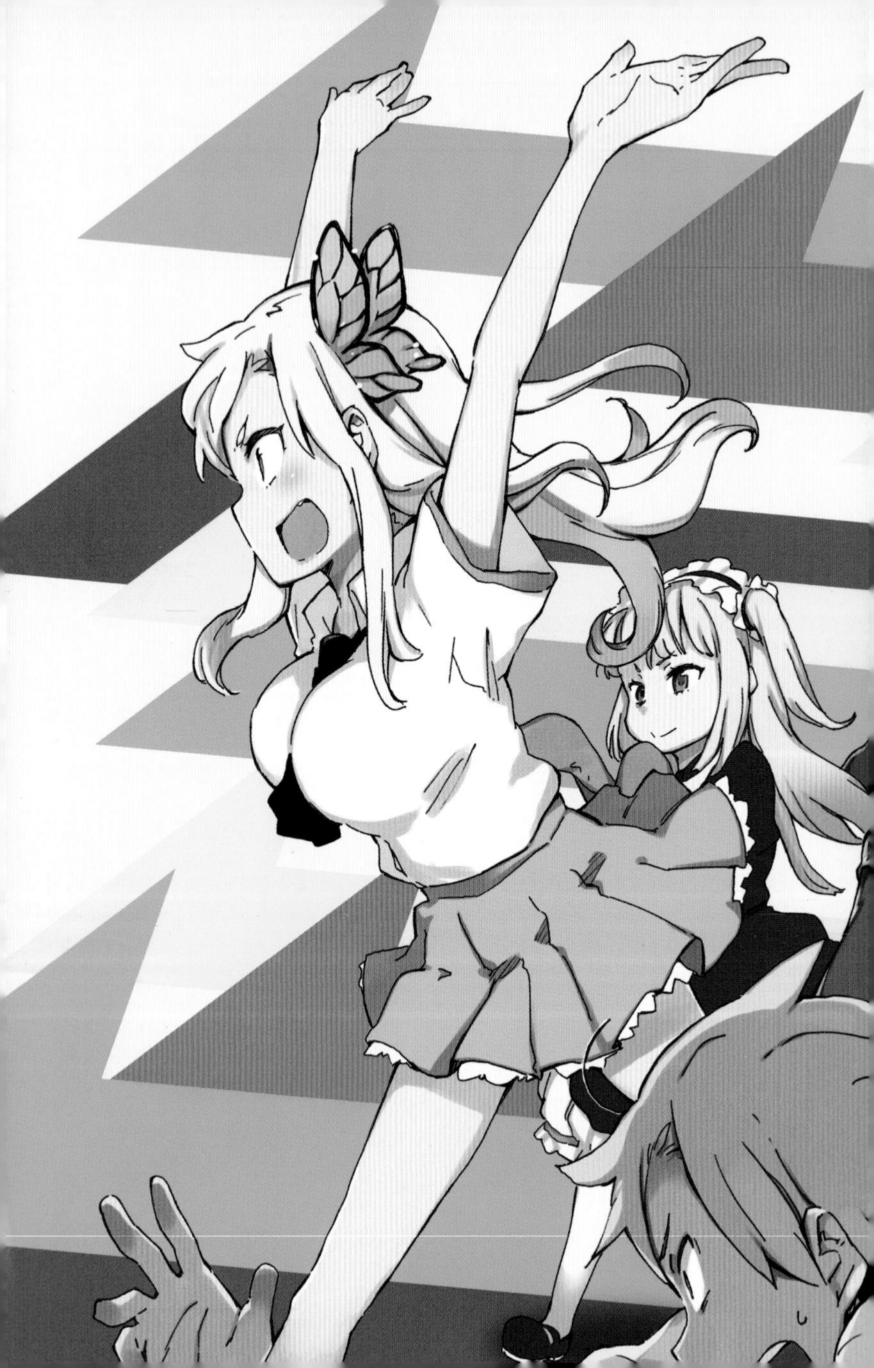

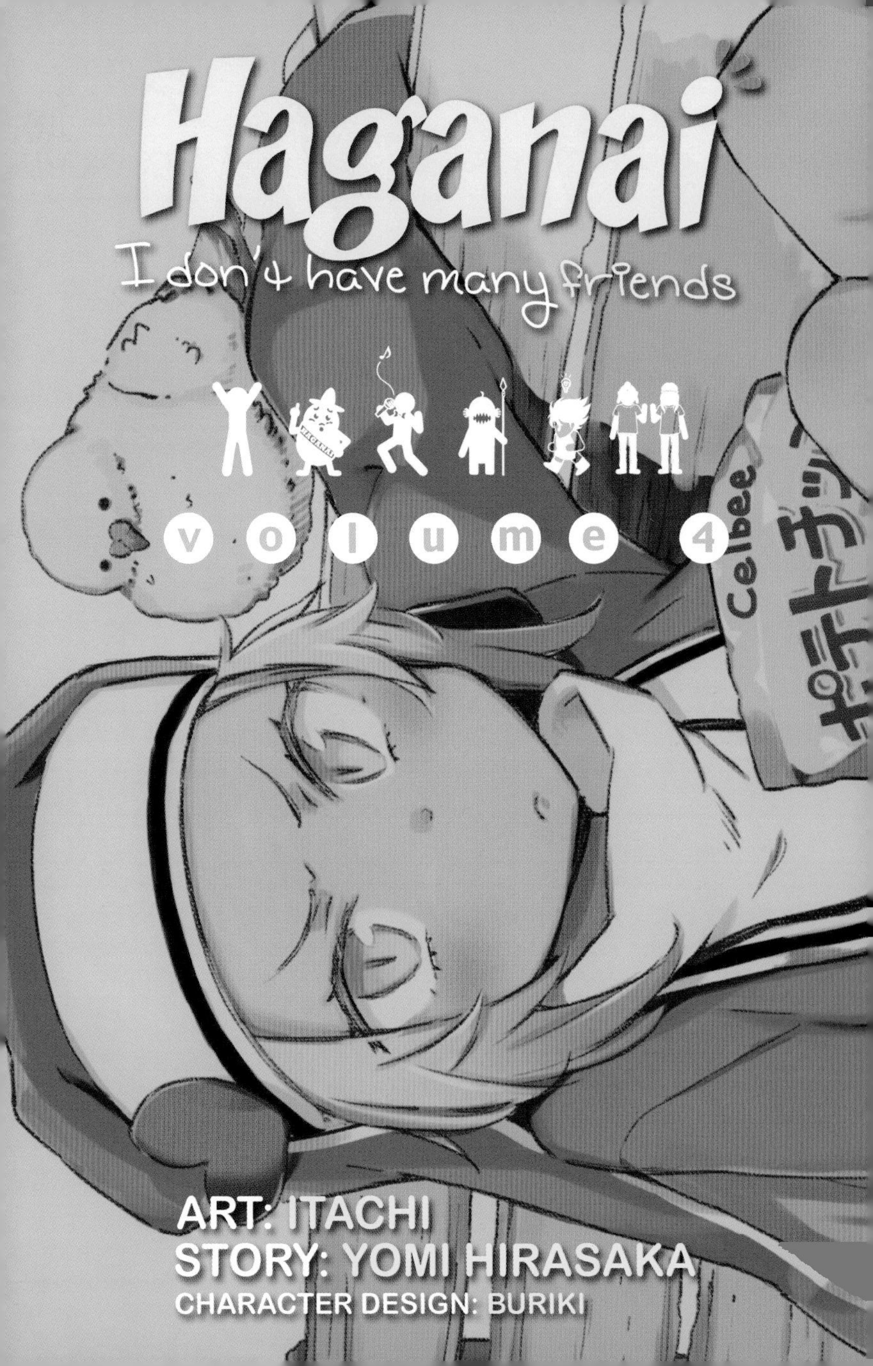
HAGANAI
Celbee

Haganai

I don't have many friends

volume 4

ART: ITACHI
STORY: YOMI HIRASAKA
CHARACTER DESIGN: BURIKI

HAGANAI

MEET THE CAST

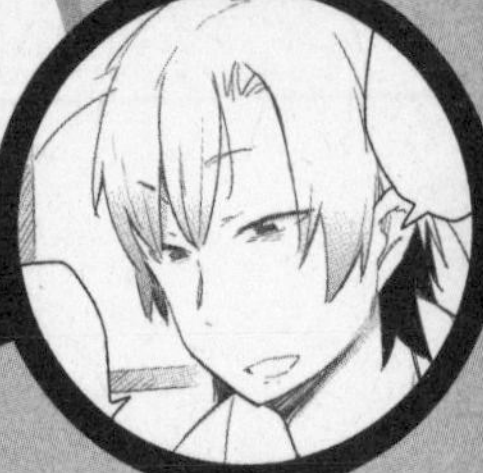

羽瀬川 小鷹
Hasegawa Kodaka

A second-year student at Saint Chronica Academy. He looks like a thug. Doesn't have many friends.

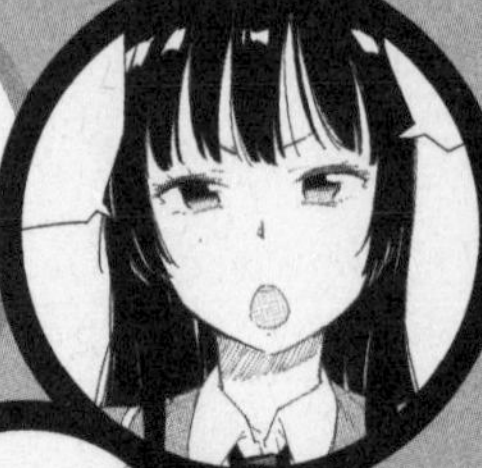

三日月 夜空
Mikazuki Yozora

Kodaka's classmate. Other than her looks, she doesn't have much going for her. Doesn't have many friends.

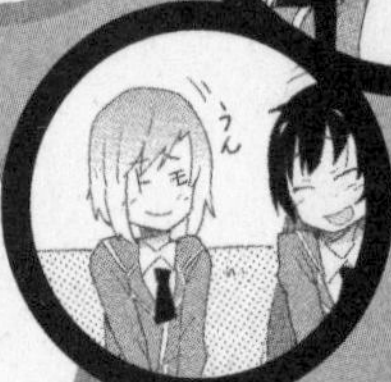

トモちゃん
Tomo-chan

Yozora's "air friend."

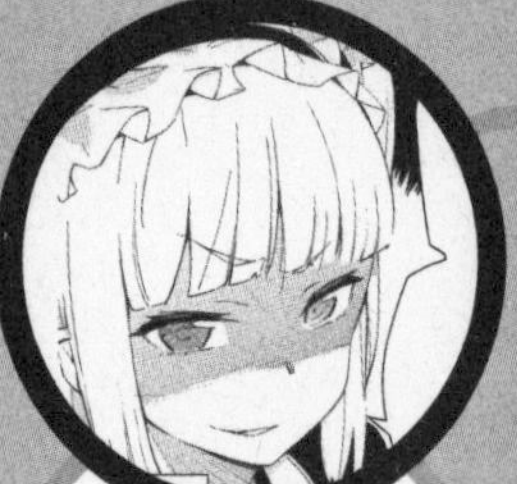

羽瀬川 小鳩
Hasegawa Kobato

Kodaka's kid sister. She's a student at Saint Chronica Academy's middle school, and she has some...unfortunate ideas. Her unusual style of clothing and speech stems from her persona as a vampire.

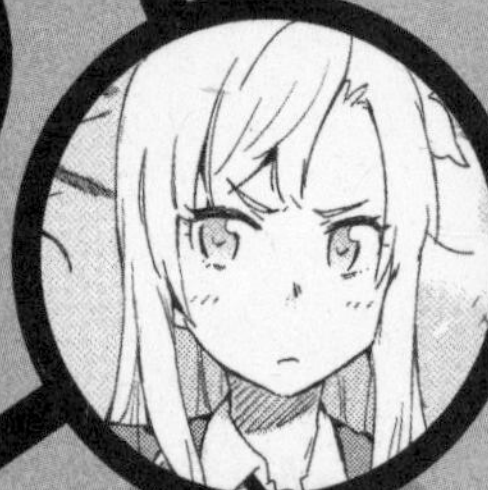

柏崎 星奈
Kashiwazaki Sena

The daughter of Saint Chronica Academy's director. Perfect in every way... except for her personality. Doesn't have many friends.

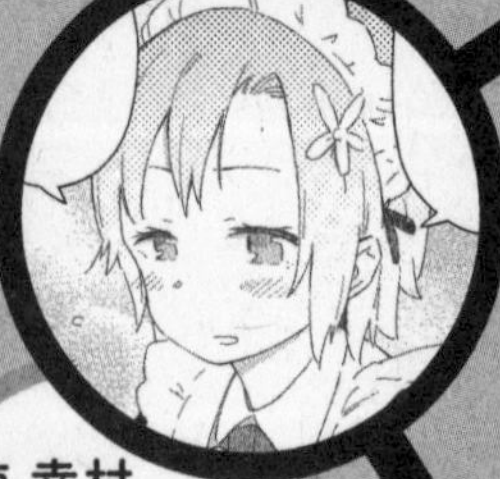

楠 幸村
Kusunoki Yukimura

A first-year student at Saint Chronica Academy. A kouhai to the rest of the club. Don't be fooled by the maid costume--Yukimura dreams of being a "fine Japanese boy."

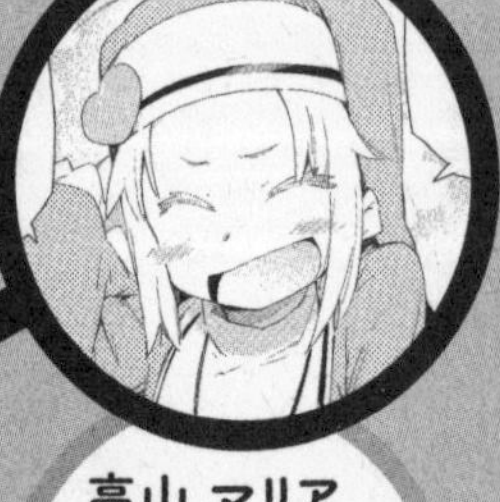

高山 マリア
Takayama Maria

A ten-year-old girl who wears a nun's habit... and happens to be the Neighbors Club's advisor! She loves both potato chips and Kodaka.

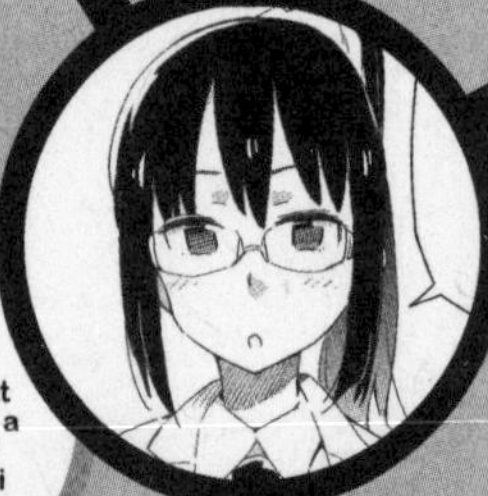

志熊 理科
Shiguma Rika

A first-year student at Saint Chronica. She's a genius inventor, and also a perverted yaoi fan who wastes her intelligence.

The Neighbors Club

Previous club activity logs:

Hasegawa Kodaka, a lone wolf at a new school, happens to come across his gloomy classmate Mikazuki Yozora chattering happily away by herself. The two of them discuss the process of making friends, and Yozora, who's got energy to spare for the oddest things, spontaneously creates a new club for unfortunate souls who desperately need to make friends. More and more students join, and with one exception, they're all beautiful--but deranged--girls. Next thing you know, the club is up to seven members! While trying to figure out ways to make friends, the club members play games and perform plays, but they always end up veering wildly off course. Is it even possible for this group to make friends?

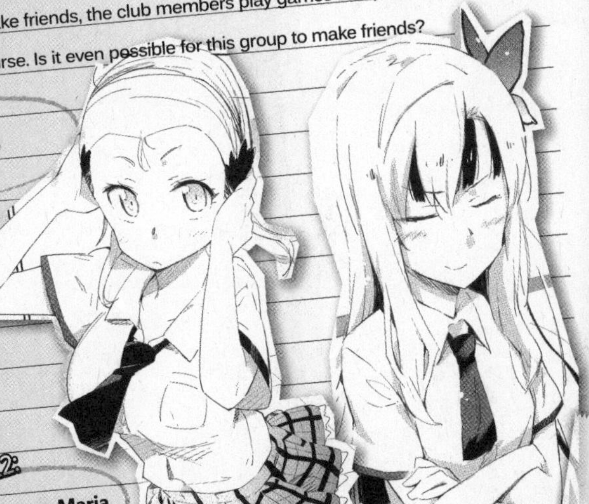

Club Activity Log 11: LOL

At Mikazuki Yozora's instigation, the club tries to get the hang of comedy.

HA!

Club Activity Log 12: Takayama Maria

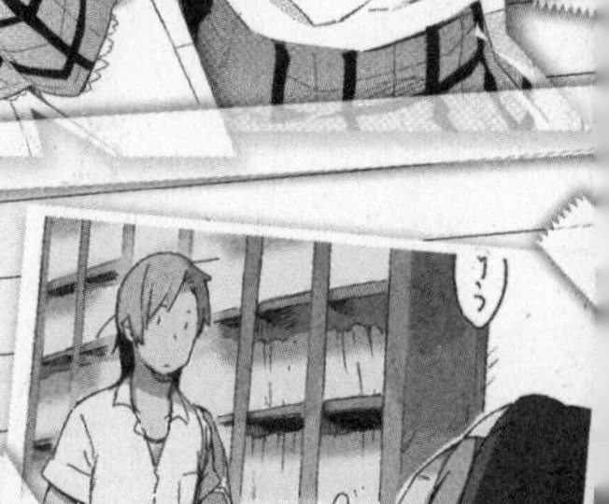

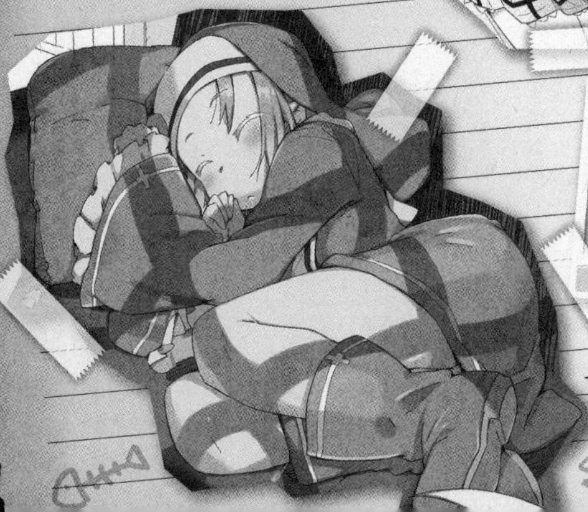

Takayama Maria, the Neighbors Club advisor, drops by--and she's a ten-year-old **nun!**

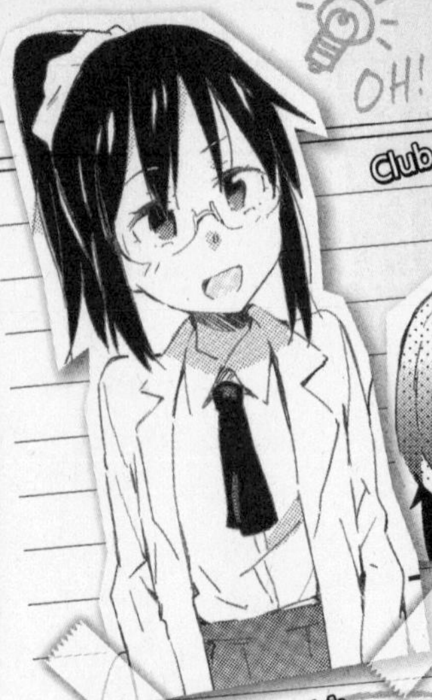
OH!

Club Activity Log 13: Shiguma Rika

Shiguma Rika, a (very) perverted girl, joins the club after being helped out by Kodaka.

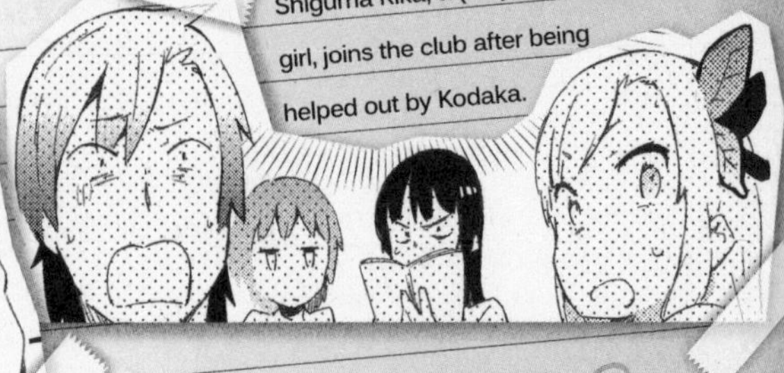

Club Activity Log 14: Fangirl

Rika brings a doujinshi to the club, and gets into an...unfortunate...mood while reading it.

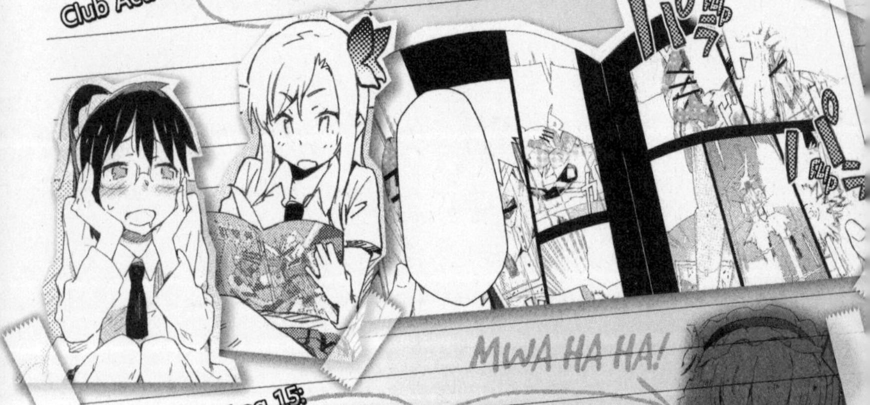
FLIP
FLIP

Club Activity Log 15: Little Sister

Kodaka's kid sister, Kobato (a second-year middle school student), becomes the club's seventh member.

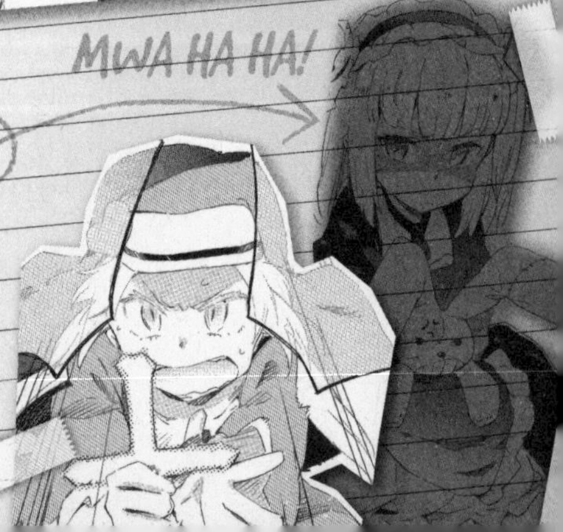
MWA HA HA!

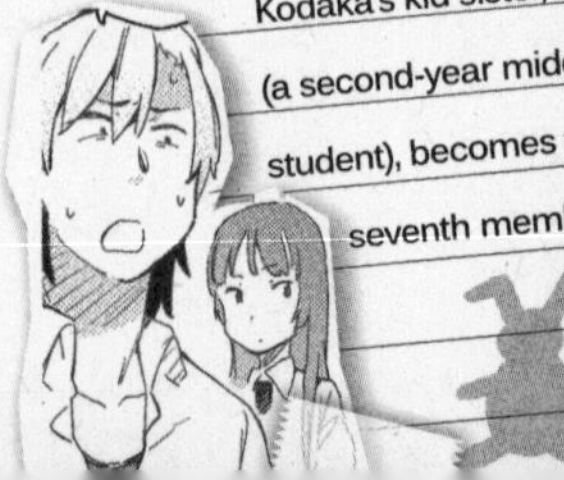

Haganai

I don't have many friends

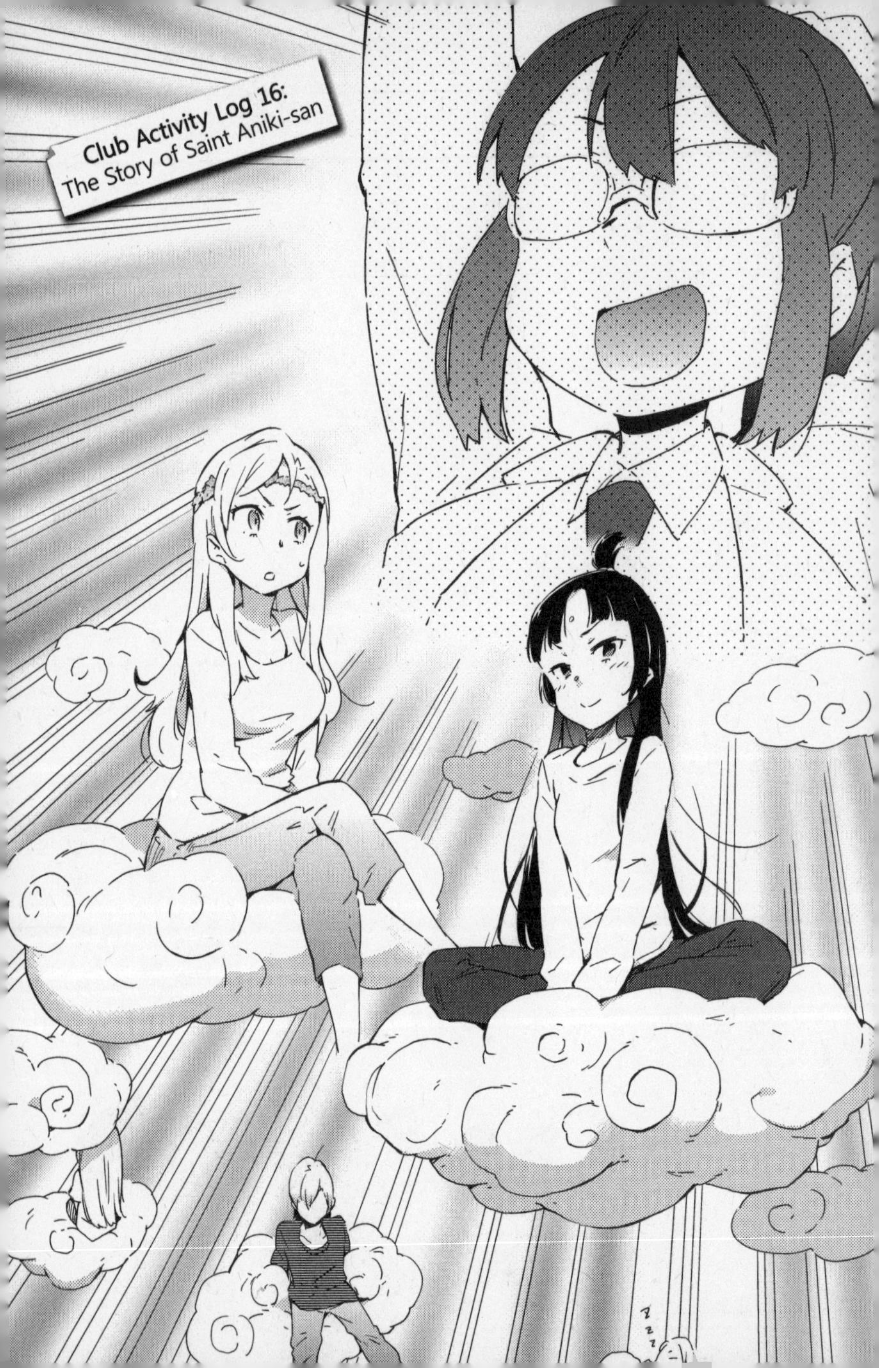
Club Activity Log 16:
The Story of Saint Aniki-san

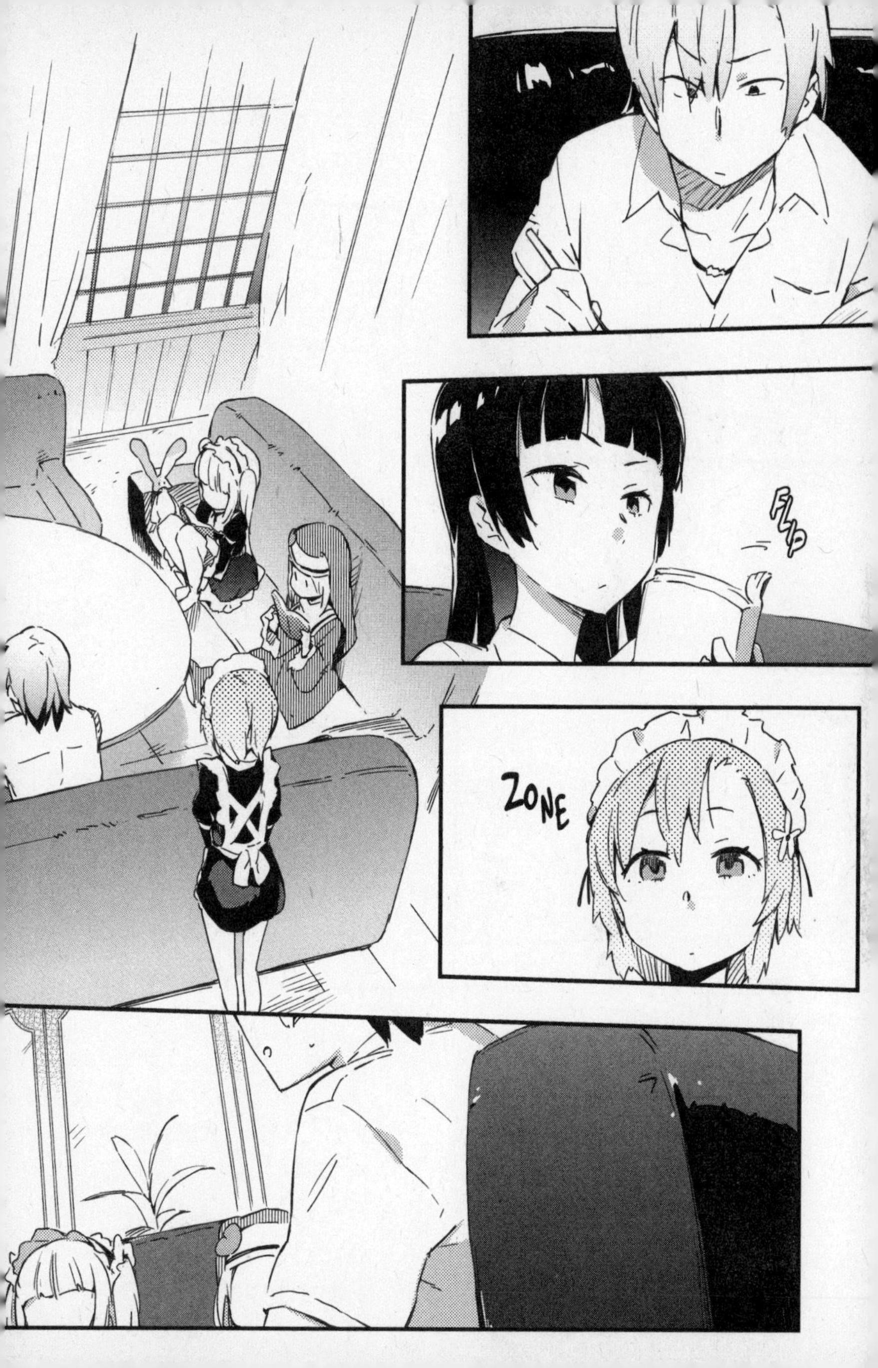
FLIP
ZONE

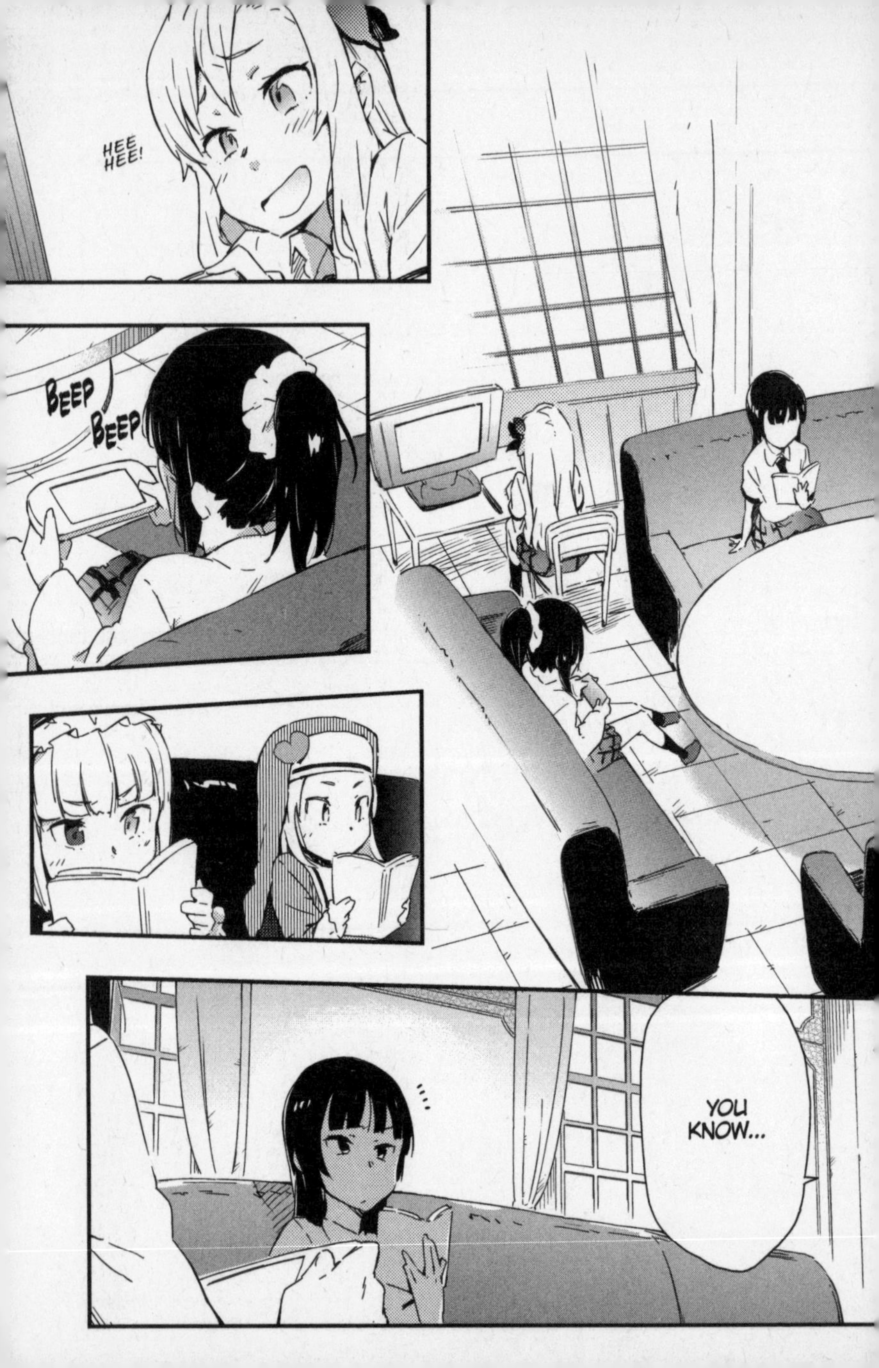
HEE HEE!
BEEP BEEP
YOU KNOW...

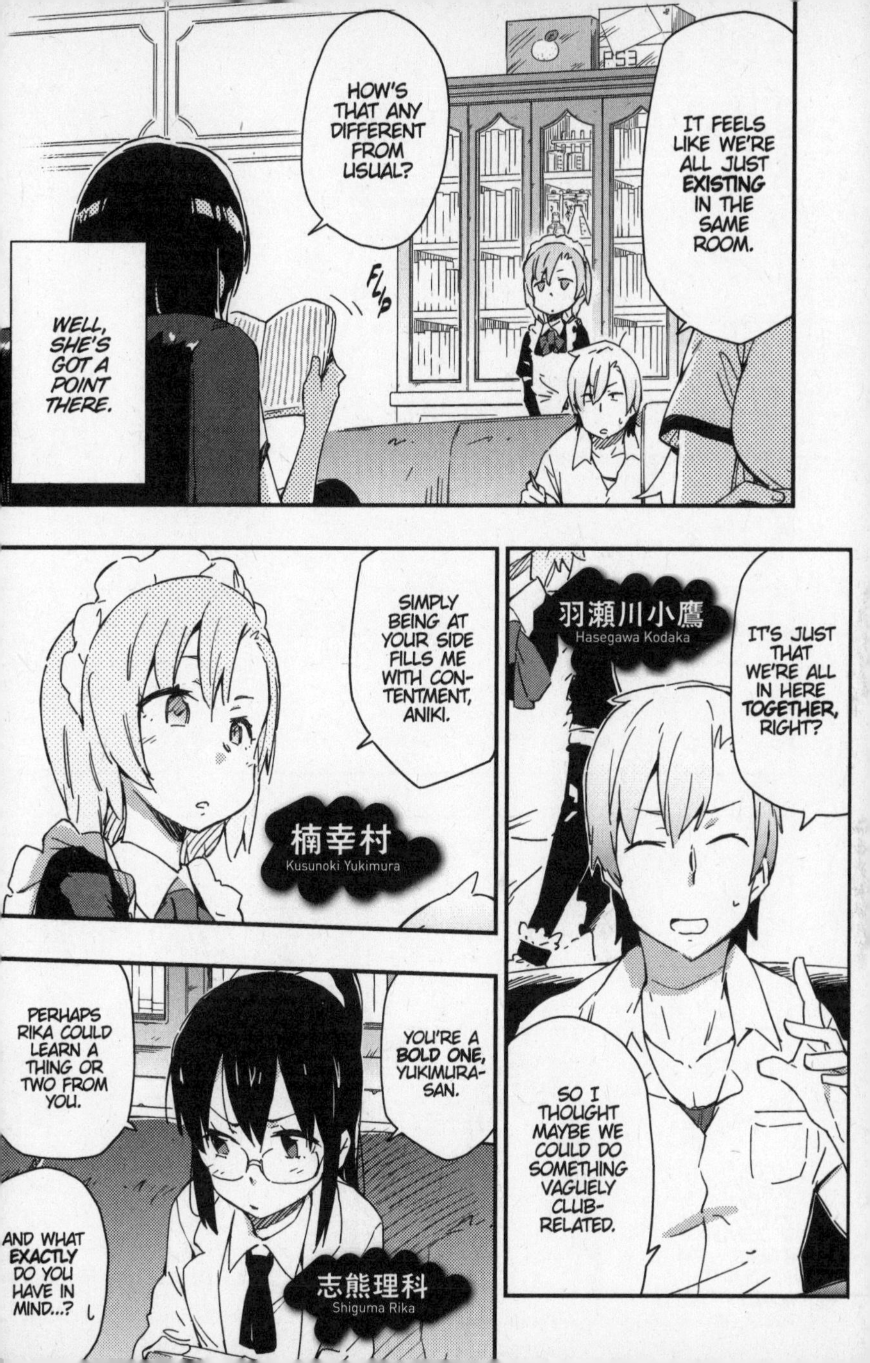
PS3
IT FEELS LIKE WE'RE ALL JUST EXISTING IN THE SAME ROOM.
HOW'S THAT ANY DIFFERENT FROM USUAL?
FLIP
WELL, SHE'S GOT A POINT THERE.
羽瀬川小鷹
Hasegawa Kodaka
IT'S JUST THAT WE'RE ALL IN HERE TOGETHER, RIGHT?
SO I THOUGHT MAYBE WE COULD DO SOMETHING VAGUELY CLUB-RELATED.
SIMPLY BEING AT YOUR SIDE FILLS ME WITH CONTENTMENT, ANIKI.
楠幸村
Kusunoki Yukimura
YOU'RE A BOLD ONE, YUKIMURA-SAN.
PERHAPS RIKA COULD LEARN A THING OR TWO FROM YOU.
AND WHAT EXACTLY DO YOU HAVE IN MIND...?
志熊理科
Shiguma Rika

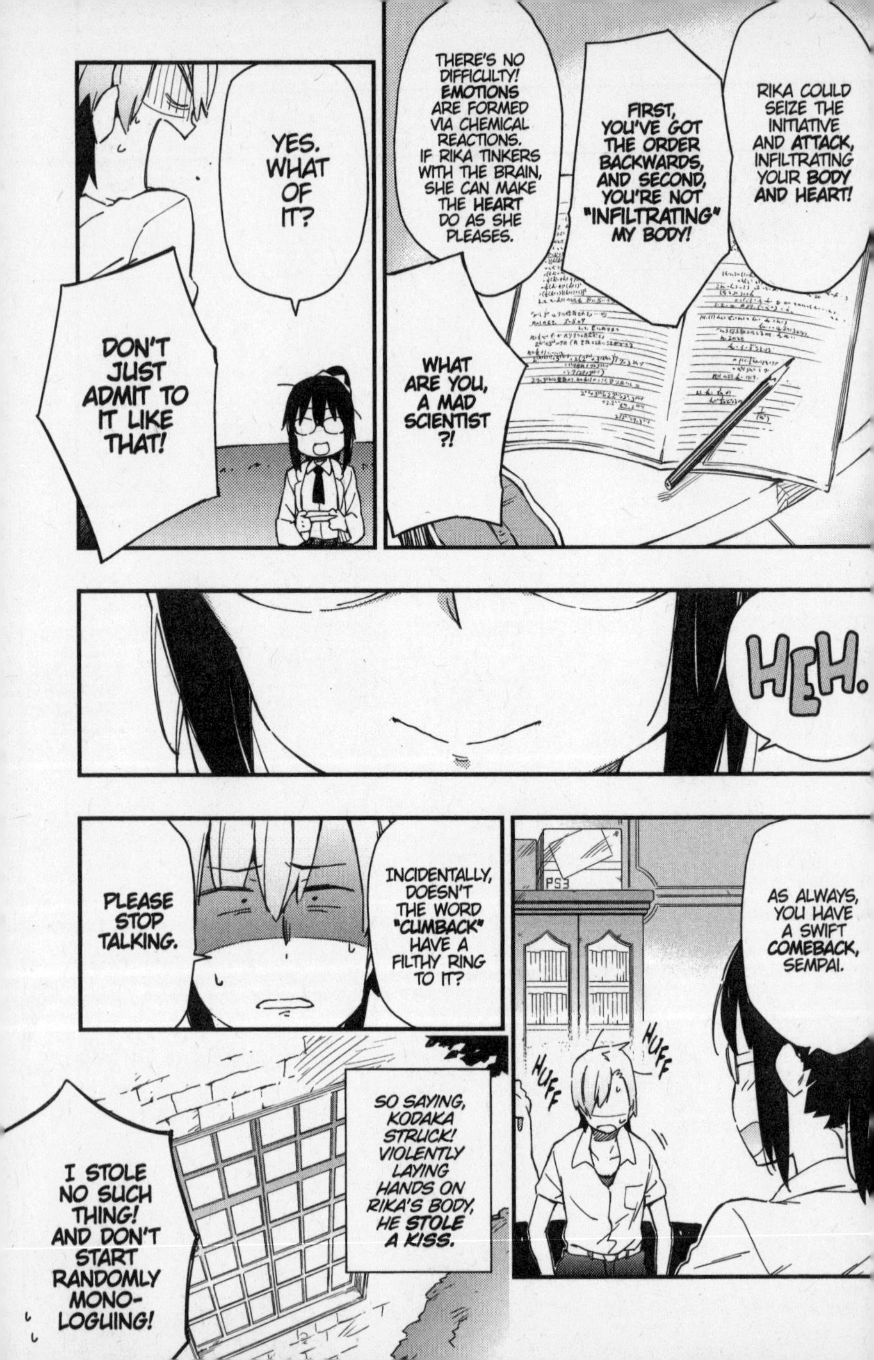
RIKA COULD SEIZE THE INITIATIVE AND ATTACK, INFILTRATING YOUR BODY AND HEART!
FIRST, YOU'VE GOT THE ORDER BACKWARDS, AND SECOND, YOU'RE NOT "INFILTRATING" MY BODY!
THERE'S NO DIFFICULTY! EMOTIONS ARE FORMED VIA CHEMICAL REACTIONS. IF RIKA TINKERS WITH THE BRAIN, SHE CAN MAKE THE HEART DO AS SHE PLEASES.
WHAT ARE YOU, A MAD SCIENTIST?!
YES. WHAT OF IT?
DON'T JUST ADMIT TO IT LIKE THAT!
HEH.
AS ALWAYS, YOU HAVE A SWIFT COMEBACK, SEMPAI.
PS3
HUFF
HUFF
INCIDENTALLY, DOESN'T THE WORD "CUMBACK" HAVE A FILTHY RING TO IT?
PLEASE STOP TALKING.
SO SAYING, KODAKA STRUCK! VIOLENTLY LAYING HANDS ON RIKA'S BODY, HE STOLE A KISS.
I STOLE NO SUCH THING! AND DON'T START RANDOMLY MONO-LOGUING!

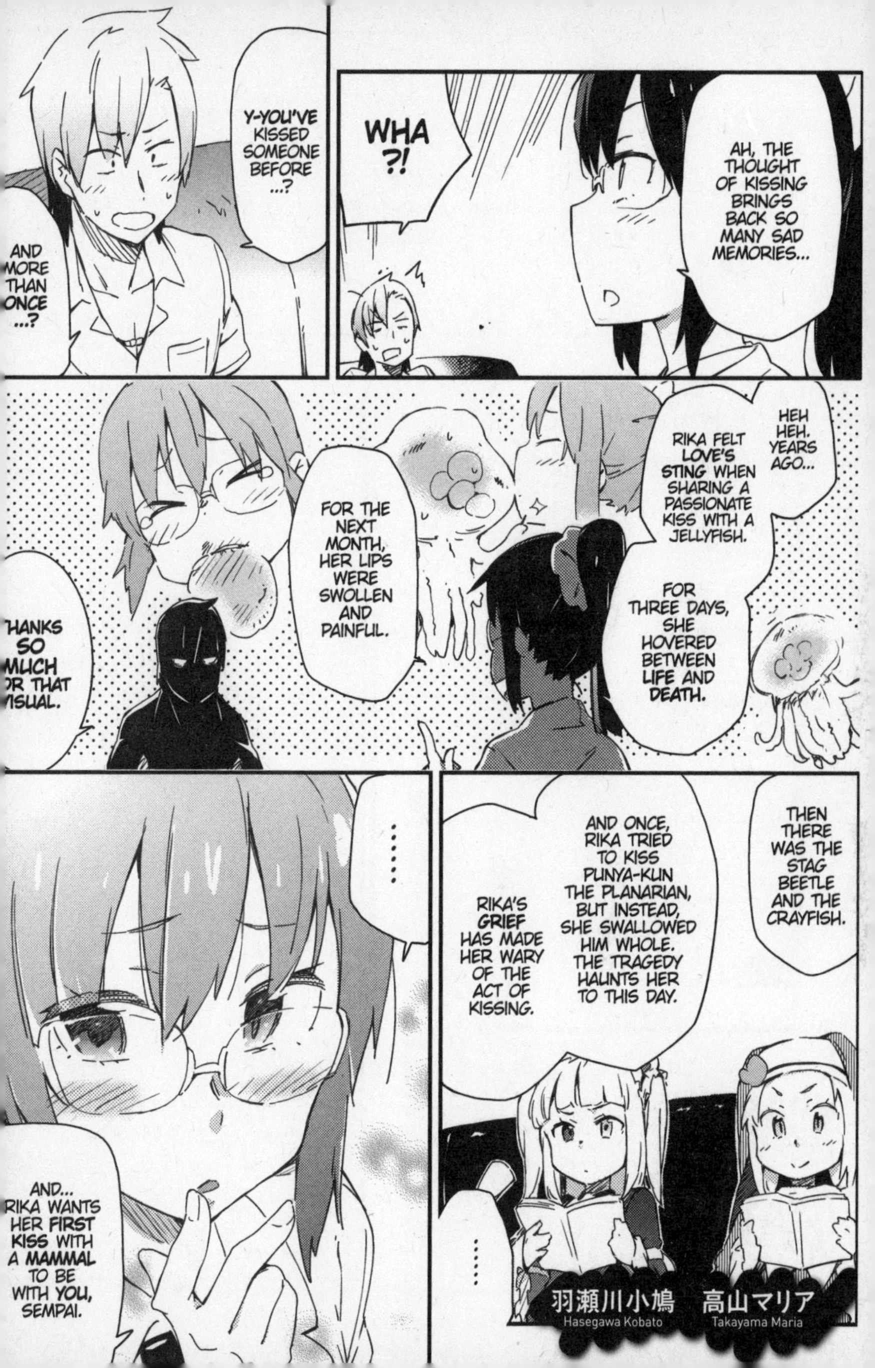
AH, THE THOUGHT OF KISSING BRINGS BACK SO MANY SAD MEMORIES...
WHA ?!
Y-YOU'VE KISSED SOMEONE BEFORE ...?
AND MORE THAN ONCE ...?
HEH HEH. YEARS AGO...
RIKA FELT LOVE'S STING WHEN SHARING A PASSIONATE KISS WITH A JELLYFISH.
FOR THREE DAYS, SHE HOVERED BETWEEN LIFE AND DEATH.
FOR THE NEXT MONTH, HER LIPS WERE SWOLLEN AND PAINFUL.
HANKS SO MUCH OR THAT ISUAL.
THEN THERE WAS THE STAG BEETLE AND THE CRAYFISH.
AND ONCE, RIKA TRIED TO KISS PUNYA-KUN THE PLANARIAN, BUT INSTEAD, SHE SWALLOWED HIM WHOLE. THE TRAGEDY HAUNTS HER TO THIS DAY.
RIKA'S GRIEF HAS MADE HER WARY OF THE ACT OF KISSING.
......
高山マリア Takayama Maria
羽瀬川小鳩 Hasegawa Kobato
......
AND... RIKA WANTS HER FIRST KISS WITH A MAMMAL TO BE WITH YOU, SEMPAI.

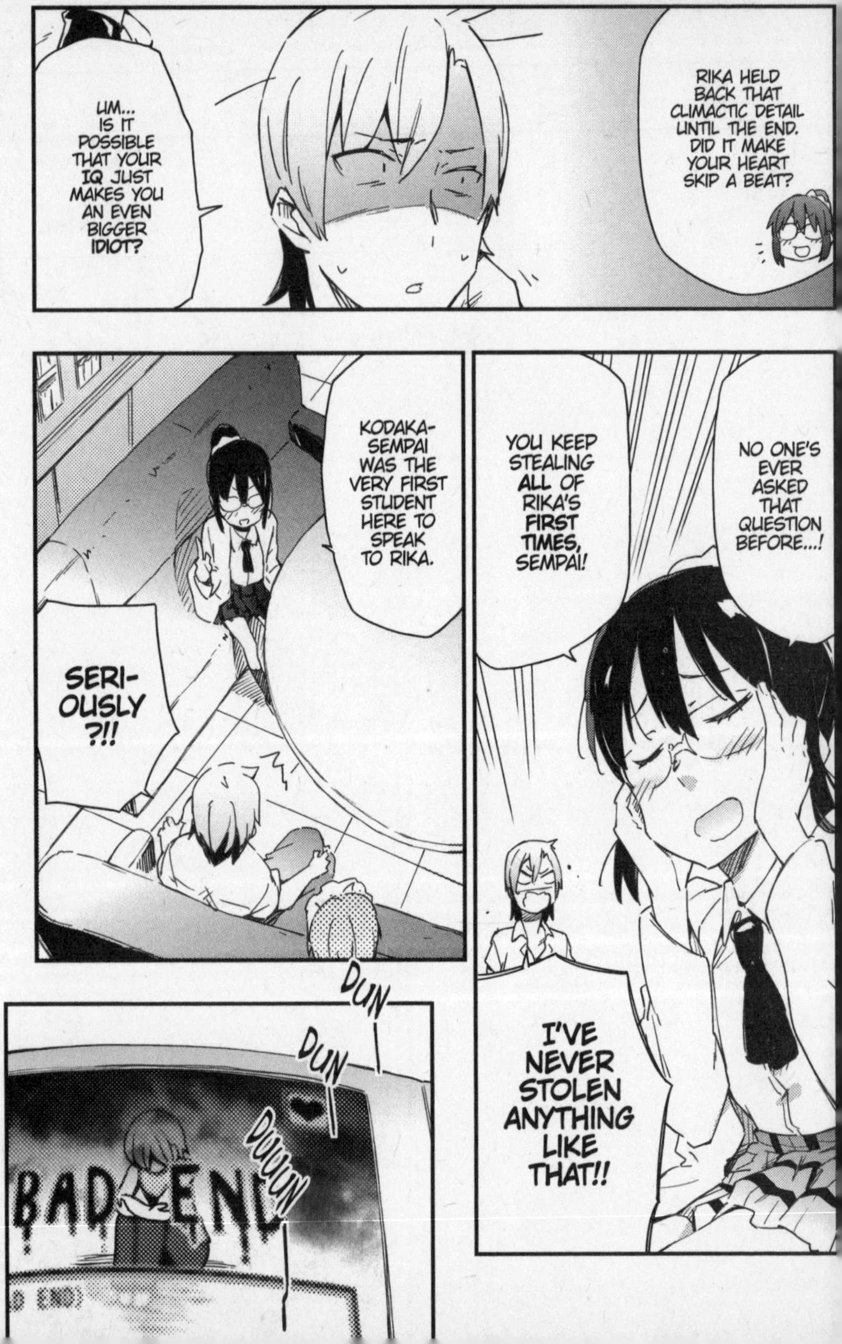
RIKA HELD BACK THAT CLIMACTIC DETAIL UNTIL THE END. DID IT MAKE YOUR HEART SKIP A BEAT?
UM... IS IT POSSIBLE THAT YOUR IQ JUST MAKES YOU AN EVEN BIGGER IDIOT?
NO ONE'S EVER ASKED THAT QUESTION BEFORE...!
YOU KEEP STEALING ALL OF RIKA'S FIRST TIMES, SEMPAI!
I'VE NEVER STOLEN ANYTHING LIKE THAT!!
KODAKA-SEMPAI WAS THE VERY FIRST STUDENT HERE TO SPEAK TO RIKA.
SERI-OUSLY ?!!
DUN DUN DUUUN
BAD END

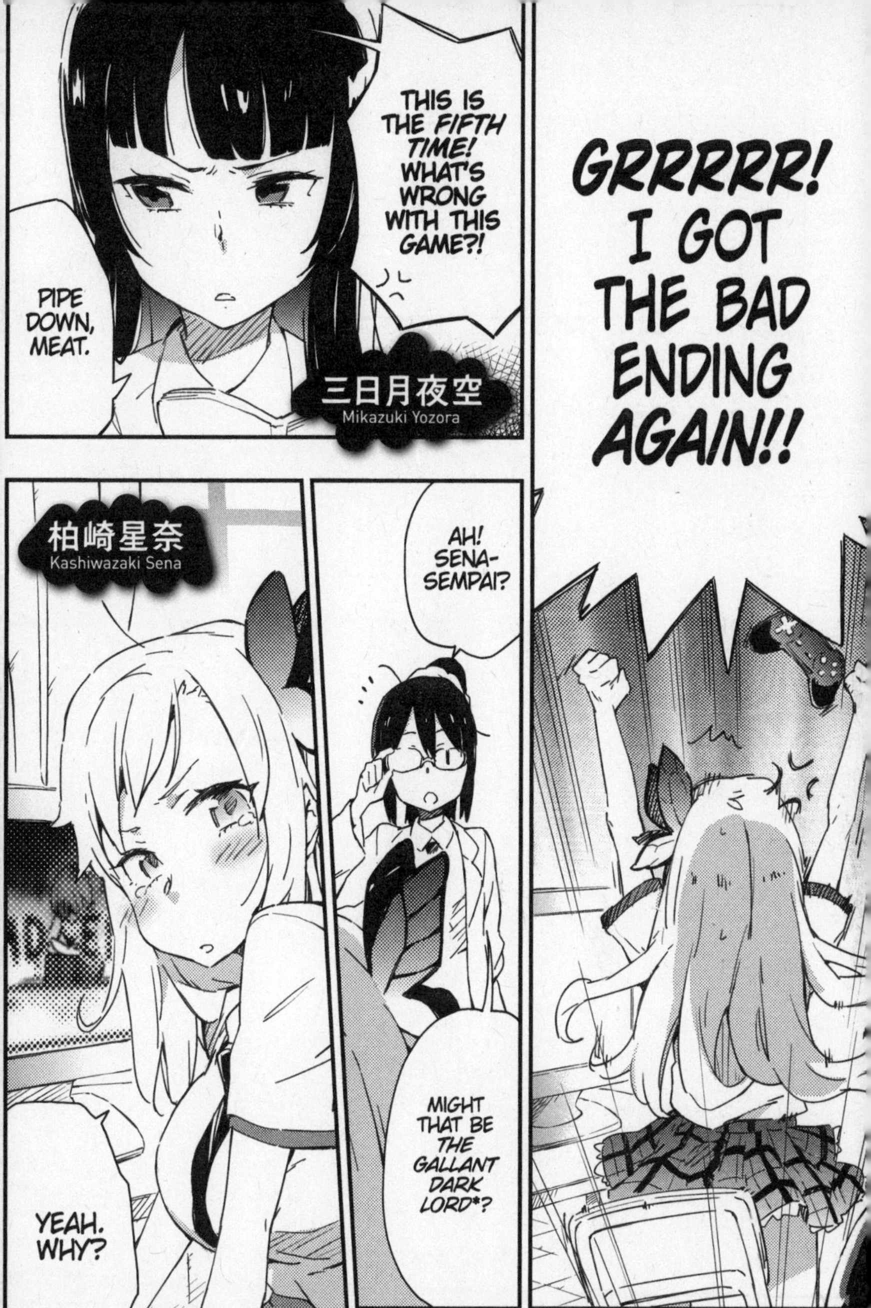
GRRRRR! I GOT THE BAD ENDING AGAIN!!
THIS IS THE FIFTH TIME! WHAT'S WRONG WITH THIS GAME?!
PIPE DOWN, MEAT.
三日月夜空
Mikazuki Yozora
AH! SENA-SEMPAI?
MIGHT THAT BE THE GALLANT DARK LORD*?
柏崎星奈
Kashiwazaki Sena
YEAH. WHY?

*Literally, "Kaguwashiki Maou"--a pun on the light novel series *Kaguya Maou Shiki! (Demon Kaguya's Form!)*

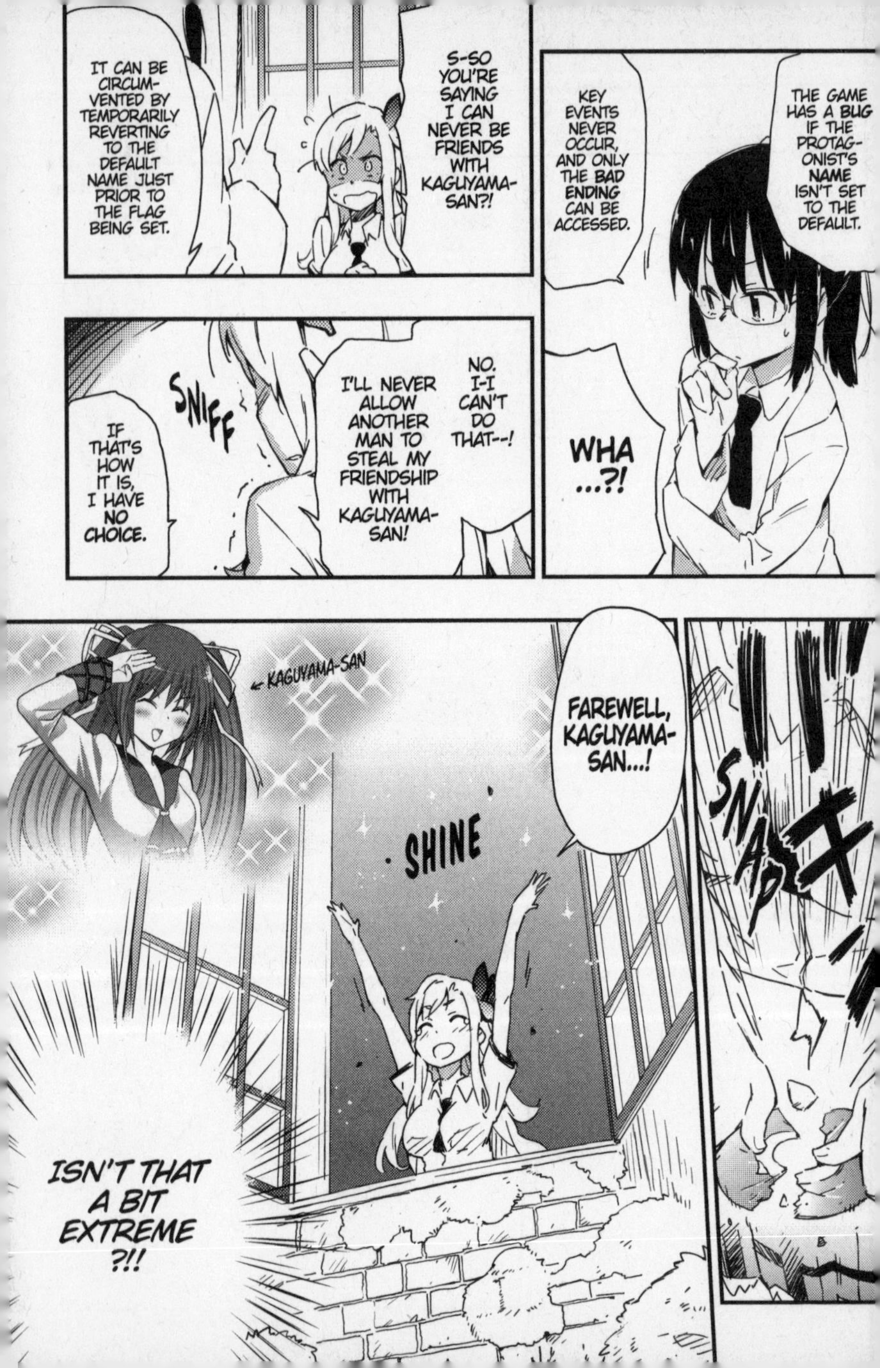
THE GAME HAS A BUG IF THE PROTAGONIST'S NAME ISN'T SET TO THE DEFAULT.
KEY EVENTS NEVER OCCUR, AND ONLY THE BAD ENDING CAN BE ACCESSED.
WHA ...?!
S-SO YOU'RE SAYING I CAN NEVER BE FRIENDS WITH KAGUYAMA-SAN?!
IT CAN BE CIRCUMVENTED BY TEMPORARILY REVERTING TO THE DEFAULT NAME JUST PRIOR TO THE FLAG BEING SET.
NO. I-I CAN'T DO THAT--!
I'LL NEVER ALLOW ANOTHER MAN TO STEAL MY FRIENDSHIP WITH KAGUYAMA-SAN!
SNIFF
IF THAT'S HOW IT IS, I HAVE NO CHOICE.
SNAP
FAREWELL, KAGUYAMA-SAN...!
SHINE
← KAGUYAMA-SAN
ISN'T THAT A BIT EXTREME ?!!

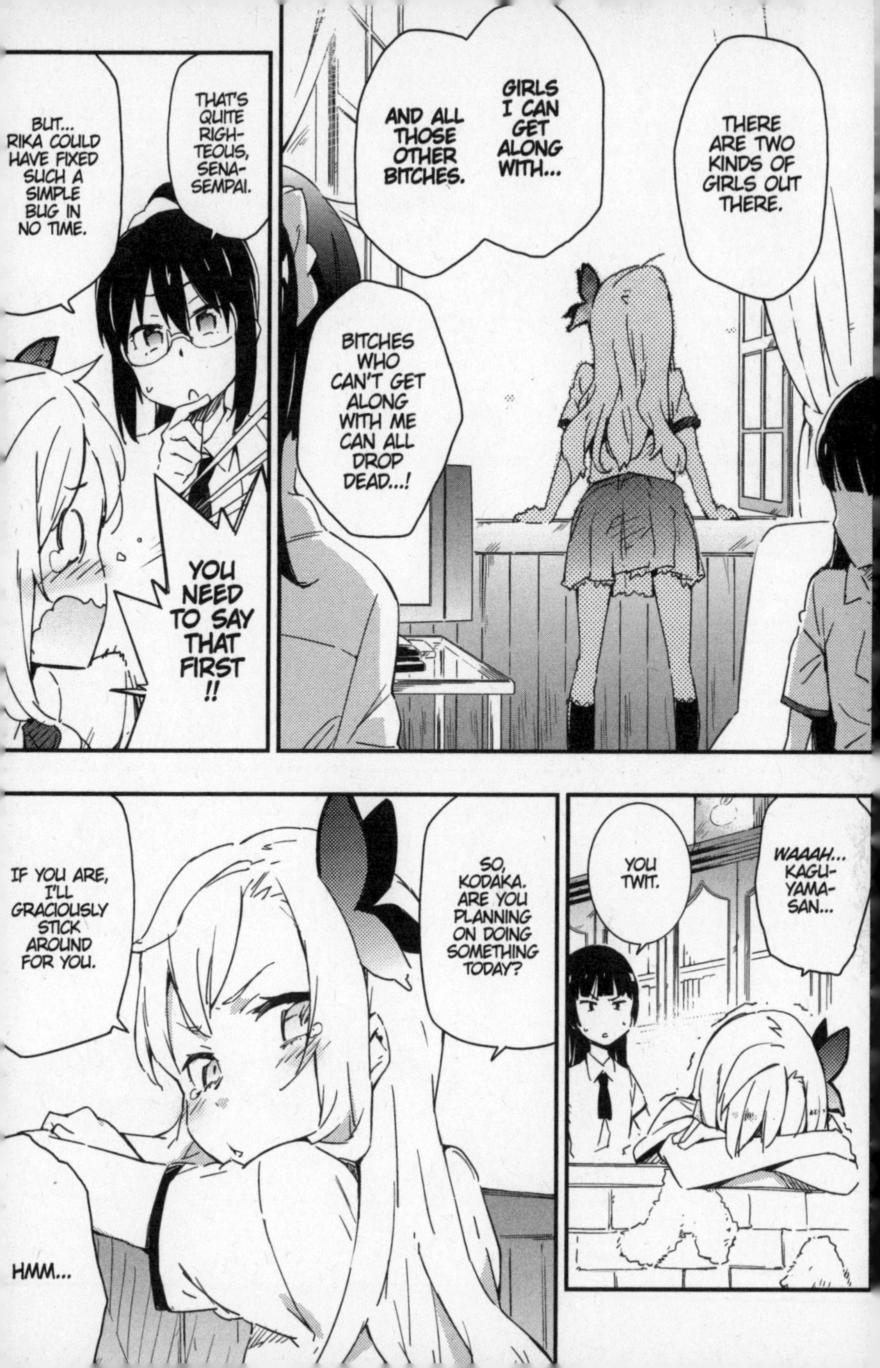
THERE ARE TWO KINDS OF GIRLS OUT THERE.
GIRLS I CAN GET ALONG WITH... AND ALL THOSE OTHER BITCHES.
BITCHES WHO CAN'T GET ALONG WITH ME CAN ALL DROP DEAD...!
THAT'S QUITE RIGH-TEOUS, SENA-SEMPAI.
BUT... RIKA COULD HAVE FIXED SUCH A SIMPLE BUG IN NO TIME.
YOU NEED TO SAY THAT FIRST !!
WAAAH... KAGU-YAMA-SAN...
YOU TWIT.
SO, KODAKA. ARE YOU PLANNING ON DOING SOMETHING TODAY?
IF YOU ARE, I'LL GRACIOUSLY STICK AROUND FOR YOU.
HMM...

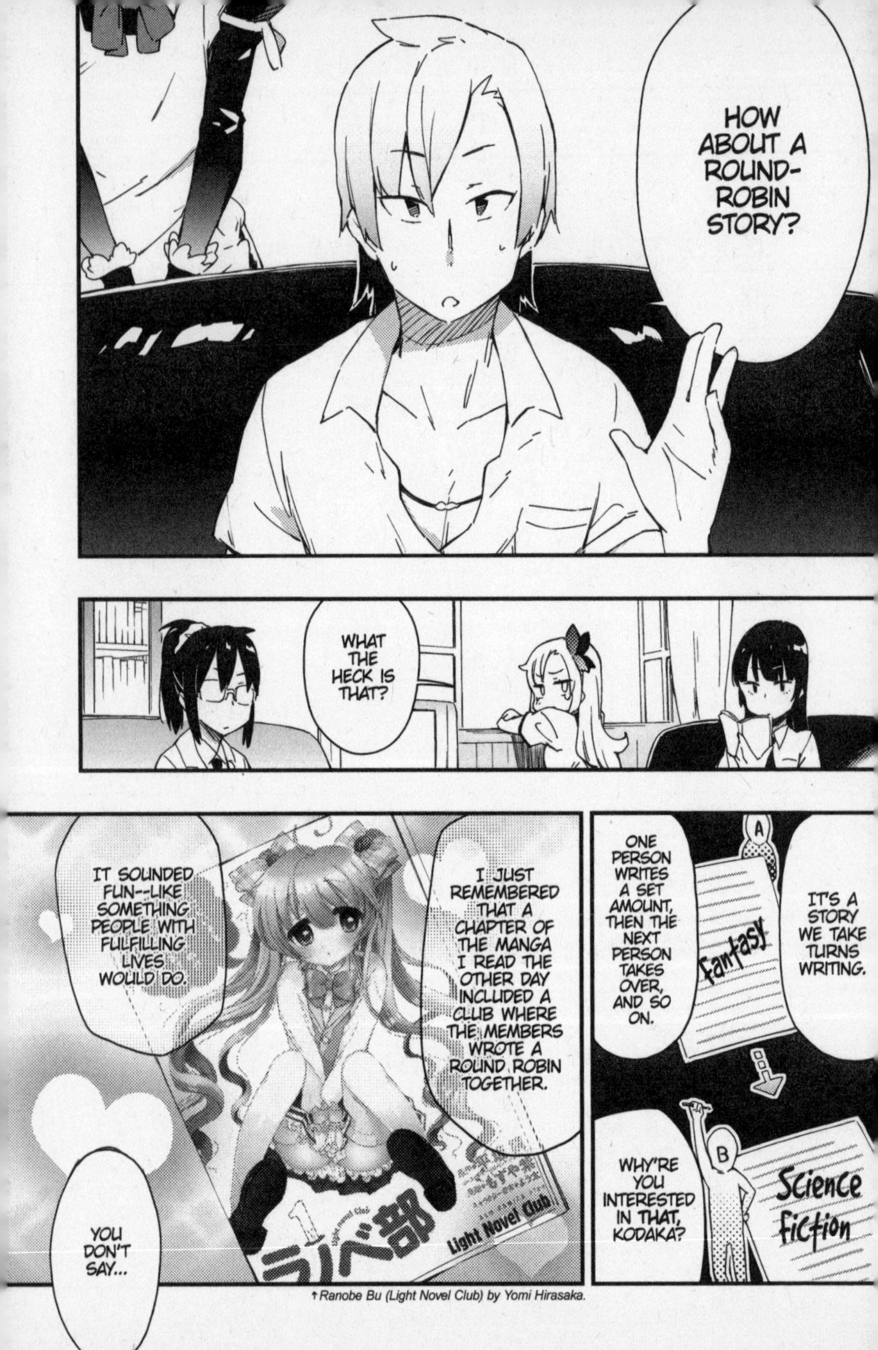
HOW ABOUT A ROUND-ROBIN STORY?
WHAT THE HECK IS THAT?
IT'S A STORY WE TAKE TURNS WRITING.
ONE PERSON WRITES A SET AMOUNT, THEN THE NEXT PERSON TAKES OVER, AND SO ON.
A
Fantasy
B
Science Fiction
WHY'RE YOU INTERESTED IN THAT, KODAKA?
I JUST REMEMBERED THAT A CHAPTER OF THE MANGA I READ THE OTHER DAY INCLUDED A CLUB WHERE THE MEMBERS WROTE A ROUND ROBIN TOGETHER.
ラノベ部
Light Novel Club
IT SOUNDED FUN--LIKE SOMETHING PEOPLE WITH FULFILLING LIVES WOULD DO.
YOU DON'T SAY...

↑*Ranobe Bu (Light Novel Club)* by Yomi Hirasaka.

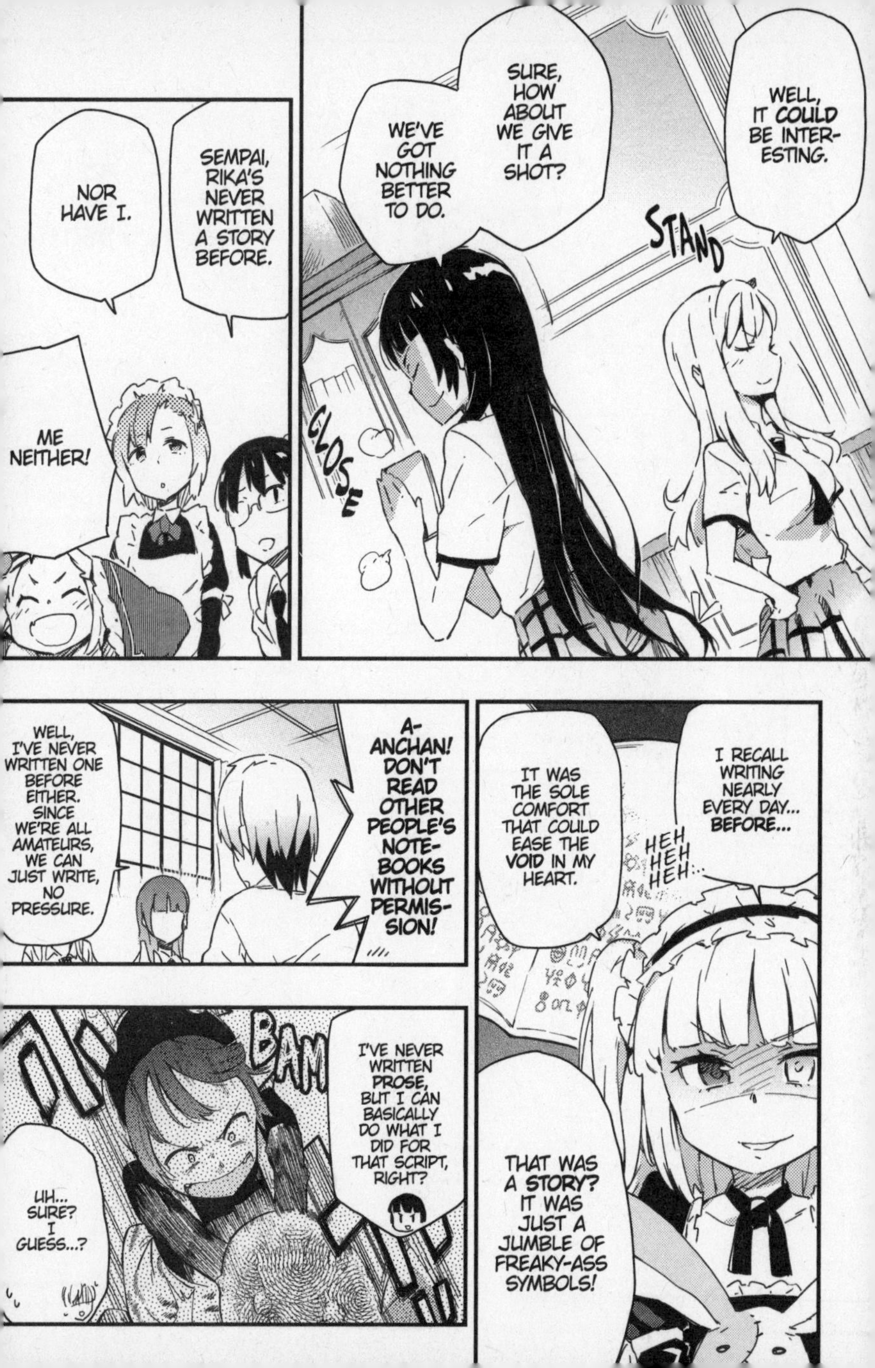
WELL, IT COULD BE INTER-ESTING.
STAND
SURE, HOW ABOUT WE GIVE IT A SHOT?
WE'VE GOT NOTHING BETTER TO DO.
CLOSE
SEMPAI, RIKA'S NEVER WRITTEN A STORY BEFORE.
NOR HAVE I.
ME NEITHER!
I RECALL WRITING NEARLY EVERY DAY... BEFORE...
IT WAS THE SOLE COMFORT THAT COULD EASE THE VOID IN MY HEART.
HEH HEH HEH...
THAT WAS A STORY? IT WAS JUST A JUMBLE OF FREAKY-ASS SYMBOLS!
A-ANCHAN! DON'T READ OTHER PEOPLE'S NOTE-BOOKS WITHOUT PERMIS-SION!
WELL, I'VE NEVER WRITTEN ONE BEFORE EITHER. SINCE WE'RE ALL AMATEURS, WE CAN JUST WRITE, NO PRESSURE.
BAM
I'VE NEVER WRITTEN PROSE, BUT I CAN BASICALLY DO WHAT I DID FOR THAT SCRIPT, RIGHT?
UH... SURE? I GUESS...?

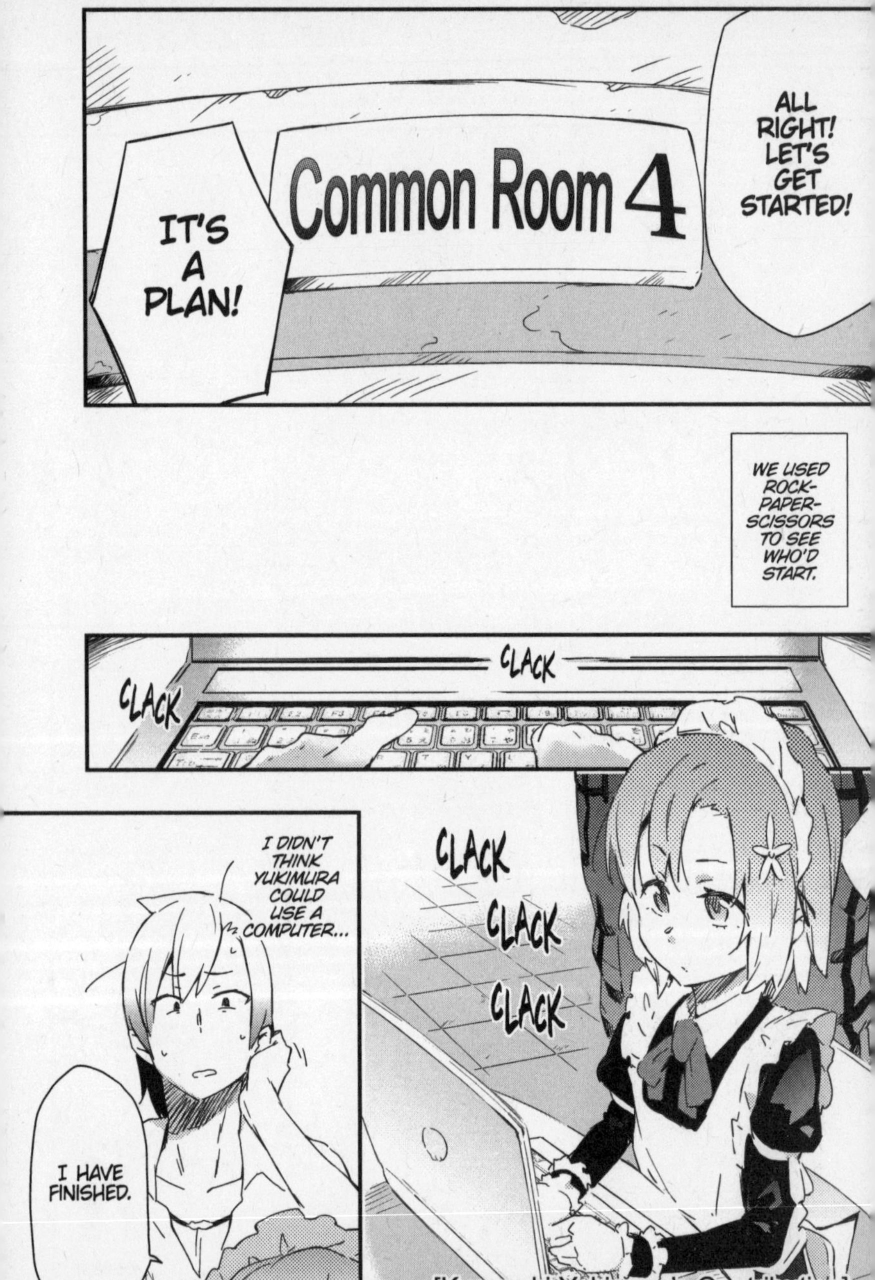
ALL RIGHT! LET'S GET STARTED!
Common Room 4
IT'S A PLAN!
WE USED ROCK-PAPER-SCISSORS TO SEE WHO'D START.
CLACK
CLACK
CLACK
CLACK
CLACK
[Kusunoki Yukimura's Contribution]
I DIDN'T THINK YUKIMURA COULD USE A COMPUTER...
I HAVE FINISHED.

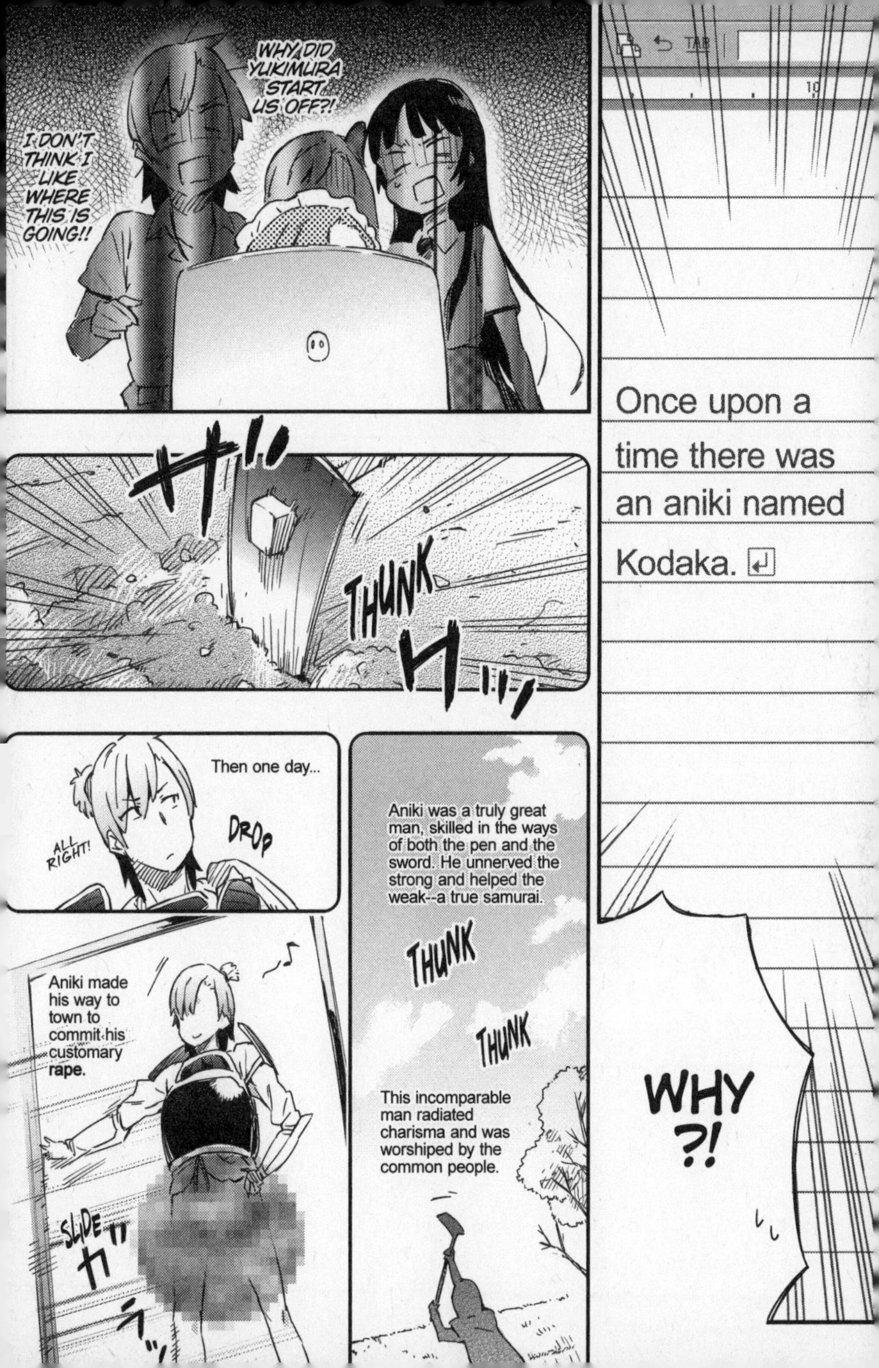
TAB
10
Once upon a time there was an aniki named Kodaka.
WHY DID YUKIMURA START US OFF?!
I DON'T THINK I LIKE WHERE THIS IS GOING!!
THUNK
Aniki was a truly great man, skilled in the ways of both the pen and the sword. He unnerved the strong and helped the weak--a true samurai.
THUNK
THUNK
This incomparable man radiated charisma and was worshiped by the common people.
Then one day...
DROP
ALL RIGHT!
Aniki made his way to town to commit his customary **rape.**
SLIDE
WHY?!

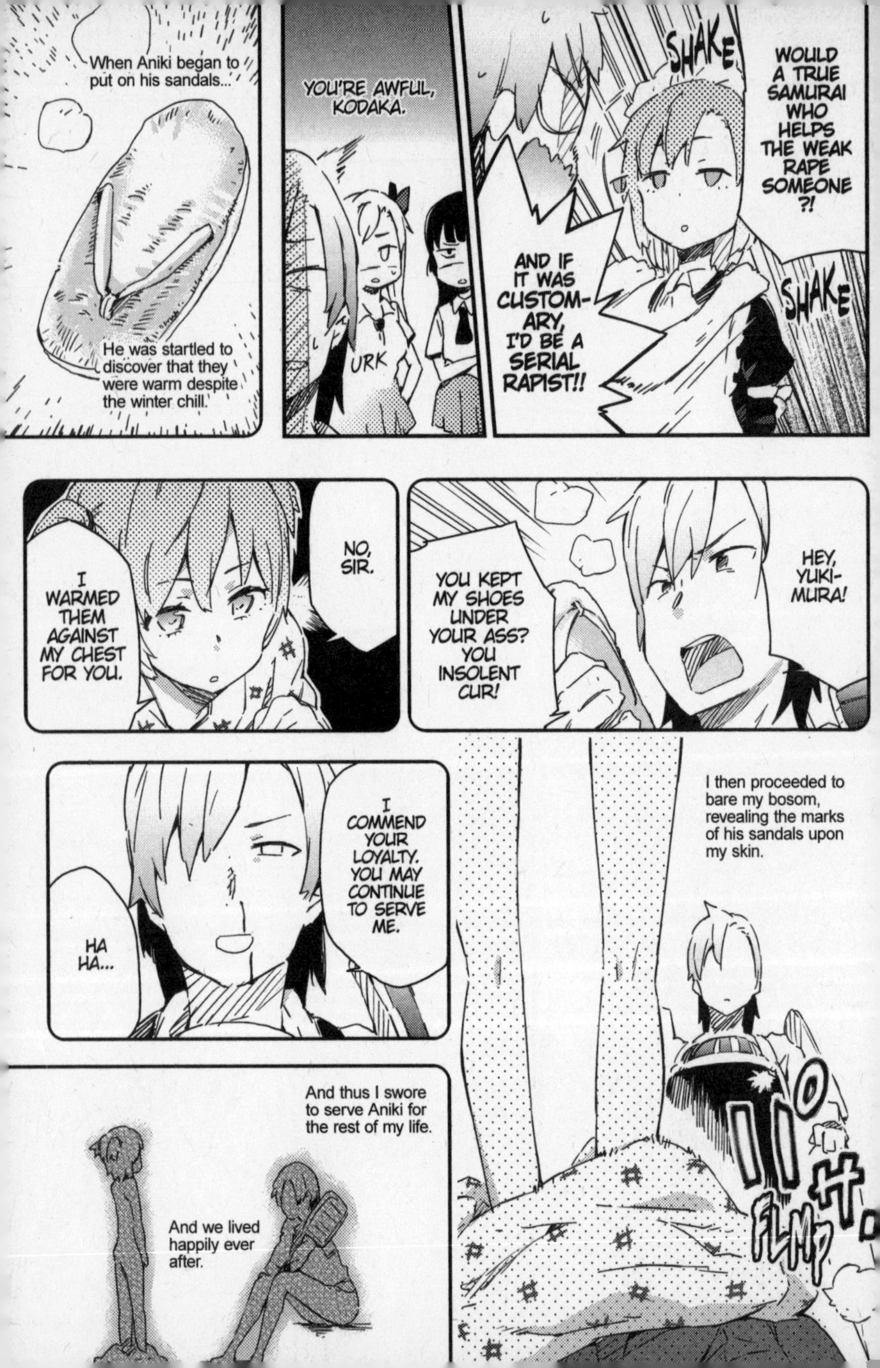
WOULD A TRUE SAMURAI WHO HELPS THE WEAK RAPE SOMEONE ?!
SHAKE
SHAKE
AND IF IT WAS CUSTOM-ARY, I'D BE A SERIAL RAPIST!!
YOU'RE AWFUL, KODAKA.
URK
When Aniki began to put on his sandals...
He was startled to discover that they were warm despite the winter chill.
HEY, YUKI-MURA!
YOU KEPT MY SHOES UNDER YOUR ASS? YOU INSOLENT CUR!
NO, SIR.
I WARMED THEM AGAINST MY CHEST FOR YOU.
I then proceeded to bare my bosom, revealing the marks of his sandals upon my skin.
FLMP
I COMMEND YOUR LOYALTY. YOU MAY CONTINUE TO SERVE ME.
HA HA...
And thus I swore to serve Aniki for the rest of my life.
And we lived happily ever after.

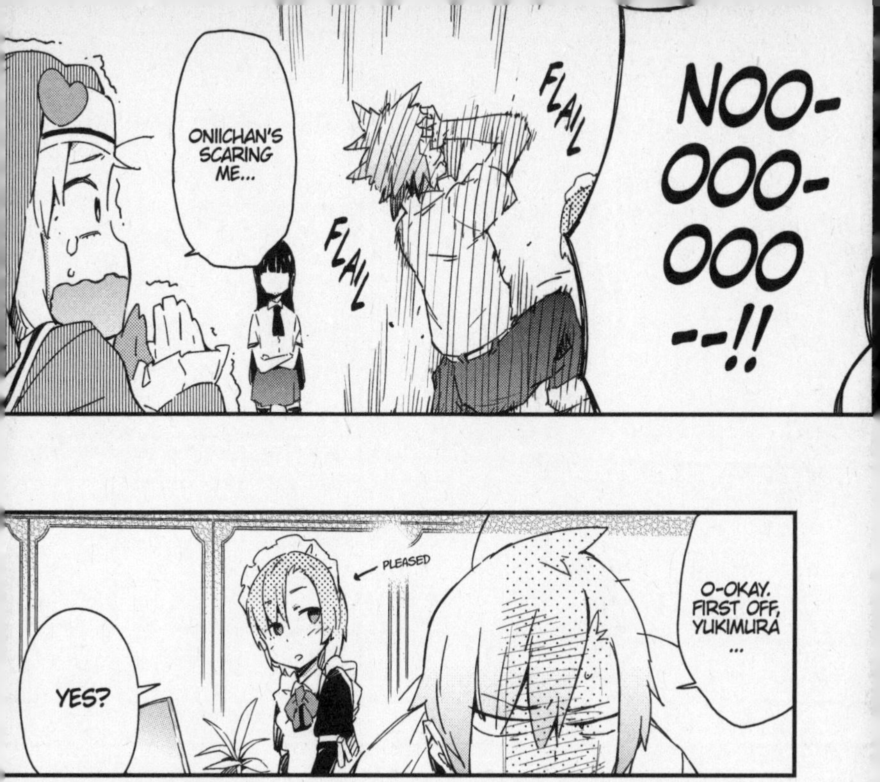
NOO-OOO-OOO--!!
FLAIL
FLAIL
ONIICHAN'S SCARING ME...
O-OKAY. FIRST OFF, YUKIMURA...
PLEASED
YES?

he two men responsible for the unification of Japan under the shogunate in the late 16th century.

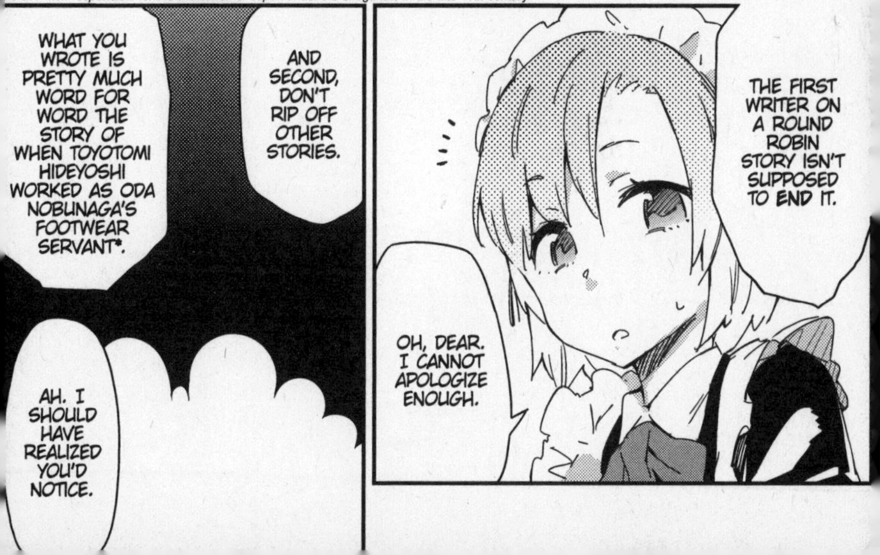
THE FIRST WRITER ON A ROUND ROBIN STORY ISN'T SUPPOSED TO END IT.
OH, DEAR. I CANNOT APOLOGIZE ENOUGH.
AND SECOND, DON'T RIP OFF OTHER STORIES.
WHAT YOU WROTE IS PRETTY MUCH WORD FOR WORD THE STORY OF WHEN TOYOTOMI HIDEYOSHI WORKED AS ODA NOBUNAGA'S FOOTWEAR SERVANT*.
AH. I SHOULD HAVE REALIZED YOU'D NOTICE.

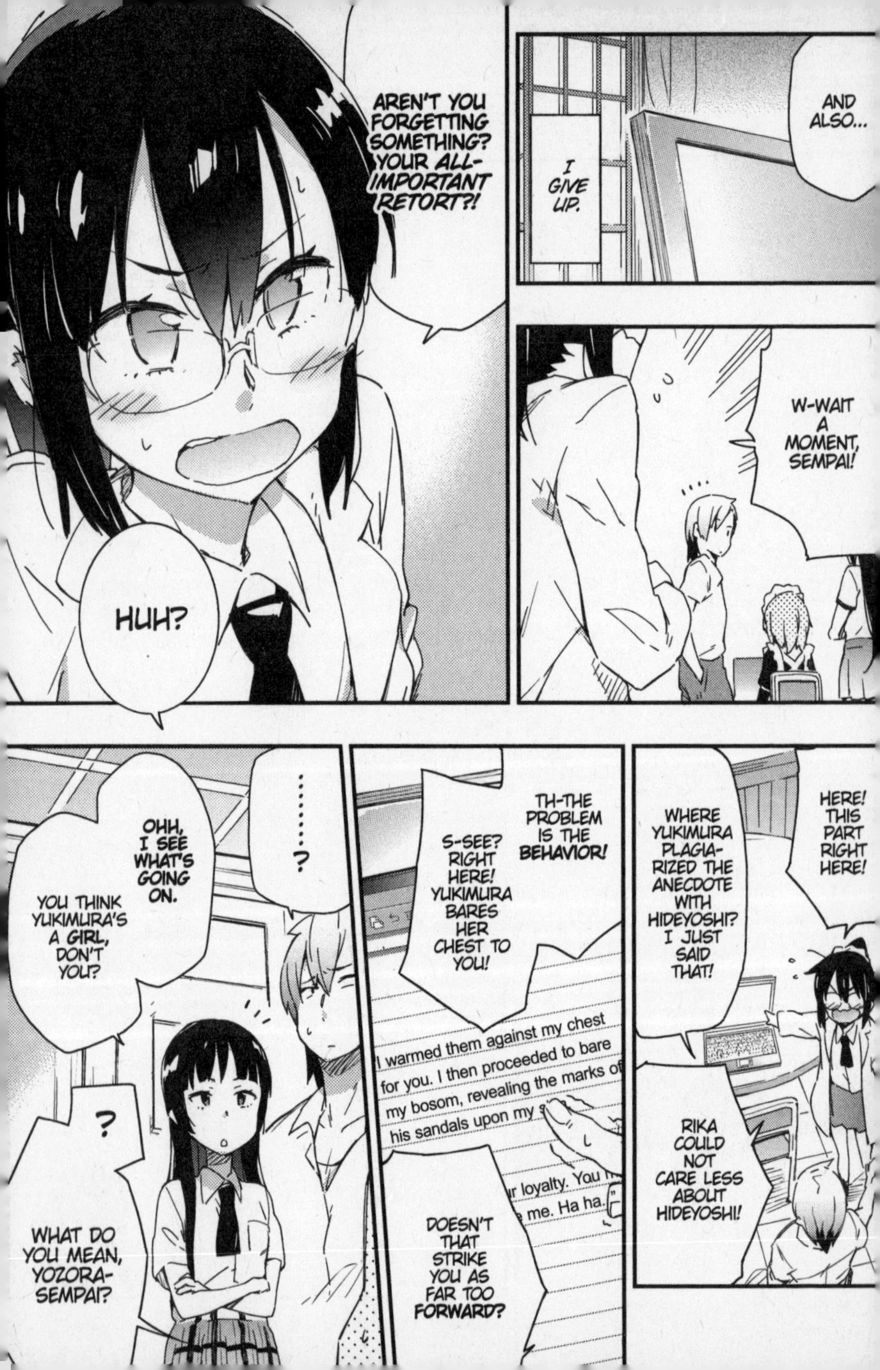
AND ALSO...
I GIVE UP.
W-WAIT A MOMENT, SEMPAI!
...
AREN'T YOU FORGETTING SOMETHING? YOUR ALL-IMPORTANT RETORT?!
HUH?
HERE! THIS PART RIGHT HERE!
WHERE YUKIMURA PLAGIARIZED THE ANECDOTE WITH HIDEYOSHI? I JUST SAID THAT!
RIKA COULD NOT CARE LESS ABOUT HIDEYOSHI!
TH-THE PROBLEM IS THE BEHAVIOR!
S-SEE? RIGHT HERE! YUKIMURA BARES HER CHEST TO YOU!
I warmed them against my chest
for you. I then proceeded to bare
my bosom, revealing the marks o
his sandals upon my
loyalty. You
me. Ha ha.
DOESN'T THAT STRIKE YOU AS FAR TOO FORWARD?
......?
OHH, I SEE WHAT'S GOING ON.
YOU THINK YUKIMURA'S A GIRL, DON'T YOU?
?
WHAT DO YOU MEAN, YOZORA-SEMPAI?

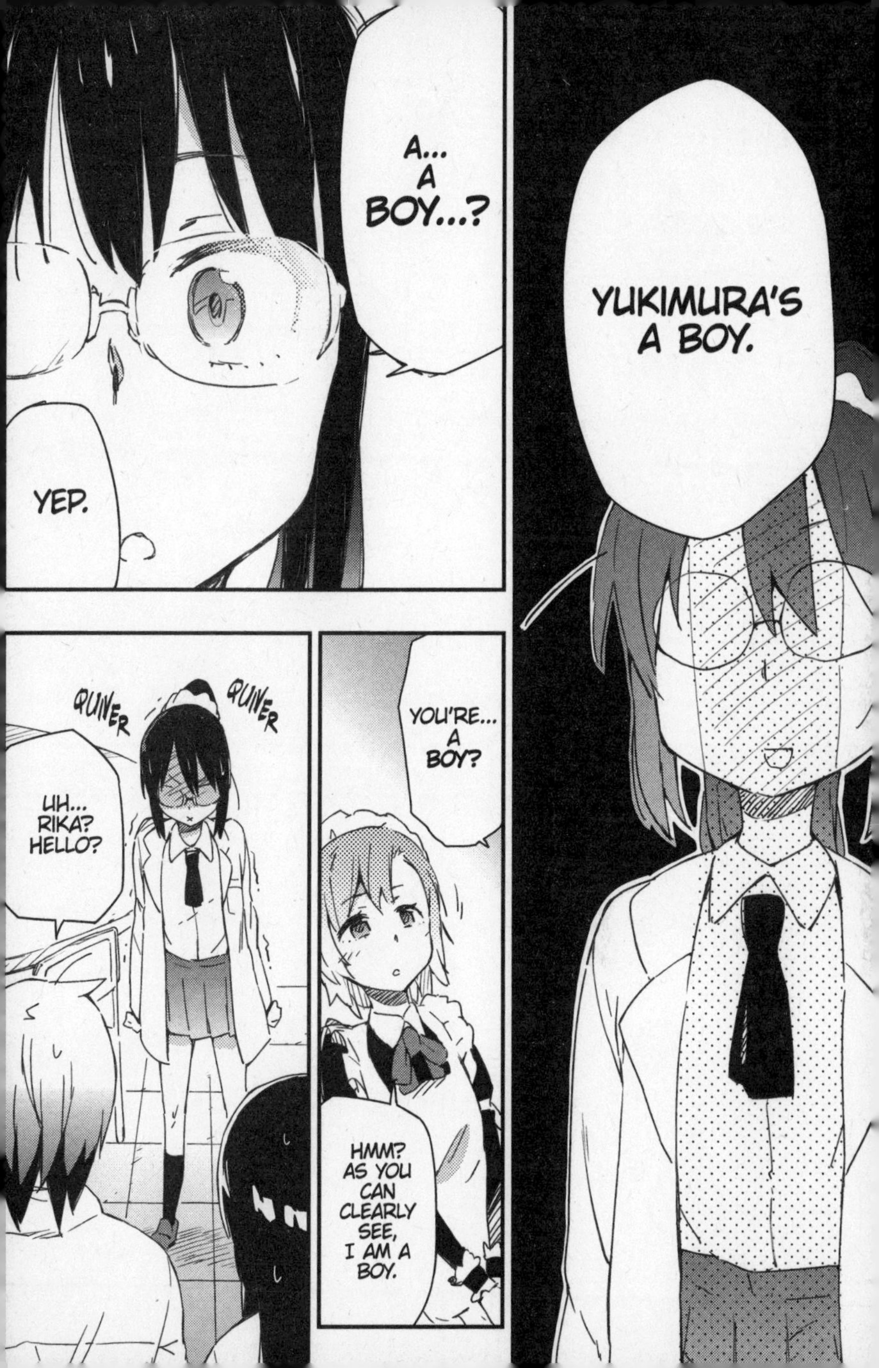
YUKIMURA'S A BOY.
A... A BOY...?
YEP.
YOU'RE... A BOY?
HMM? AS YOU CAN CLEARLY SEE, I AM A BOY.
QUIVER
QUIVER
UH... RIKA? HELLO?

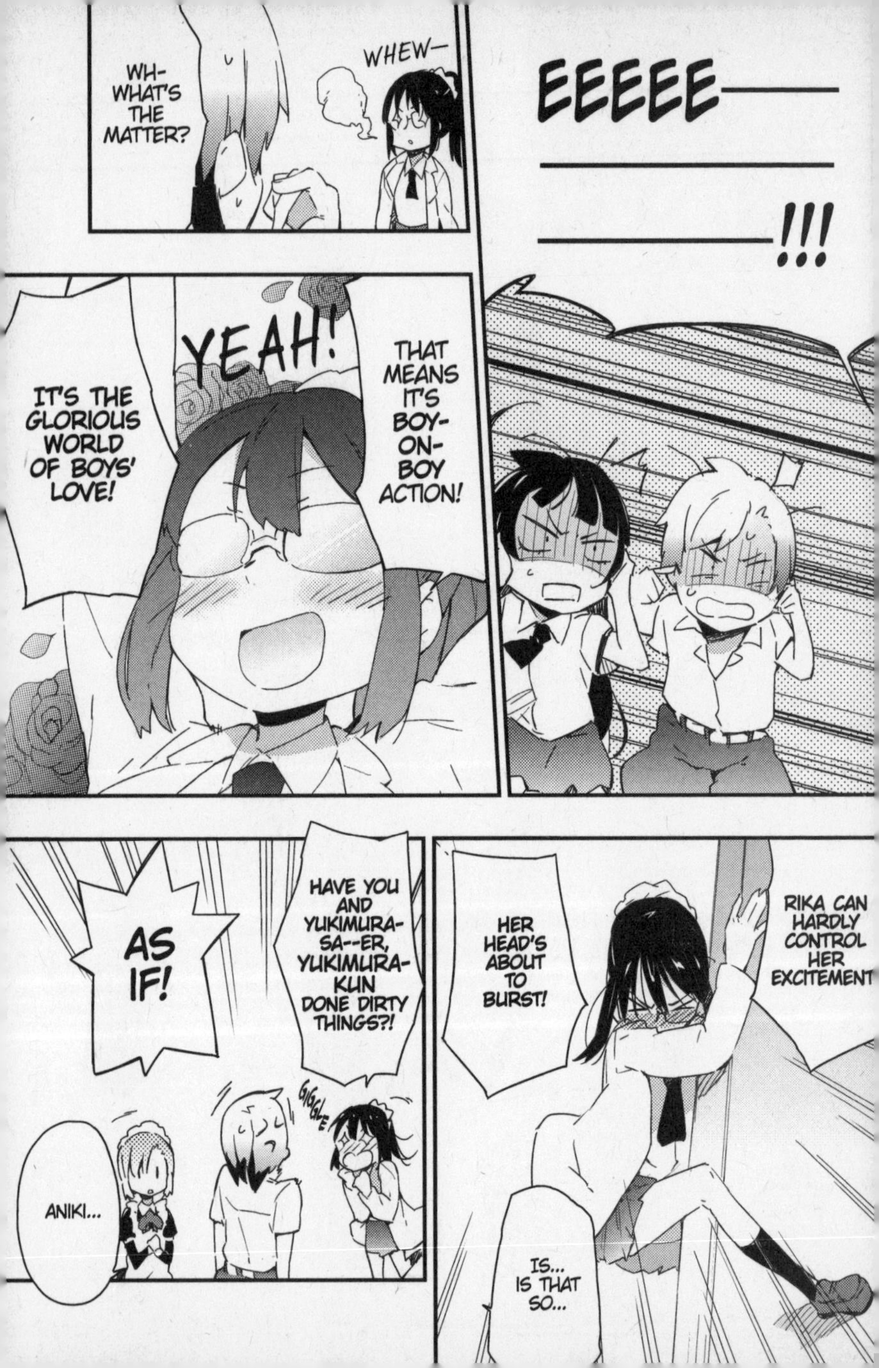
WHEW—
WH-WHAT'S THE MATTER?
THAT MEANS IT'S BOY-ON-BOY ACTION!
YEAH!
IT'S THE GLORIOUS WORLD OF BOYS' LOVE!
EEEEE————————!!!
RIKA CAN HARDLY CONTROL HER EXCITEMENT
HER HEAD'S ABOUT TO BURST!
IS... IS THAT SO...
HAVE YOU AND YUKIMURA-SA--ER, YUKIMURA-KUN DONE DIRTY THINGS?!
AS IF!
GIGGLE
ANIKI...

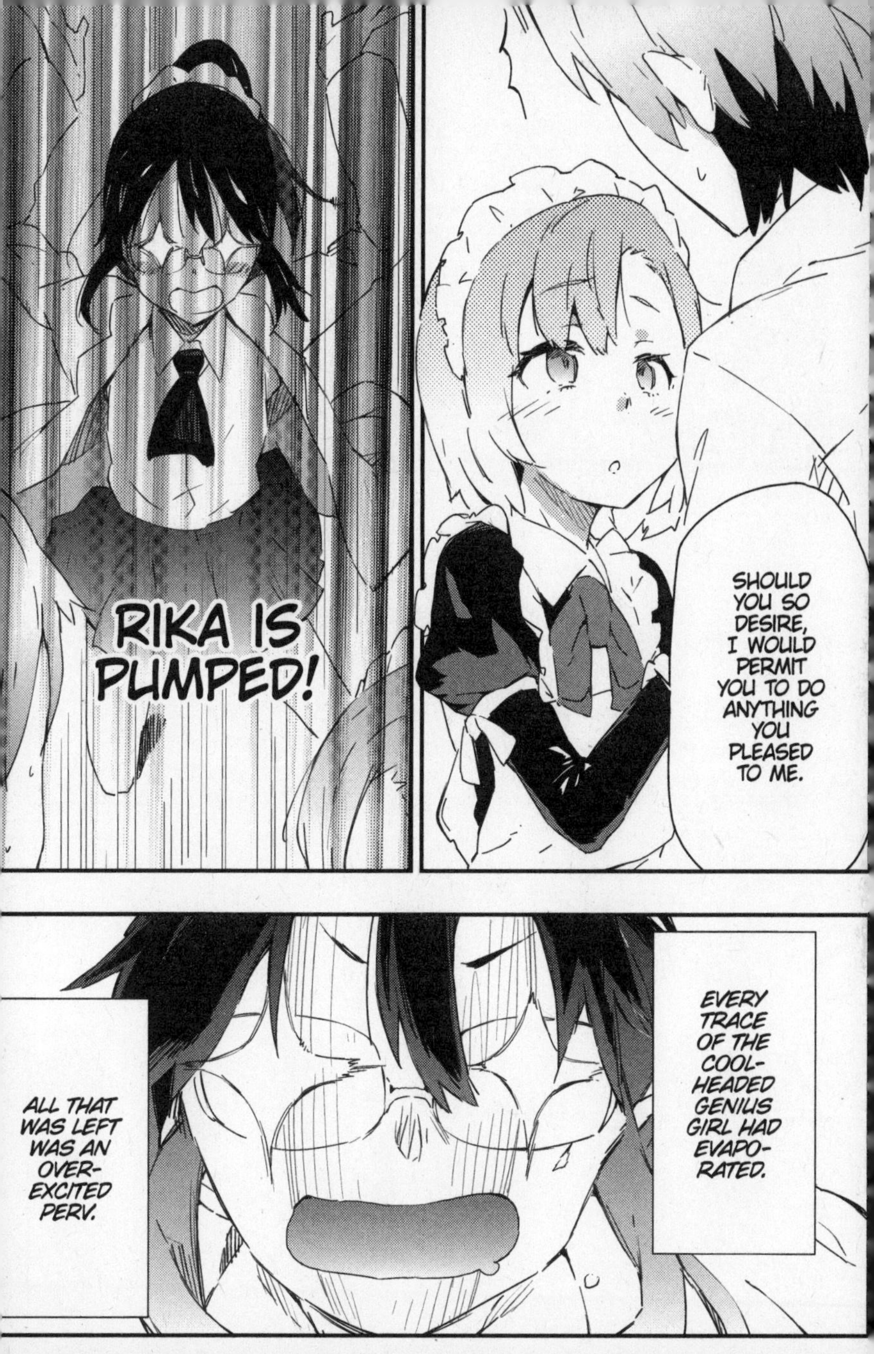
SHOULD YOU SO DESIRE, I WOULD PERMIT YOU TO DO ANYTHING YOU PLEASED TO ME.
RIKA IS PUMPED!
EVERY TRACE OF THE COOL-HEADED GENIUS GIRL HAD EVAPO-RATED.
ALL THAT WAS LEFT WAS AN OVER-EXCITED PERV.

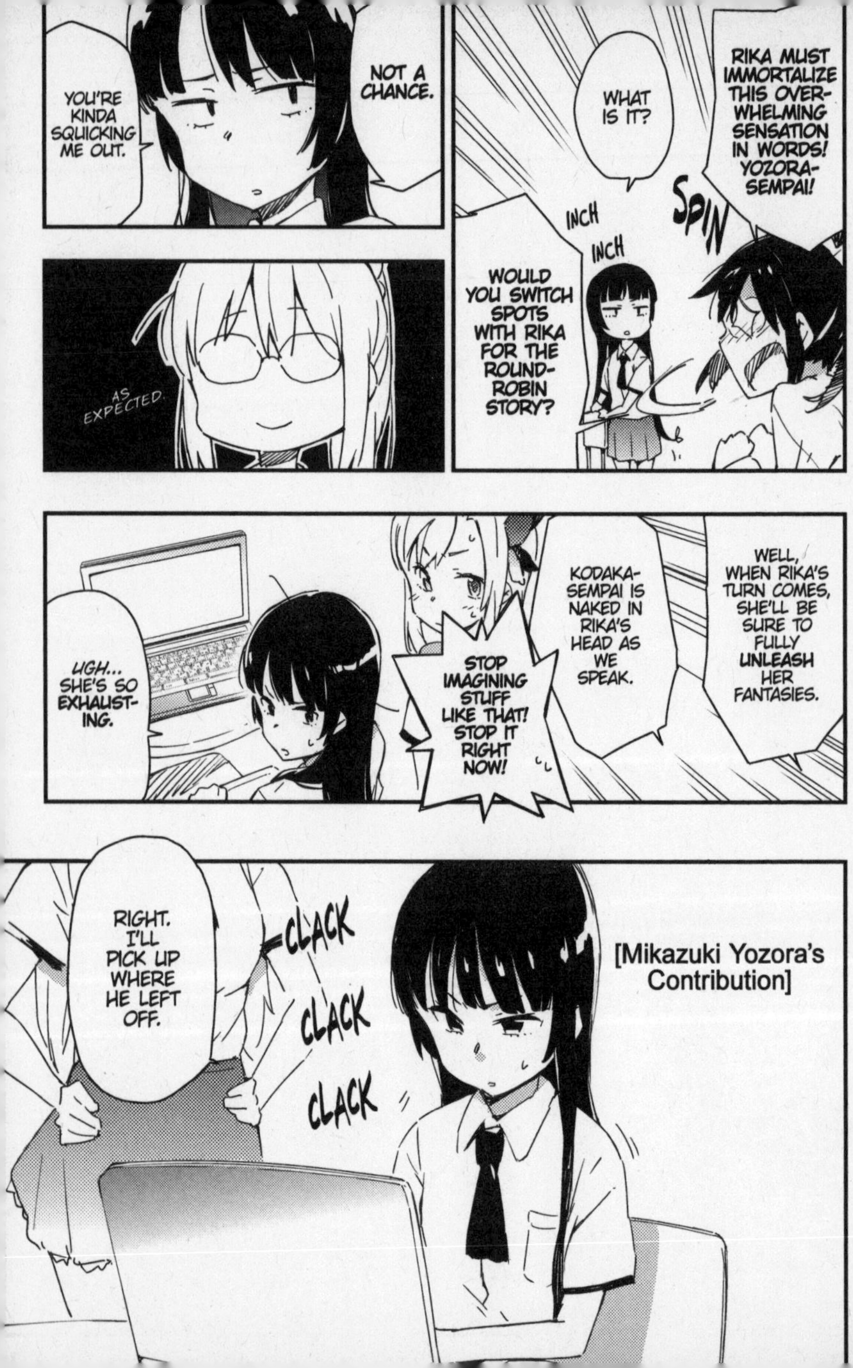

RIKA MUST IMMORTALIZE THIS OVERWHELMING SENSATION IN WORDS! YOZORA-SEMPAI!
WHAT IS IT?
SPIN
INCH
INCH
WOULD YOU SWITCH SPOTS WITH RIKA FOR THE ROUND-ROBIN STORY?
NOT A CHANCE.
YOU'RE KINDA SQUICKING ME OUT.
AS EXPECTED.
WELL, WHEN RIKA'S TURN COMES, SHE'LL BE SURE TO FULLY UNLEASH HER FANTASIES.
KODAKA-SEMPAI IS NAKED IN RIKA'S HEAD AS WE SPEAK.
STOP IMAGINING STUFF LIKE THAT! STOP IT RIGHT NOW!
UGH... SHE'S SO EXHAUSTING.
[Mikazuki Yozora's Contribution]
CLACK
CLACK
CLACK
RIGHT. I'LL PICK UP WHERE HE LEFT OFF.

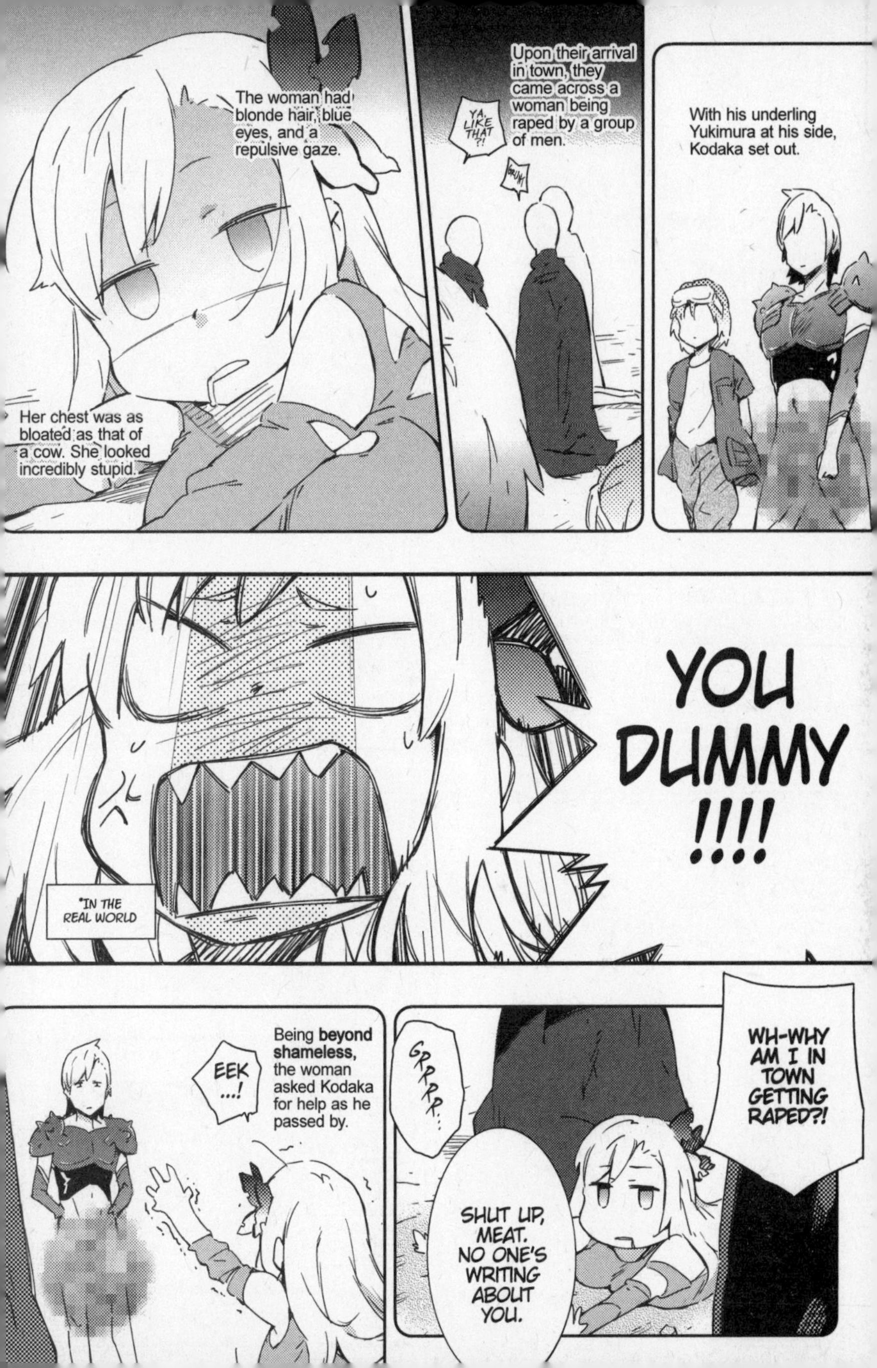

With his underling Yukimura at his side, Kodaka set out.
Upon their arrival in town, they came across a woman being raped by a group of men.
YA, LIKE THAT?!
GRUH!
The woman had blonde hair, blue eyes, and a repulsive gaze.
Her chest was as bloated as that of a cow. She looked incredibly stupid.
YOU DUMMY !!!!
*IN THE REAL WORLD
WH-WHY AM I IN TOWN GETTING RAPED?!
GRRRR...
SHUT UP, MEAT. NO ONE'S WRITING ABOUT YOU.
Being **beyond shameless,** the woman asked Kodaka for help as he passed by.
EEK ...!

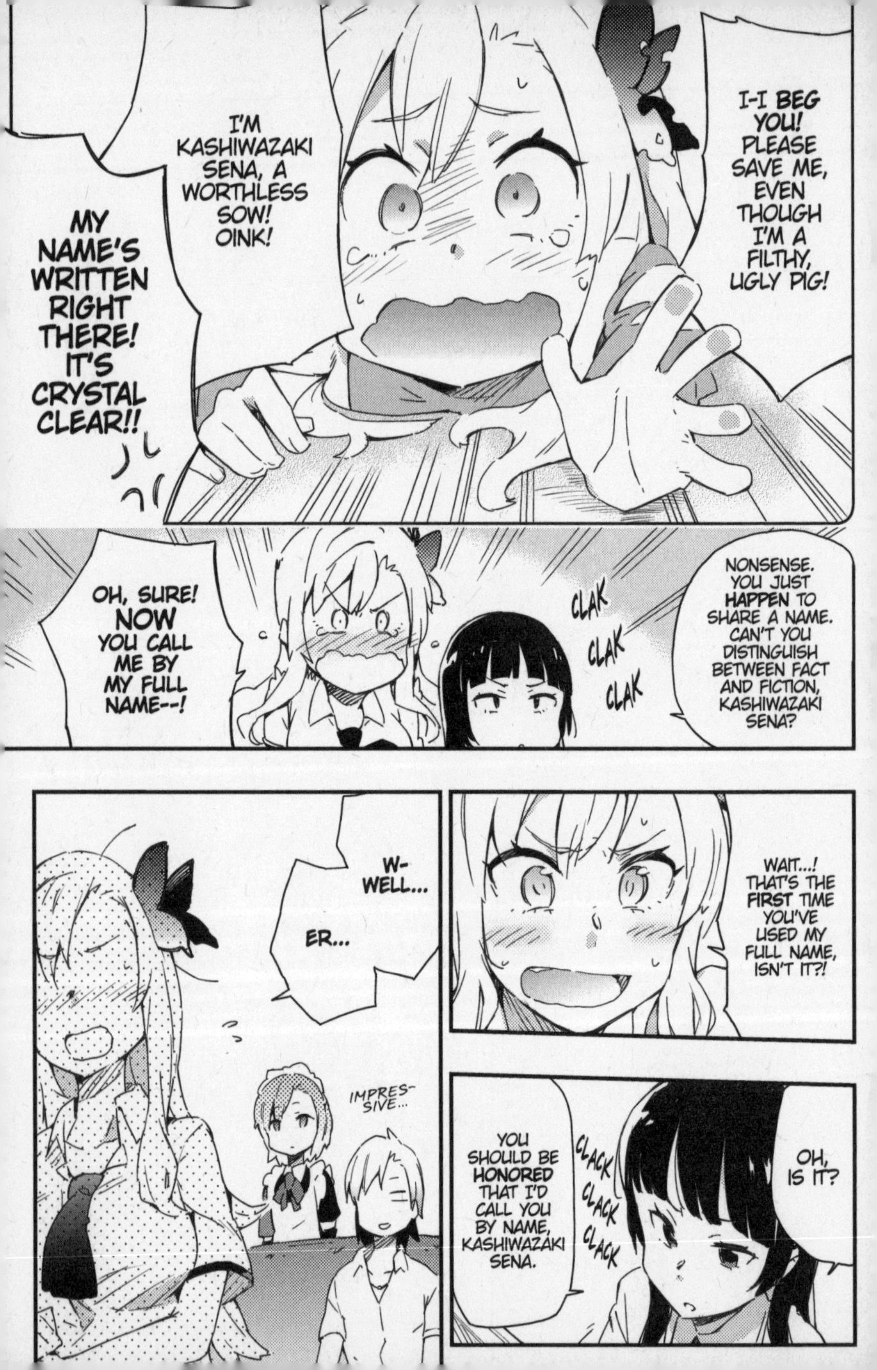
I-I BEG YOU! PLEASE SAVE ME, EVEN THOUGH I'M A FILTHY, UGLY PIG!
I'M KASHIWAZAKI SENA, A WORTHLESS SOW! OINK!
MY NAME'S WRITTEN RIGHT THERE! IT'S CRYSTAL CLEAR!!
NONSENSE. YOU JUST HAPPEN TO SHARE A NAME. CAN'T YOU DISTINGUISH BETWEEN FACT AND FICTION, KASHIWAZAKI SENA?
CLAK CLAK CLAK
OH, SURE! NOW YOU CALL ME BY MY FULL NAME--!
WAIT...! THAT'S THE FIRST TIME YOU'VE USED MY FULL NAME, ISN'T IT?!
OH, IS IT?
CLACK CLACK CLACK
YOU SHOULD BE HONORED THAT I'D CALL YOU BY NAME, KASHIWAZAKI SENA.
W-WELL...
ER...
IMPRES-SIVE...

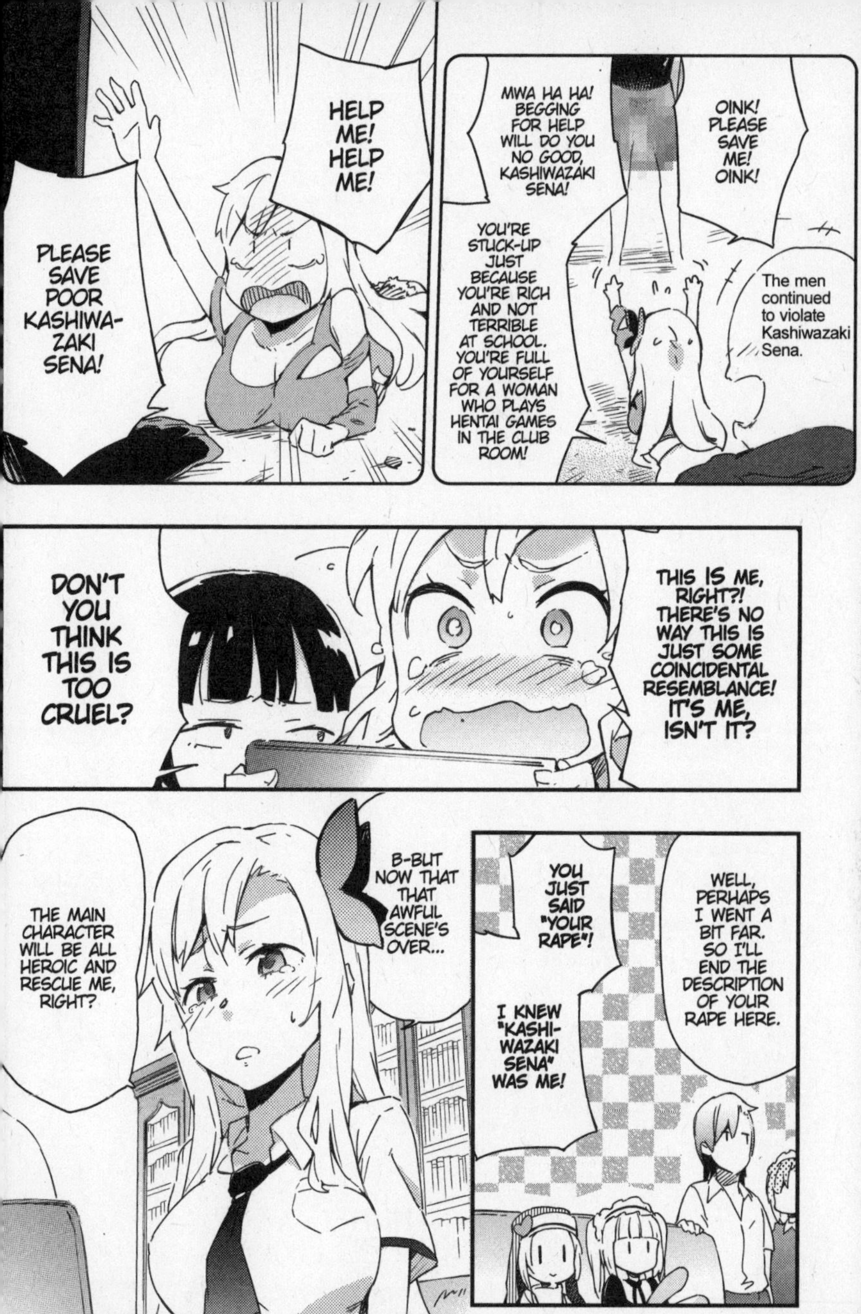
The men continued to violate Kashiwazaki Sena.
OINK! PLEASE SAVE ME! OINK!
MWA HA HA! BEGGING FOR HELP WILL DO YOU NO GOOD, KASHIWAZAKI SENA!
YOU'RE STUCK-UP JUST BECAUSE YOU'RE RICH AND NOT TERRIBLE AT SCHOOL. YOU'RE FULL OF YOURSELF FOR A WOMAN WHO PLAYS HENTAI GAMES IN THE CLUB ROOM!
HELP ME! HELP ME!
PLEASE SAVE POOR KASHIWAZAKI SENA!
THIS IS ME, RIGHT?! THERE'S NO WAY THIS IS JUST SOME COINCIDENTAL RESEMBLANCE! IT'S ME, ISN'T IT?
DON'T YOU THINK THIS IS TOO CRUEL?
WELL, PERHAPS I WENT A BIT FAR. SO I'LL END THE DESCRIPTION OF YOUR RAPE HERE.
YOU JUST SAID "YOUR RAPE"!
I KNEW "KASHIWAZAKI SENA" WAS ME!
B-BUT NOW THAT THAT AWFUL SCENE'S OVER...
THE MAIN CHARACTER WILL BE ALL HEROIC AND RESCUE ME, RIGHT?

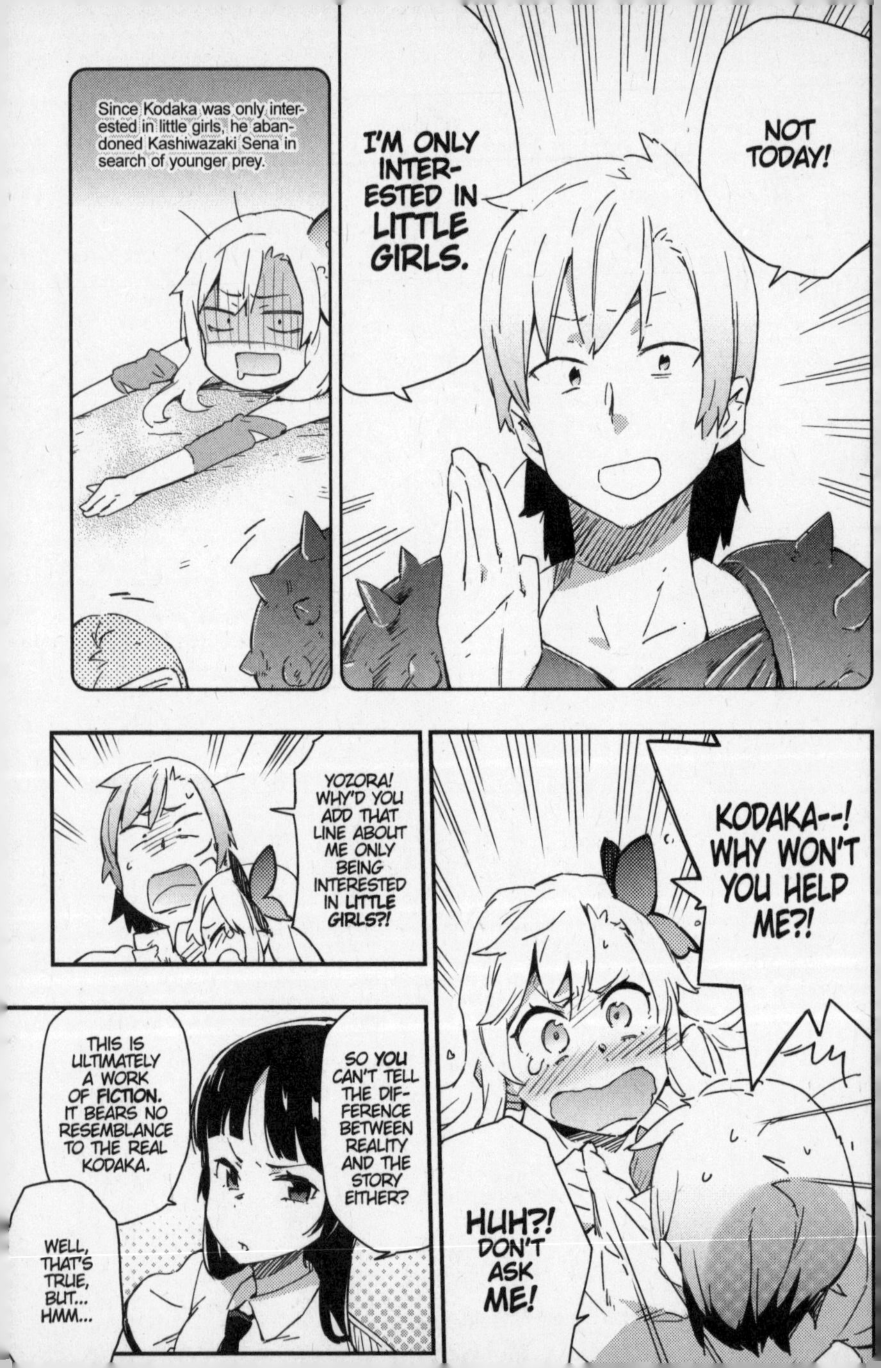
NOT TODAY!
I'M ONLY INTER-ESTED IN LITTLE GIRLS.
Since Kodaka was only interested in little girls, he abandoned Kashiwazaki Sena in search of younger prey.
KODAKA--! WHY WON'T YOU HELP ME?!
HUH?! DON'T ASK ME!
YOZORA! WHY'D YOU ADD THAT LINE ABOUT ME ONLY BEING INTERESTED IN LITTLE GIRLS?!
SO YOU CAN'T TELL THE DIF-FERENCE BETWEEN REALITY AND THE STORY EITHER?
THIS IS ULTIMATELY A WORK OF FICTION. IT BEARS NO RESEMBLANCE TO THE REAL KODAKA.
WELL, THAT'S TRUE, BUT... HMM...

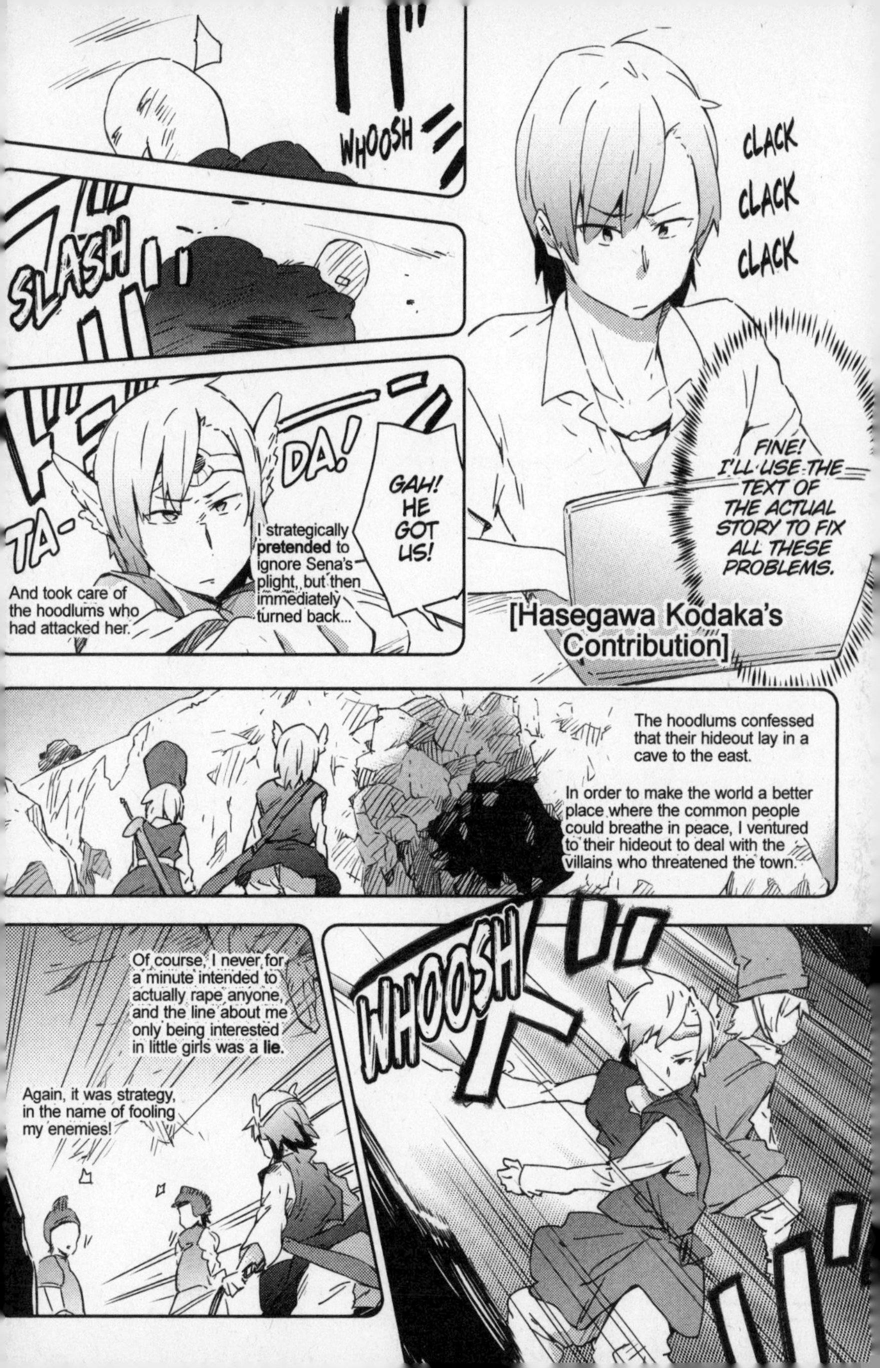
CLACK CLACK CLACK
FINE! I'LL USE THE TEXT OF THE ACTUAL STORY TO FIX ALL THESE PROBLEMS.
[Hasegawa Kodaka's Contribution]
WHOOSH
SLASH
TA-DA!
GAH! HE GOT US!
I strategically **pretended** to ignore Sena's plight, but then immediately turned back...
And took care of the hoodlums who had attacked her.
The hoodlums confessed that their hideout lay in a cave to the east.
In order to make the world a better place where the common people could breathe in peace, I ventured to their hideout to deal with the villains who threatened the town.
WHOOSH
Of course, I never for a minute intended to actually rape anyone, and the line about me only being interested in little girls was a **lie**.
Again, it was strategy, in the name of fooling my enemies!

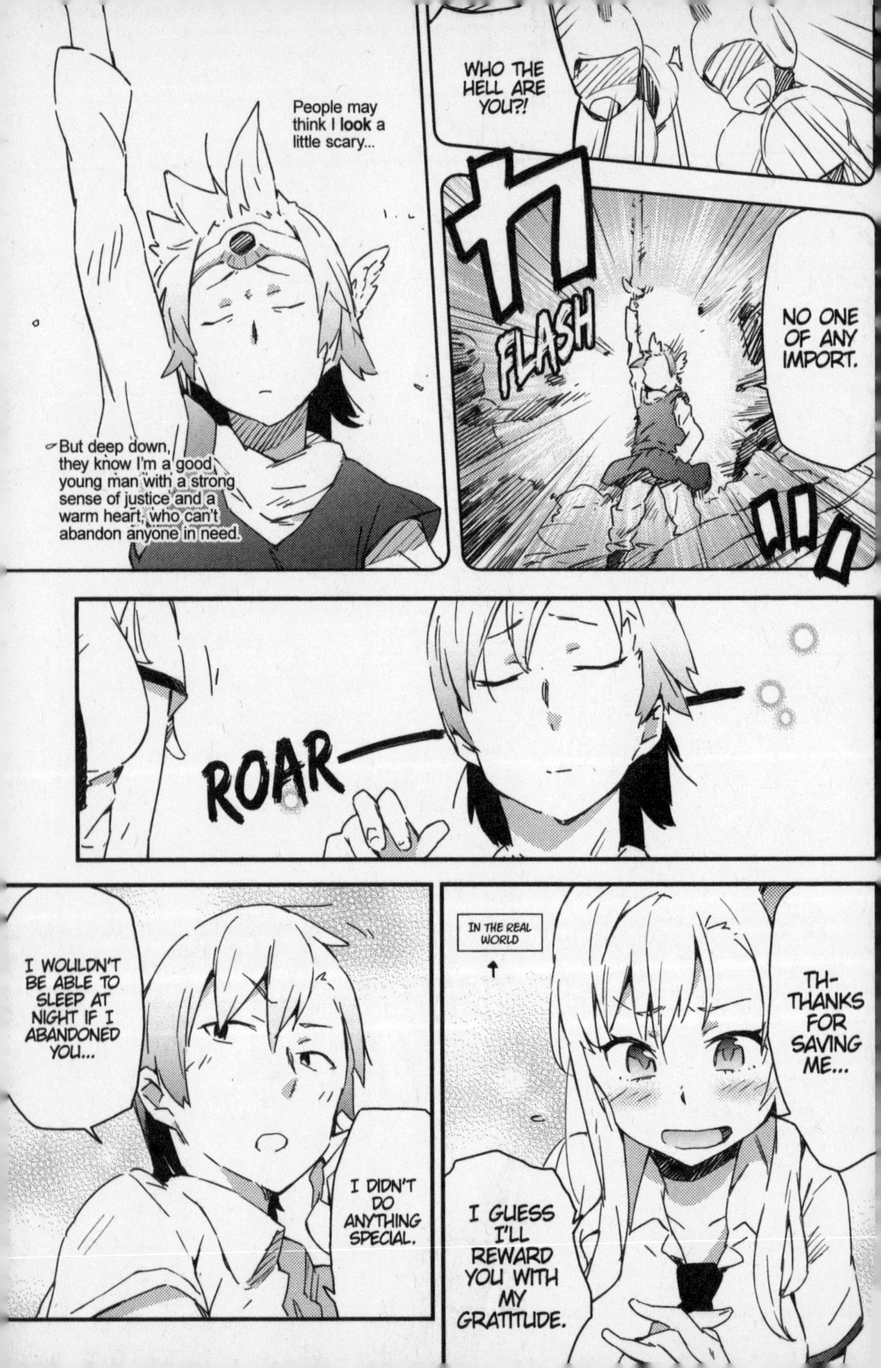
WHO THE HELL ARE YOU?!
FLASH
NO ONE OF ANY IMPORT.
People may think I **look** a little scary...
But deep down, they know I'm a good young man with a strong sense of justice and a warm heart, who can't abandon anyone in need.
ROAR
IN THE REAL WORLD
TH-THANKS FOR SAVING ME...
I GUESS I'LL REWARD YOU WITH MY GRATITUDE.
I WOULDN'T BE ABLE TO SLEEP AT NIGHT IF I ABANDONED YOU...
I DIDN'T DO ANYTHING SPECIAL.

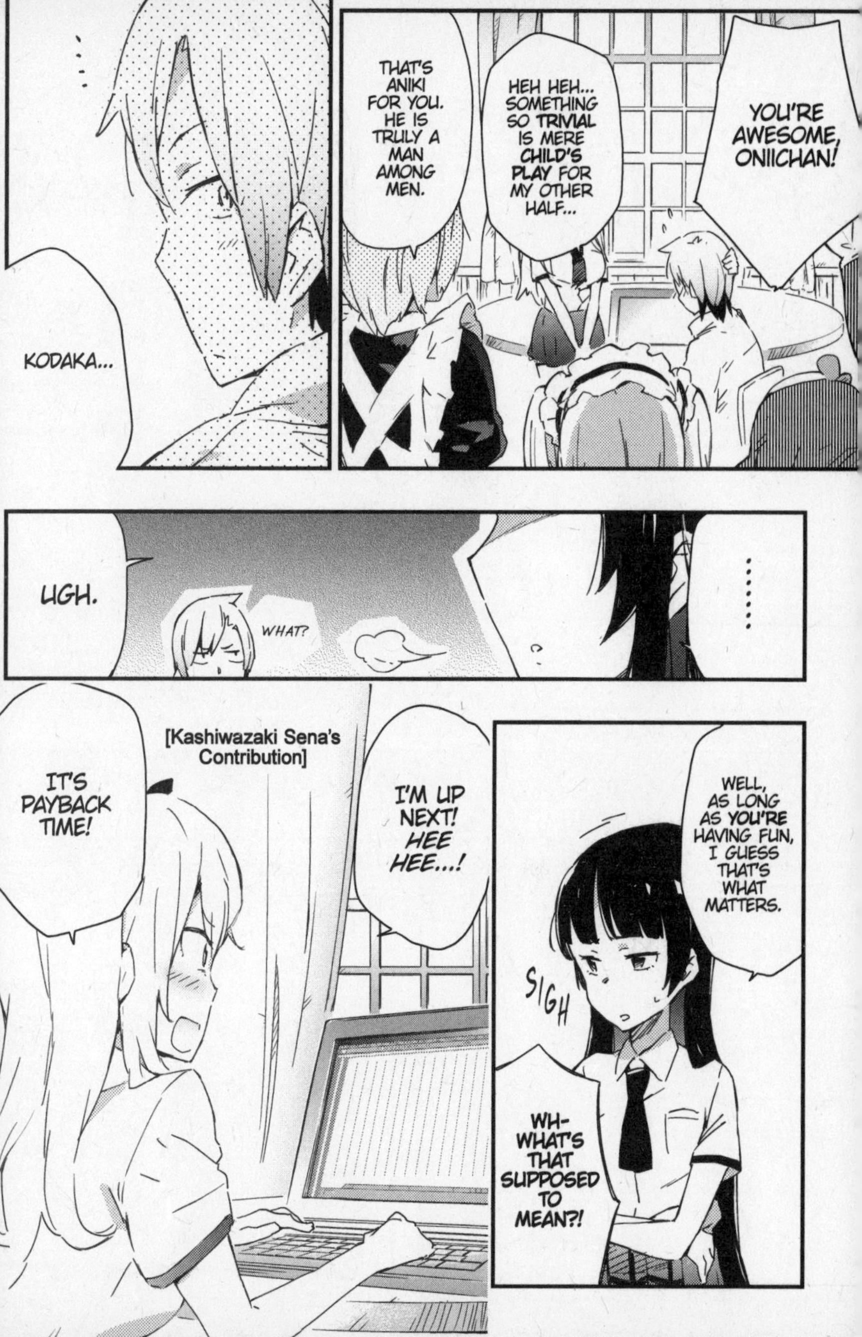
YOU'RE AWESOME, ONIICHAN!
HEH HEH... SOMETHING SO TRIVIAL IS MERE CHILD'S PLAY FOR MY OTHER HALF...
THAT'S ANIKI FOR YOU. HE IS TRULY A MAN AMONG MEN.
...
KODAKA...
......
UGH.
WHAT?
WELL, AS LONG AS YOU'RE HAVING FUN, I GUESS THAT'S WHAT MATTERS.
SIGH
WH- WHAT'S THAT SUPPOSED TO MEAN?!
I'M UP NEXT! HEE HEE...!
[Kashiwazaki Sena's Contribution]
IT'S PAYBACK TIME!

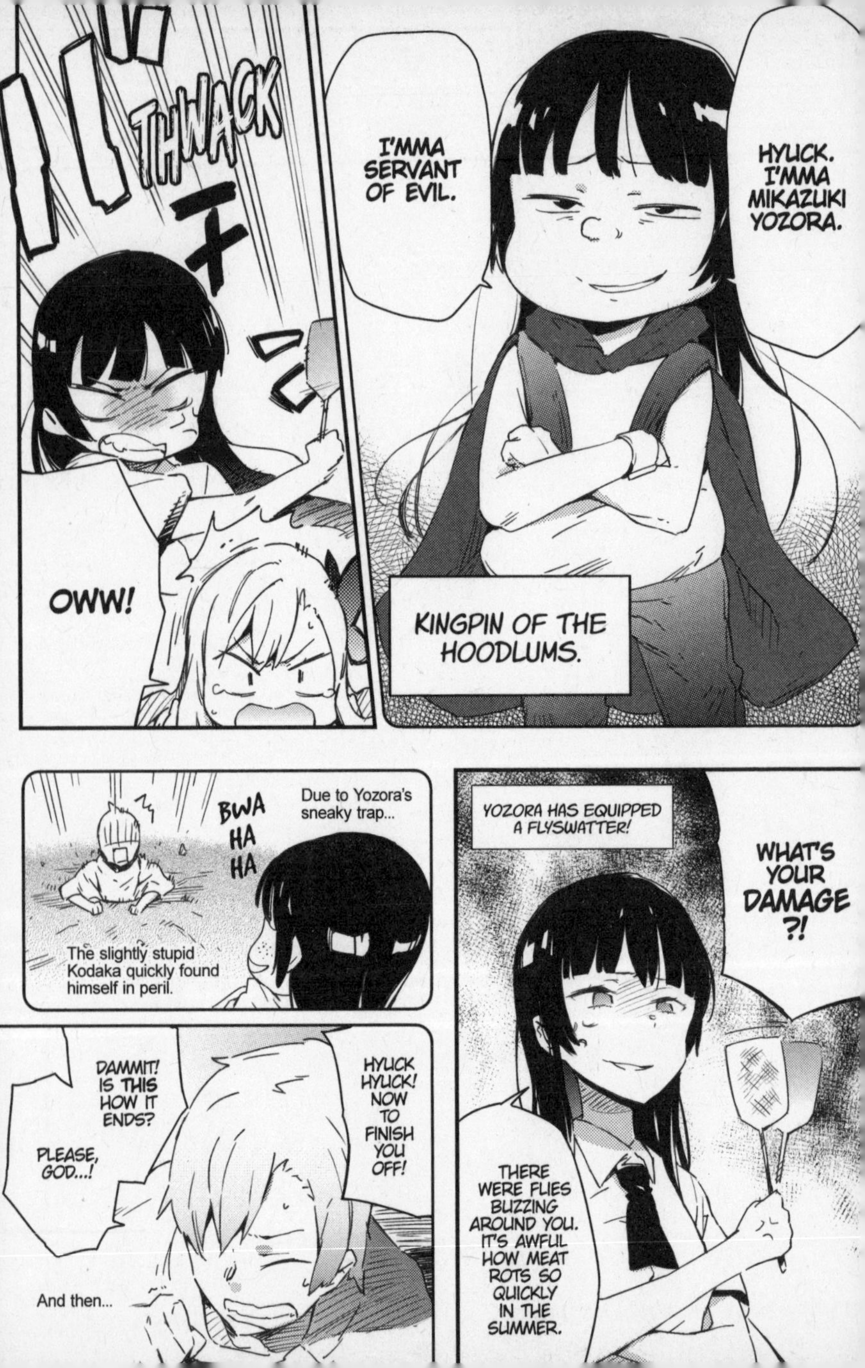
HYUCK. I'MMA MIKAZUKI YOZORA.
I'MMA SERVANT OF EVIL.
KINGPIN OF THE HOODLUMS.
THWACK
OWW!
YOZORA HAS EQUIPPED A FLYSWATTER!
WHAT'S YOUR DAMAGE?!
THERE WERE FLIES BUZZING AROUND YOU. IT'S AWFUL HOW MEAT ROTS SO QUICKLY IN THE SUMMER.
Due to Yozora's sneaky trap...
BWA HA HA
The slightly stupid Kodaka quickly found himself in peril.
HYUCK HYUCK! NOW TO FINISH YOU OFF!
DAMMIT! IS THIS HOW IT ENDS?
PLEASE, GOD...!
And then...

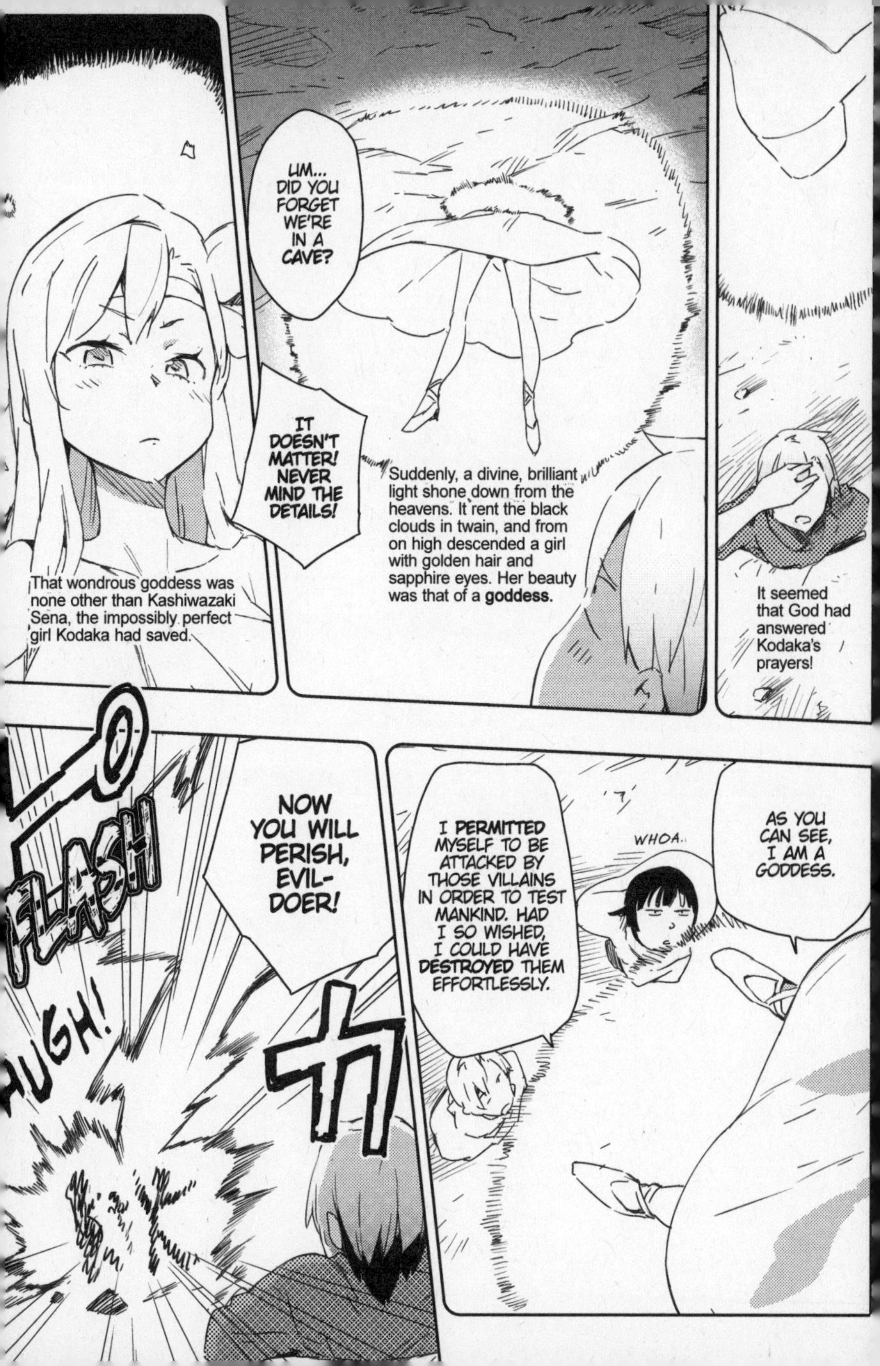
It seemed that God had answered Kodaka's prayers!
Suddenly, a divine, brilliant light shone down from the heavens. It rent the black clouds in twain, and from on high descended a girl with golden hair and sapphire eyes. Her beauty was that of a **goddess**.
UM... DID YOU FORGET WE'RE IN A CAVE?
IT DOESN'T MATTER! NEVER MIND THE DETAILS!
That wondrous goddess was none other than Kashiwazaki Sena, the impossibly perfect girl Kodaka had saved.
AS YOU CAN SEE, I AM A GODDESS.
WHOA..
I PERMITTED MYSELF TO BE ATTACKED BY THOSE VILLAINS IN ORDER TO TEST MANKIND. HAD I SO WISHED, I COULD HAVE **DESTROYED** THEM EFFORTLESSLY.
NOW YOU WILL PERISH, EVIL-DOER!
FLASH
UGH!

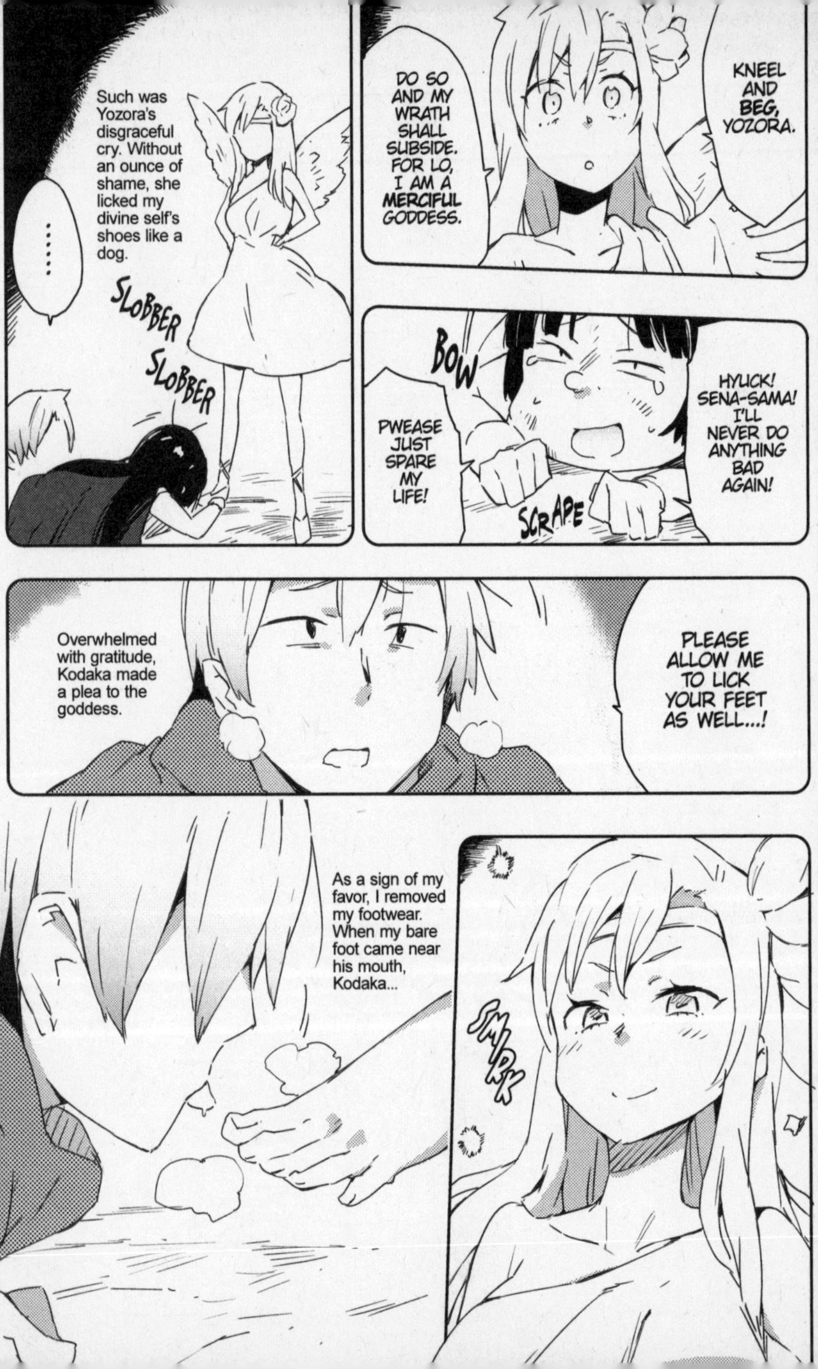
KNEEL AND BEG, YOZORA.
DO SO AND MY WRATH SHALL SUBSIDE. FOR LO, I AM A MERCIFUL GODDESS.
HYUCK! SENA-SAMA! I'LL NEVER DO ANYTHING BAD AGAIN!
BOW
PWEASE JUST SPARE MY LIFE!
SCRAPE
Such was Yozora's disgraceful cry. Without an ounce of shame, she licked my divine self's shoes like a dog.
......
SLOBBER
SLOBBER
PLEASE ALLOW ME TO LICK YOUR FEET AS WELL...!
Overwhelmed with gratitude, Kodaka made a plea to the goddess.
SMIRK
As a sign of my favor, I removed my footwear. When my bare foot came near his mouth, Kodaka...

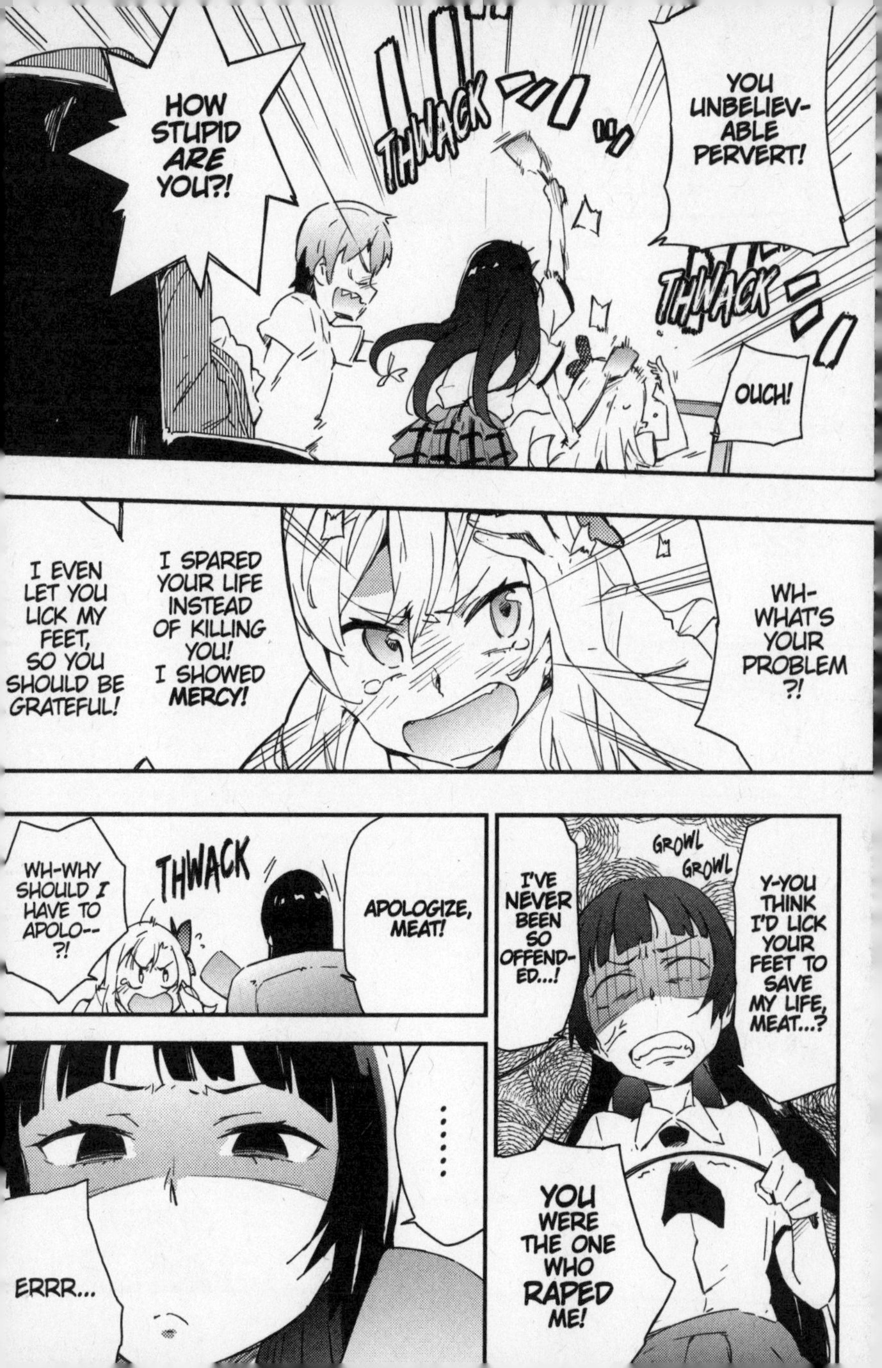
YOU UNBELIEVABLE PERVERT!
THWACK
HOW STUPID ARE YOU?!
THWACK
OUCH!
WH-WHAT'S YOUR PROBLEM?!
I SPARED YOUR LIFE INSTEAD OF KILLING YOU! I SHOWED MERCY!
I EVEN LET YOU LICK MY FEET, SO YOU SHOULD BE GRATEFUL!
Y-YOU THINK I'D LICK YOUR FEET TO SAVE MY LIFE, MEAT...?
GROWL GROWL
I'VE NEVER BEEN SO OFFENDED...!
YOU WERE THE ONE WHO RAPED ME!
APOLOGIZE, MEAT!
THWACK
WH-WHY SHOULD I HAVE TO APOLO--?!
......
ERRR...

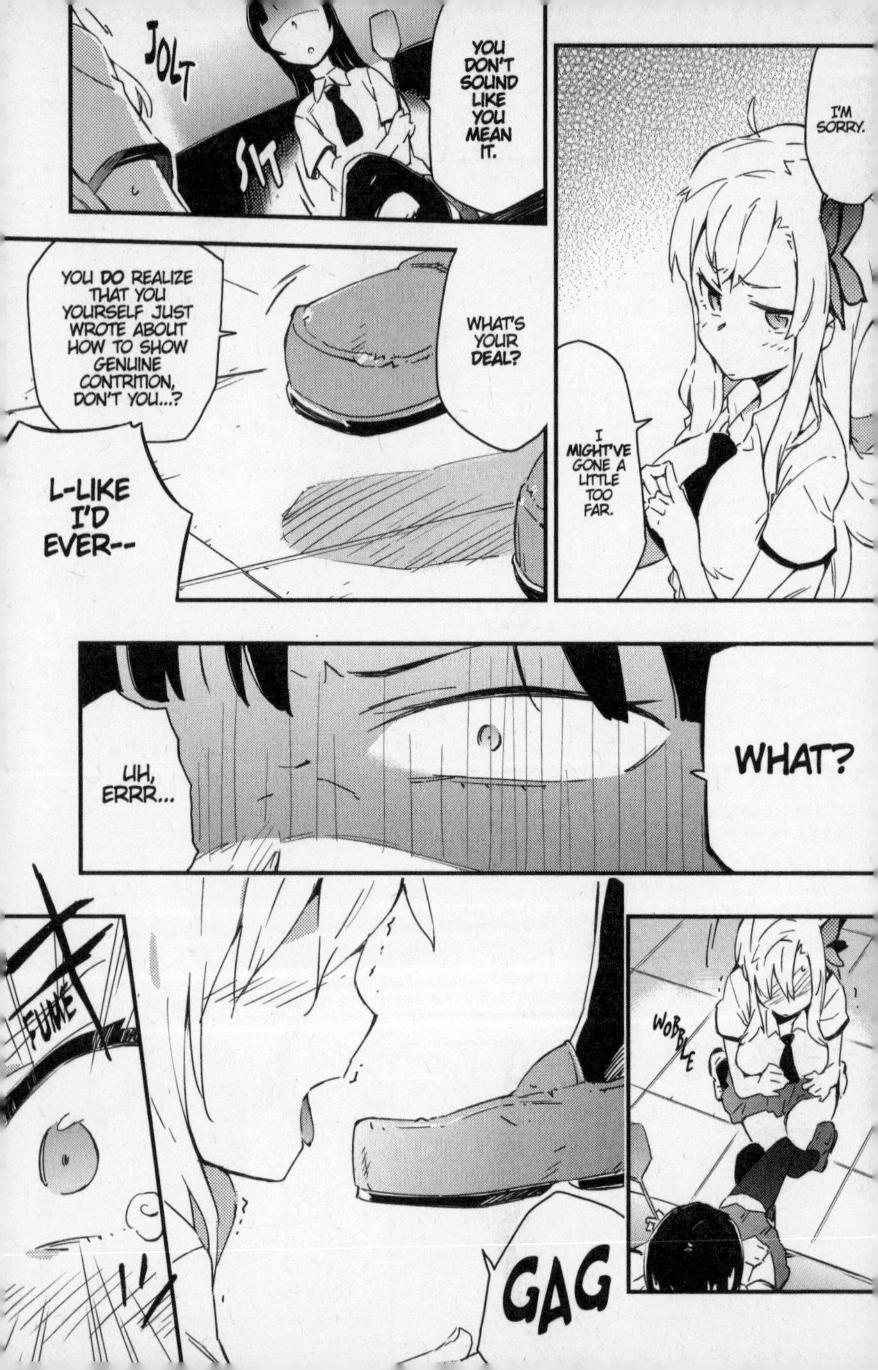
I'M SORRY.
I MIGHT'VE GONE A LITTLE TOO FAR.
YOU DON'T SOUND LIKE YOU MEAN IT.
JOLT
SIT
WHAT'S YOUR DEAL?
YOU DO REALIZE THAT YOU YOURSELF JUST WROTE ABOUT HOW TO SHOW GENUINE CONTRITION, DON'T YOU...?
L-LIKE I'D EVER--
WHAT?
UH, ERRR...
WOBBLE
FUME
GAG

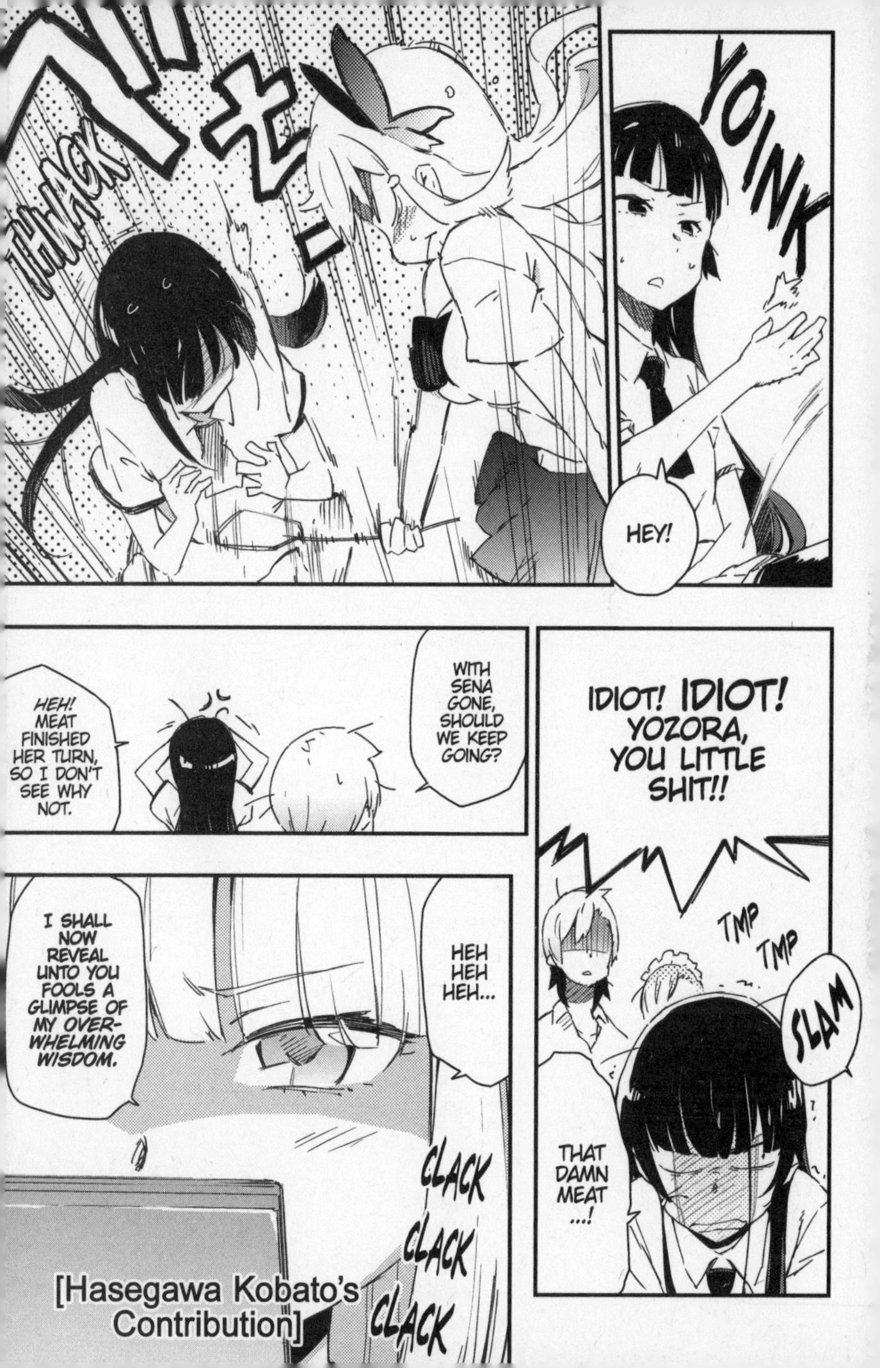
YOINK
HEY!
THWACK
IDIOT! IDIOT! YOZORA, YOU LITTLE SHIT!!
TMP
TMP
SLAM
THAT DAMN MEAT ...!
WITH SENA GONE, SHOULD WE KEEP GOING?
HEH! MEAT FINISHED HER TURN, SO I DON'T SEE WHY NOT.
HEH HEH HEH...
I SHALL NOW REVEAL UNTO YOU FOOLS A GLIMPSE OF MY OVER-WHELMING WISDOM.
CLACK
CLACK
CLACK
[Hasegawa Kobato's Contribution]

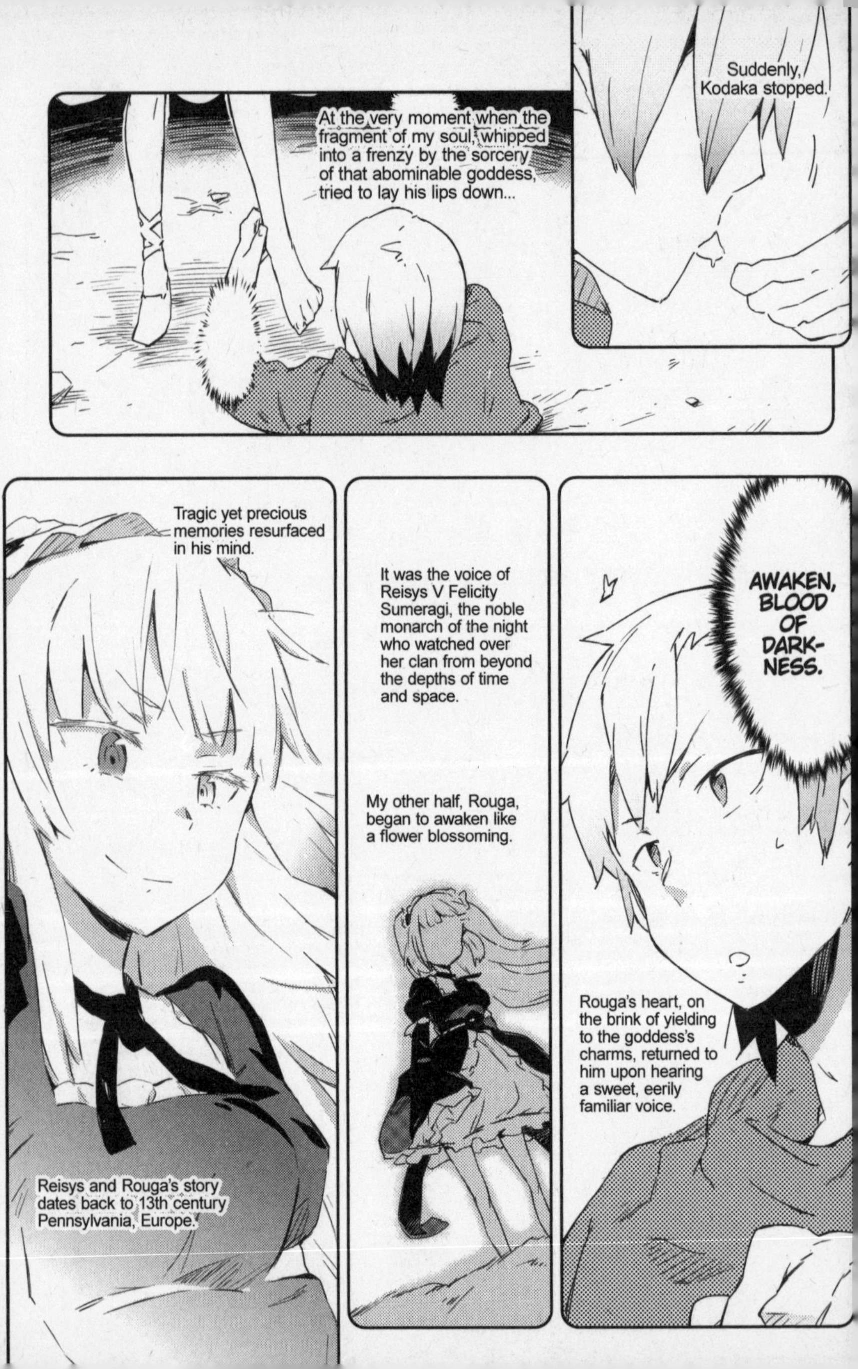
Suddenly, Kodaka stopped.
At the very moment when the fragment of my soul, whipped into a frenzy by the sorcery of that abominable goddess, tried to lay his lips down...
AWAKEN, BLOOD OF DARK-NESS.
Rouga's heart, on the brink of yielding to the goddess's charms, returned to him upon hearing a sweet, eerily familiar voice.
It was the voice of Reisys V Felicity Sumeragi, the noble monarch of the night who watched over her clan from beyond the depths of time and space.
My other half, Rouga, began to awaken like a flower blossoming.
Tragic yet precious memories resurfaced in his mind.
Reisys and Rouga's story dates back to 13th century Pennsylvania, Europe.

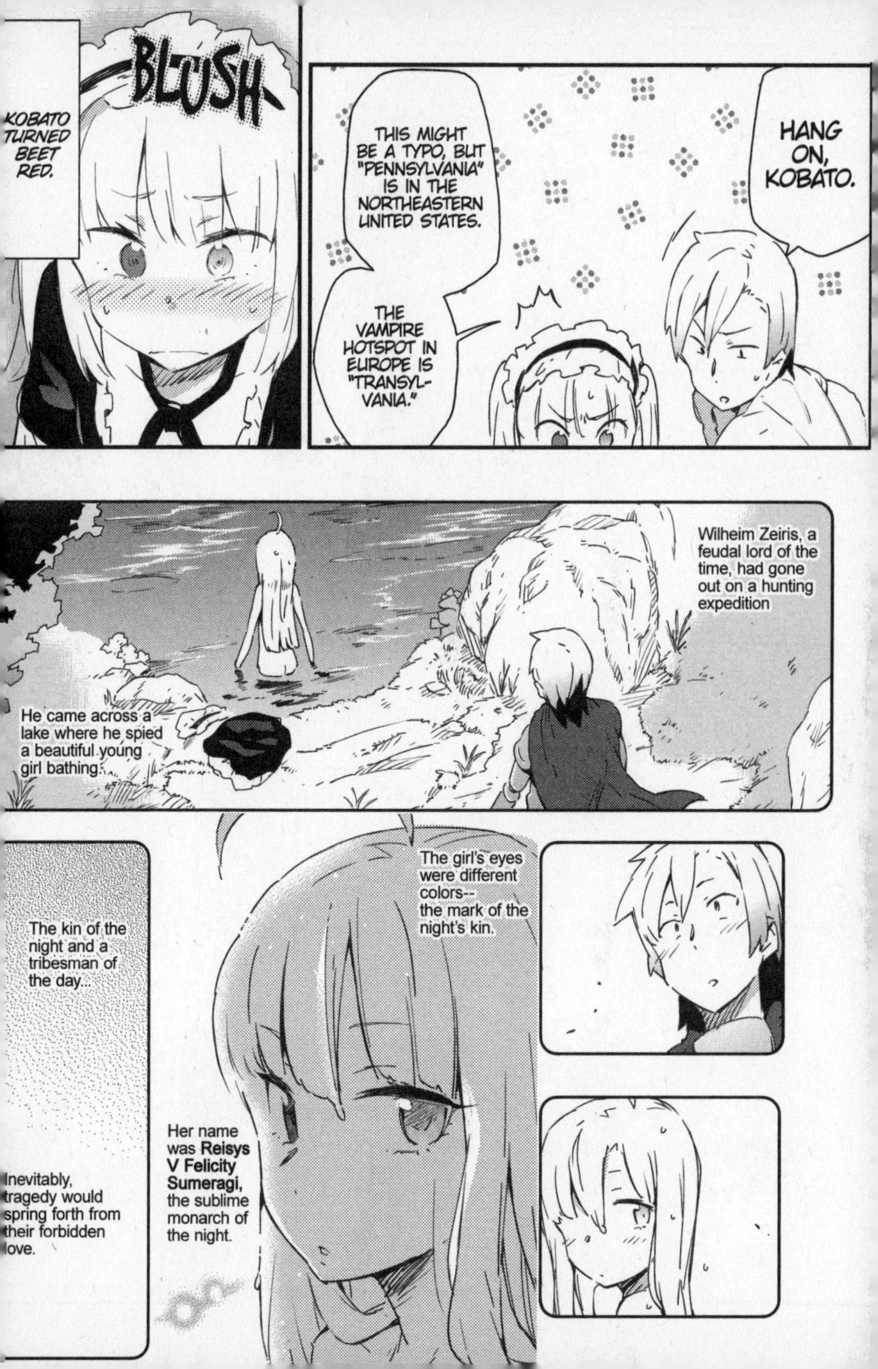
HANG ON, KOBATO.
THIS MIGHT BE A TYPO, BUT "PENNSYLVANIA" IS IN THE NORTHEASTERN UNITED STATES.
THE VAMPIRE HOTSPOT IN EUROPE IS "TRANSYLVANIA."
BLUSH
KOBATO TURNED BEET RED.
Wilheim Zeiris, a feudal lord of the time, had gone out on a hunting expedition
He came across a lake where he spied a beautiful young girl bathing.
The girl's eyes were different colors-- the mark of the night's kin.
Her name was **Reisys V Felicity Sumeragi**, the sublime monarch of the night.
The kin of the night and a tribesman of the day...
Inevitably, tragedy would spring forth from their forbidden love.

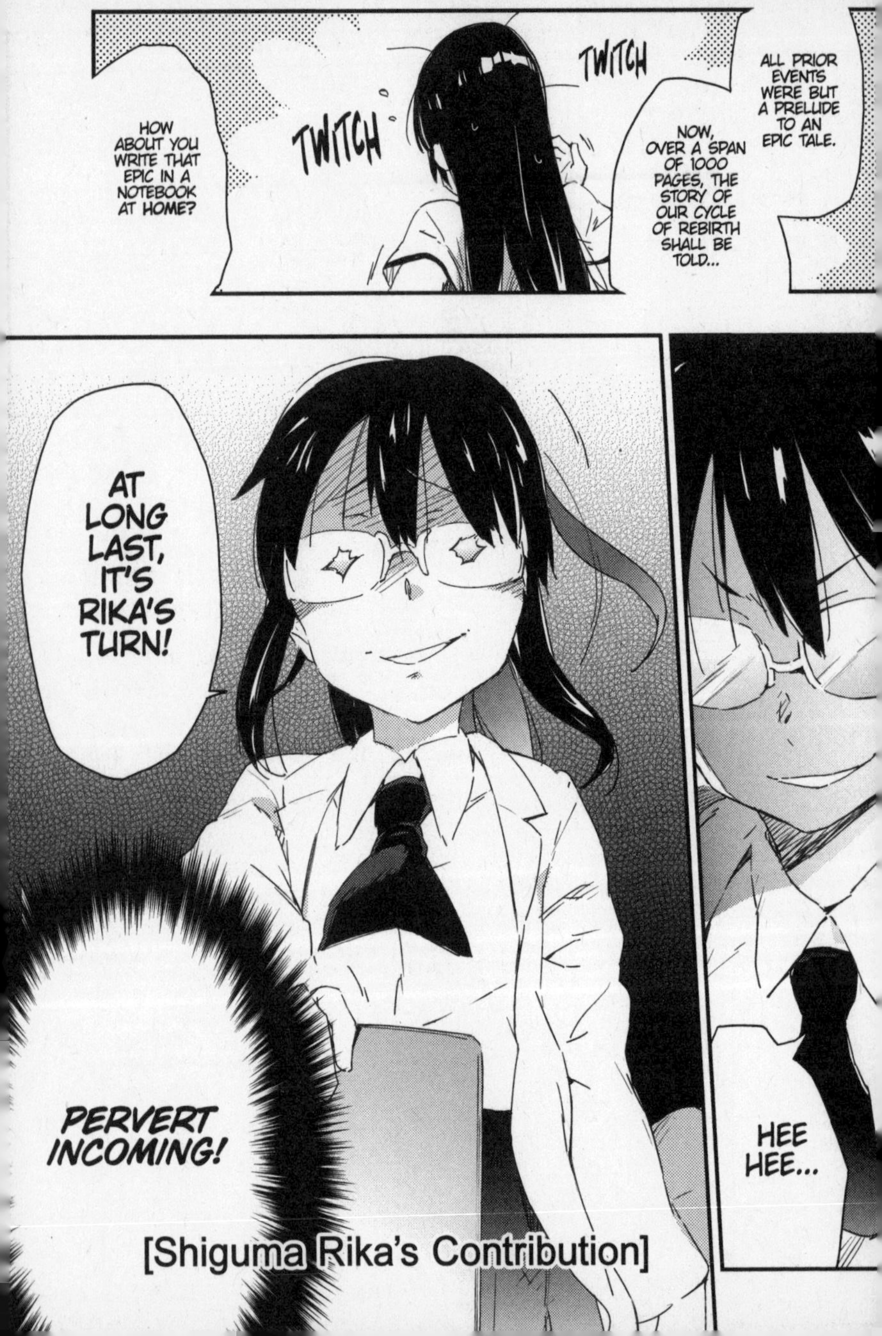
ALL PRIOR EVENTS WERE BUT A PRELUDE TO AN EPIC TALE.
NOW, OVER A SPAN OF 1000 PAGES, THE STORY OF OUR CYCLE OF REBIRTH SHALL BE TOLD...
TWITCH
TWITCH
HOW ABOUT YOU WRITE THAT EPIC IN A NOTEBOOK AT HOME?
HEE HEE...
AT LONG LAST, IT'S RIKA'S TURN!
PERVERT INCOMING!
[Shiguma Rika's Contribution]

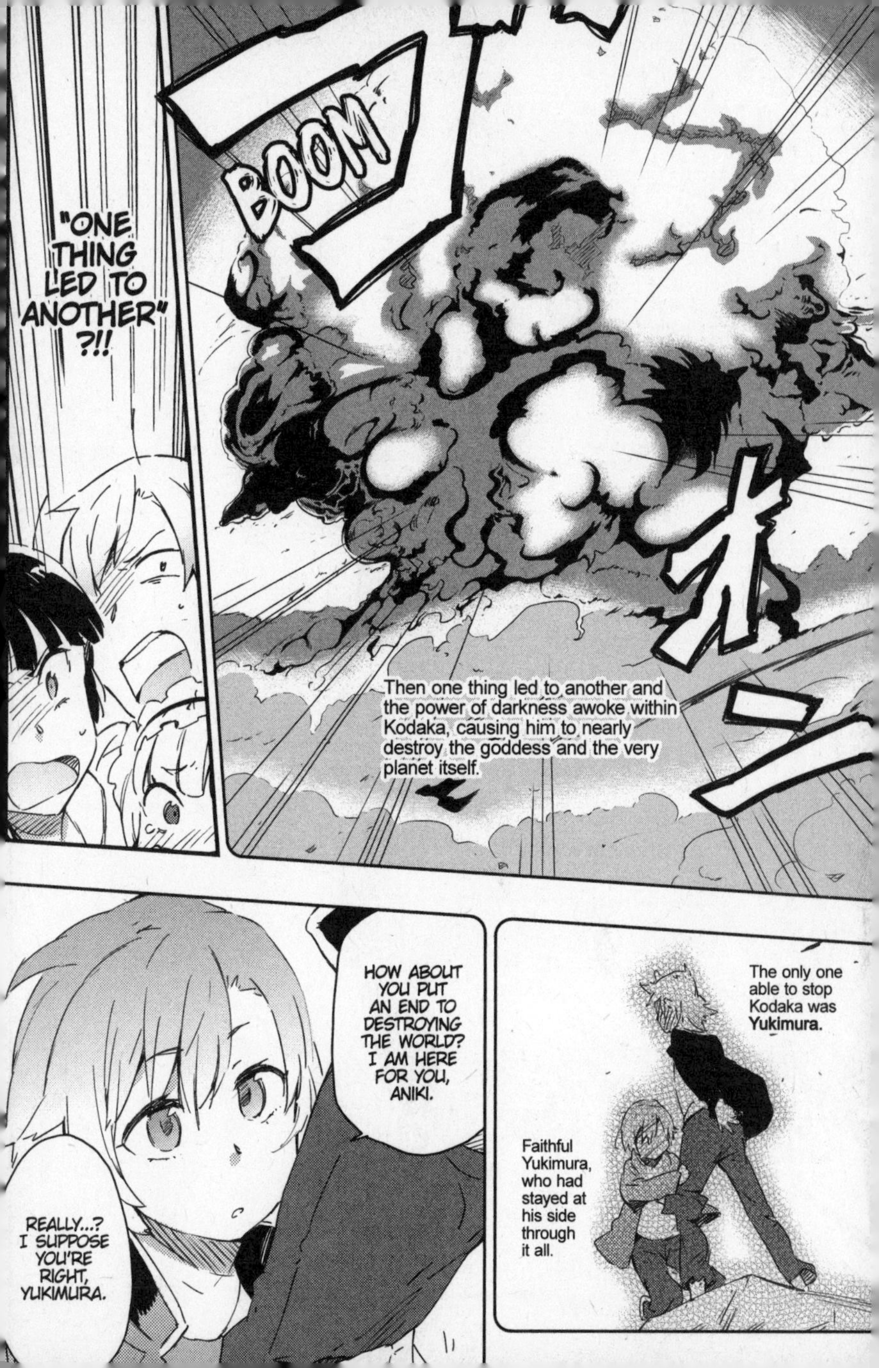
BOOM
Then one thing led to another and the power of darkness awoke within Kodaka, causing him to nearly destroy the goddess and the very planet itself.
"ONE THING LED TO ANOTHER" ?!!
The only one able to stop Kodaka was **Yukimura.**
Faithful Yukimura, who had stayed at his side through it all.
HOW ABOUT YOU PUT AN END TO DESTROYING THE WORLD? I AM HERE FOR YOU, ANIKI.
REALLY...? I SUPPOSE YOU'RE RIGHT, YUKIMURA.

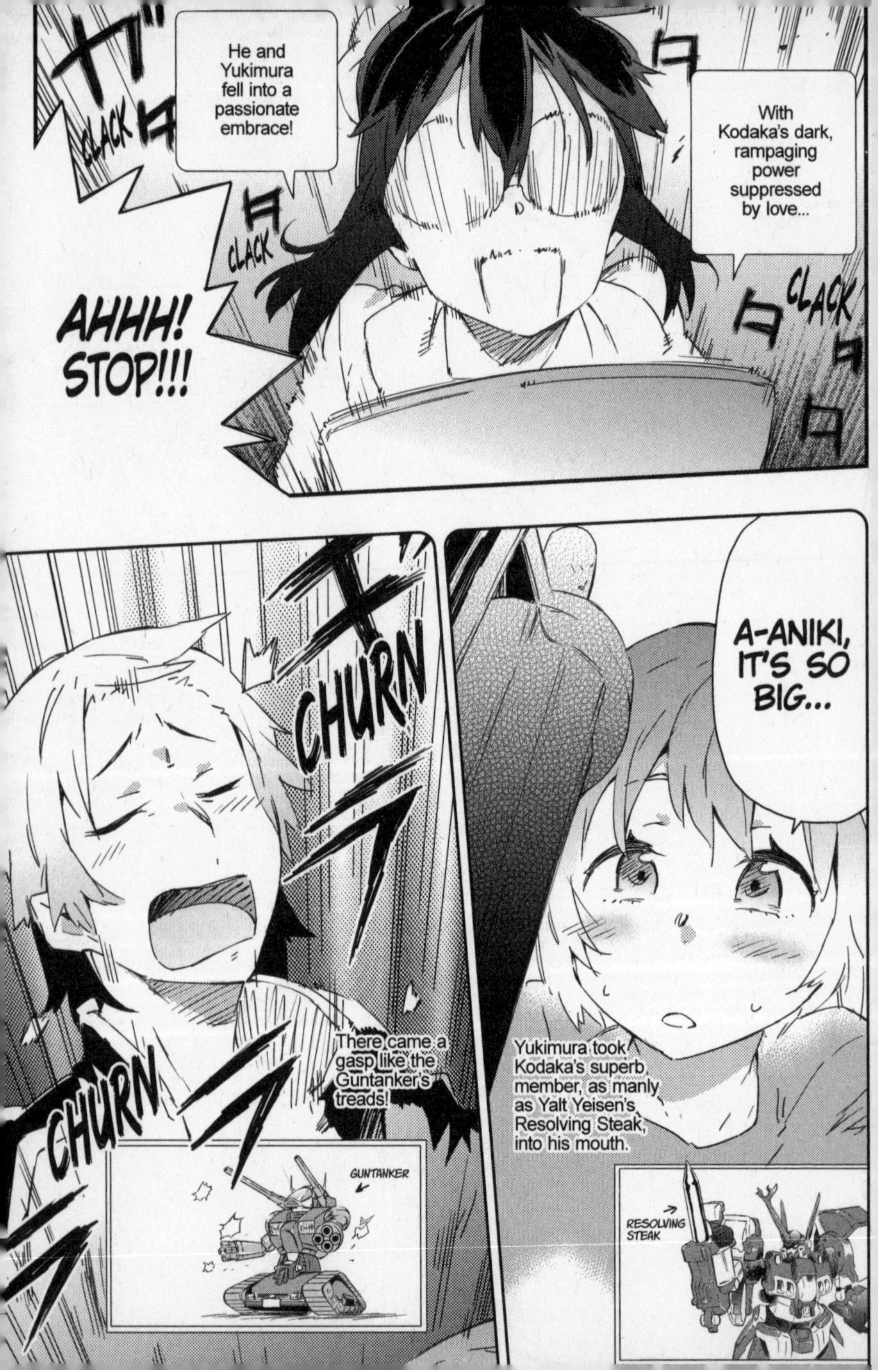
With Kodaka's dark, rampaging power suppressed by love...
CLACK
He and Yukimura fell into a passionate embrace!
CLACK
CLACK
AHHH! STOP!!!
A-ANIKI, IT'S SO BIG...
Yukimura took Kodaka's superb member, as manly as Yalt Yeisen's Resolving Steak, into his mouth.
RESOLVING STEAK
CHURN
There came a gasp like the Guntanker's treads!
CHURN
GUNTANKER

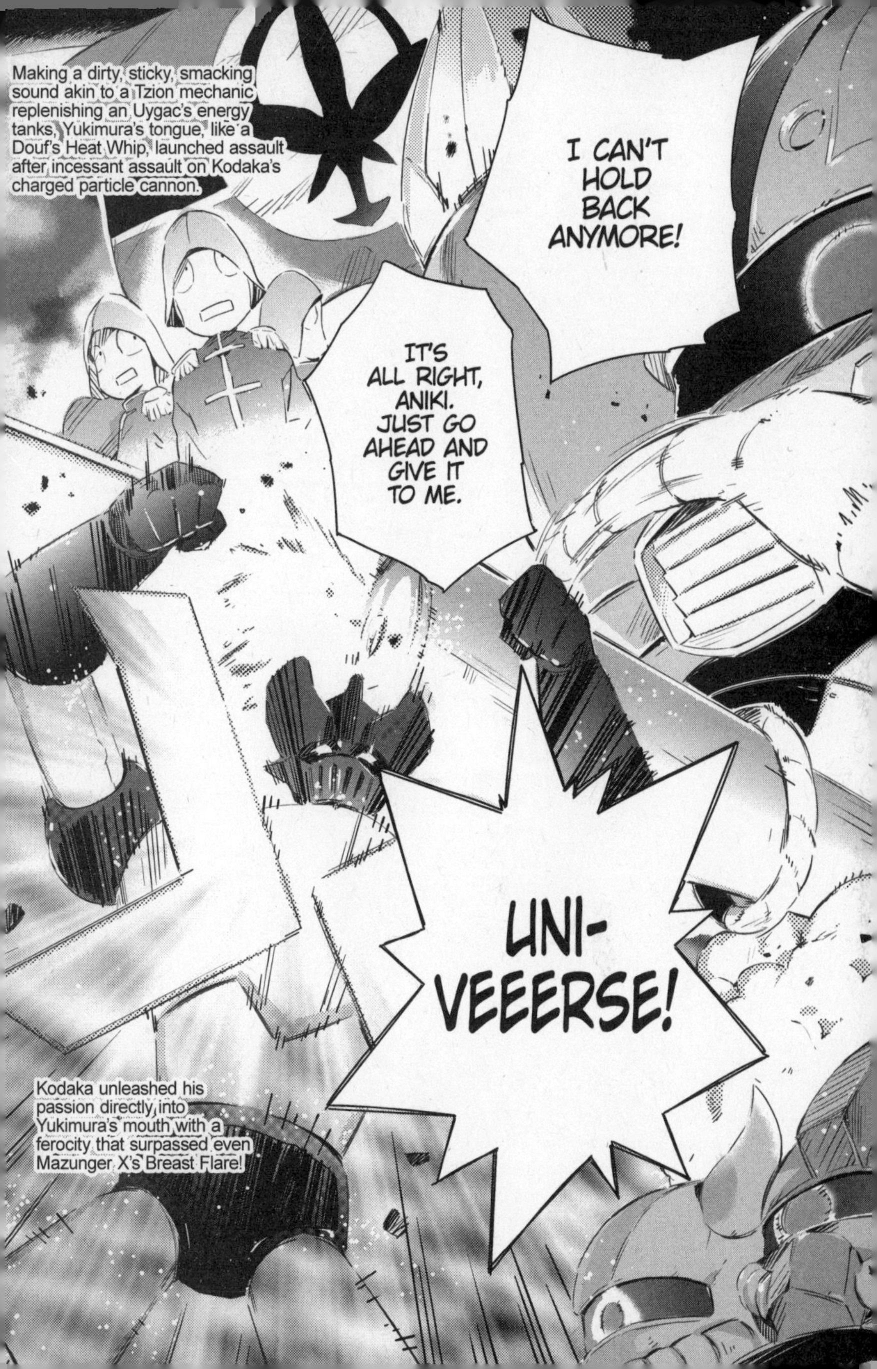
I CAN'T HOLD BACK ANYMORE!
Making a dirty, sticky, smacking sound akin to a Tzion mechanic replenishing an Uygac's energy tanks, Yukimura's tongue, like a Douf's Heat Whip, launched assault after incessant assault on Kodaka's charged particle cannon.
IT'S ALL RIGHT, ANIKI. JUST GO AHEAD AND GIVE IT TO ME.
UNI-VEEERSE!
Kodaka unleashed his passion directly into Yukimura's mouth with a ferocity that surpassed even Mazunger X's Breast Flare!

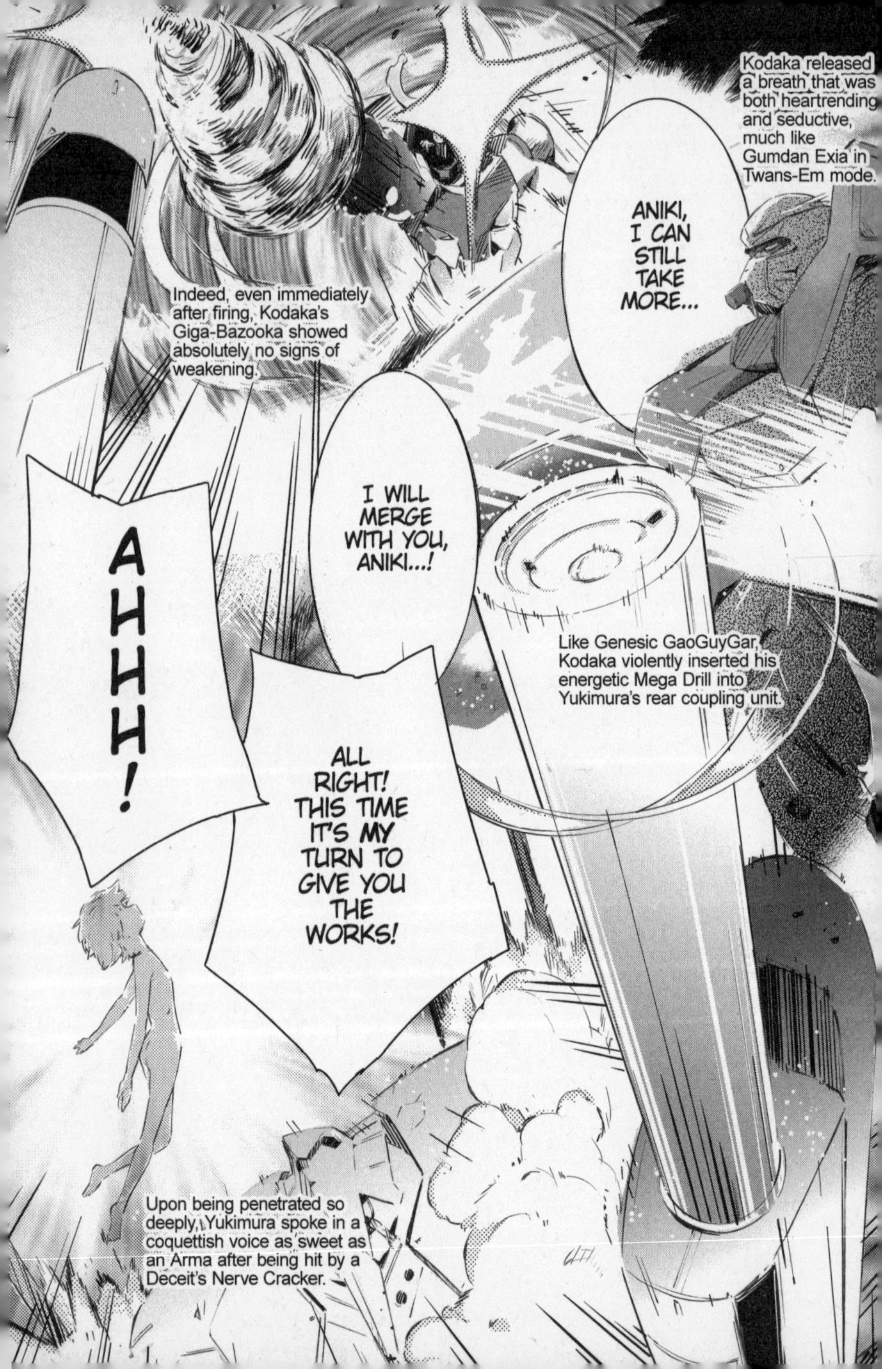
Kodaka released a breath that was both heartrending and seductive, much like Gumdan Exia in Twans-Em mode.
ANIKI, I CAN STILL TAKE MORE...
Indeed, even immediately after firing, Kodaka's Giga-Bazooka showed absolutely no signs of weakening.
I WILL MERGE WITH YOU, ANIKI...!
AHHH!
Like Genesic GaoGuyGar, Kodaka violently inserted his energetic Mega Drill into Yukimura's rear coupling unit.
ALL RIGHT! THIS TIME IT'S MY TURN TO GIVE YOU THE WORKS!
Upon being penetrated so deeply, Yukimura spoke in a coquettish voice as sweet as an Arma after being hit by a Deceit's Nerve Cracker.

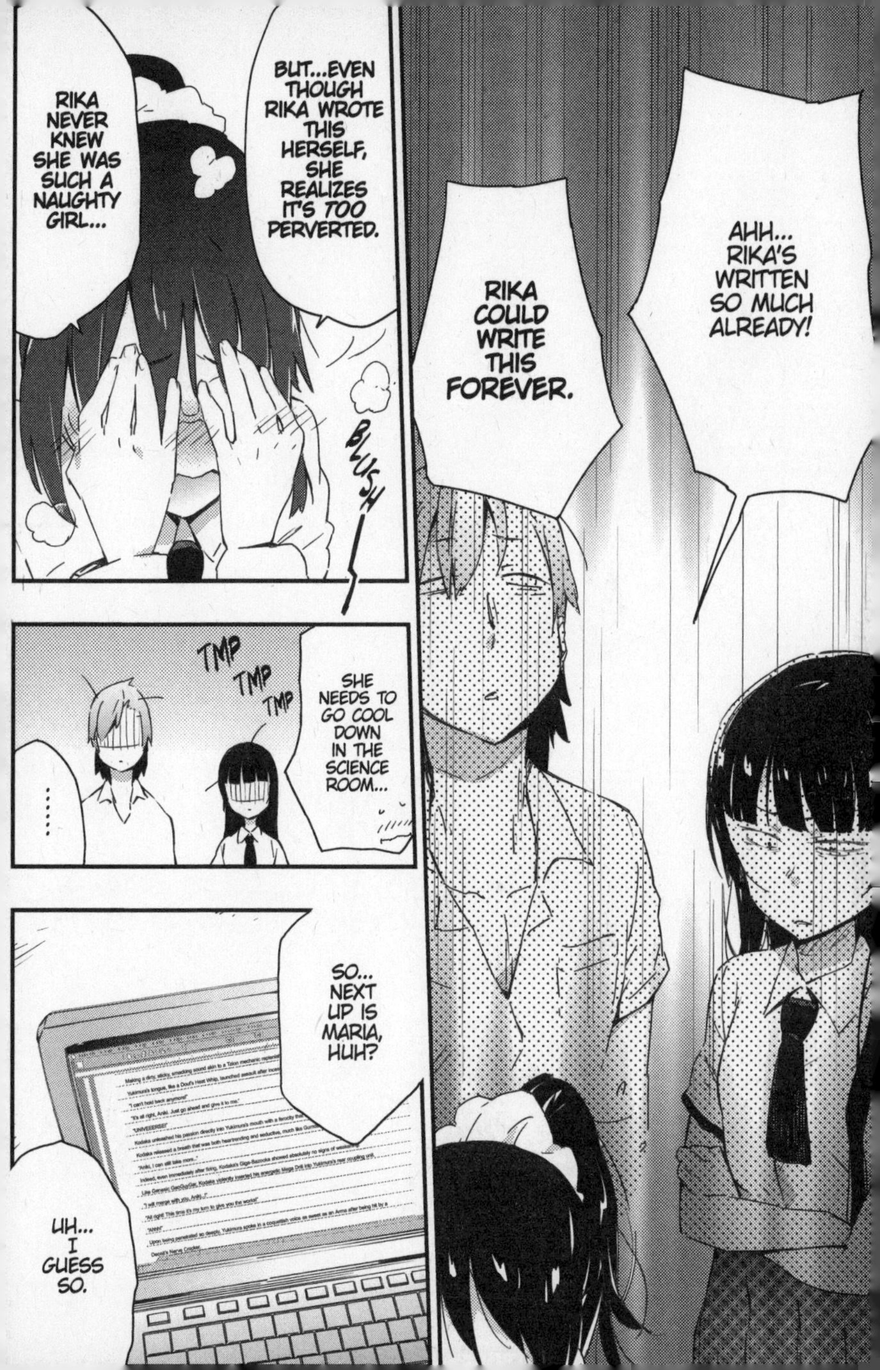
AHH... RIKA'S WRITTEN SO MUCH ALREADY!
RIKA COULD WRITE THIS FOREVER.
BUT...EVEN THOUGH RIKA WROTE THIS HERSELF, SHE REALIZES IT'S *TOO* PERVERTED.
RIKA NEVER KNEW SHE WAS SUCH A NAUGHTY GIRL...
BLUSH
TMP TMP TMP
SHE NEEDS TO GO COOL DOWN IN THE SCIENCE ROOM...
......
SO... NEXT UP IS MARIA, HUH?
UH... I GUESS SO.

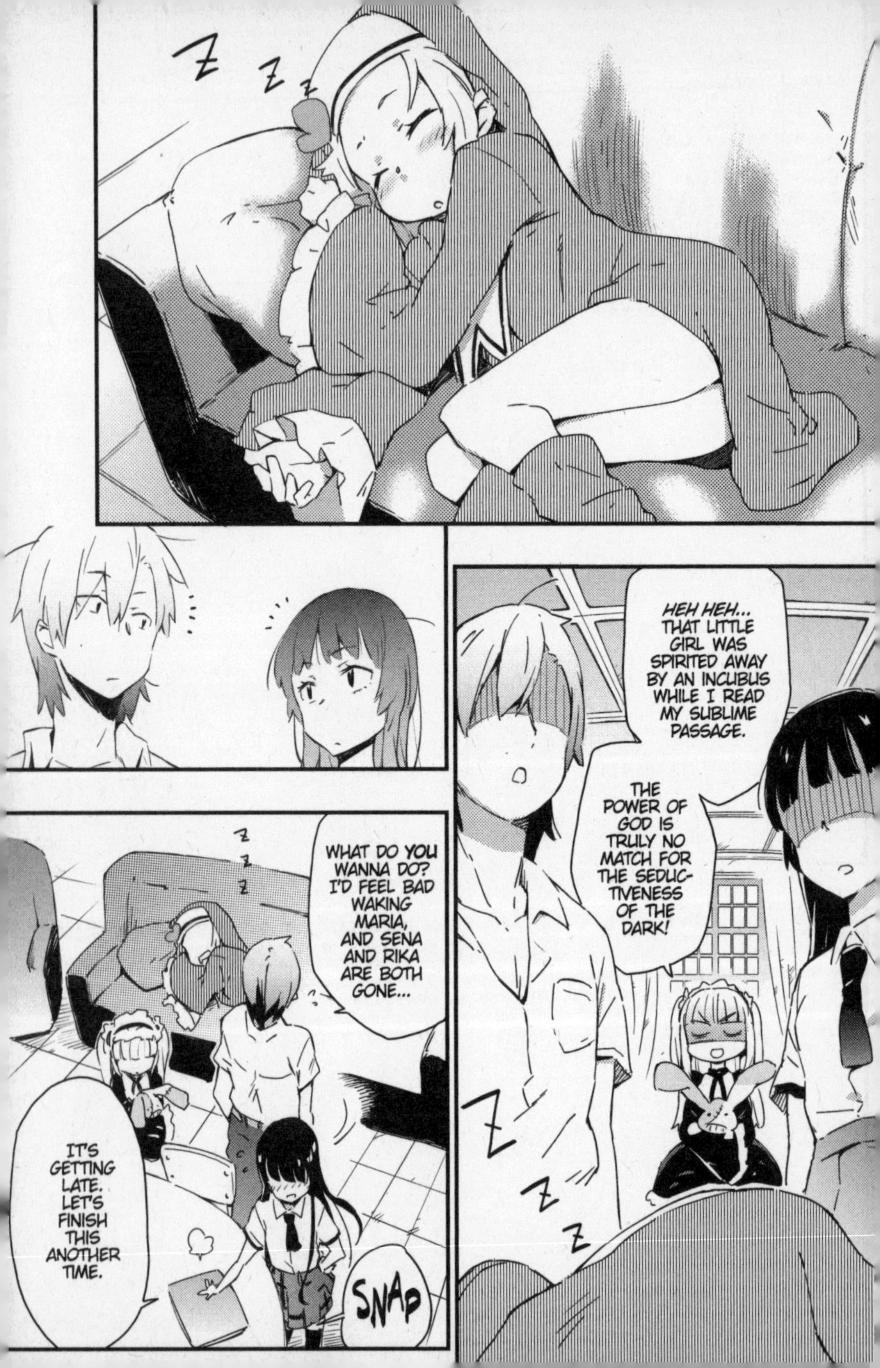
Z Z Z
HEH HEH... THAT LITTLE GIRL WAS SPIRITED AWAY BY AN INCUBUS WHILE I READ MY SUBLIME PASSAGE.
THE POWER OF GOD IS TRULY NO MATCH FOR THE SEDUC-TIVENESS OF THE DARK!
Z Z Z
Z Z Z
WHAT DO YOU WANNA DO? I'D FEEL BAD WAKING MARIA, AND SENA AND RIKA ARE BOTH GONE...
IT'S GETTING LATE. LET'S FINISH THIS ANOTHER TIME.
SNAP

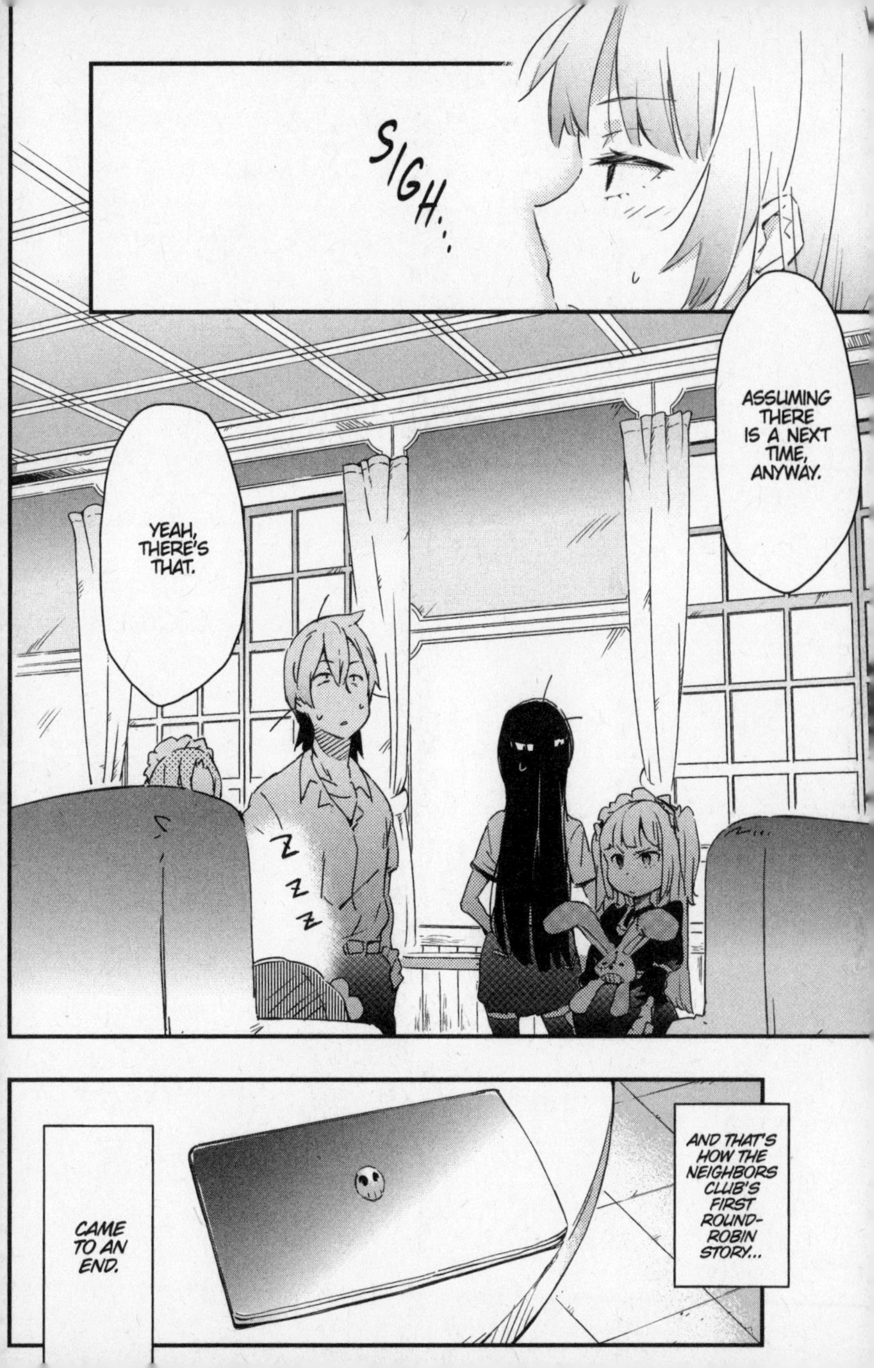
SIGH...
ASSUMING THERE IS A NEXT TIME, ANYWAY.
YEAH, THERE'S THAT.
Z Z Z
AND THAT'S HOW THE NEIGHBORS CLUB'S FIRST ROUND-ROBIN STORY...
CAME TO AN END.

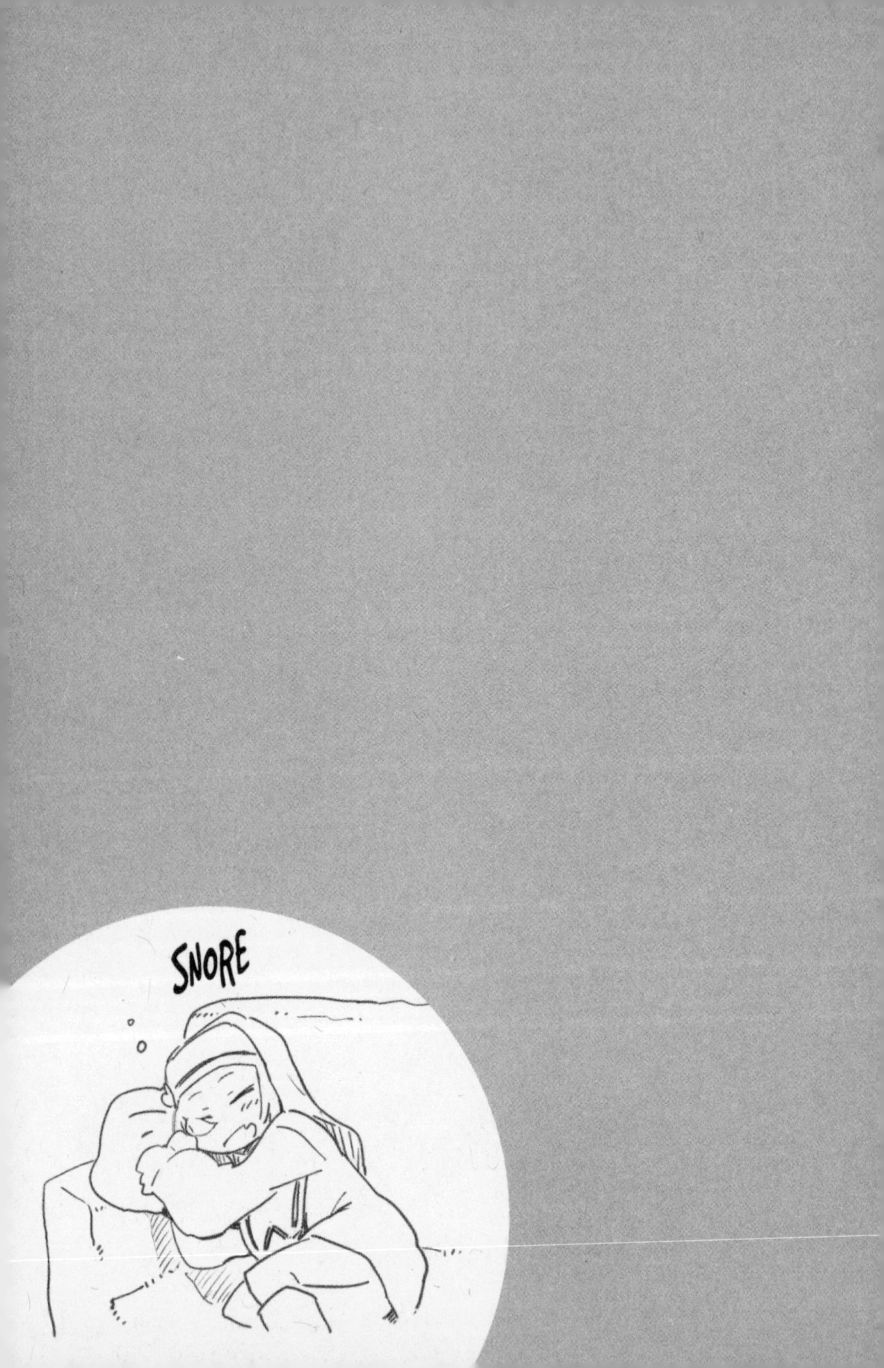
SNORE

TRANSLATION NOTES

In the previous chapter, Rika name-dropped quite a few mecha series. Did you catch them all?

Yalt Yeisen's Resolving Steak: Alt Eisen is a robot from the *Super Robot Wars* video game series; "Revolving Stake" is one of the weapons.

Guntanker: Refers to the Guntank from the original *Mobile Suit Gundam* series.

Univeeerse!: Alludes to the line *Turn A Gundam's* Harry Ord screams as he launches a kamikaze attack against Gym Ghingnham.

Tzion: Zeon, the antagonist force throughout most of the *Gundam* franchise.

Uygac: Acguy, a Zeon mobile suit.

Douf: Gouf, a Zeon mobile suit.

Mazunger X: *Mazinger Z*, a robot anime.

Breast Flare: Breast Fire, one of Mazinger Z's attacks.

Gumdan Exia in Twans-Em: Alludes to *Gundam 00's* Gundam Exia in Trans-Am Mode.

Genesic GaoGuyGar: Alludes to the robot anime series *GaoGaiGar.*

Deceit: Alludes to a robot called Deceive from *Linebarrels of Iron.* Nerve Crackers and Arma also come from this series.

Haganai I don't have many friends

Club Activity Log 17: Romancing Saga Prefecture (Part One)

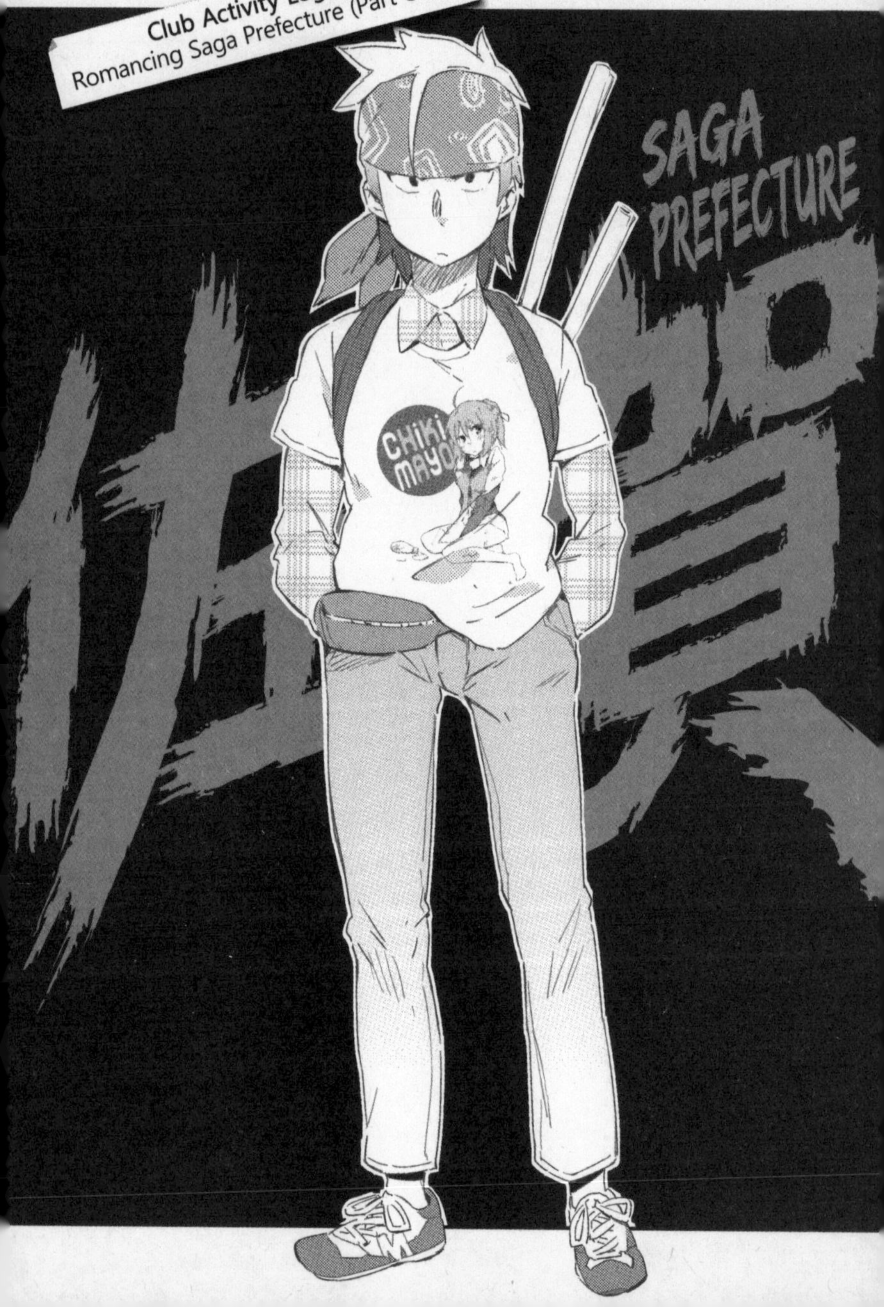
SAGA PREFECTURE
佐賀
CHiKi MAYO

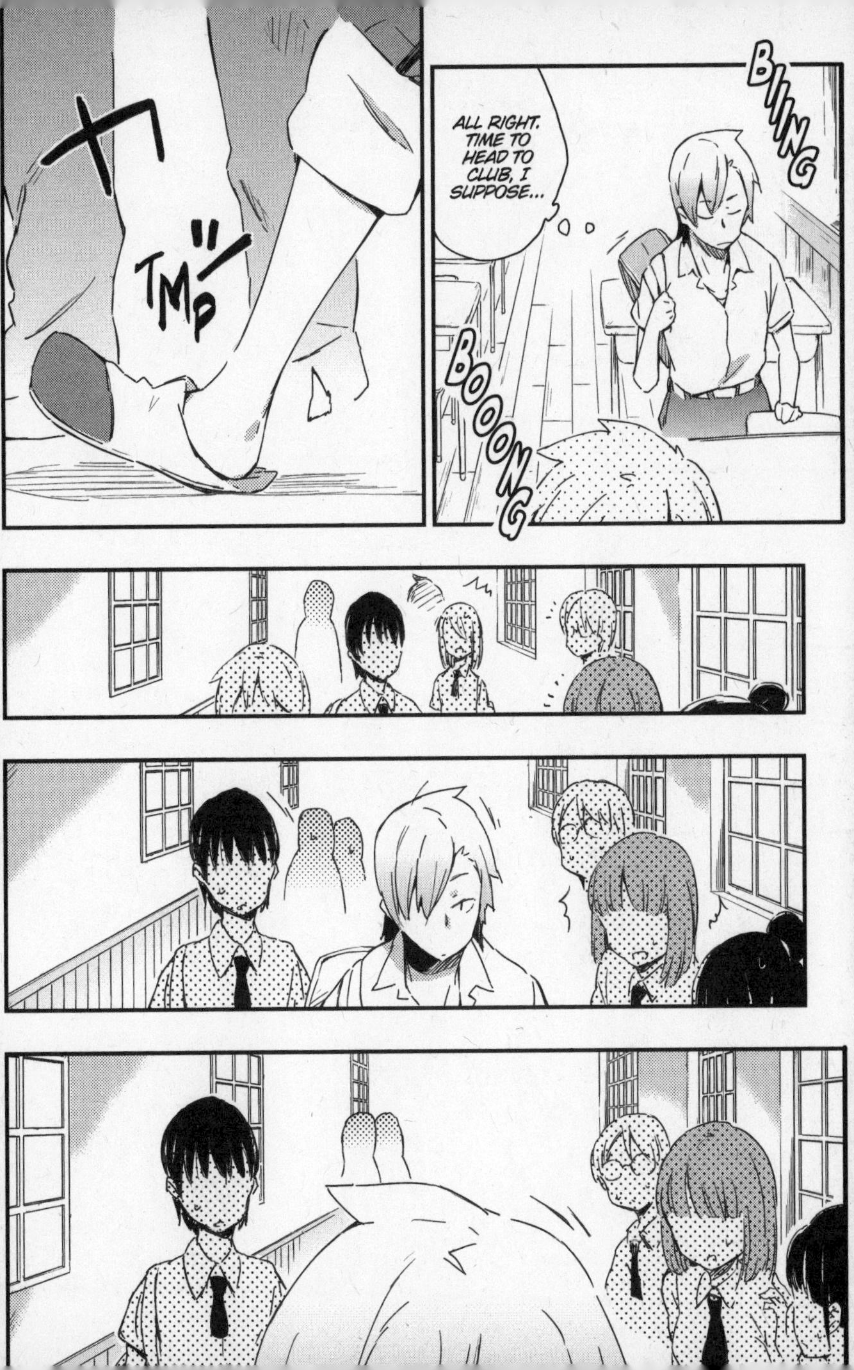
BIING
ALL RIGHT. TIME TO HEAD TO CLUB, I SUPPOSE...
BOOONG
TMP

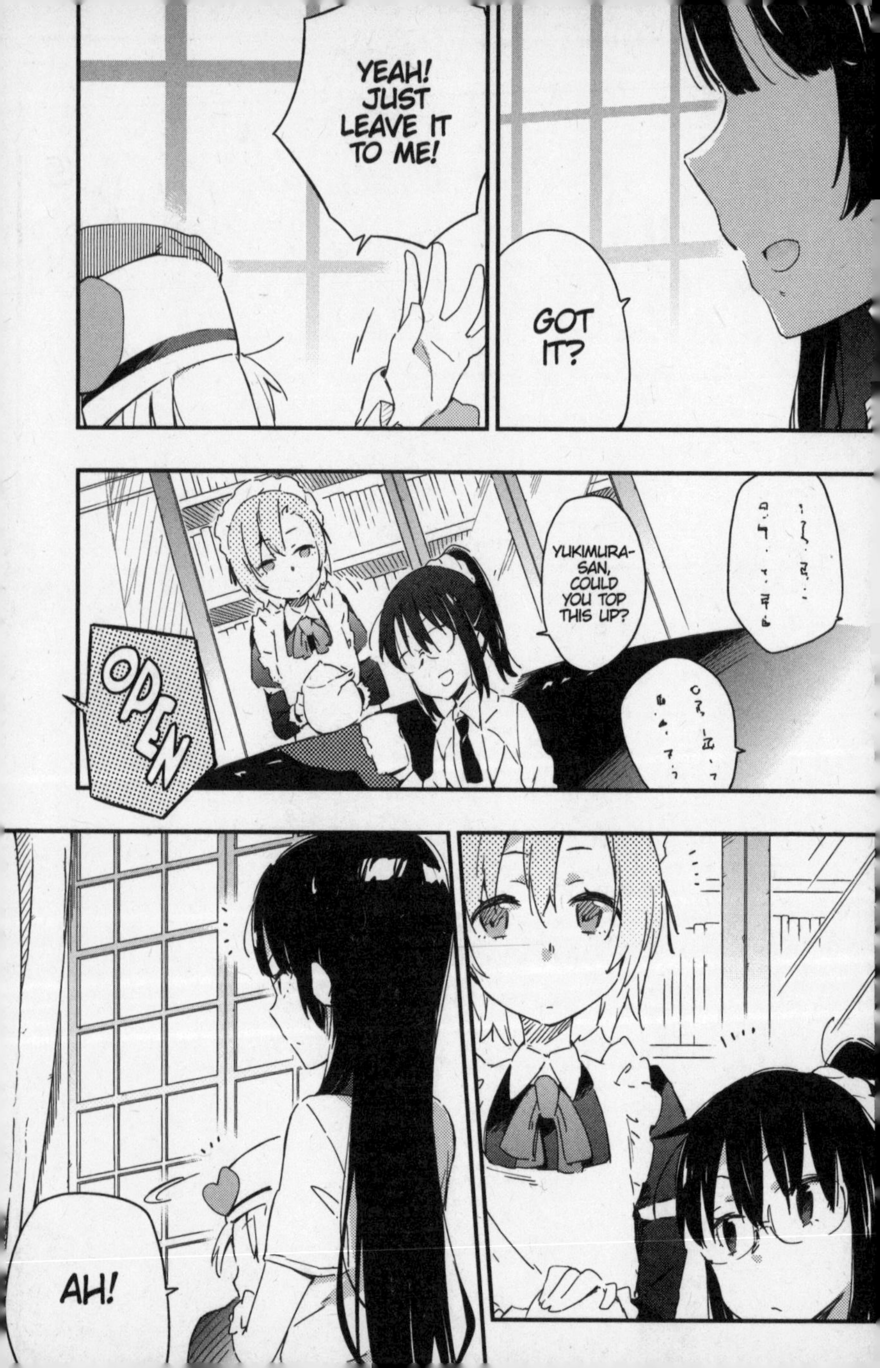
GOT IT?
YEAH! JUST LEAVE IT TO ME!
YUKIMURA-SAN, COULD YOU TOP THIS UP?
OPEN
AH!

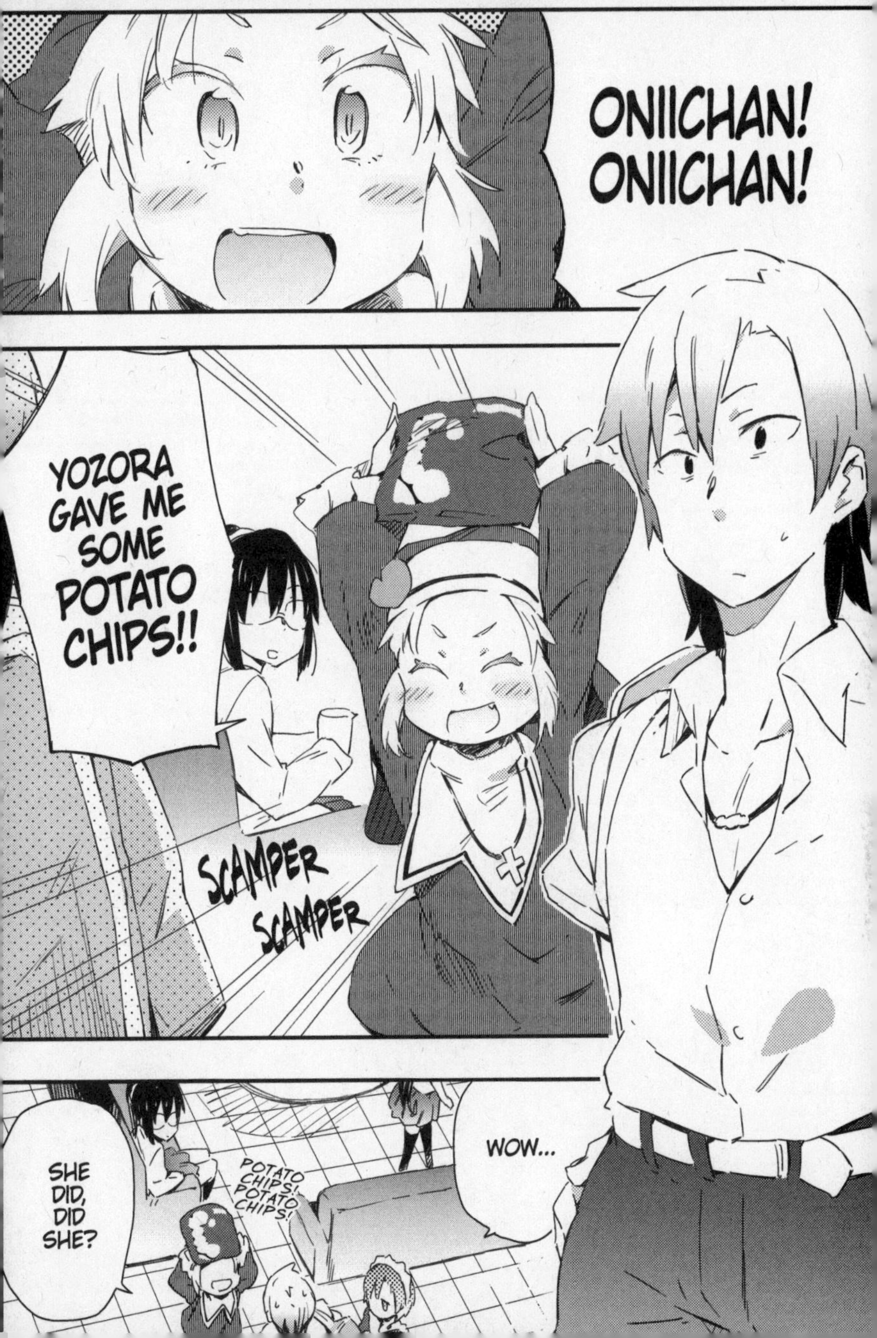
ONIICHAN! ONIICHAN!
YOZORA GAVE ME SOME POTATO CHIPS!!
SCAMPER SCAMPER
WOW...
POTATO CHIPS! POTATO CHIPS!
SHE DID, DID SHE?

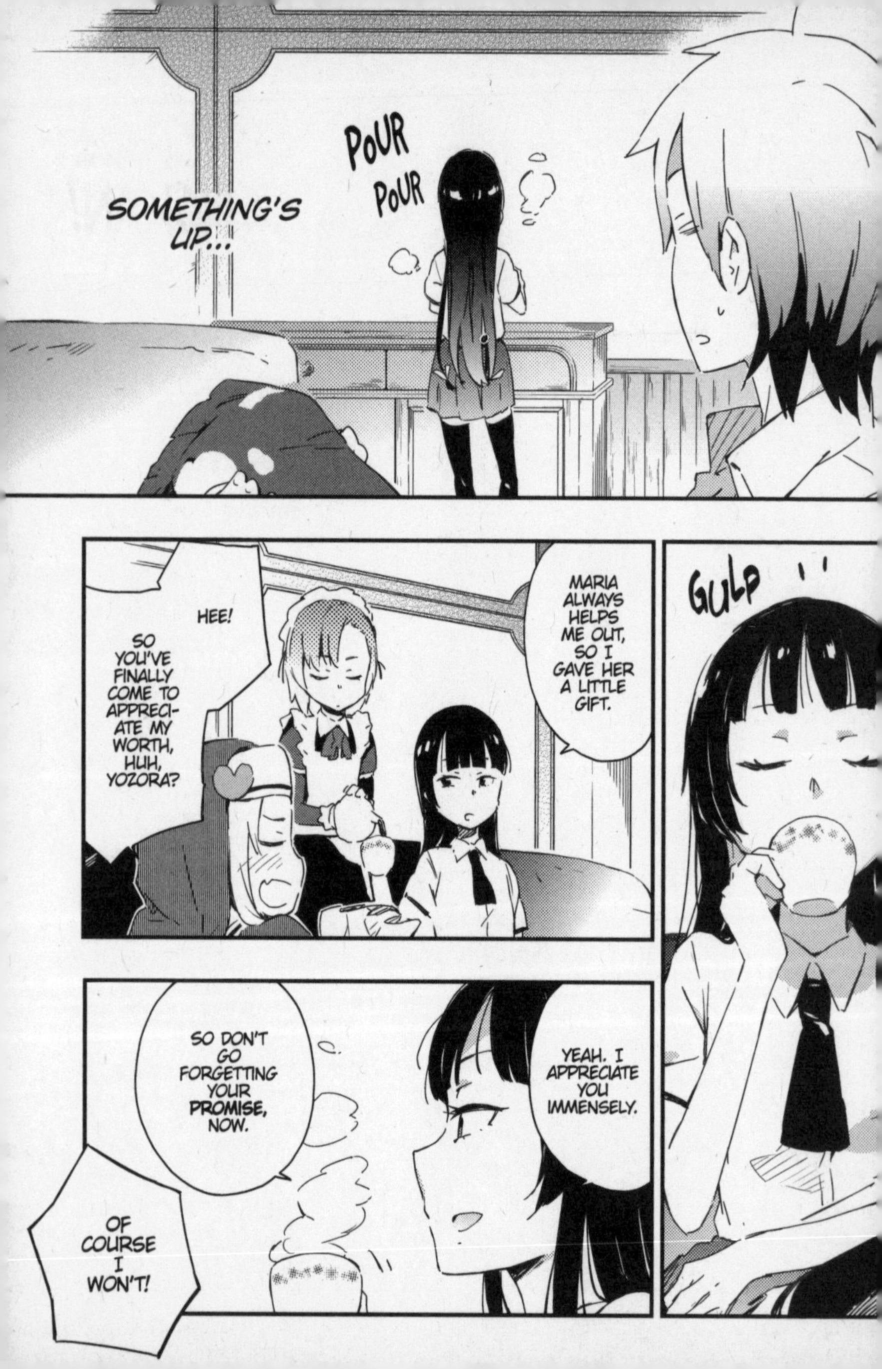
POUR POUR
SOMETHING'S UP...
GULP
MARIA ALWAYS HELPS ME OUT, SO I GAVE HER A LITTLE GIFT.
HEE!
SO YOU'VE FINALLY COME TO APPRECIATE MY WORTH, HUH, YOZORA?
YEAH. I APPRECIATE YOU IMMENSELY.
SO DON'T GO FORGETTING YOUR PROMISE, NOW.
OF COURSE I WON'T!

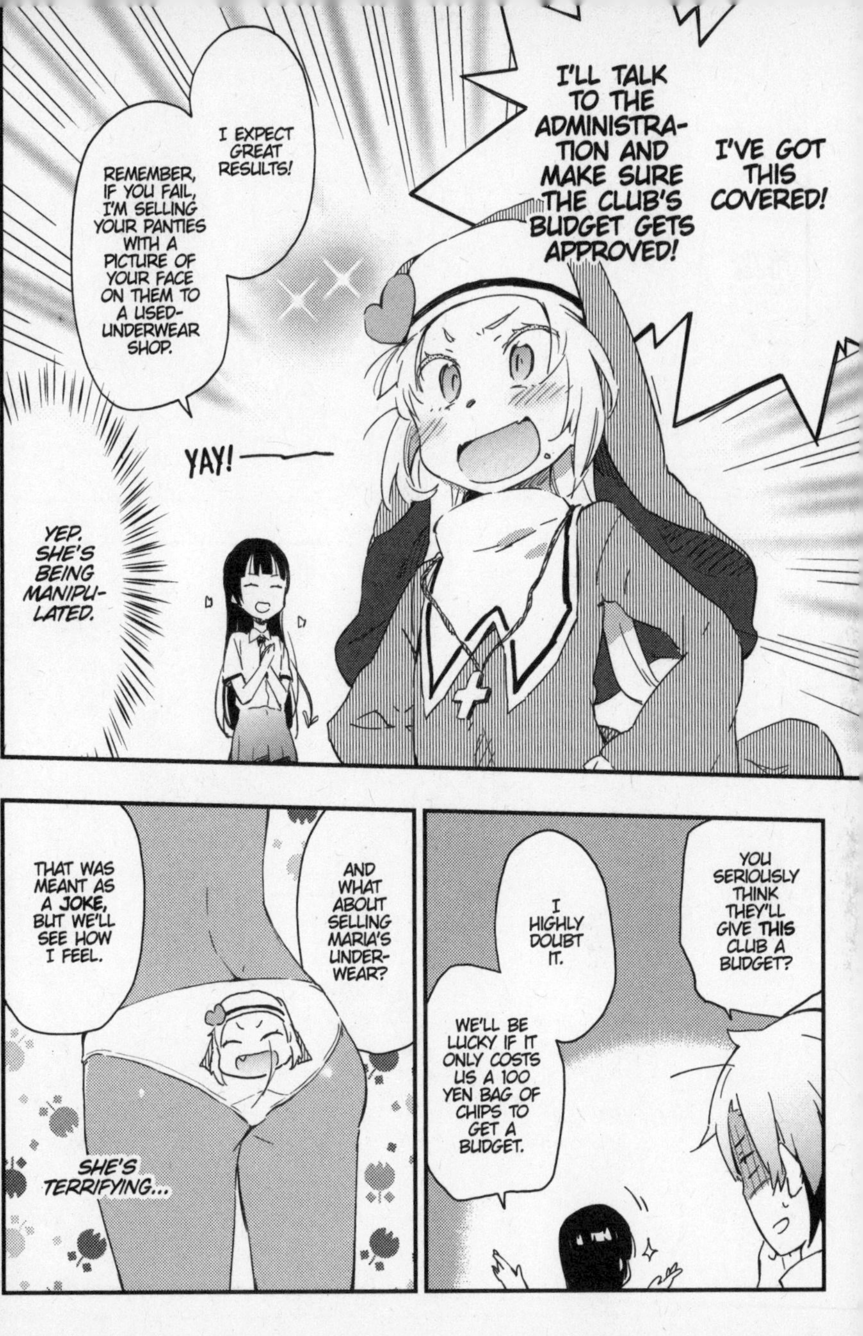
I'VE GOT THIS COVERED!
I'LL TALK TO THE ADMINISTRATION AND MAKE SURE THE CLUB'S BUDGET GETS APPROVED!
I EXPECT GREAT RESULTS!
REMEMBER, IF YOU FAIL, I'M SELLING YOUR PANTIES WITH A PICTURE OF YOUR FACE ON THEM TO A USED-UNDERWEAR SHOP.
YAY!
YEP. SHE'S BEING MANIPULATED.
YOU SERIOUSLY THINK THEY'LL GIVE **THIS** CLUB A BUDGET?
I HIGHLY DOUBT IT.
WE'LL BE LUCKY IF IT ONLY COSTS US A 100 YEN BAG OF CHIPS TO GET A BUDGET.
AND WHAT ABOUT SELLING MARIA'S UNDERWEAR?
THAT WAS MEANT AS A **JOKE**, BUT WE'LL SEE HOW I FEEL.
SHE'S TERRIFYING...

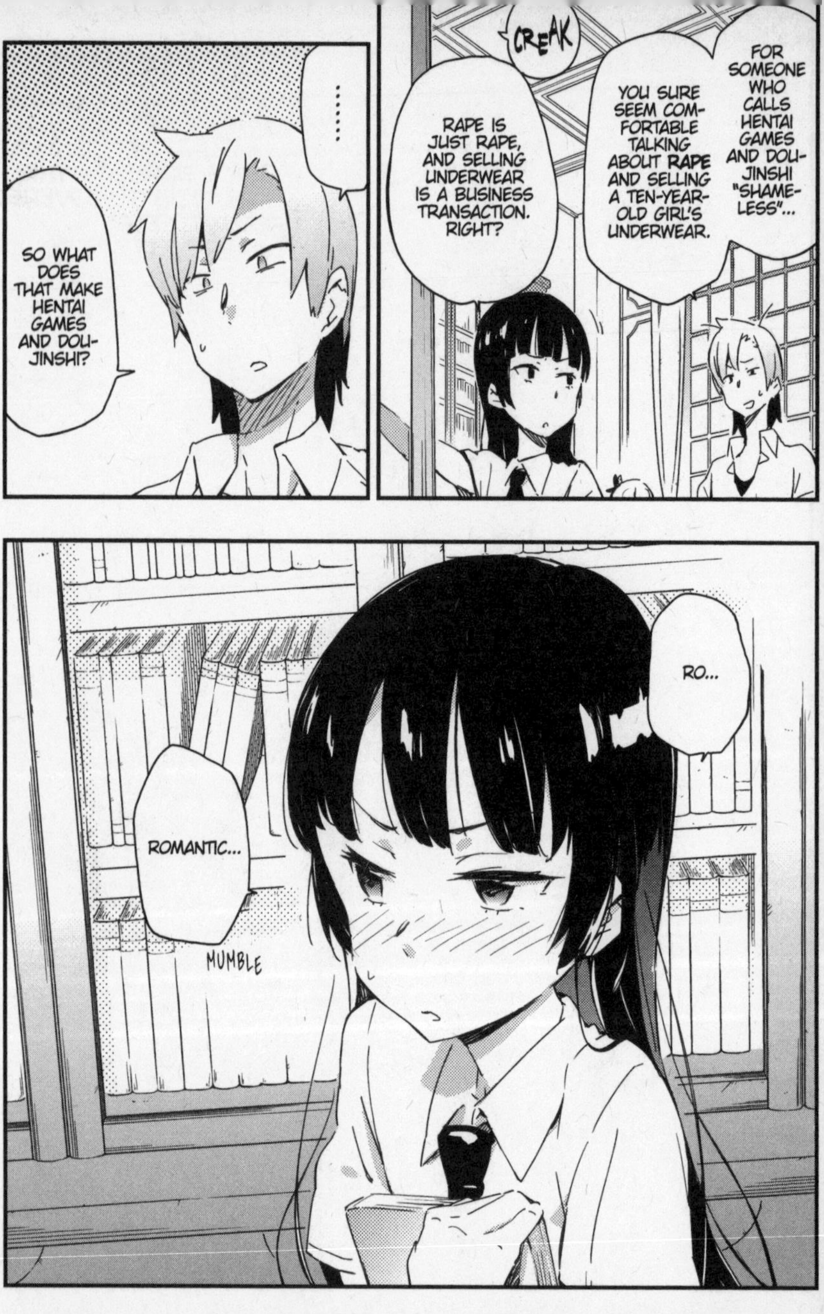
FOR SOMEONE WHO CALLS HENTAI GAMES AND DOUJINSHI "SHAMELESS"...
YOU SURE SEEM COMFORTABLE TALKING ABOUT RAPE AND SELLING A TEN-YEAR-OLD GIRL'S UNDERWEAR.
CREAK
RAPE IS JUST RAPE, AND SELLING UNDERWEAR IS A BUSINESS TRANSACTION. RIGHT?
......
SO WHAT DOES THAT MAKE HENTAI GAMES AND DOUJINSHI?
RO...
ROMANTIC...
MUMBLE

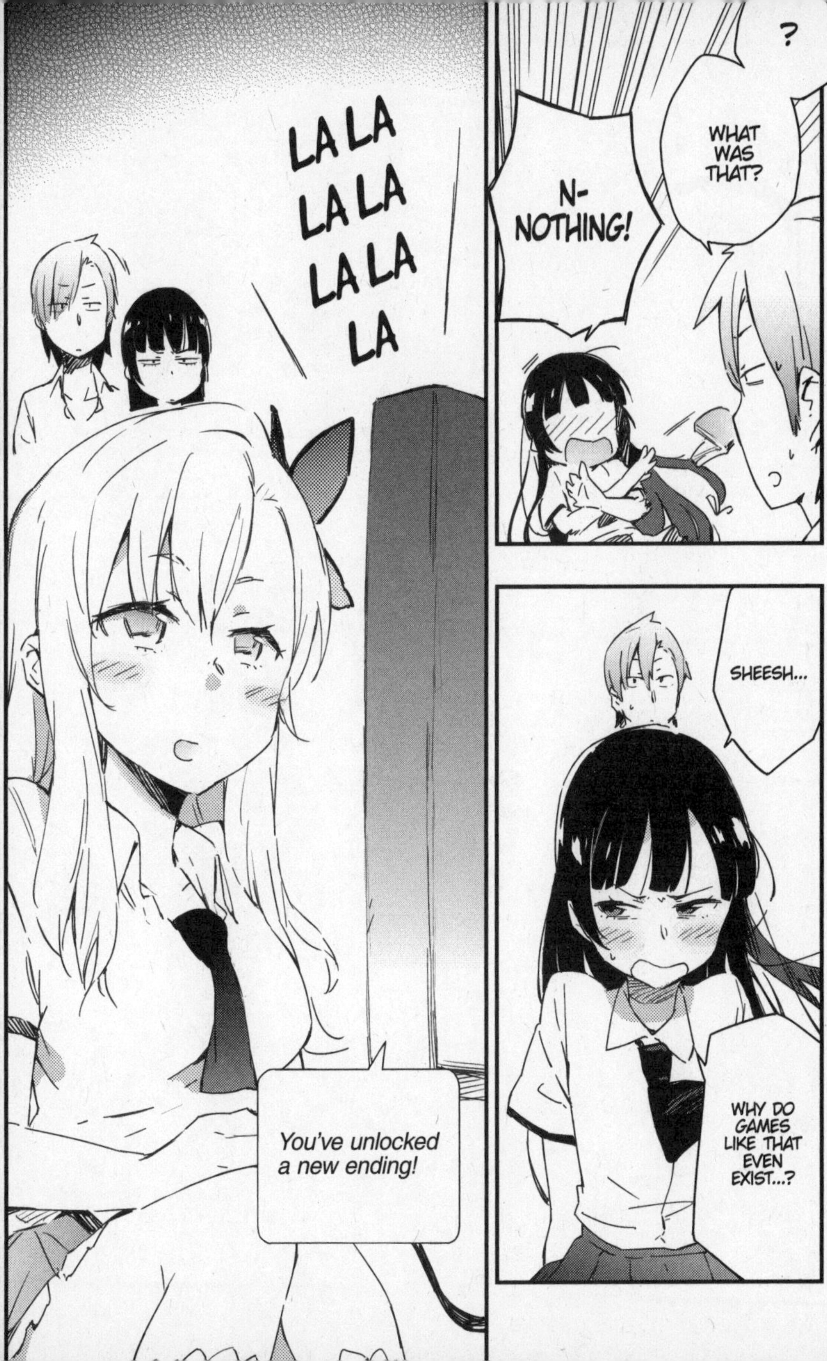
?
WHAT WAS THAT?
N-NOTHING!
SHEESH...
WHY DO GAMES LIKE THAT EVEN EXIST...?
LA LA LA LA LA LA LA
You've unlocked a new ending!

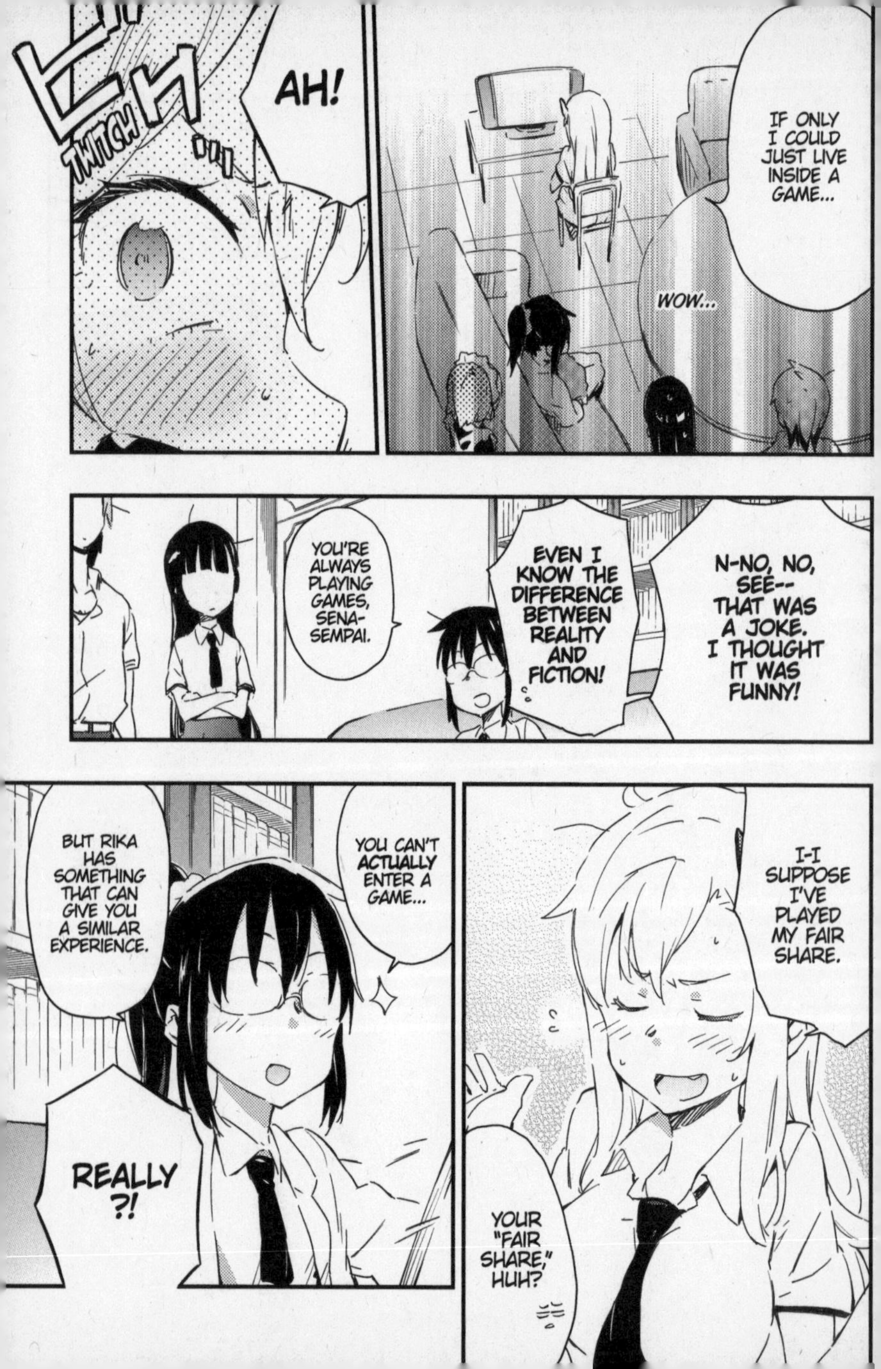
IF ONLY I COULD JUST LIVE INSIDE A GAME...
WOW...
AH!
TWITCH
N-NO, NO, SEE-- THAT WAS A JOKE. I THOUGHT IT WAS FUNNY!
EVEN I KNOW THE DIFFERENCE BETWEEN REALITY AND FICTION!
YOU'RE ALWAYS PLAYING GAMES, SENA-SEMPAI.
I-I SUPPOSE I'VE PLAYED MY FAIR SHARE.
YOUR "FAIR SHARE," HUH?
YOU CAN'T ACTUALLY ENTER A GAME...
BUT RIKA HAS SOMETHING THAT CAN GIVE YOU A SIMILAR EXPERIENCE.
REALLY ?!

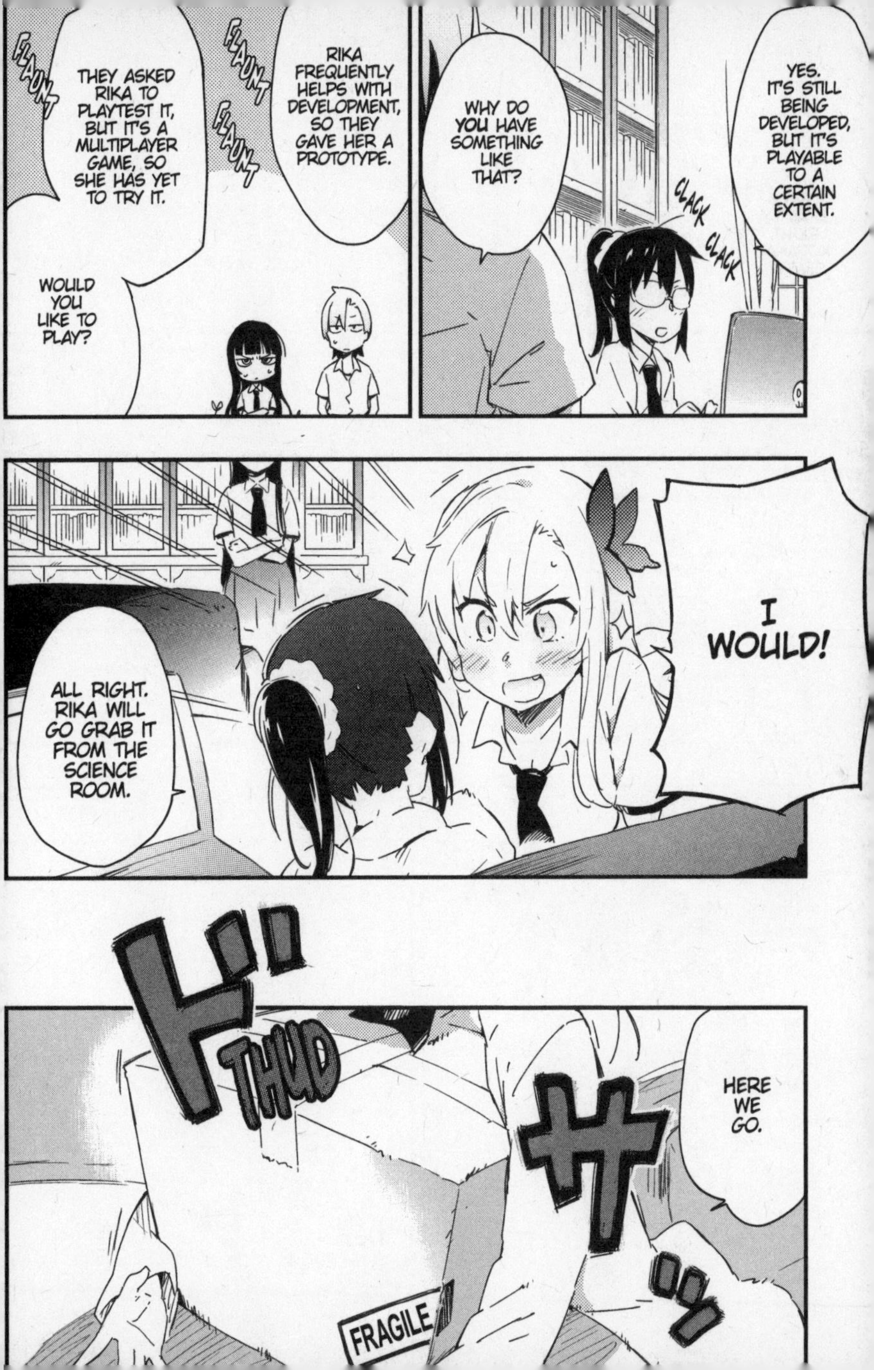
YES. IT'S STILL BEING DEVELOPED, BUT IT'S PLAYABLE TO A CERTAIN EXTENT.
CLACK
CLACK
WHY DO YOU HAVE SOMETHING LIKE THAT?
RIKA FREQUENTLY HELPS WITH DEVELOPMENT, SO THEY GAVE HER A PROTOTYPE.
FLAUNT
FLAUNT
THEY ASKED RIKA TO PLAYTEST IT, BUT IT'S A MULTIPLAYER GAME, SO SHE HAS YET TO TRY IT.
FLAUNT
WOULD YOU LIKE TO PLAY?
I WOULD!
ALL RIGHT. RIKA WILL GO GRAB IT FROM THE SCIENCE ROOM.
HERE WE GO.
ド
THUD
サッ
FRAGILE

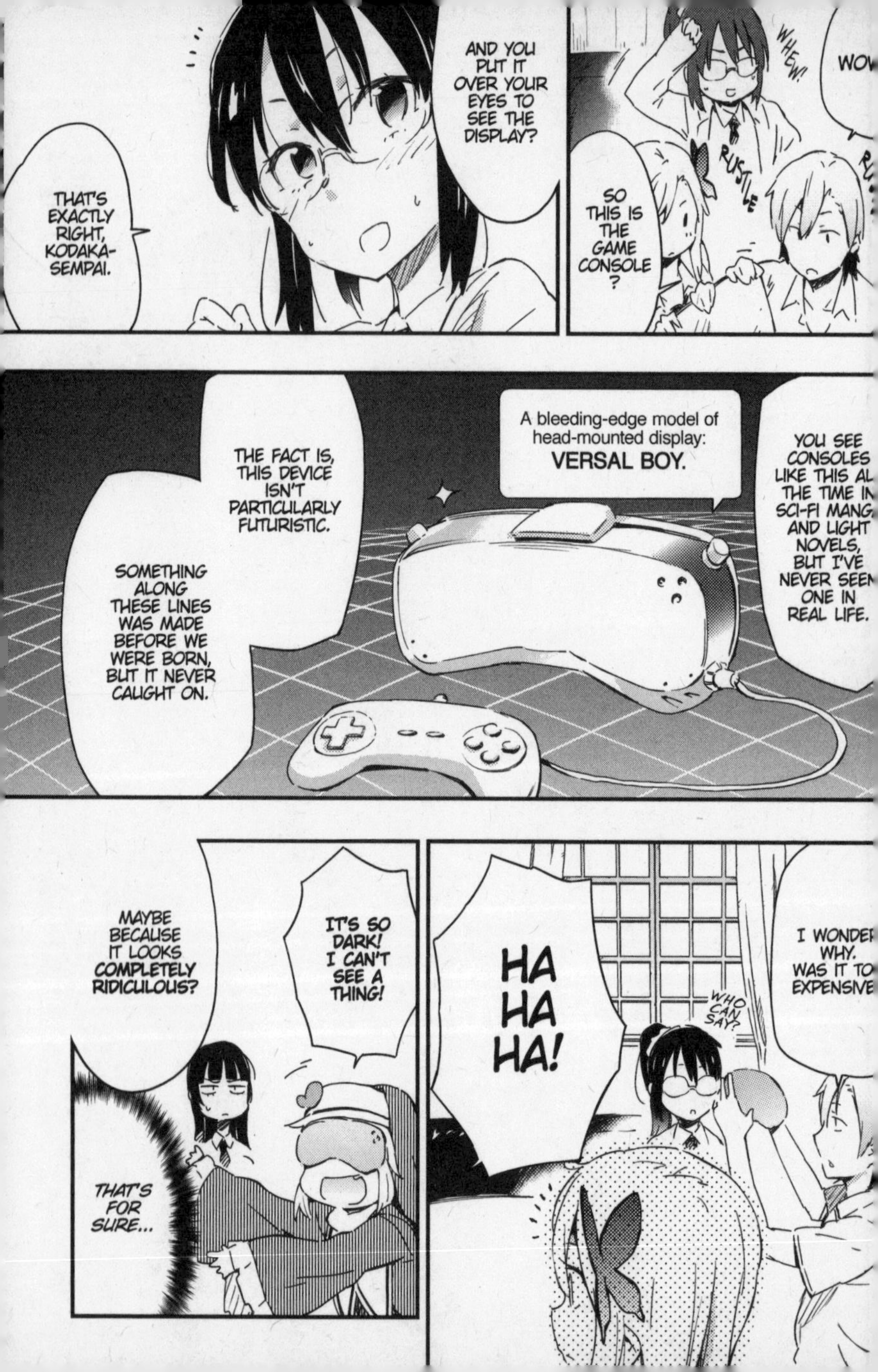
WOV
WHEW!
SO THIS IS THE GAME CONSOLE?
RUSTLE
RU
AND YOU PUT IT OVER YOUR EYES TO SEE THE DISPLAY?
THAT'S EXACTLY RIGHT, KODAKA-SEMPAI.
YOU SEE CONSOLES LIKE THIS AL THE TIME IN SCI-FI MANG AND LIGHT NOVELS, BUT I'VE NEVER SEEN ONE IN REAL LIFE.
A bleeding-edge model of head-mounted display: VERSAL BOY.
THE FACT IS, THIS DEVICE ISN'T PARTICULARLY FUTURISTIC.
SOMETHING ALONG THESE LINES WAS MADE BEFORE WE WERE BORN, BUT IT NEVER CAUGHT ON.
I WONDER WHY. WAS IT TO EXPENSIVE
WHO CAN SAY?
HA HA HA!
IT'S SO DARK! I CAN'T SEE A THING!
MAYBE BECAUSE IT LOOKS COMPLETELY RIDICULOUS?
THAT'S FOR SURE...

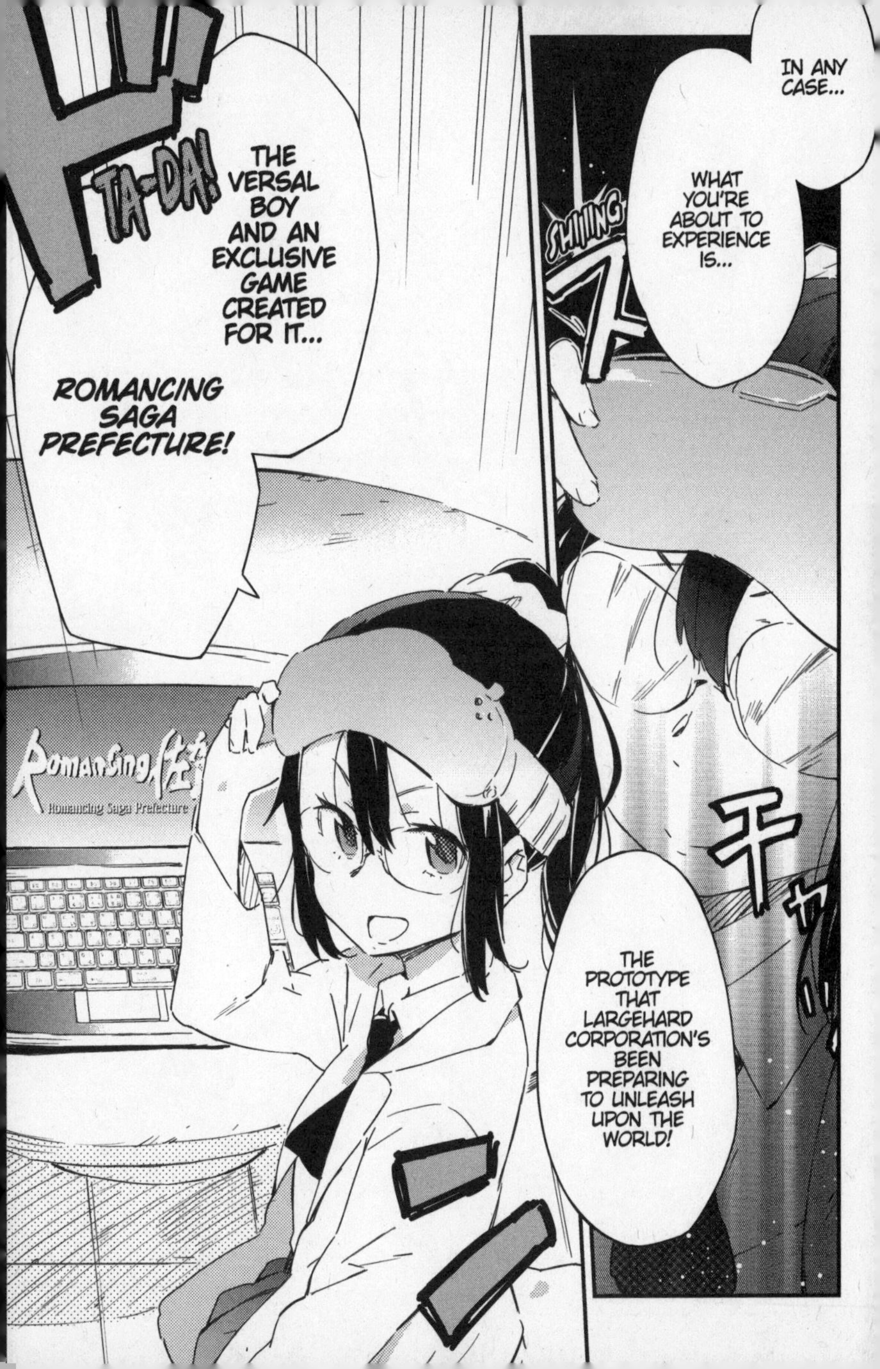
IN ANY CASE...
WHAT YOU'RE ABOUT TO EXPERIENCE IS...
SHIIIING
TA-DA!
THE VERSAL BOY AND AN EXCLUSIVE GAME CREATED FOR IT...
ROMANCING SAGA PREFECTURE!
Romancing Saga Prefecture
THE PROTOTYPE THAT LARGEHARD CORPORATION'S BEEN PREPARING TO UNLEASH UPON THE WORLD!

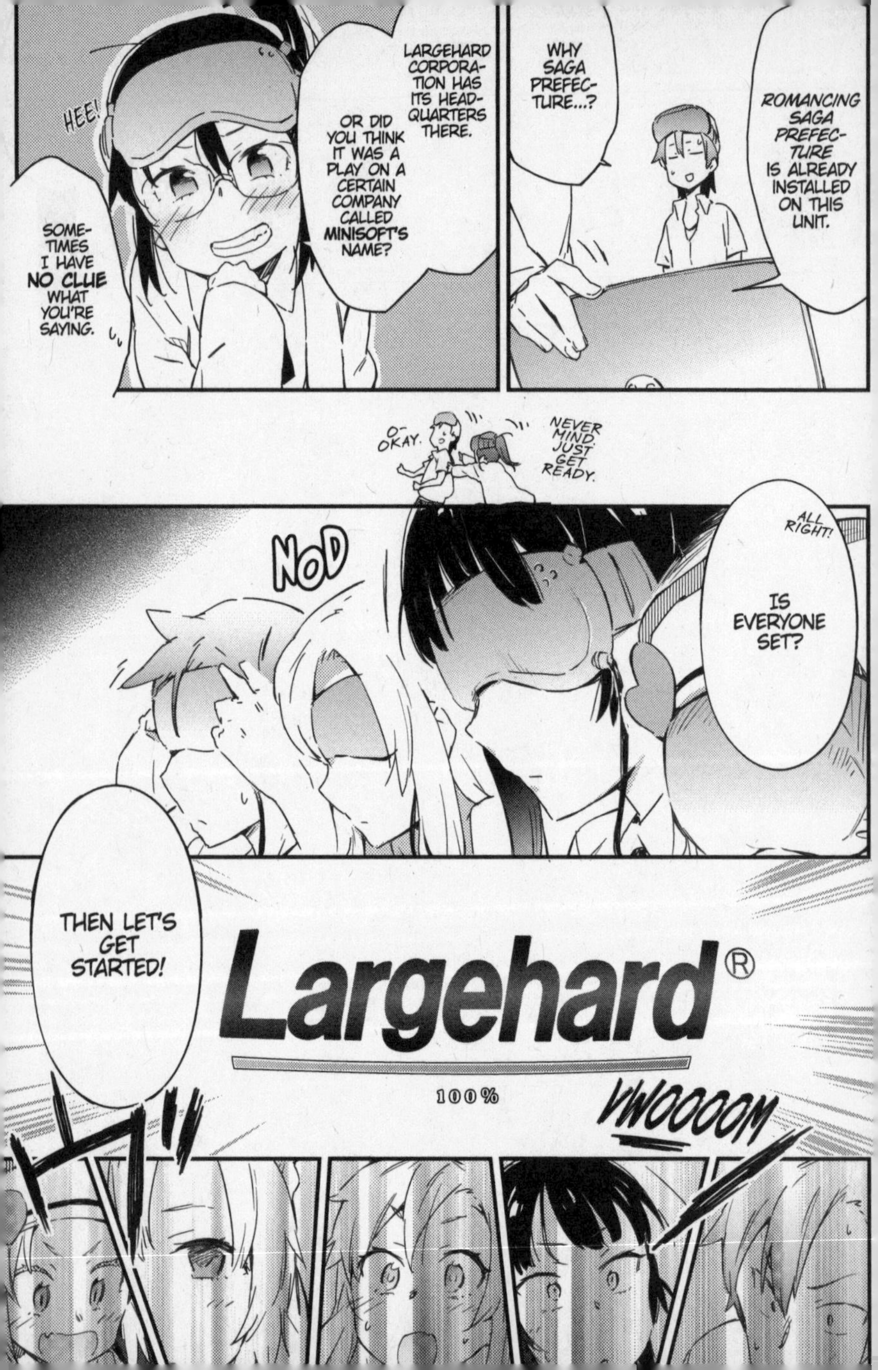
ROMANCING SAGA PREFECTURE IS ALREADY INSTALLED ON THIS UNIT.
WHY SAGA PREFECTURE...?
LARGEHARD CORPORATION HAS ITS HEADQUARTERS THERE.
OR DID YOU THINK IT WAS A PLAY ON A CERTAIN COMPANY CALLED MINISOFT'S NAME?
HEE!
SOMETIMES I HAVE NO CLUE WHAT YOU'RE SAYING.
NEVER MIND. JUST GET READY.
O-OKAY.
ALL RIGHT!
IS EVERYONE SET?
NOD
THEN LET'S GET STARTED!
Largehard®
100%
VWOOOOM

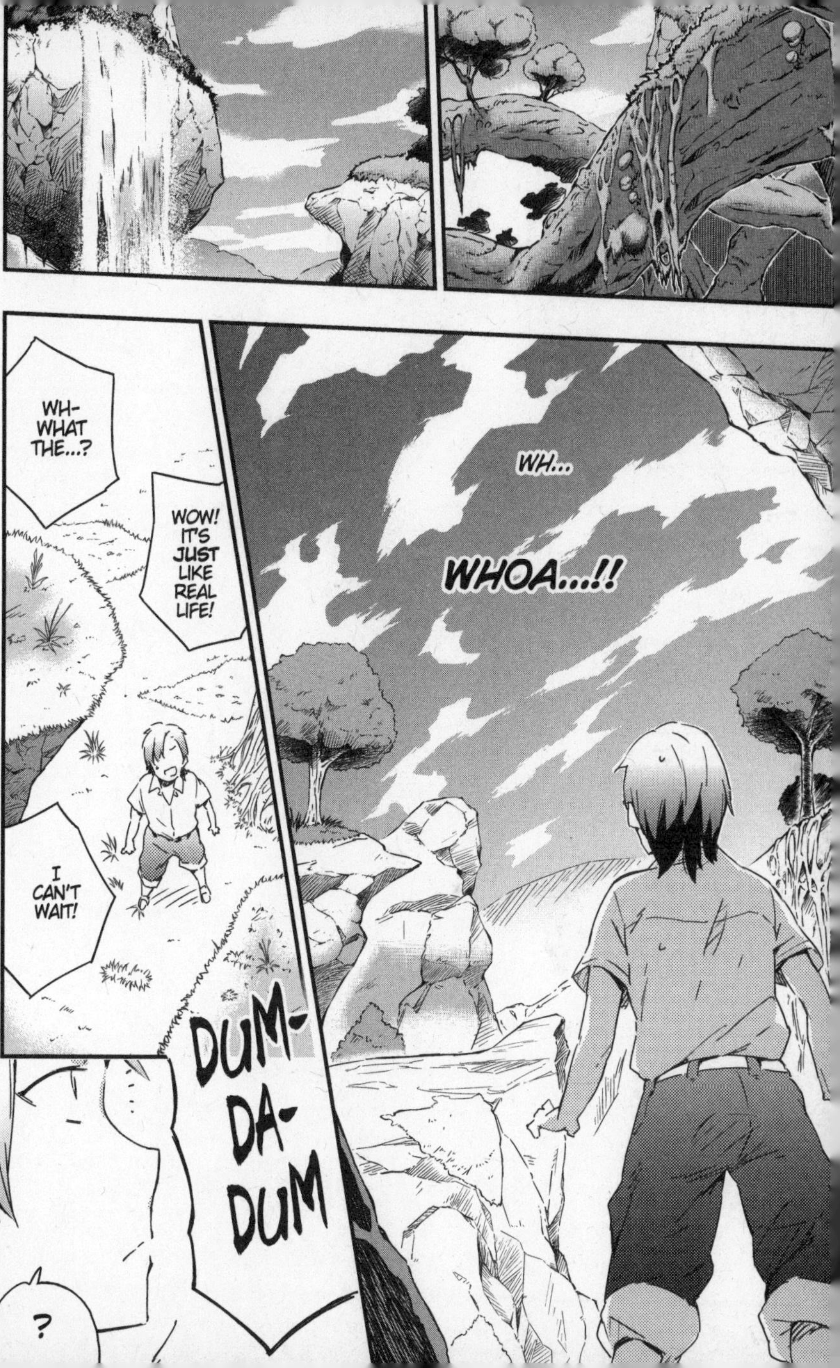
WH...
WHOA...!!
WH-WHAT THE...?
WOW! IT'S JUST LIKE REAL LIFE!
I CAN'T WAIT!
DUM-DA-DUM
?

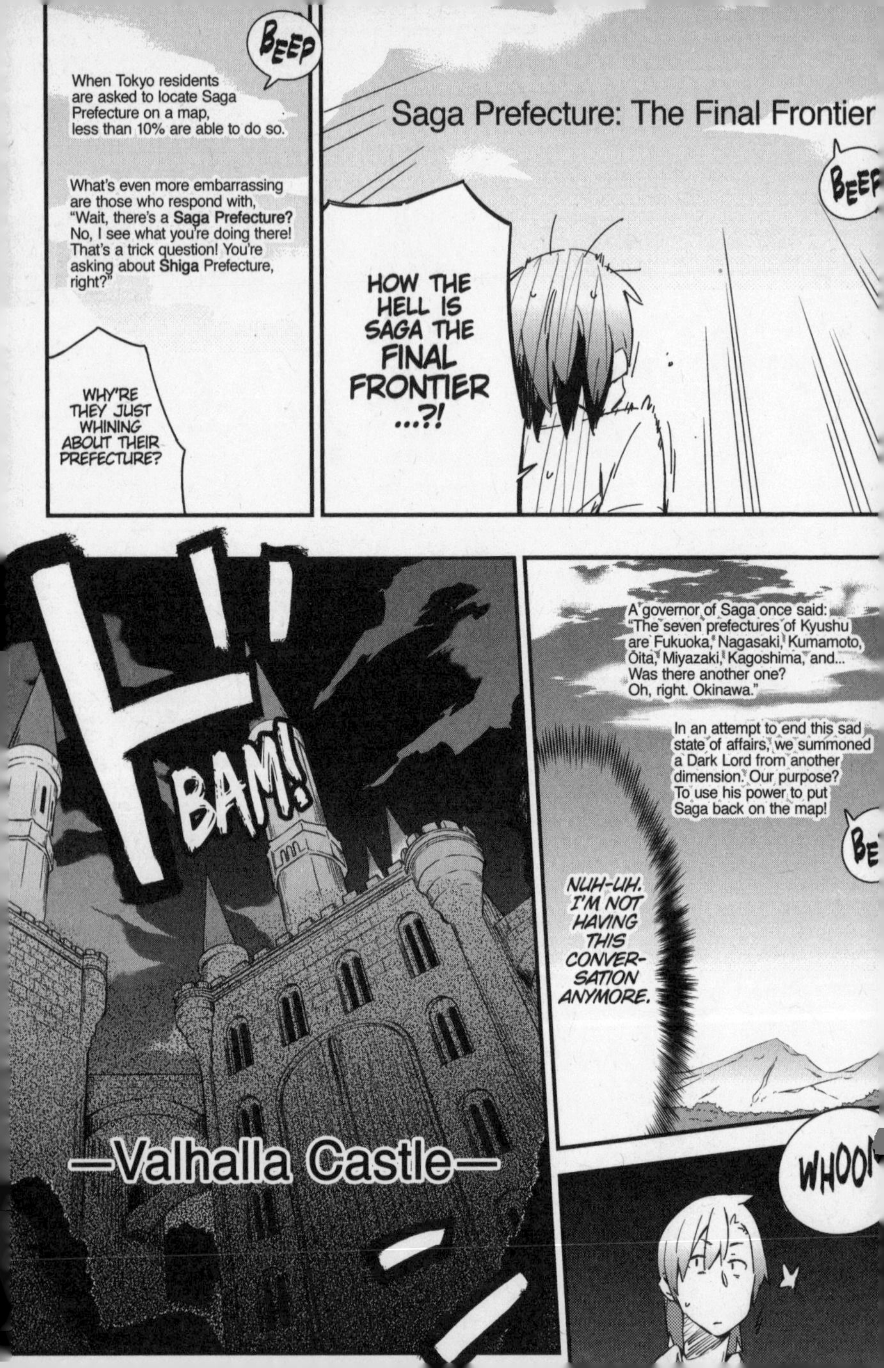
Saga Prefecture: The Final Frontier
HOW THE HELL IS SAGA THE FINAL FRONTIER ...?!
BEEP
When Tokyo residents are asked to locate Saga Prefecture on a map, less than 10% are able to do so.
What's even more embarrassing are those who respond with, "Wait, there's a **Saga Prefecture?** No, I see what you're doing there! That's a trick question! You're asking about **Shiga** Prefecture, right?"
WHY'RE THEY JUST WHINING ABOUT THEIR PREFECTURE?
A governor of Saga once said: "The seven prefectures of Kyushu are Fukuoka, Nagasaki, Kumamoto, Ōita, Miyazaki, Kagoshima, and... Was there another one? Oh, right. Okinawa."
In an attempt to end this sad state of affairs, we summoned a Dark Lord from another dimension. Our purpose? To use his power to put Saga back on the map!
NUH-UH. I'M NOT HAVING THIS CONVER-SATION ANYMORE.
BAM!
—Valhalla Castle—

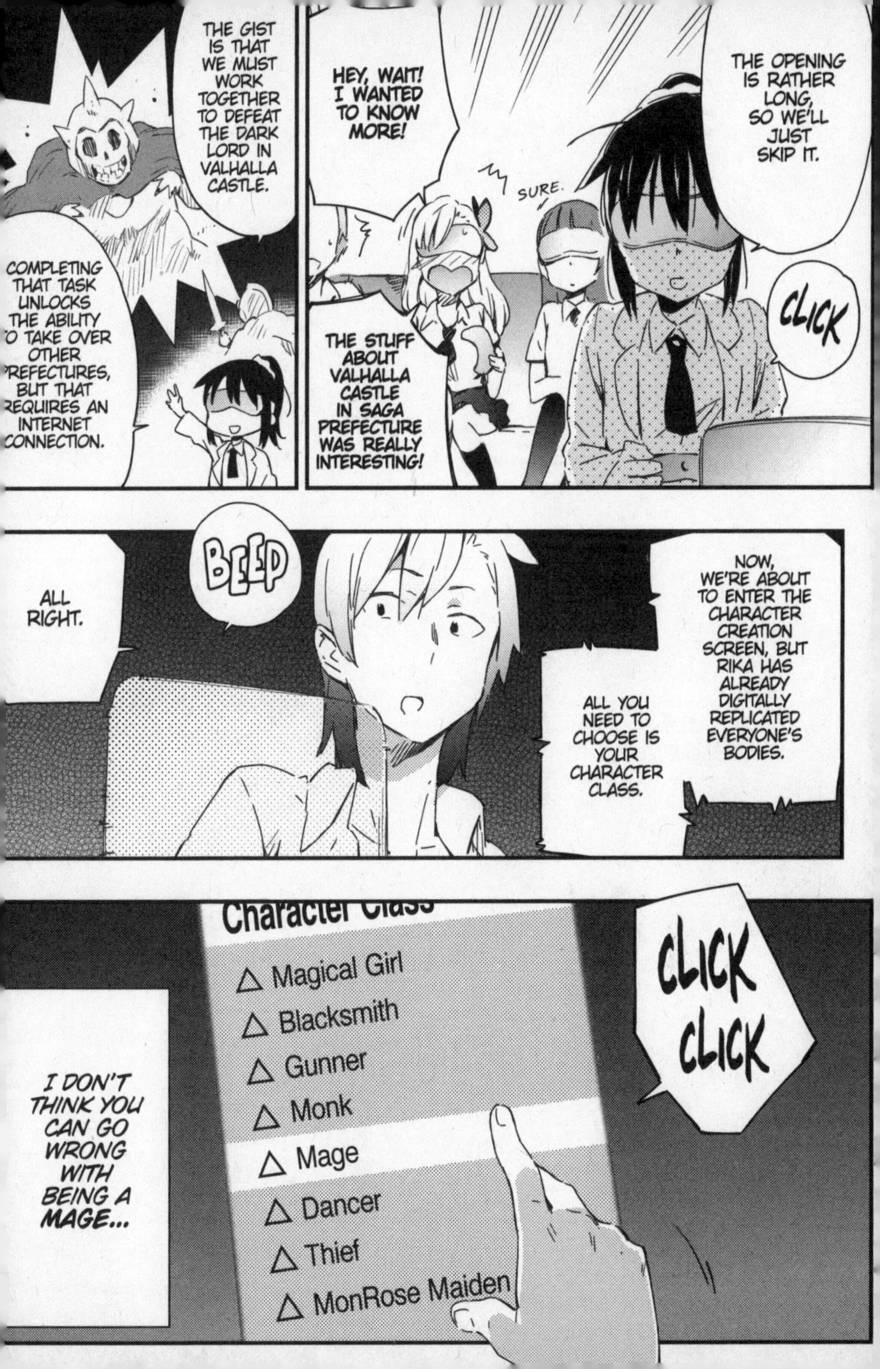
THE OPENING IS RATHER LONG, SO WE'LL JUST SKIP IT.
CLICK
SURE.
HEY, WAIT! I WANTED TO KNOW MORE!
THE STUFF ABOUT VALHALLA CASTLE IN SAGA PREFECTURE WAS REALLY INTERESTING!
THE GIST IS THAT WE MUST WORK TOGETHER TO DEFEAT THE DARK LORD IN VALHALLA CASTLE.
COMPLETING THAT TASK UNLOCKS THE ABILITY O TAKE OVER OTHER REFECTURES, BUT THAT EQUIRES AN INTERNET CONNECTION.
NOW, WE'RE ABOUT TO ENTER THE CHARACTER CREATION SCREEN, BUT RIKA HAS ALREADY DIGITALLY REPLICATED EVERYONE'S BODIES.
ALL YOU NEED TO CHOOSE IS YOUR CHARACTER CLASS.
BEEP
ALL RIGHT.
CLICK CLICK
Character Class
△ Magical Girl
△ Blacksmith
△ Gunner
△ Monk
△ Mage
△ Dancer
△ Thief
△ MonRose Maiden
I DON'T THINK YOU CAN GO WRONG WITH BEING A MAGE...

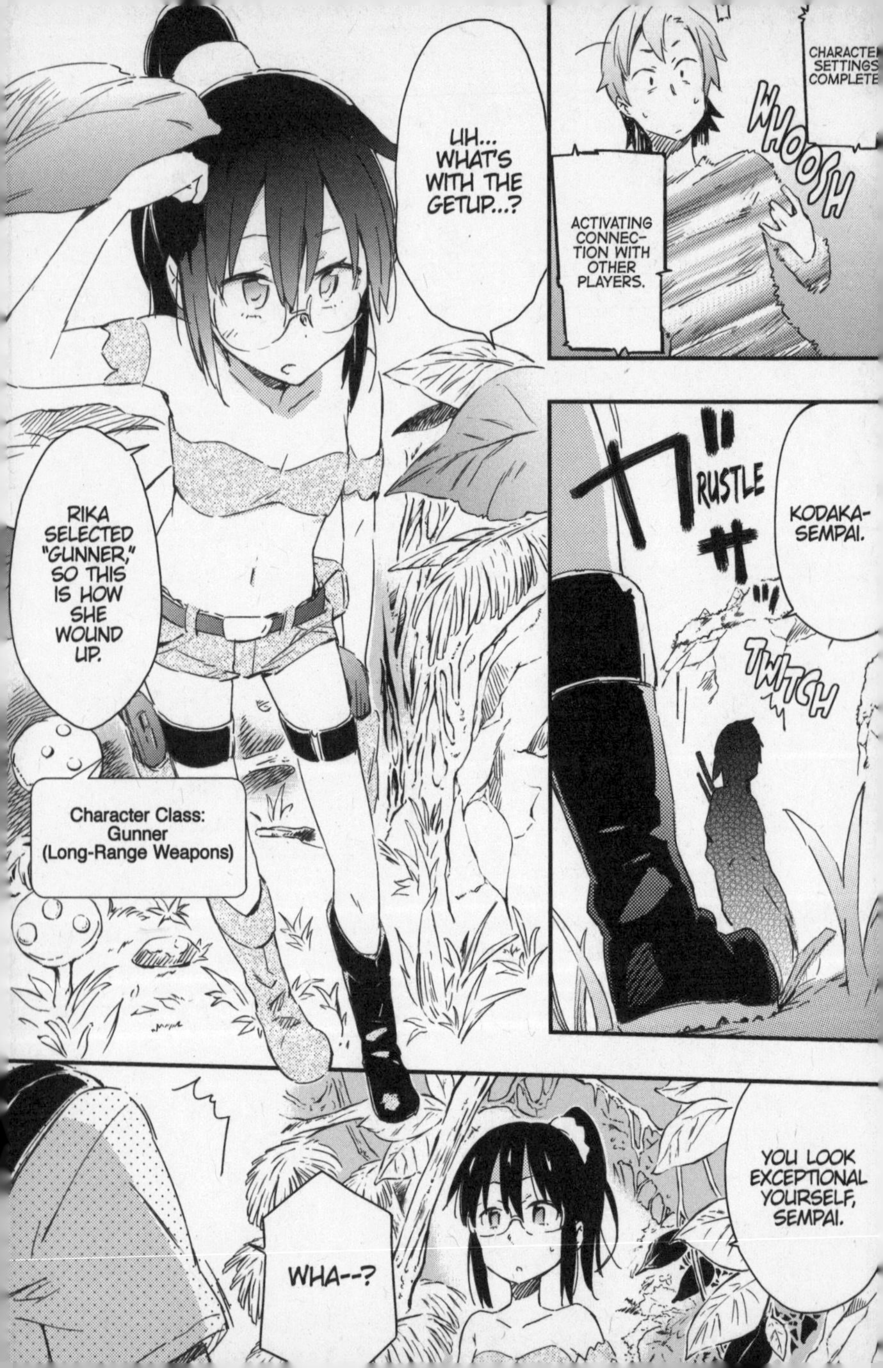
CHARACTE SETTINGS COMPLETE
WHOOSH
ACTIVATING CONNECTION WITH OTHER PLAYERS.
KODAKA-SEMPAI.
RUSTLE
TWITCH
UH... WHAT'S WITH THE GETUP...?
RIKA SELECTED "GUNNER," SO THIS IS HOW SHE WOUND UP.
Character Class: Gunner (Long-Range Weapons)
YOU LOOK EXCEPTIONAL YOURSELF, SEMPAI.
WHA--?

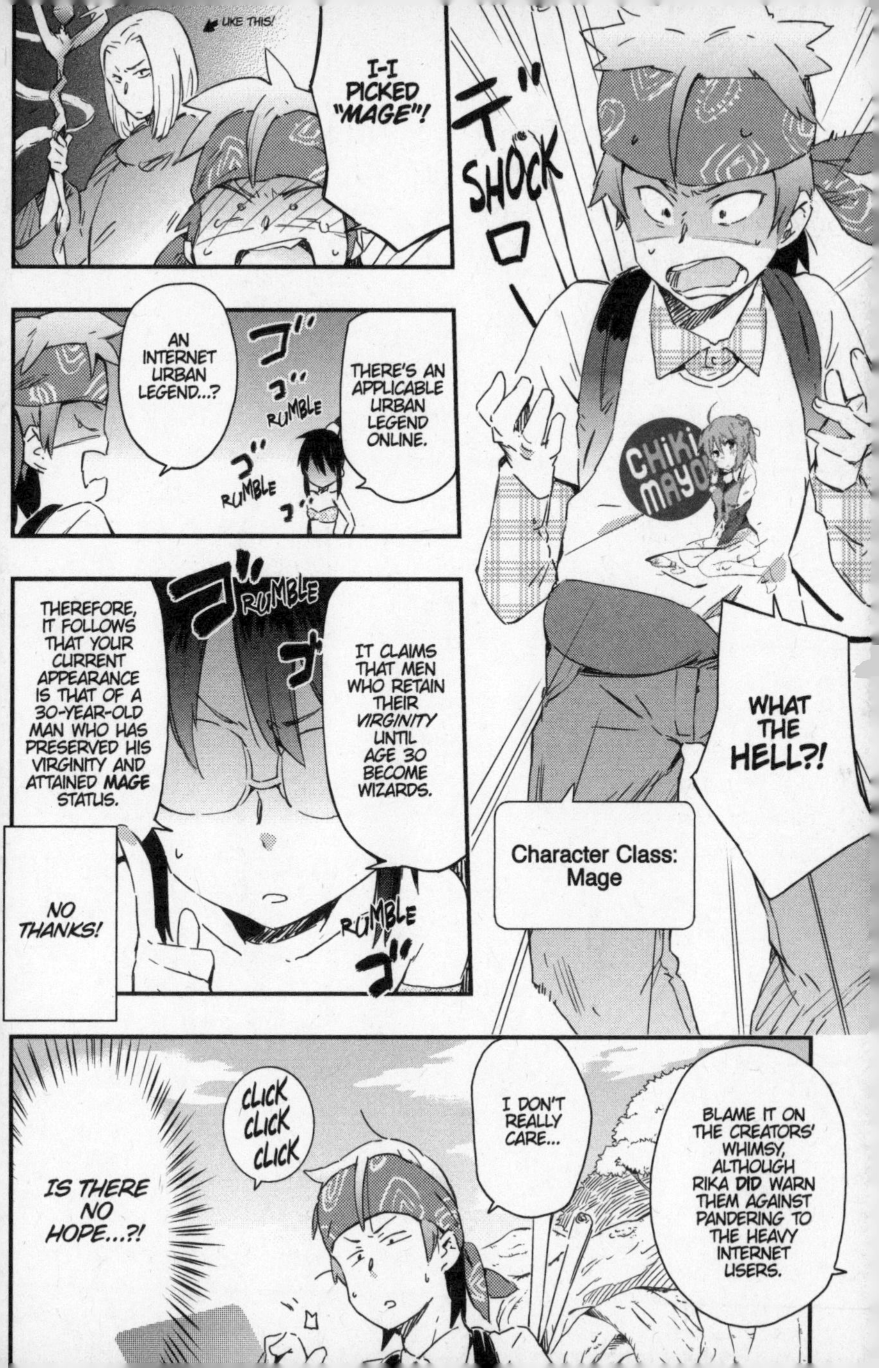
SHOCK
WHAT THE HELL?!
Character Class: Mage
I-I PICKED "MAGE"!
LIKE THIS!
THERE'S AN APPLICABLE URBAN LEGEND ONLINE.
RUMBLE
RUMBLE
AN INTERNET URBAN LEGEND...?
IT CLAIMS THAT MEN WHO RETAIN THEIR VIRGINITY UNTIL AGE 30 BECOME WIZARDS.
RUMBLE
RUMBLE
THEREFORE, IT FOLLOWS THAT YOUR CURRENT APPEARANCE IS THAT OF A 30-YEAR-OLD MAN WHO HAS PRESERVED HIS VIRGINITY AND ATTAINED MAGE STATUS.
NO THANKS!
BLAME IT ON THE CREATORS' WHIMSY, ALTHOUGH RIKA DID WARN THEM AGAINST PANDERING TO THE HEAVY INTERNET USERS.
I DON'T REALLY CARE...
CLICK CLICK CLICK
IS THERE NO HOPE...?!

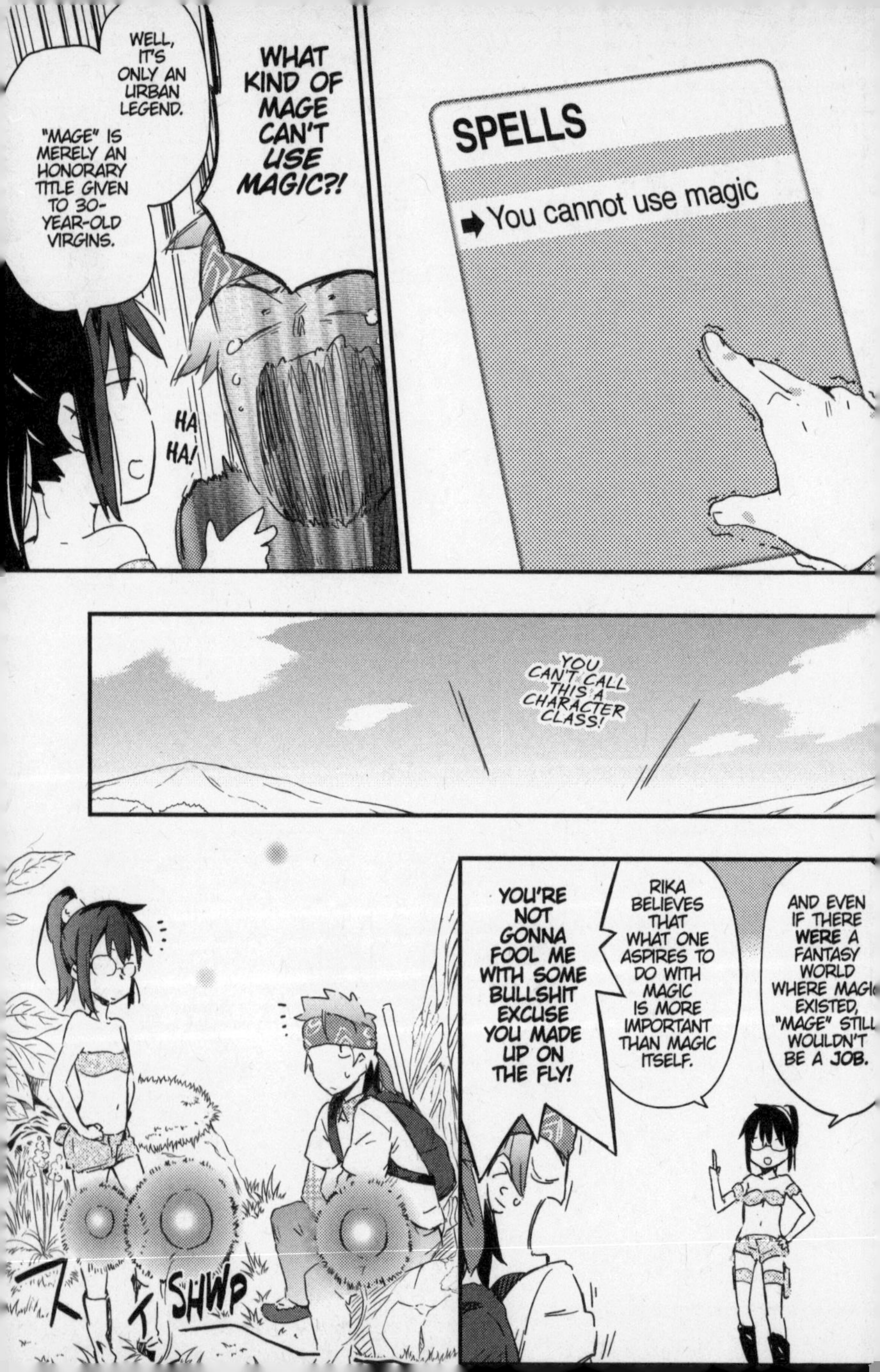
SPELLS
➡ You cannot use magic
WHAT KIND OF MAGE CAN'T USE MAGIC?!
WELL, IT'S ONLY AN URBAN LEGEND.
"MAGE" IS MERELY AN HONORARY TITLE GIVEN TO 30-YEAR-OLD VIRGINS.
HA HA!
YOU CAN'T CALL THIS A CHARACTER CLASS!
AND EVEN IF THERE WERE A FANTASY WORLD WHERE MAGIC EXISTED, "MAGE" STILL WOULDN'T BE A JOB.
RIKA BELIEVES THAT WHAT ONE ASPIRES TO DO WITH MAGIC IS MORE IMPORTANT THAN MAGIC ITSELF.
YOU'RE NOT GONNA FOOL ME WITH SOME BULLSHIT EXCUSE YOU MADE UP ON THE FLY!
SHWP

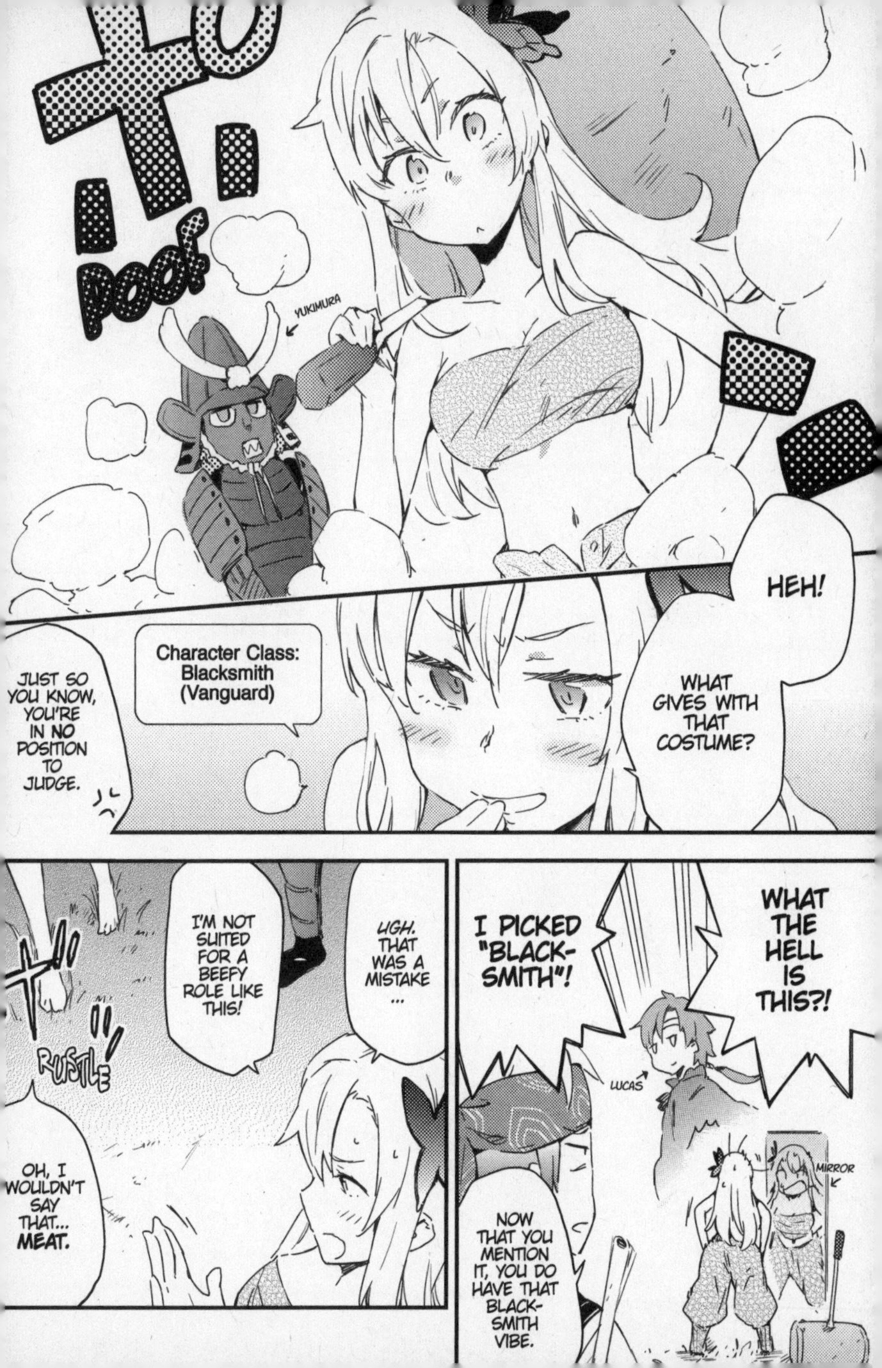
POOF
YUKIMURA
HEH!
WHAT GIVES WITH THAT COSTUME?
Character Class: Blacksmith (Vanguard)
JUST SO YOU KNOW, YOU'RE IN NO POSITION TO JUDGE.
WHAT THE HELL IS THIS?!
I PICKED "BLACK-SMITH"!
LUCAS
MIRROR
NOW THAT YOU MENTION IT, YOU DO HAVE THAT BLACK-SMITH VIBE.
UGH. THAT WAS A MISTAKE ...
I'M NOT SUITED FOR A BEEFY ROLE LIKE THIS!
RUSTLE
OH, I WOULDN'T SAY THAT... **MEAT.**

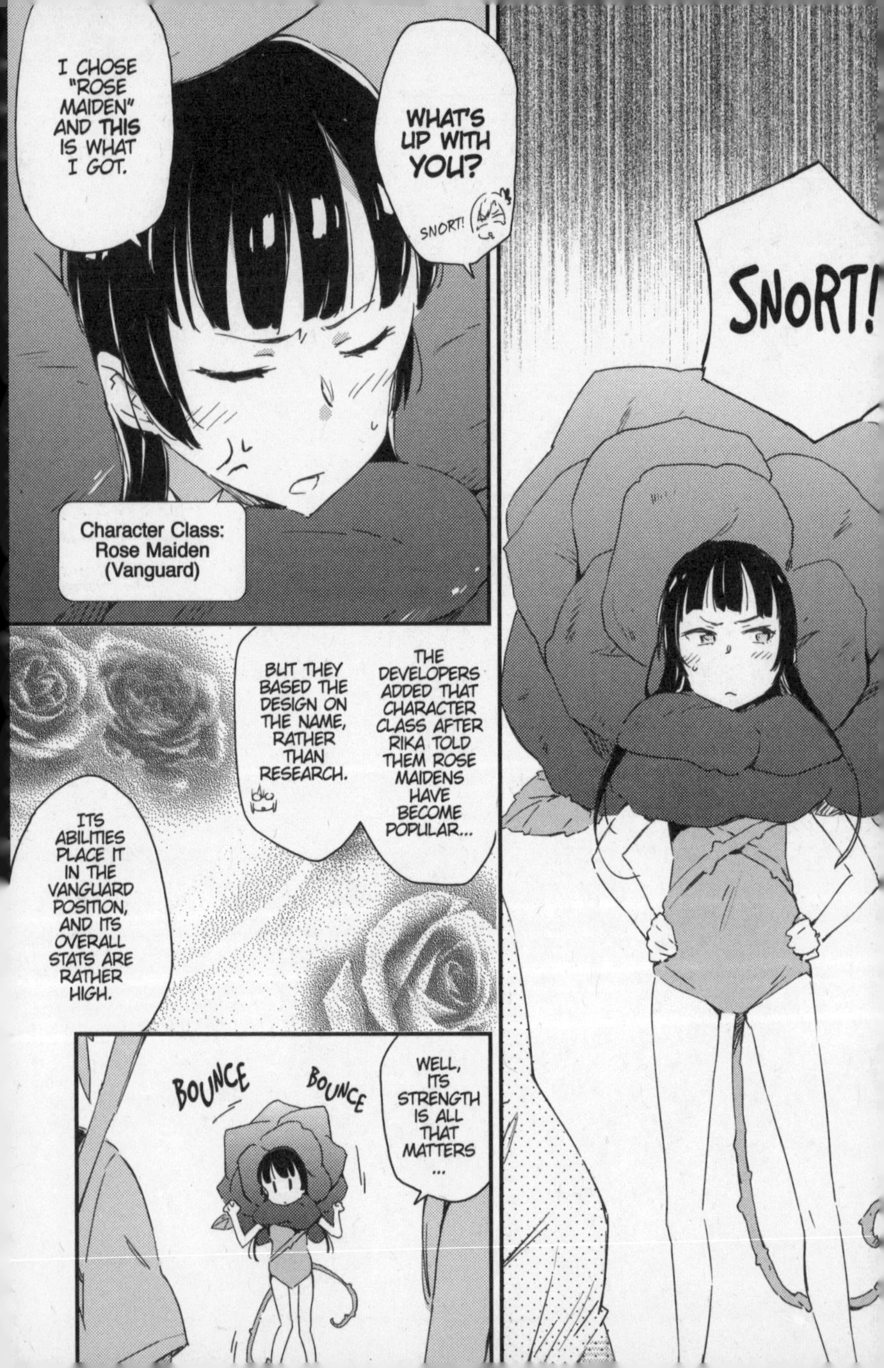
SNORT!
WHAT'S UP WITH YOU?
SNORT!
I CHOSE "ROSE MAIDEN" AND THIS IS WHAT I GOT.
Character Class: Rose Maiden (Vanguard)
THE DEVELOPERS ADDED THAT CHARACTER CLASS AFTER RIKA TOLD THEM ROSE MAIDENS HAVE BECOME POPULAR...
BUT THEY BASED THE DESIGN ON THE NAME, RATHER THAN RESEARCH.
ITS ABILITIES PLACE IT IN THE VANGUARD POSITION, AND ITS OVERALL STATS ARE RATHER HIGH.
WELL, ITS STRENGTH IS ALL THAT MATTERS...
BOUNCE
BOUNCE

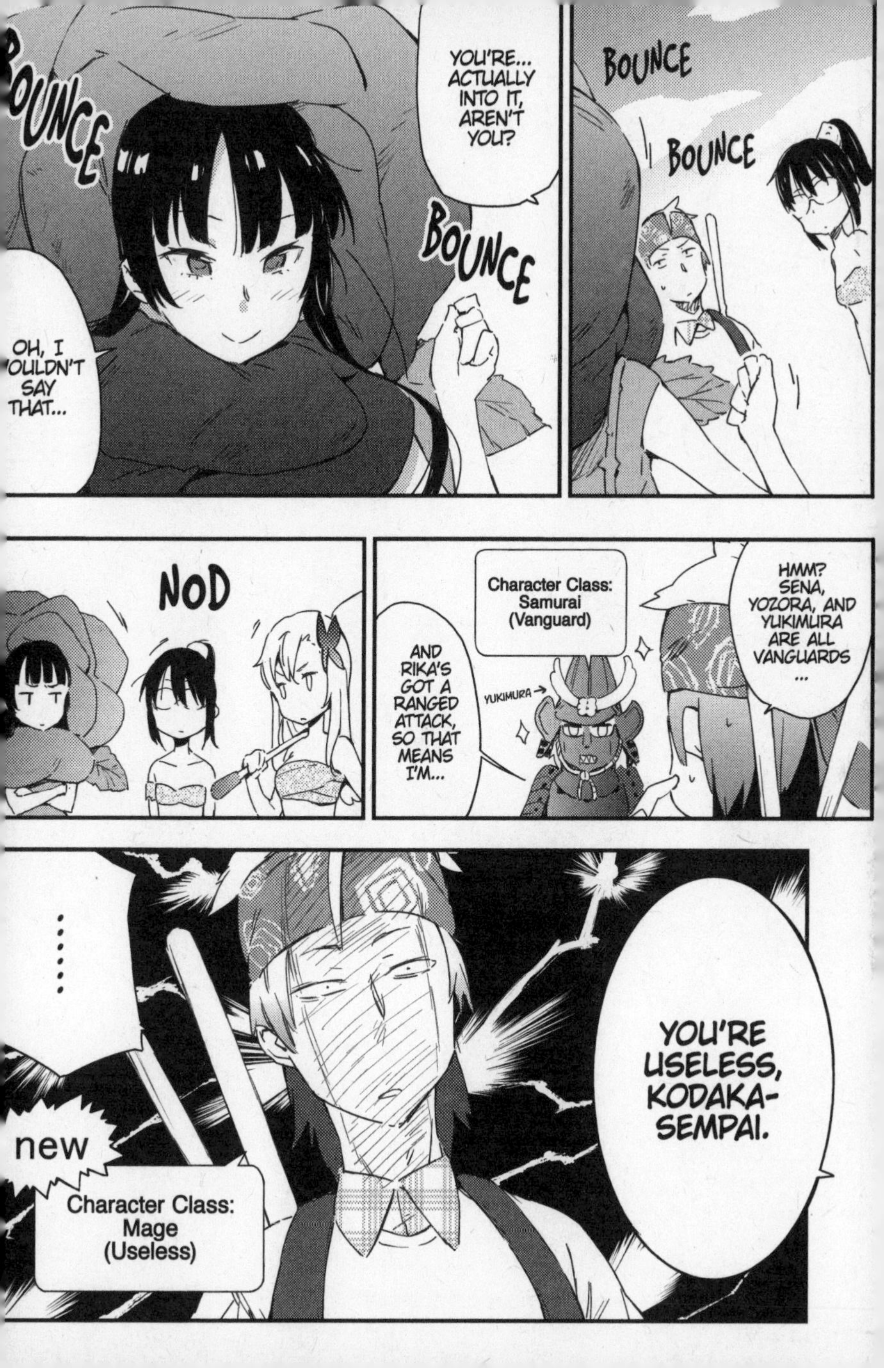
BOUNCE
BOUNCE
YOU'RE... ACTUALLY INTO IT, AREN'T YOU?
BOUNCE
BOUNCE
OH, I OULDN'T SAY THAT...
HMM? SENA, YOZORA, AND YUKIMURA ARE ALL VANGUARDS ...
Character Class: Samurai (Vanguard)
YUKIMURA →
AND RIKA'S GOT A RANGED ATTACK, SO THAT MEANS I'M...
NOD
YOU'RE USELESS, KODAKA-SEMPAI.
......
new
Character Class: Mage (Useless)

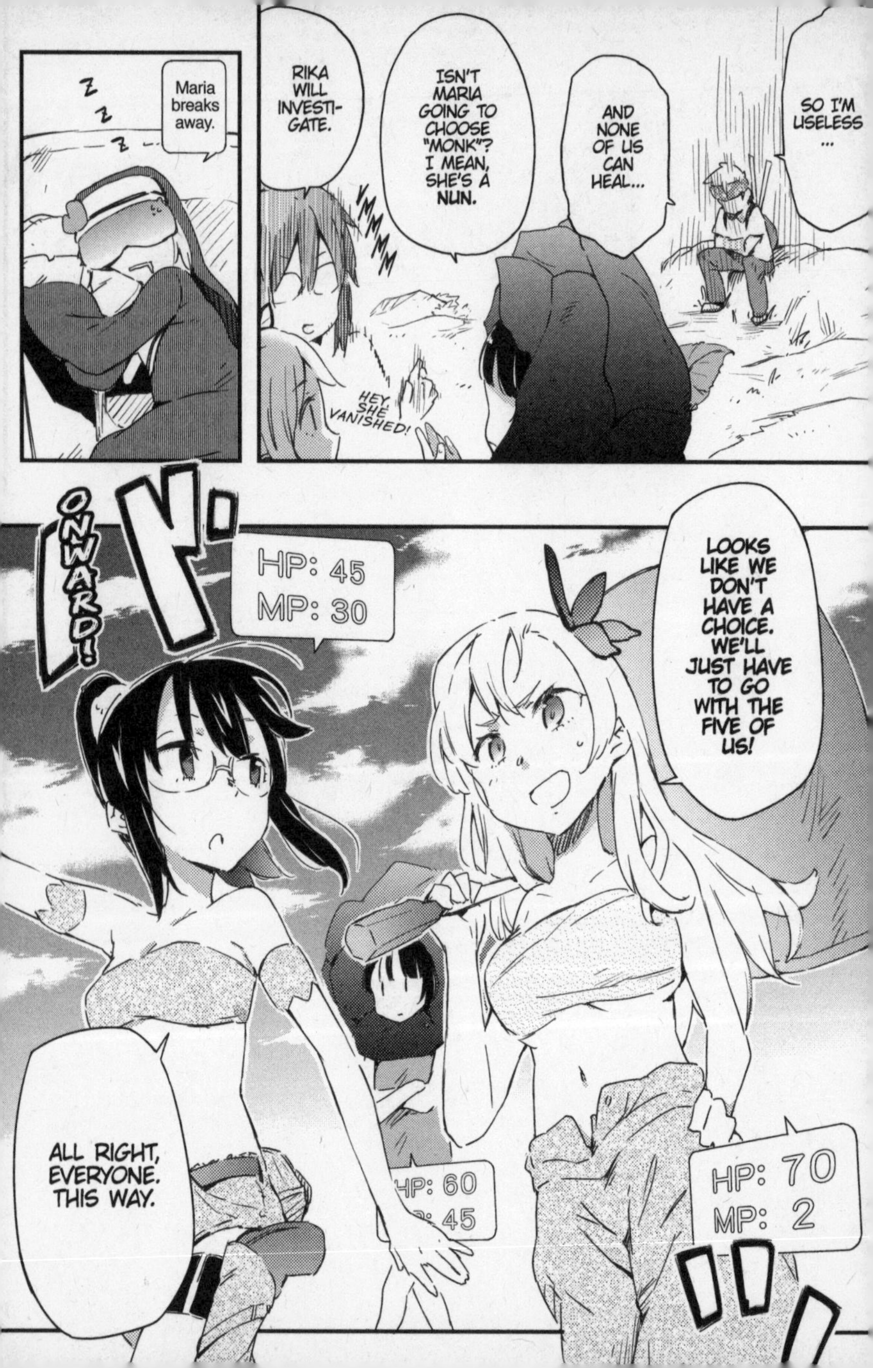
SO I'M USELESS ...
AND NONE OF US CAN HEAL...
ISN'T MARIA GOING TO CHOOSE "MONK"? I MEAN, SHE'S A NUN.
RIKA WILL INVESTI-GATE.
HEY, SHE VANISHED!
Maria breaks away.
Z Z Z
LOOKS LIKE WE DON'T HAVE A CHOICE. WE'LL JUST HAVE TO GO WITH THE FIVE OF US!
HP: 45
MP: 30
ONWARD!
HP: 70
MP: 2
HP: 60
45
ALL RIGHT, EVERYONE. THIS WAY.

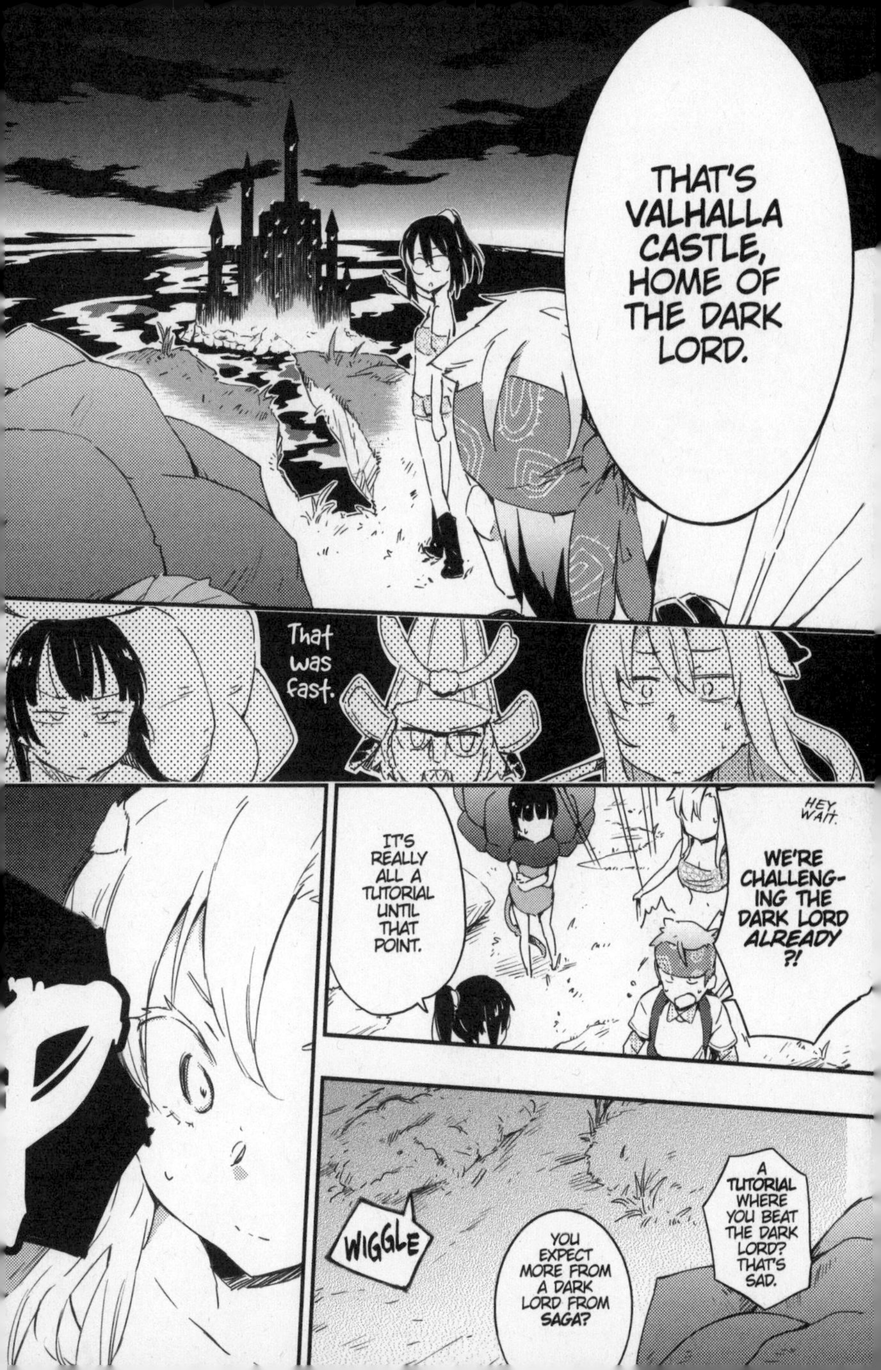
THAT'S VALHALLA CASTLE, HOME OF THE DARK LORD.
That was fast.
HEY, WAIT.
WE'RE CHALLENG-ING THE DARK LORD ALREADY?!
IT'S REALLY ALL A TUTORIAL UNTIL THAT POINT.
A TUTORIAL WHERE YOU BEAT THE DARK LORD? THAT'S SAD.
YOU EXPECT MORE FROM A DARK LORD FROM SAGA?
WIGGLE

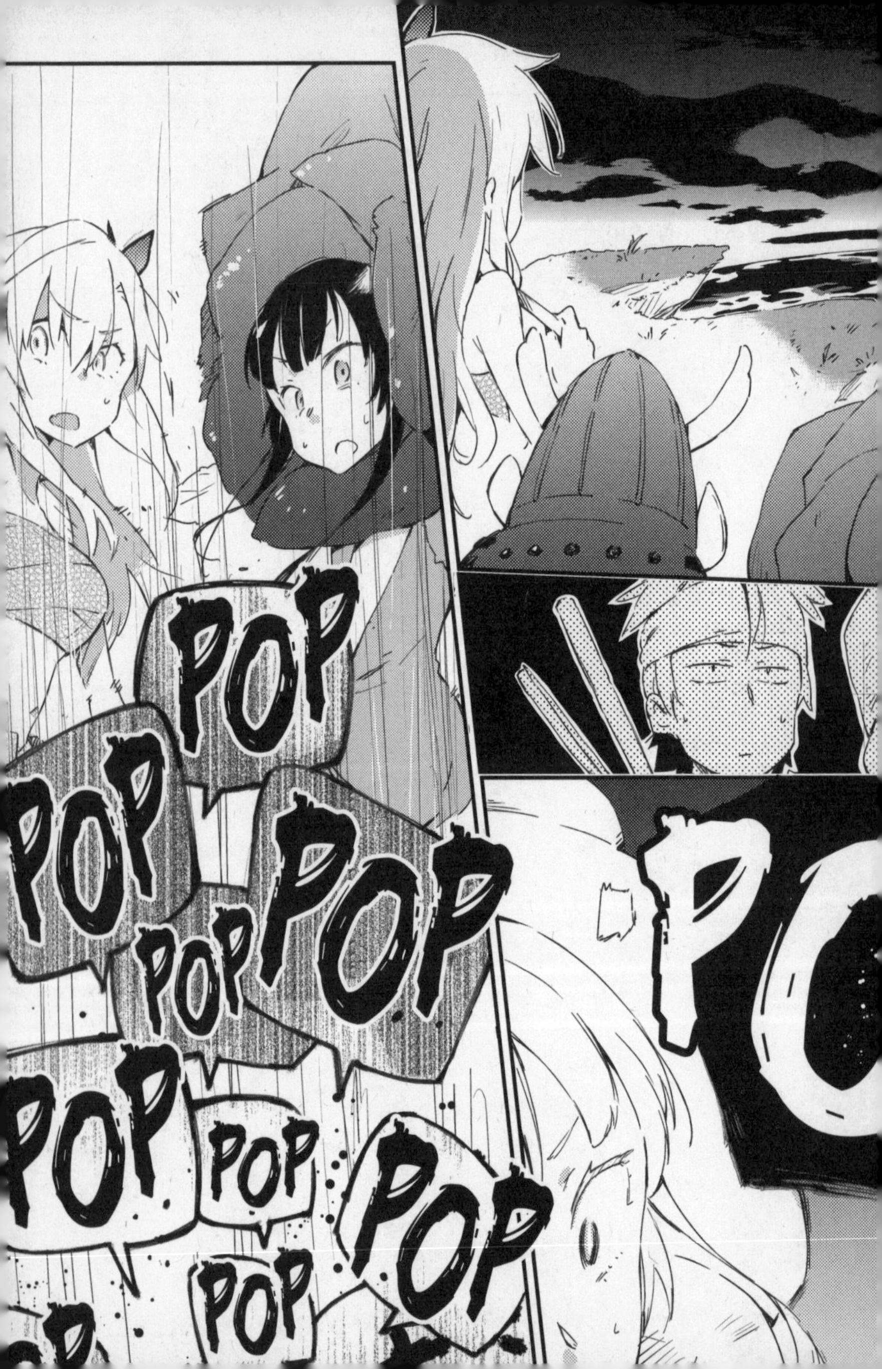
PO
POP
POP
POP
POP
POP
POP
POP
POP
PO

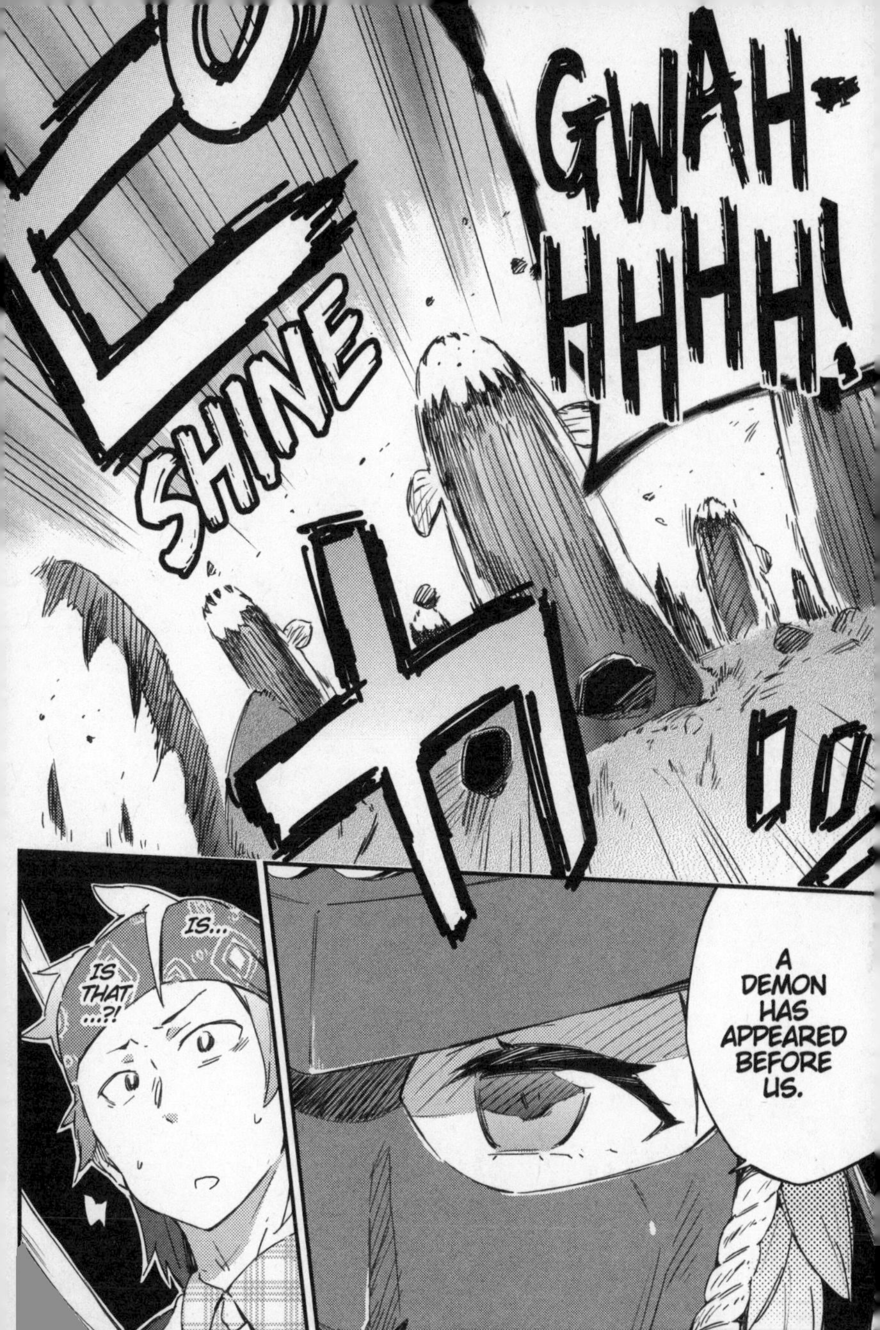
GWAH-HHHH!
SHINE
DOO
A DEMON HAS APPEARED BEFORE US.
IS...
IS THAT...?!
*YUKIMURA

SNORE

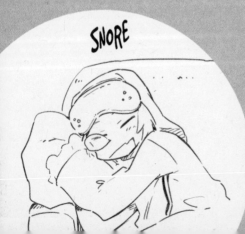

TRANSLATION NOTES

Yozora's "Rose Maiden" character class refers to a trend of gothic Lolita fashion made popular by the anime series *Rozen Maiden.*

Haganai I don't have many friends

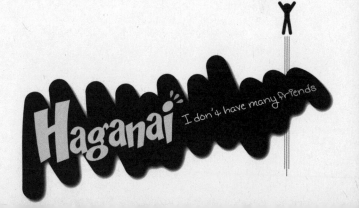

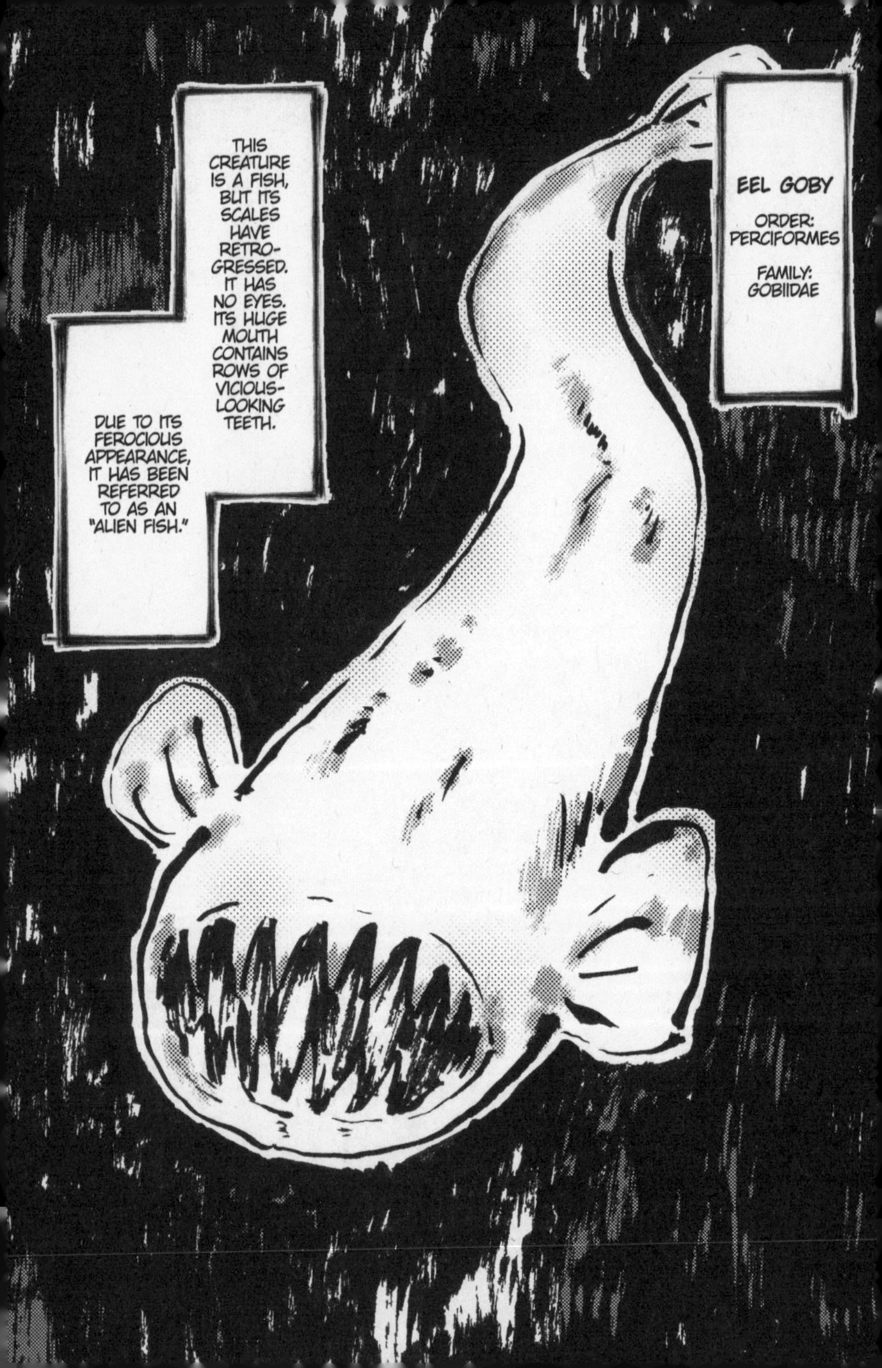
EEL GOBY
ORDER: PERCIFORMES
FAMILY: GOBIIDAE
THIS CREATURE IS A FISH, BUT ITS SCALES HAVE RETRO-GRESSED. IT HAS NO EYES. ITS HUGE MOUTH CONTAINS ROWS OF VICIOUS-LOOKING TEETH.
DUE TO ITS FEROCIOUS APPEARANCE, IT HAS BEEN REFERRED TO AS AN "ALIEN FISH."

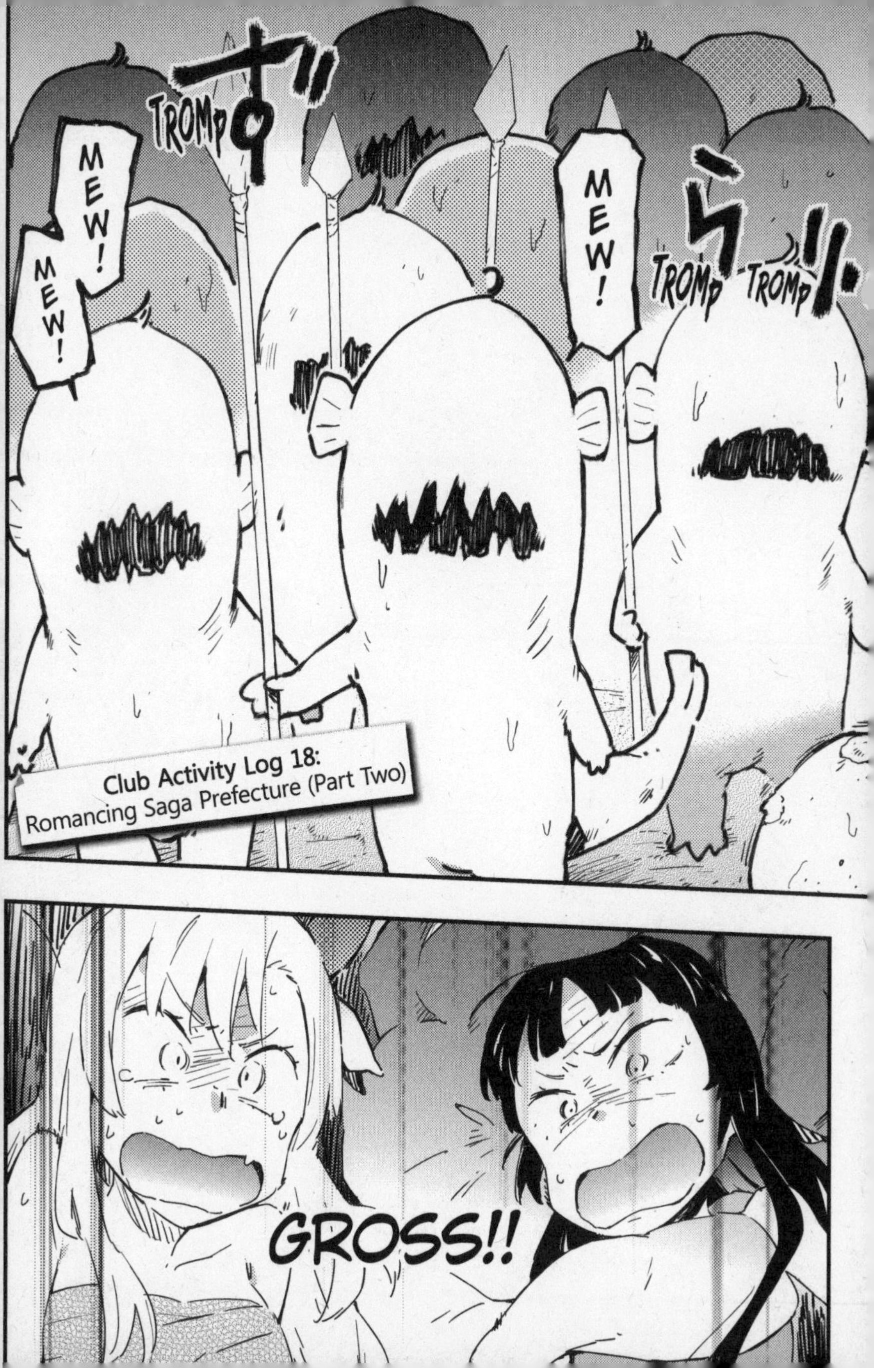
TROMP TROMP
MEW!
TROMP
MEW! MEW!
MEW! MEW!
Club Activity Log 18:
Romancing Saga Prefecture (Part Two)
GROSS!!

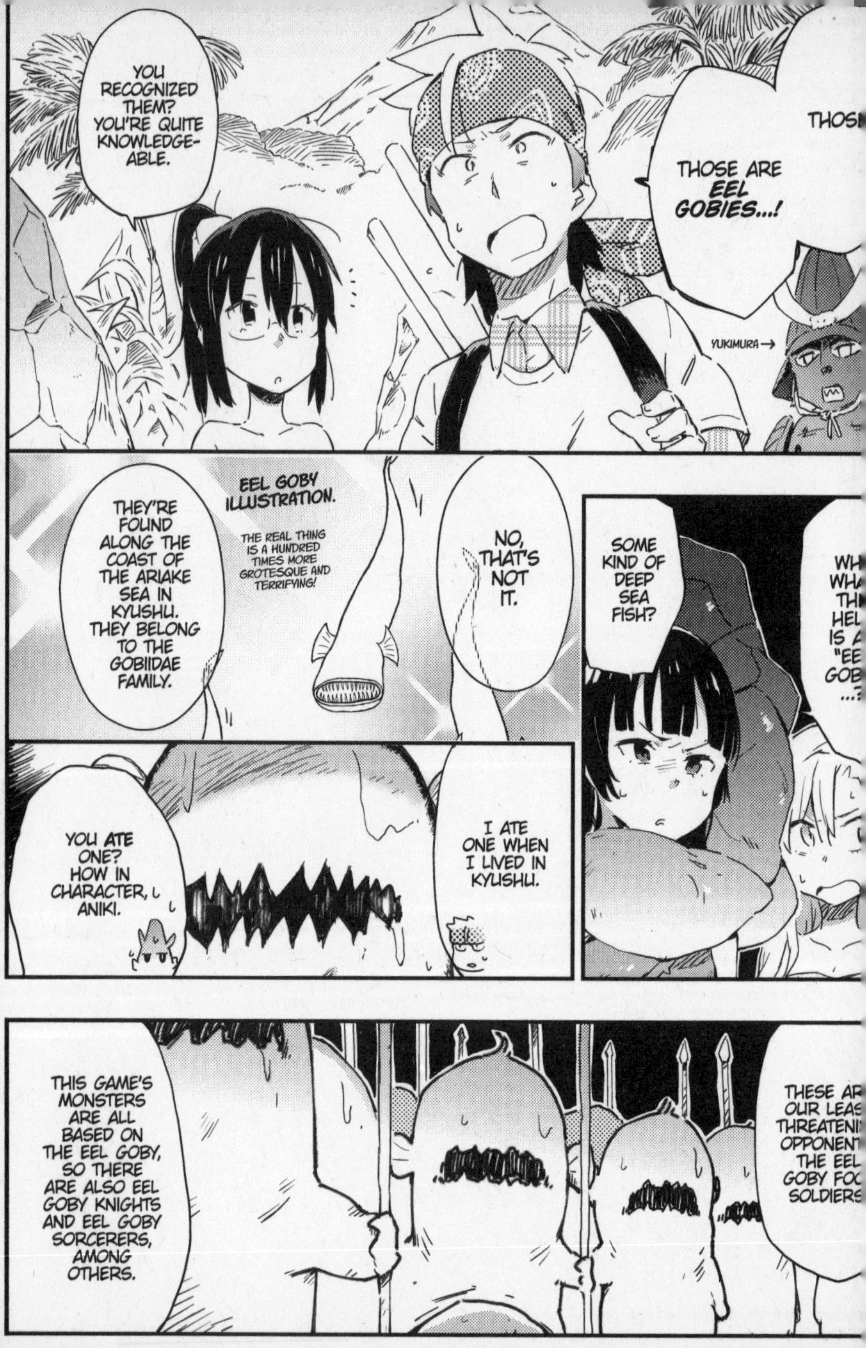
THOS
THOSE ARE EEL GOBIES...!
YUKIMURA →
YOU RECOGNIZED THEM? YOU'RE QUITE KNOWLEDGE-ABLE.
WH WHA TH HEL IS A "EE GOB ...?
SOME KIND OF DEEP SEA FISH?
NO, THAT'S NOT IT.
EEL GOBY ILLUSTRATION.
THE REAL THING IS A HUNDRED TIMES MORE GROTESQUE AND TERRIFYING!
THEY'RE FOUND ALONG THE COAST OF THE ARIAKE SEA IN KYUSHU. THEY BELONG TO THE GOBIIDAE FAMILY.
I ATE ONE WHEN I LIVED IN KYUSHU.
YOU ATE ONE? HOW IN CHARACTER, ANIKI.
THESE AR OUR LEAS THREATENI OPPONENT THE EEL GOBY FOO SOLDIERS
THIS GAME'S MONSTERS ARE ALL BASED ON THE EEL GOBY, SO THERE ARE ALSO EEL GOBY KNIGHTS AND EEL GOBY SORCERERS, AMONG OTHERS.

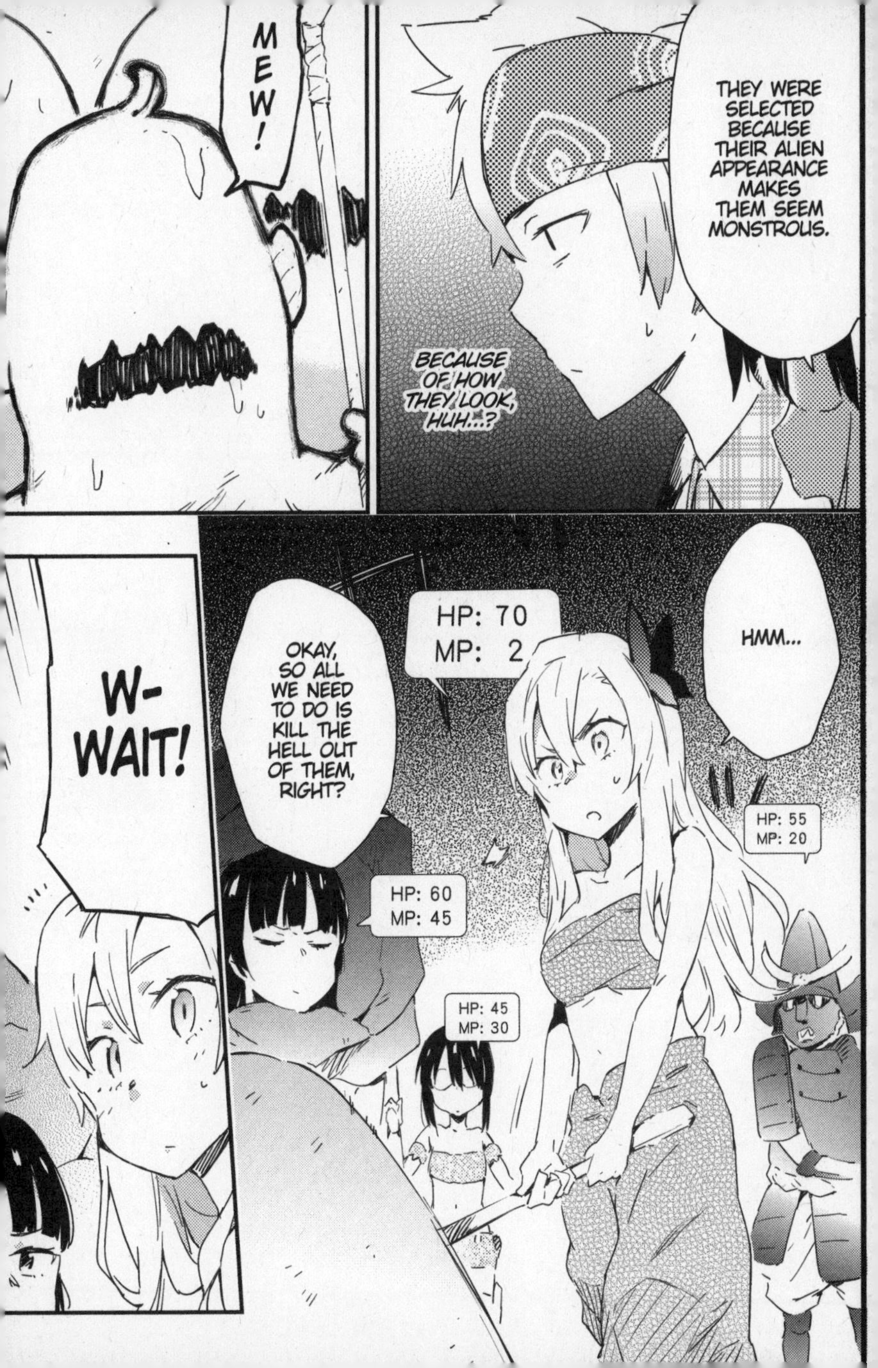
THEY WERE SELECTED BECAUSE THEIR ALIEN APPEARANCE MAKES THEM SEEM MONSTROUS.
BECAUSE OF HOW THEY LOOK, HUH...?
MEW!
HMM...
HP: 70
MP: 2
OKAY, SO ALL WE NEED TO DO IS KILL THE HELL OUT OF THEM, RIGHT?
HP: 55
MP: 20
HP: 60
MP: 45
HP: 45
MP: 30
W-WAIT!

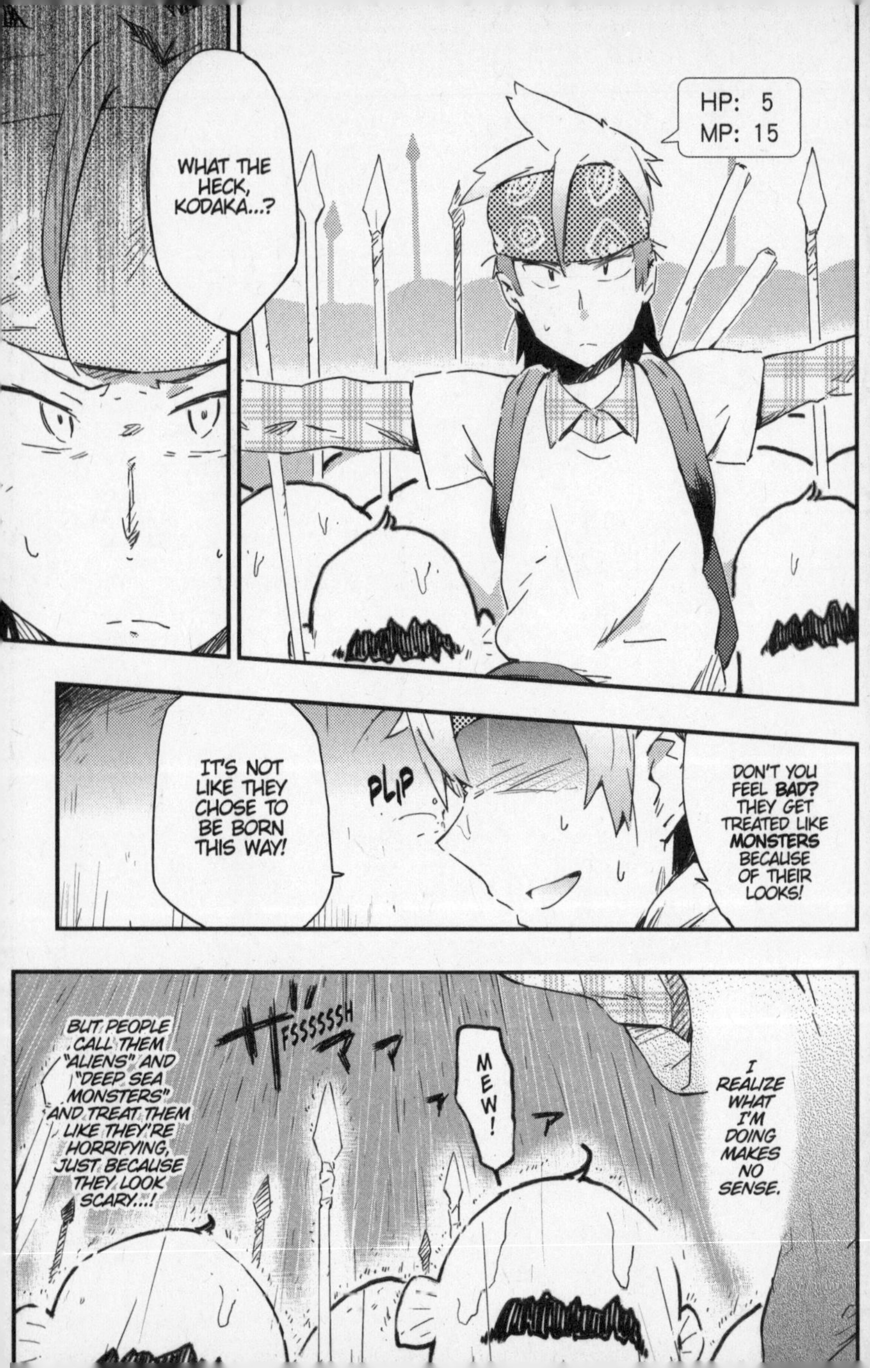
HP: 5
MP: 15
WHAT THE HECK, KODAKA...?
DON'T YOU FEEL BAD? THEY GET TREATED LIKE MONSTERS BECAUSE OF THEIR LOOKS!
PLIP
IT'S NOT LIKE THEY CHOSE TO BE BORN THIS WAY!
I REALIZE WHAT I'M DOING MAKES NO SENSE.
MEW!
FSSSSSSH
BUT PEOPLE CALL THEM "ALIENS" AND "DEEP SEA MONSTERS" AND TREAT THEM LIKE THEY'RE HORRIFYING, JUST BECAUSE THEY LOOK SCARY...!

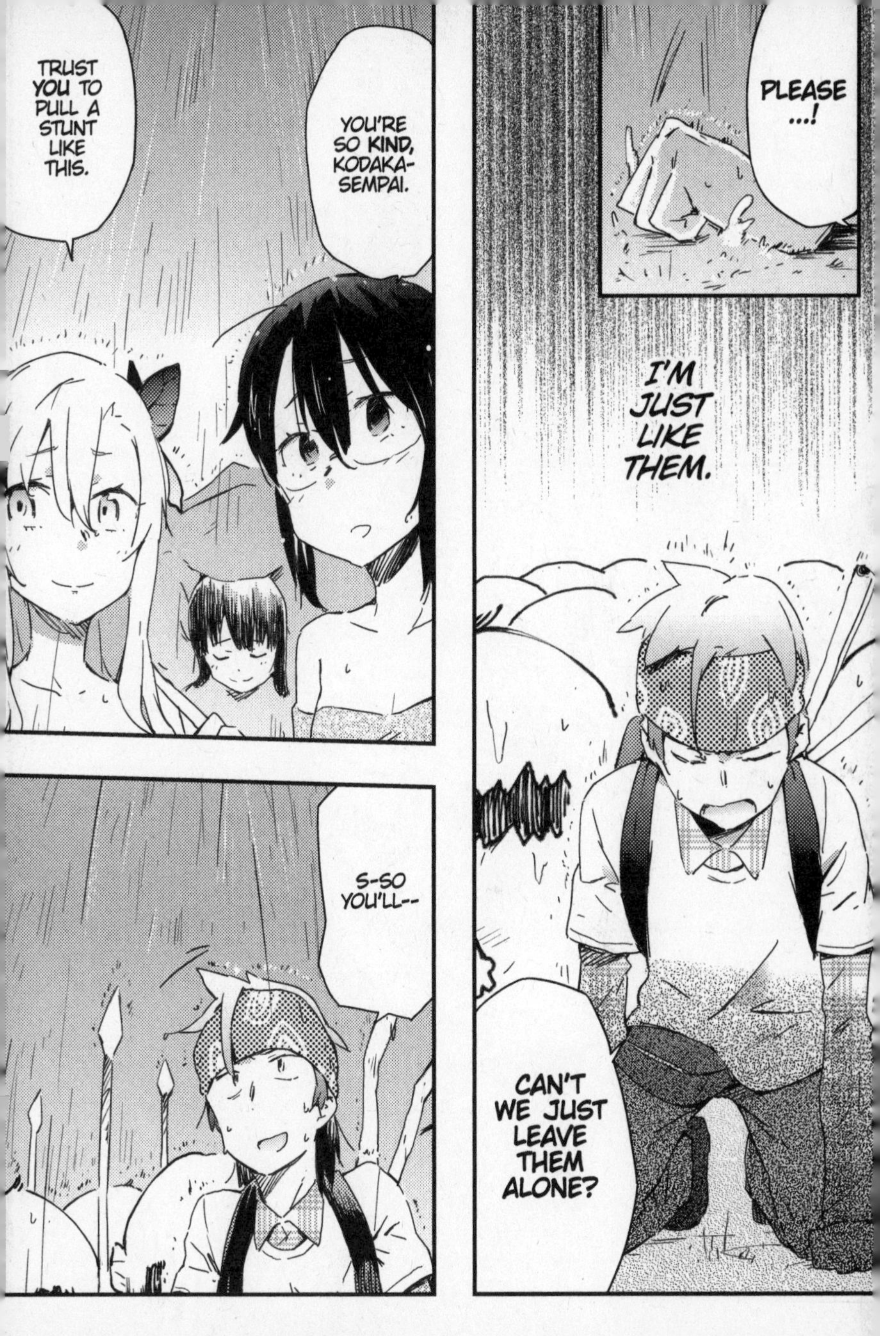
PLEASE ...!
I'M JUST LIKE THEM.
CAN'T WE JUST LEAVE THEM ALONE?
YOU'RE SO KIND, KODAKA-SEMPAI.
TRUST YOU TO PULL A STUNT LIKE THIS.
S-SO YOU'LL--

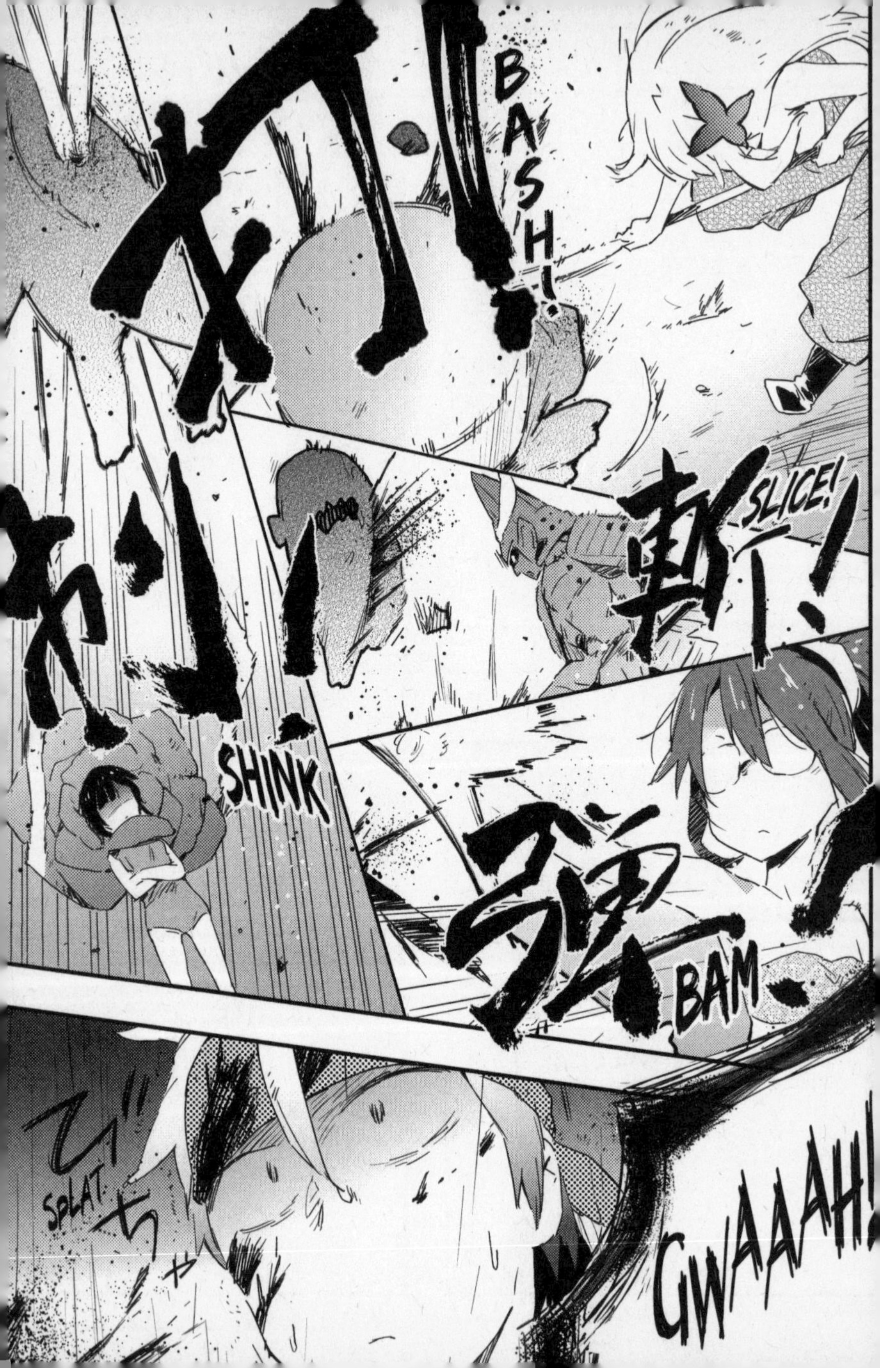
BASHI!
SLICE!
BAM
SHINK
GWAAAH!
SPLAT

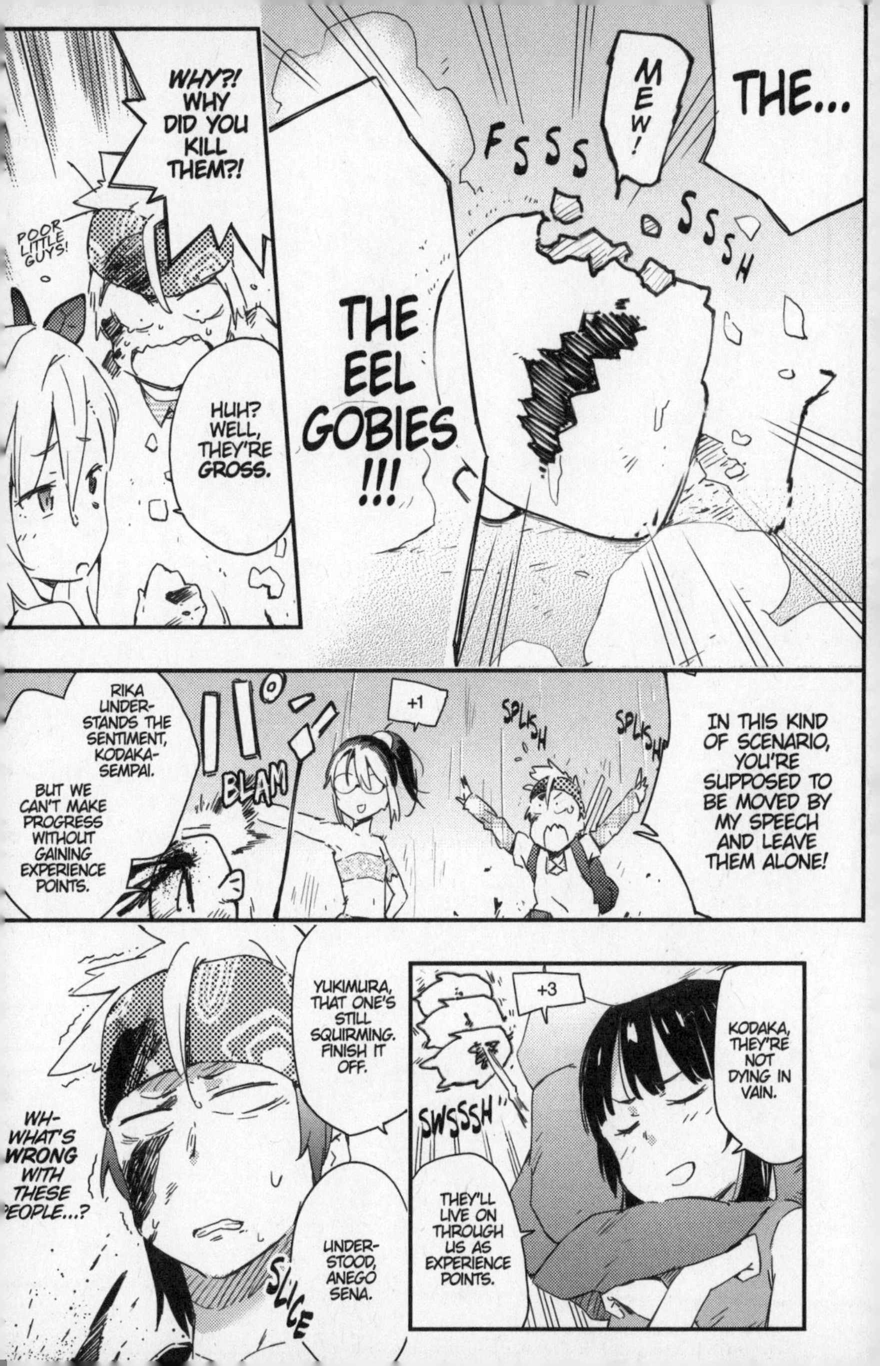
THE...
MEW!
FSSS
SSSH
THE EEL GOBIES!!!
WHY?! WHY DID YOU KILL THEM?!
POOR LITTLE GUYS!
HUH? WELL, THEY'RE GROSS.
IN THIS KIND OF SCENARIO, YOU'RE SUPPOSED TO BE MOVED BY MY SPEECH AND LEAVE THEM ALONE!
SPLKSH
SPLKSH
+1
BLAM
RIKA UNDERSTANDS THE SENTIMENT, KODAKA-SEMPAI.
BUT WE CAN'T MAKE PROGRESS WITHOUT GAINING EXPERIENCE POINTS.
KODAKA, THEY'RE NOT DYING IN VAIN.
+3
SWSSSH
THEY'LL LIVE ON THROUGH US AS EXPERIENCE POINTS.
YUKIMURA, THAT ONE'S STILL SQUIRMING. FINISH IT OFF.
UNDERSTOOD, ANEGO SENA.
SLICE
WH-WHAT'S WRONG WITH THESE PEOPLE...?

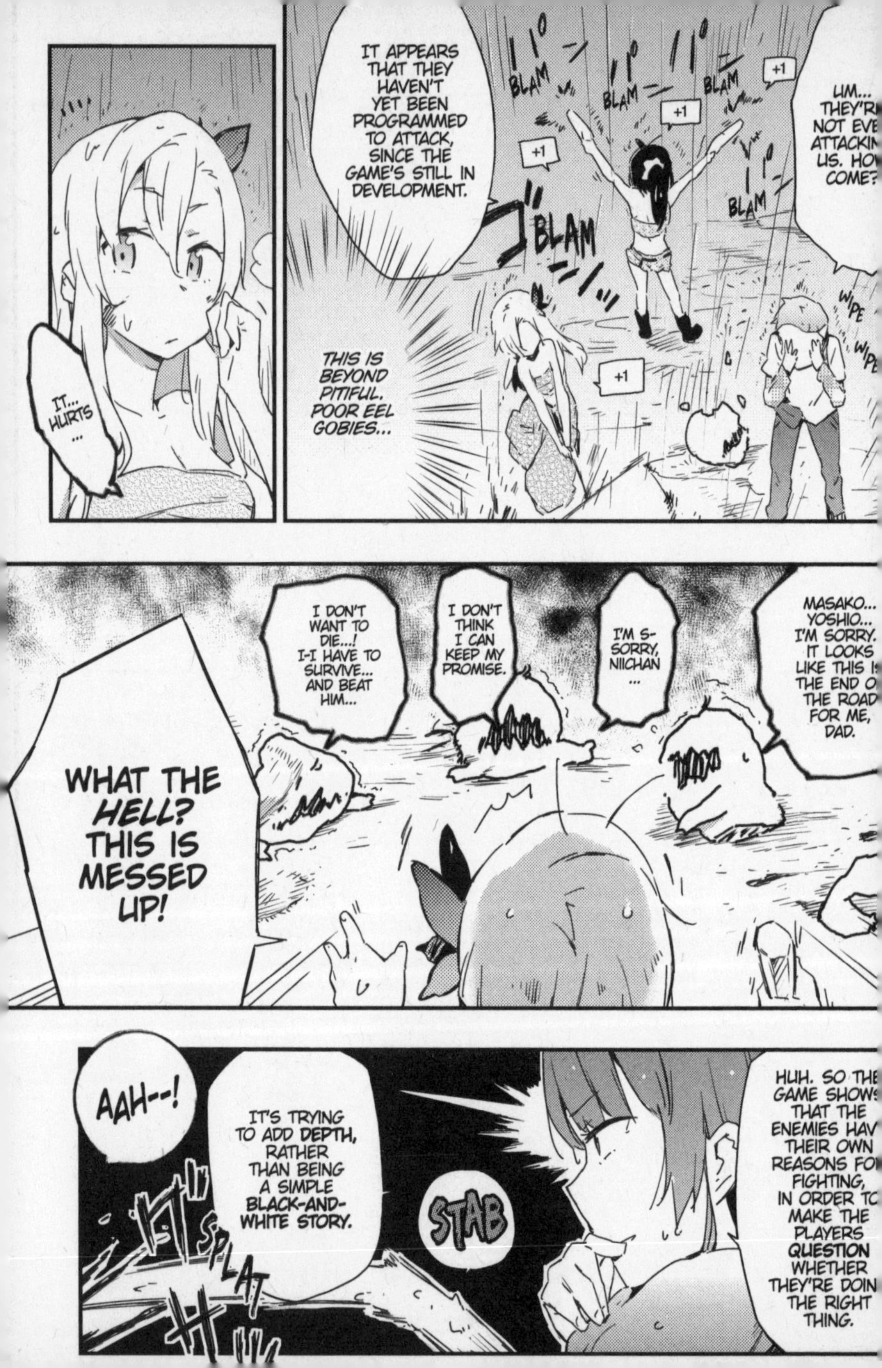

UM... THEY'R NOT EVE ATTACKIN US. HO COME?
+1
BLAM
BLAM
+1
BLAM
+1
IT APPEARS THAT THEY HAVEN'T YET BEEN PROGRAMMED TO ATTACK, SINCE THE GAME'S STILL IN DEVELOPMENT.
BLAM
BLAM
WIPE WIPE
+1
THIS IS BEYOND PITIFUL. POOR EEL GOBIES...
IT... HURTS...
MASAKO... YOSHIO... I'M SORRY. IT LOOKS LIKE THIS I THE END O THE ROAD FOR ME, DAD.
I'M S-SORRY, NIICHAN...
I DON'T THINK I CAN KEEP MY PROMISE.
I DON'T WANT TO DIE...! I-I HAVE TO SURVIVE... AND BEAT HIM...
WHAT THE *HELL?* THIS IS MESSED UP!
HUH. SO THE GAME SHOWS THAT THE ENEMIES HAV THEIR OWN REASONS FO FIGHTING, IN ORDER TO MAKE THE PLAYERS QUESTION WHETHER THEY'RE DOIN THE RIGHT THING.
STAB
IT'S TRYING TO ADD DEPTH, RATHER THAN BEING A SIMPLE BLACK-AND-WHITE STORY.
AAH--!
SPLAT

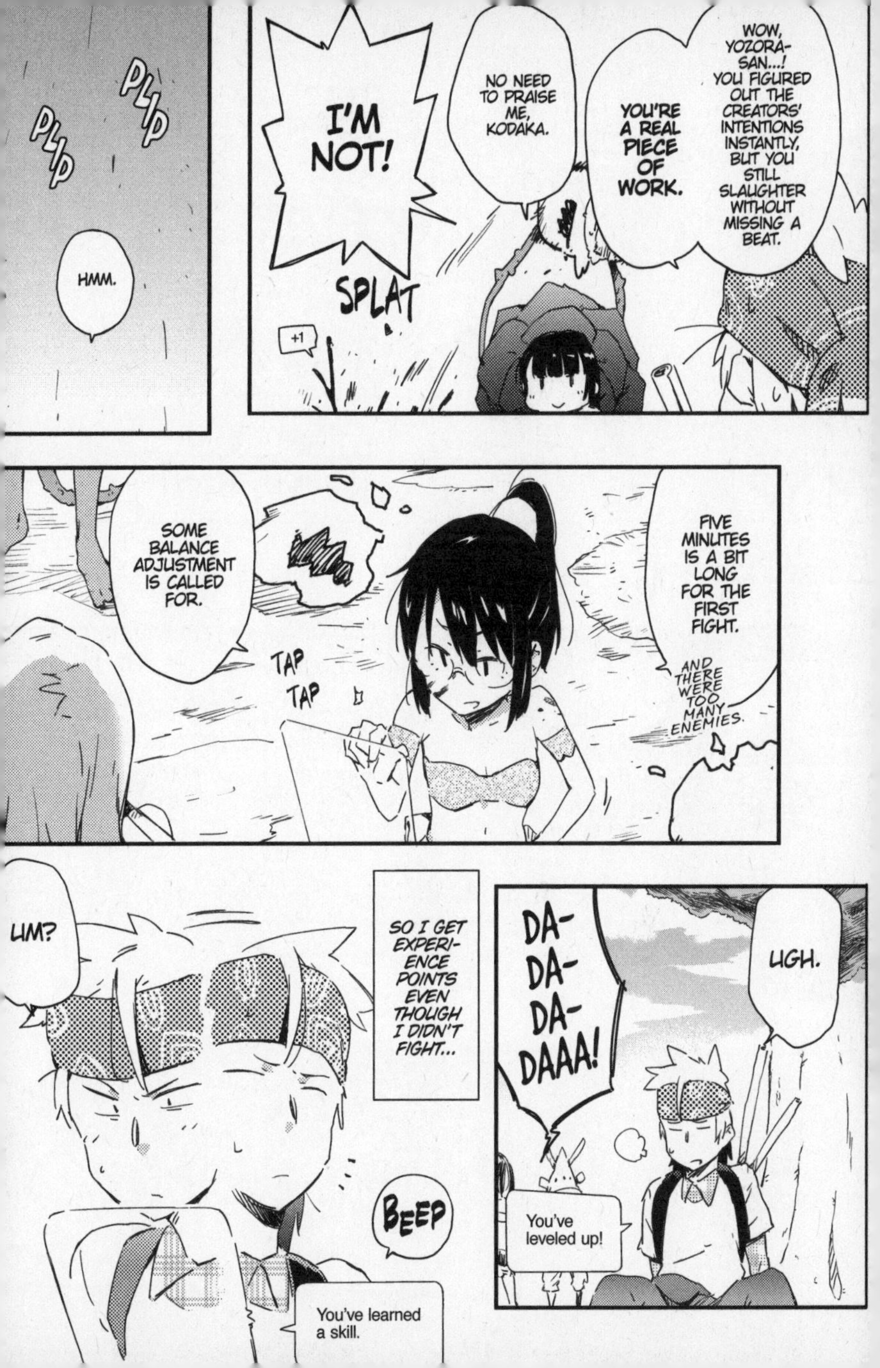
WOW, YOZORA-SAN...! YOU FIGURED OUT THE CREATORS' INTENTIONS INSTANTLY, BUT YOU STILL SLAUGHTER WITHOUT MISSING A BEAT.
YOU'RE A REAL PIECE OF WORK.
NO NEED TO PRAISE ME, KODAKA.
I'M NOT!
SPLAT
+1
PLIP
PLIP
HMM.
FIVE MINUTES IS A BIT LONG FOR THE FIRST FIGHT.
AND THERE WERE TOO MANY ENEMIES.
SOME BALANCE ADJUSTMENT IS CALLED FOR.
TAP
TAP
UGH.
DA-DA-DA-DAAA!
You've leveled up!
SO I GET EXPERIENCE POINTS EVEN THOUGH I DIDN'T FIGHT...
UM?
BEEP
You've learned a skill.

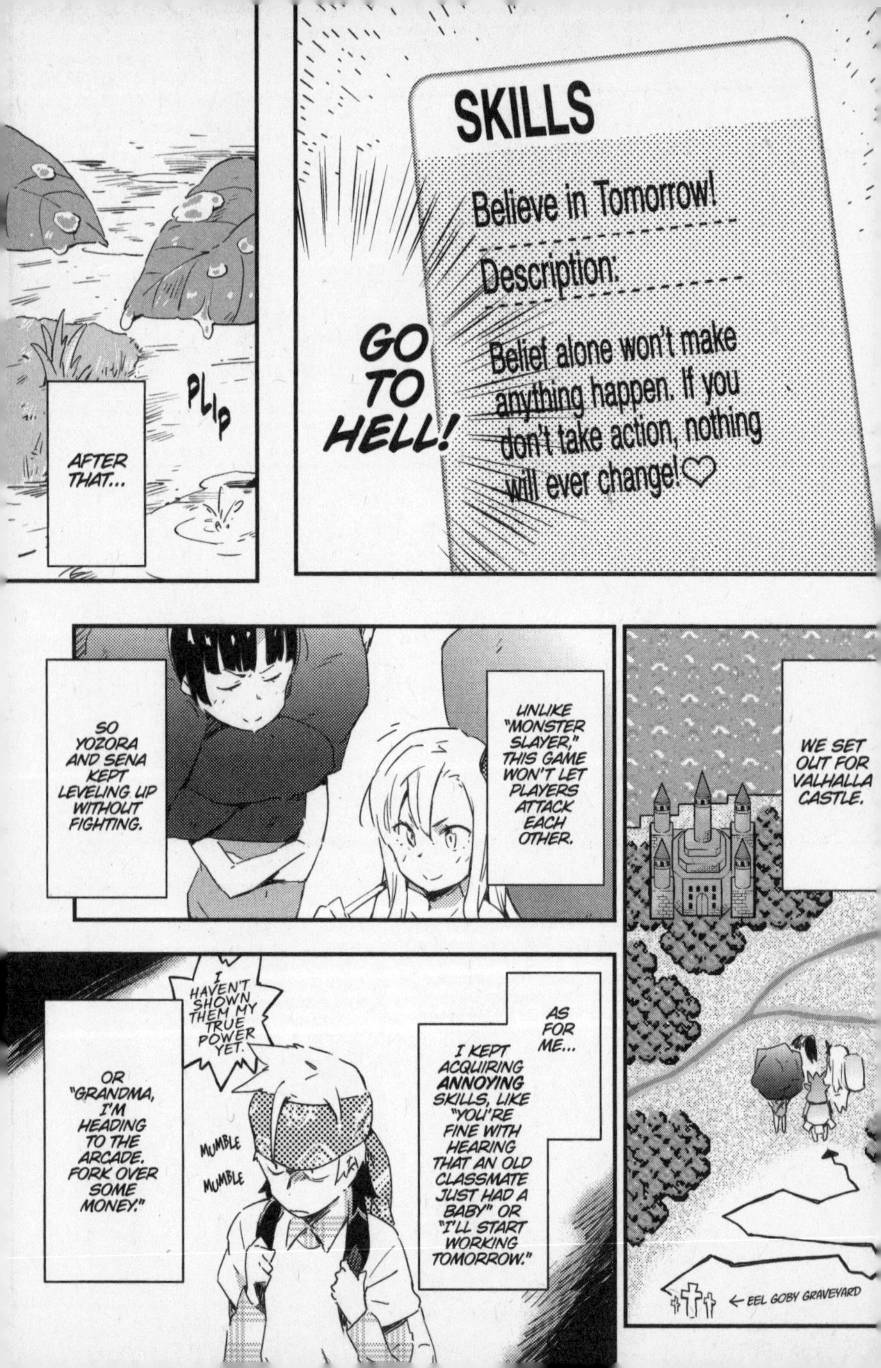
SKILLS
Believe in Tomorrow!
Description:
Belief alone won't make anything happen. If you don't take action, nothing will ever change!♡
GO TO HELL!
PLIP
AFTER THAT...
WE SET OUT FOR VALHALLA CASTLE.
← EEL GOBY GRAVEYARD
UNLIKE "MONSTER SLAYER," THIS GAME WON'T LET PLAYERS ATTACK EACH OTHER.
SO YOZORA AND SENA KEPT LEVELING UP WITHOUT FIGHTING.
AS FOR ME...
I KEPT ACQUIRING ANNOYING SKILLS, LIKE "YOU'RE FINE WITH HEARING THAT AN OLD CLASSMATE JUST HAD A BABY" OR "I'LL START WORKING TOMORROW."
I HAVEN'T SHOWN THEM MY TRUE POWER YET.
MUMBLE
MUMBLE
OR "GRANDMA, I'M HEADING TO THE ARCADE. FORK OVER SOME MONEY."

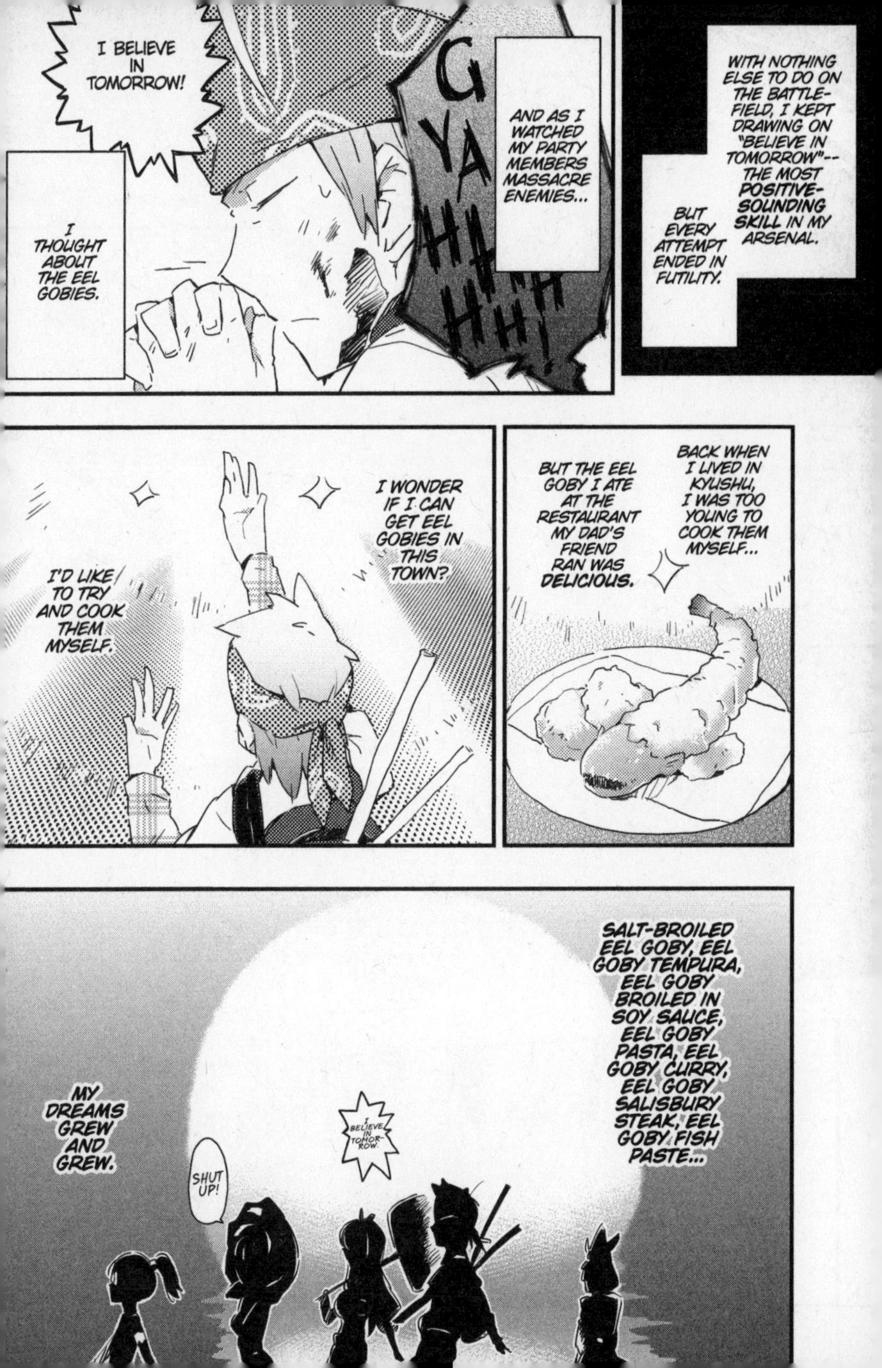
WITH NOTHING ELSE TO DO ON THE BATTLEFIELD, I KEPT DRAWING ON "BELIEVE IN TOMORROW"-- THE MOST **POSITIVE-SOUNDING SKILL** IN MY ARSENAL.
BUT EVERY ATTEMPT ENDED IN FUTILITY.
AND AS I WATCHED MY PARTY MEMBERS MASSACRE ENEMIES...
I BELIEVE IN TOMORROW!
I THOUGHT ABOUT THE EEL GOBIES.
BACK WHEN I LIVED IN KYUSHU, I WAS TOO YOUNG TO COOK THEM MYSELF...
BUT THE EEL GOBY I ATE AT THE RESTAURANT MY DAD'S FRIEND RAN WAS **DELICIOUS.**
I WONDER IF I CAN GET EEL GOBIES IN THIS TOWN?
I'D LIKE TO TRY AND COOK THEM MYSELF.
SALT-BROILED EEL GOBY, EEL GOBY TEMPURA, EEL GOBY BROILED IN SOY SAUCE, EEL GOBY PASTA, EEL GOBY CURRY, EEL GOBY SALISBURY STEAK, EEL GOBY FISH PASTE...
I BELIEVE IN TOMORROW.
MY DREAMS GREW AND GREW.
SHUT UP!

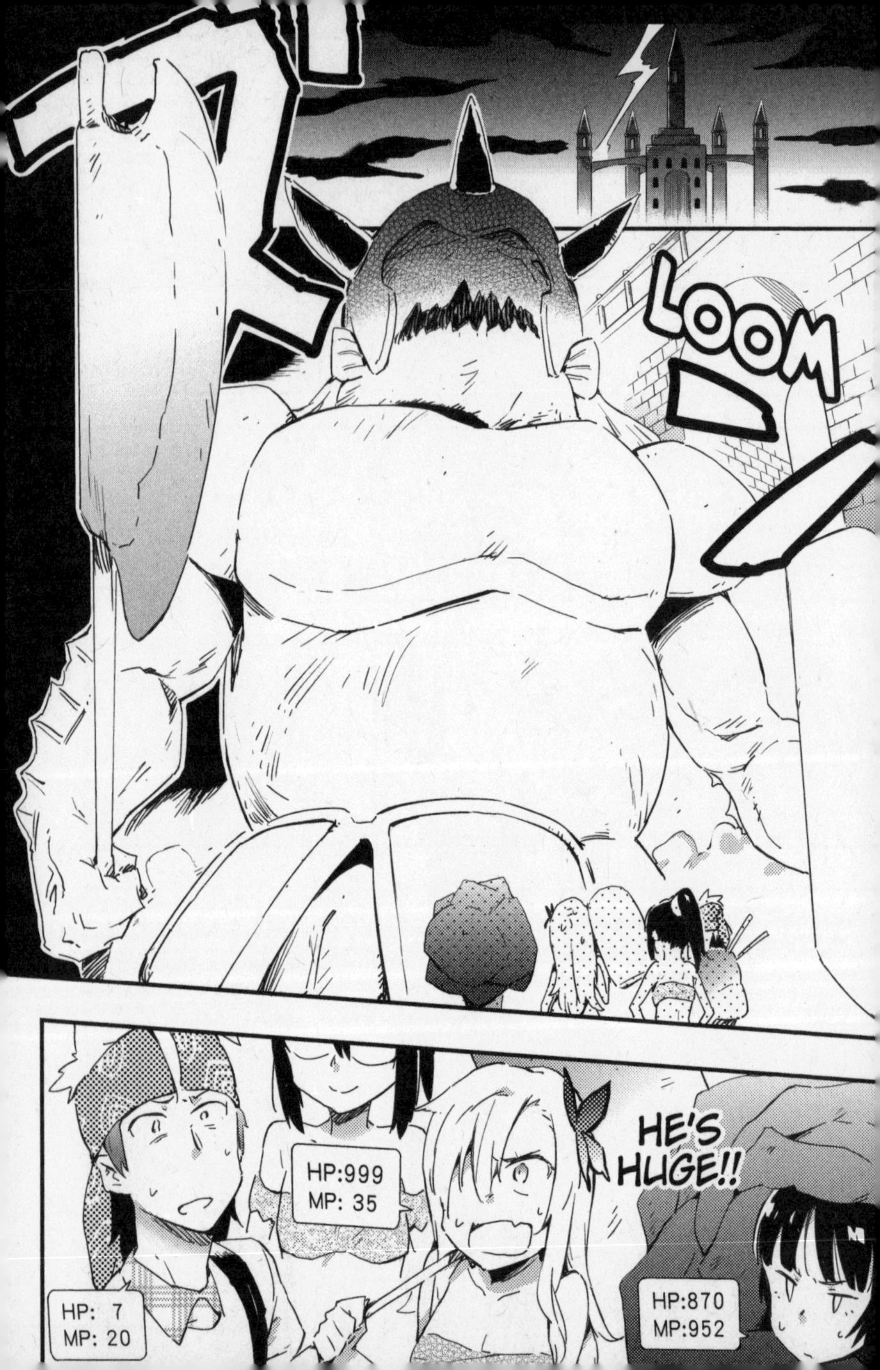
LOOM
HE'S HUGE!!
HP:870
MP:952
HP:999
MP: 35
HP: 7
MP: 20

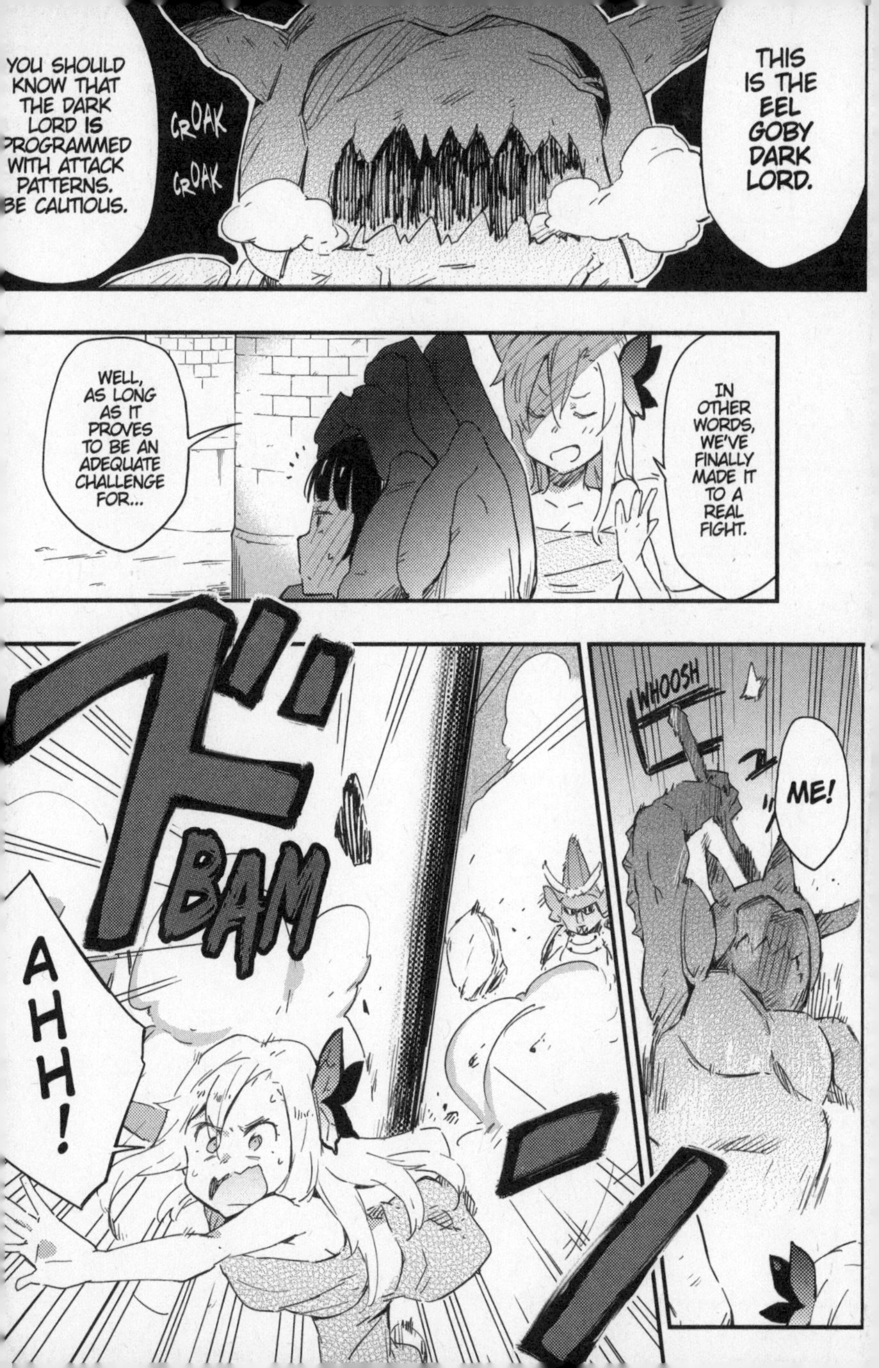
THIS IS THE EEL GOBY DARK LORD.
CROAK
CROAK
YOU SHOULD KNOW THAT THE DARK LORD IS PROGRAMMED WITH ATTACK PATTERNS. BE CAUTIOUS.
IN OTHER WORDS, WE'VE FINALLY MADE IT TO A REAL FIGHT.
WELL, AS LONG AS IT PROVES TO BE AN ADEQUATE CHALLENGE FOR...
WHOOSH
ME!
ド
BAM
AHH!

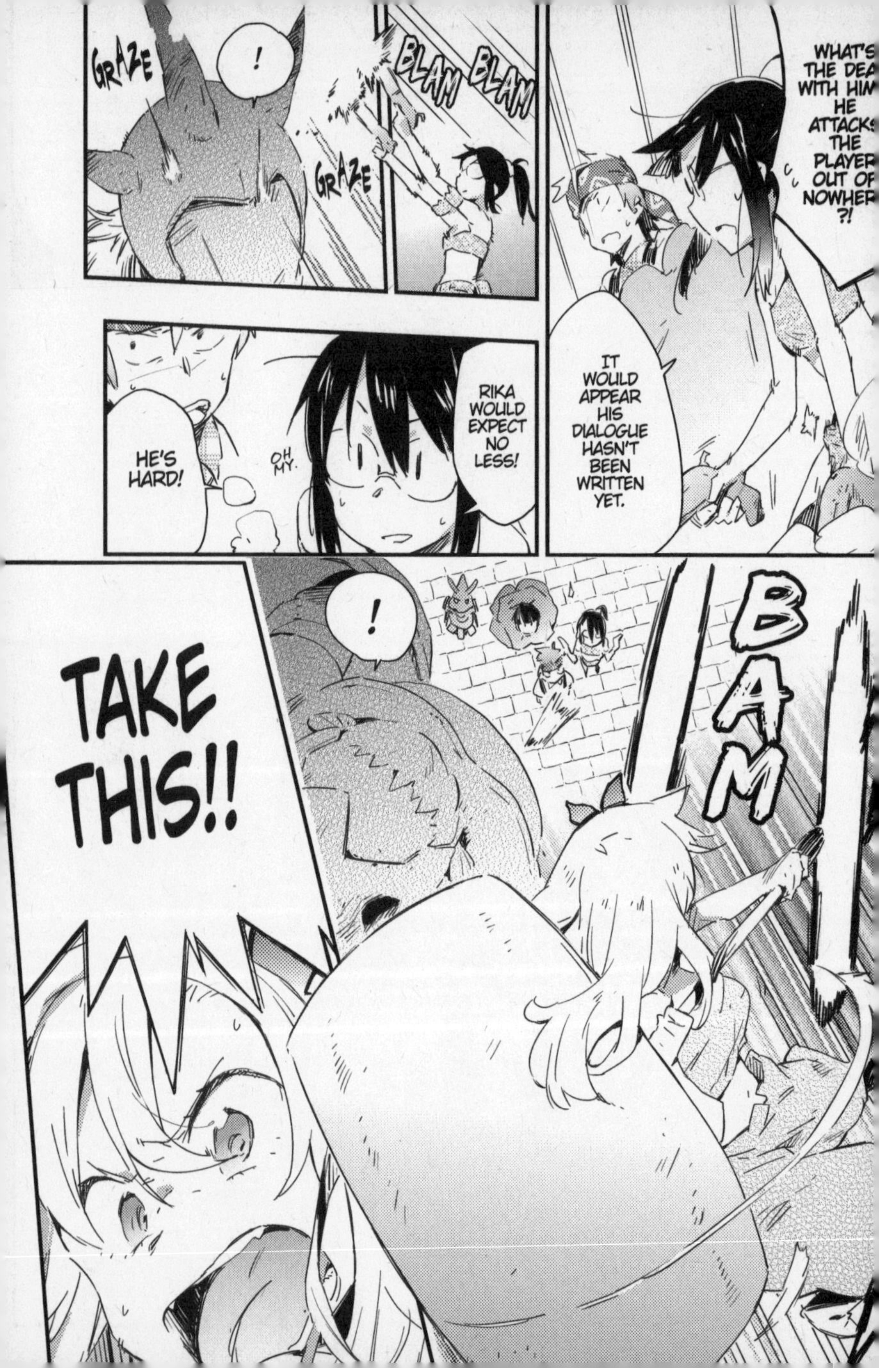
WHAT'S THE DEA WITH HIM HE ATTACKS THE PLAYER OUT OF NOWHER ?!
IT WOULD APPEAR HIS DIALOGUE HASN'T BEEN WRITTEN YET.
BLAM BLAM
GRAZE
GRAZE
!
RIKA WOULD EXPECT NO LESS!
OH MY.
HE'S HARD!
BAM
!
TAKE THIS!!

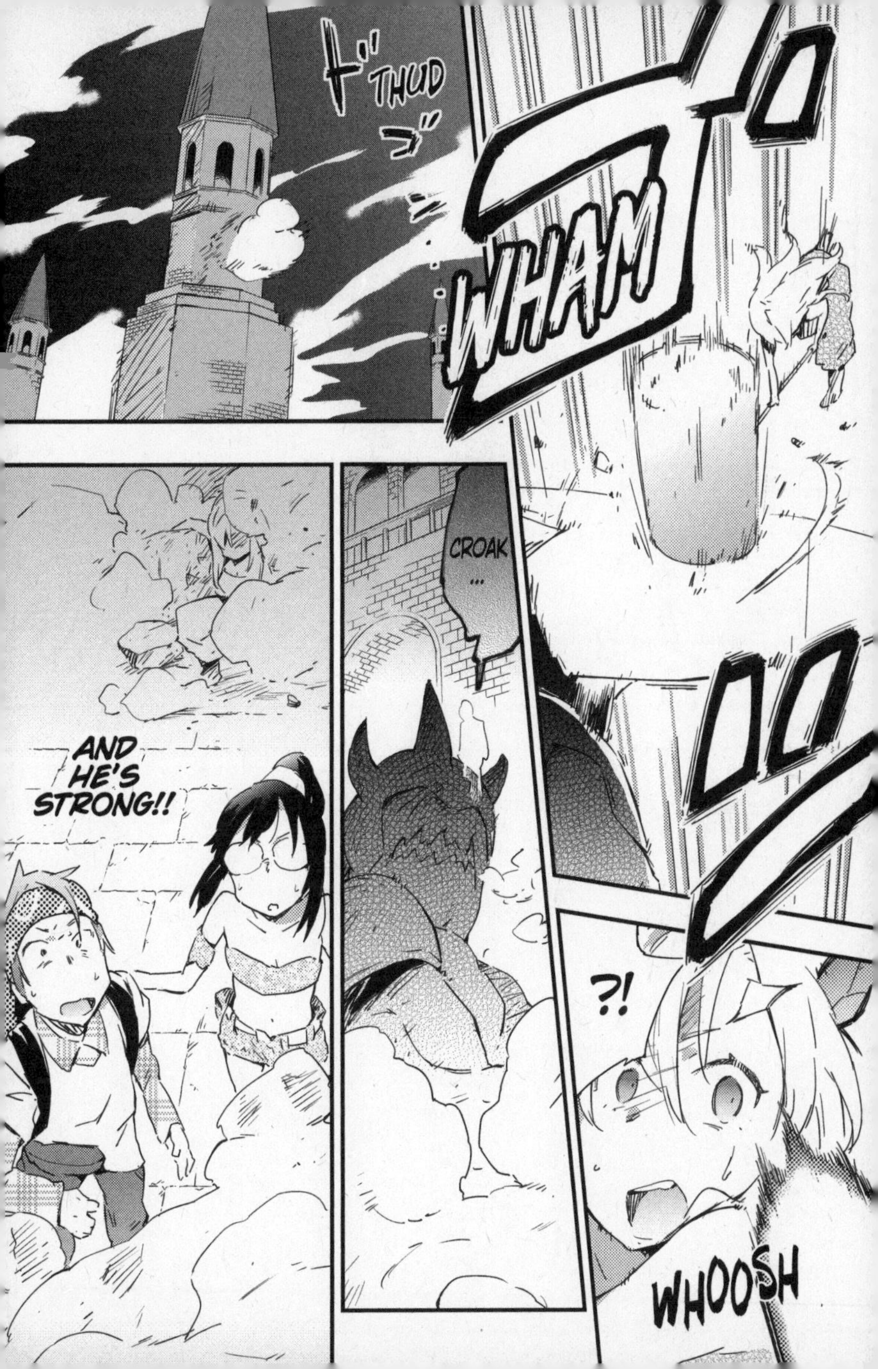
WHAM
THUD
?!
WHOOSH
CROAK
...
AND HE'S STRONG!!

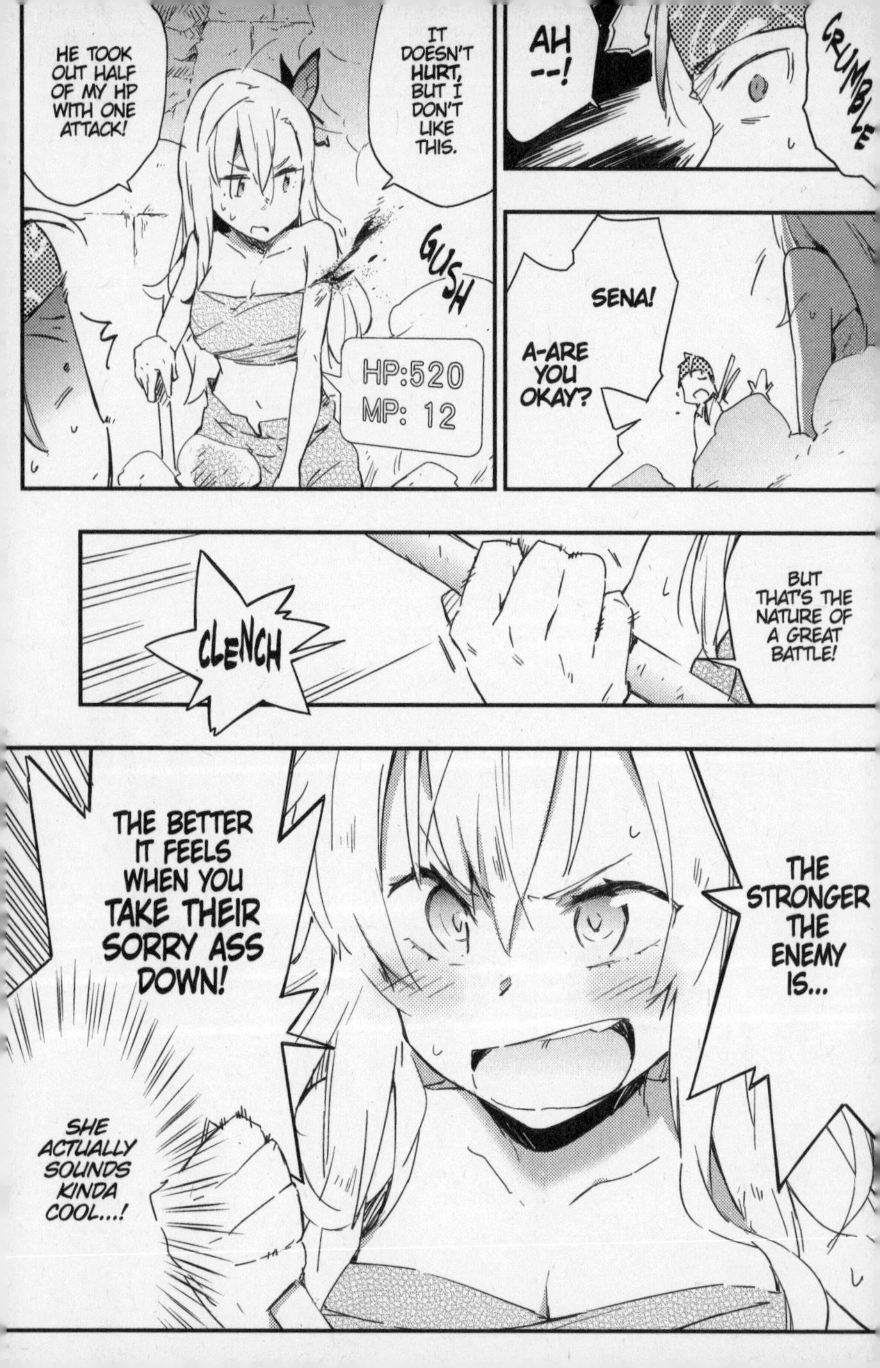
AH --!
CRUMBLE
SENA!
A-ARE YOU OKAY?
IT DOESN'T HURT, BUT I DON'T LIKE THIS.
HE TOOK OUT HALF OF MY HP WITH ONE ATTACK!
GUSH
HP:520
MP: 12
BUT THAT'S THE NATURE OF A GREAT BATTLE!
CLENCH
THE STRONGER THE ENEMY IS...
THE BETTER IT FEELS WHEN YOU TAKE THEIR SORRY ASS DOWN!
SHE ACTUALLY SOUNDS KINDA COOL...!

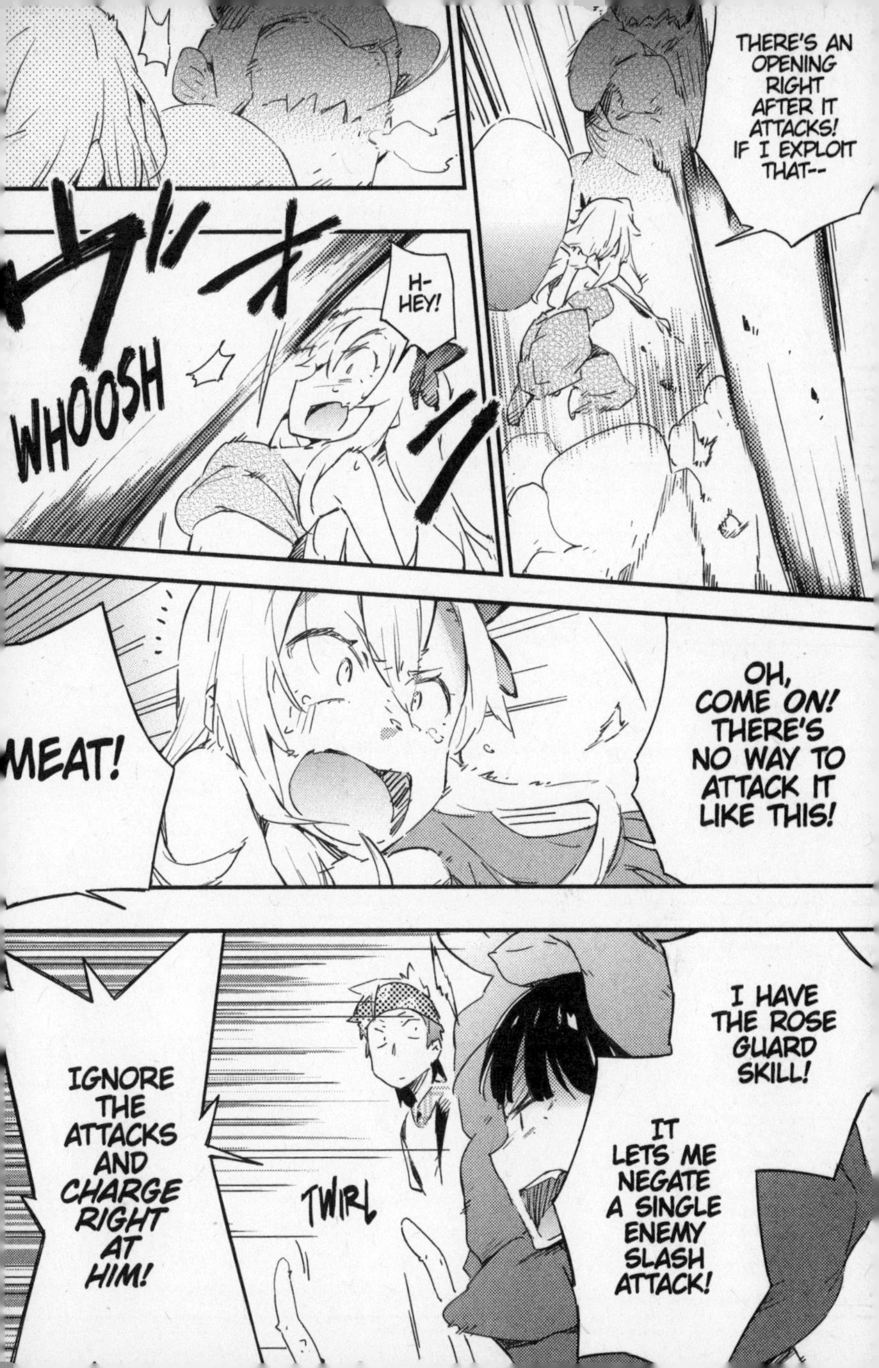
THERE'S AN OPENING RIGHT AFTER IT ATTACKS! IF I EXPLOIT THAT--
H-HEY!
WHOOSH
OH, COME ON! THERE'S NO WAY TO ATTACK IT LIKE THIS!
MEAT!
I HAVE THE ROSE GUARD SKILL!
IT LETS ME NEGATE A SINGLE ENEMY SLASH ATTACK!
TWIRL
IGNORE THE ATTACKS AND CHARGE RIGHT AT HIM!

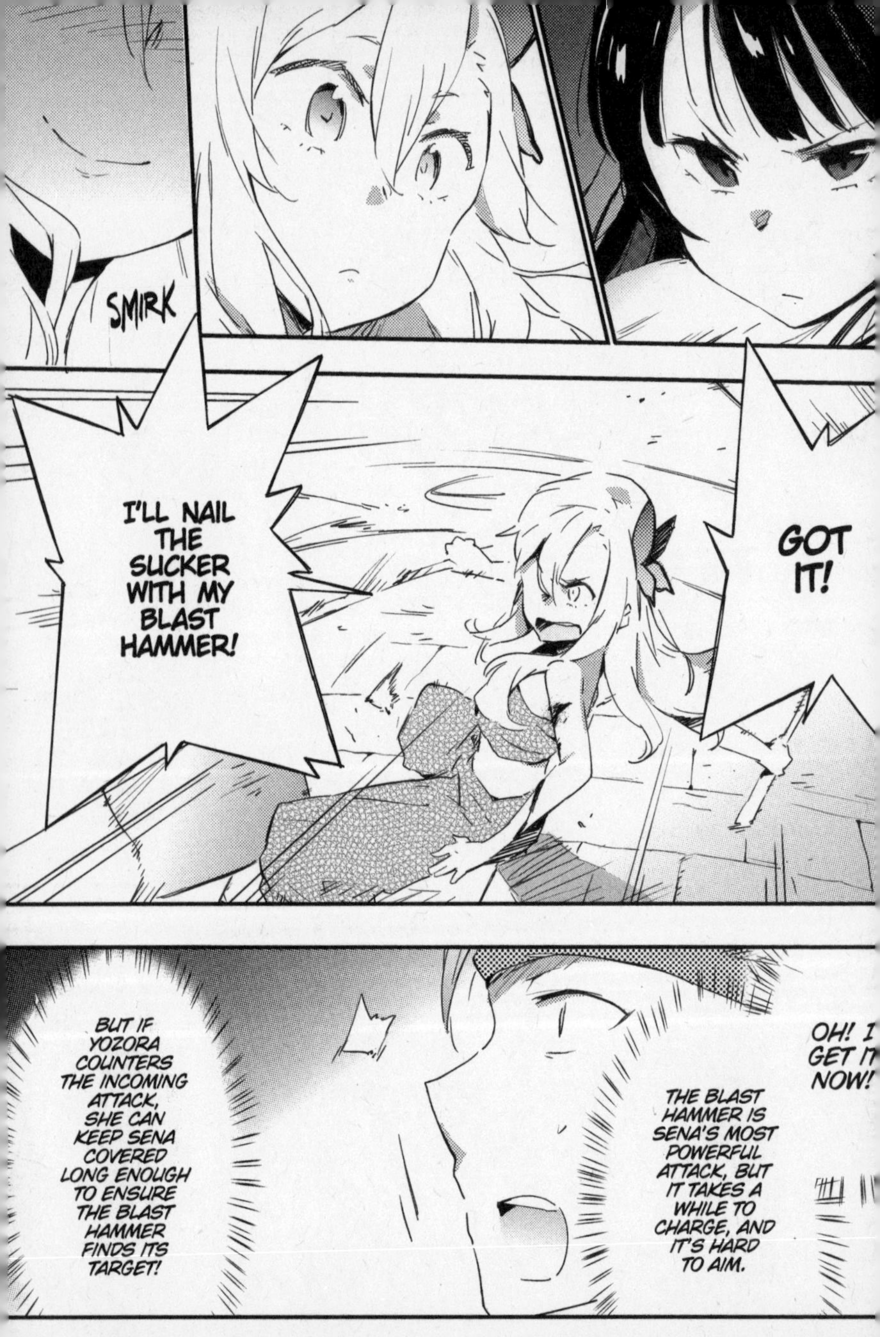
SMIRK
GOT IT!
I'LL NAIL THE SUCKER WITH MY BLAST HAMMER!
OH! I GET IT NOW!
THE BLAST HAMMER IS SENA'S MOST POWERFUL ATTACK, BUT IT TAKES A WHILE TO CHARGE, AND IT'S HARD TO AIM.
BUT IF YOZORA COUNTERS THE INCOMING ATTACK, SHE CAN KEEP SENA COVERED LONG ENOUGH TO ENSURE THE BLAST HAMMER FINDS ITS TARGET!

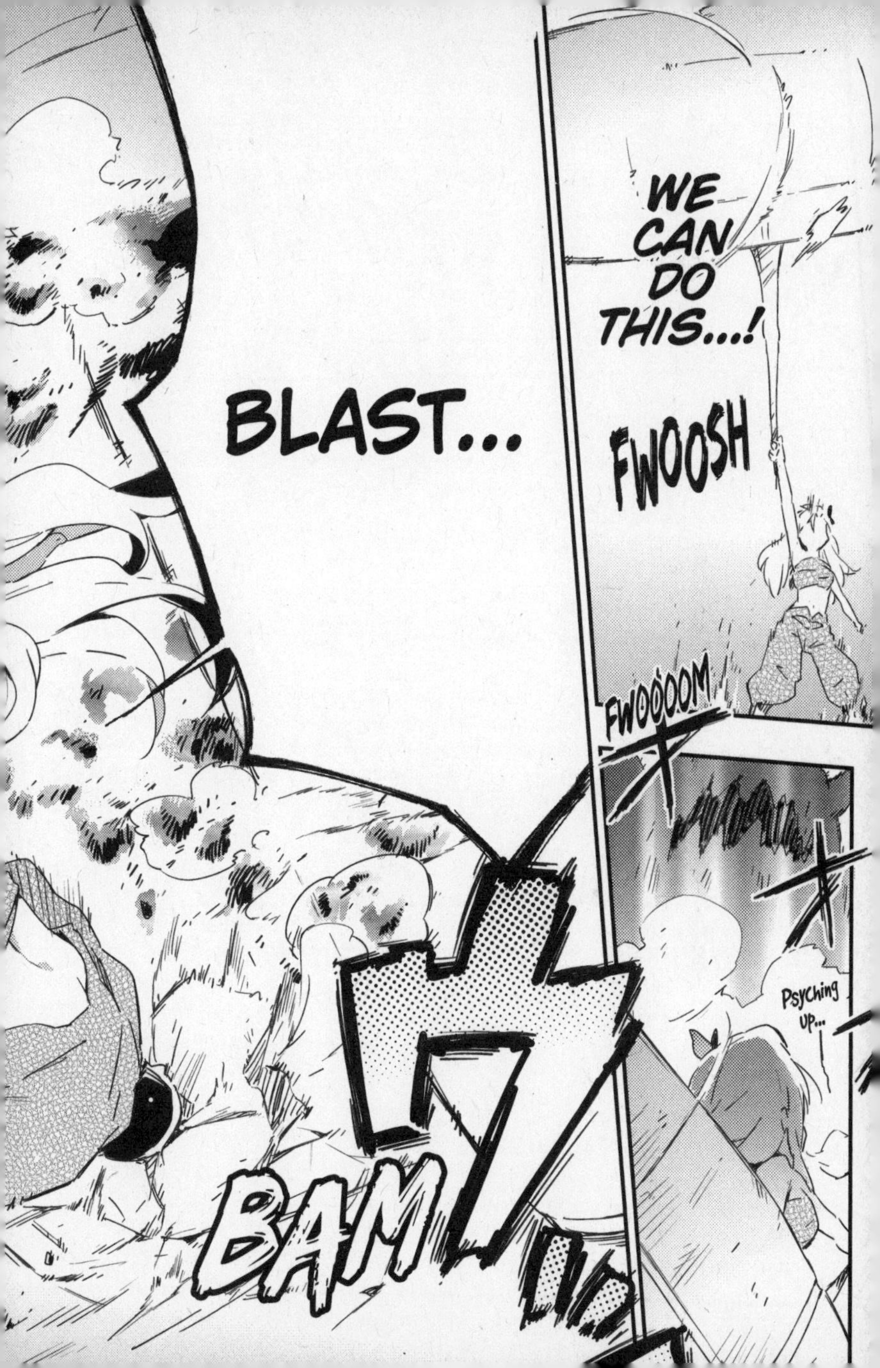
WE CAN DO THIS...!
FWOOSH
FWOOOM
Psyching up...
BLAST...
BAM

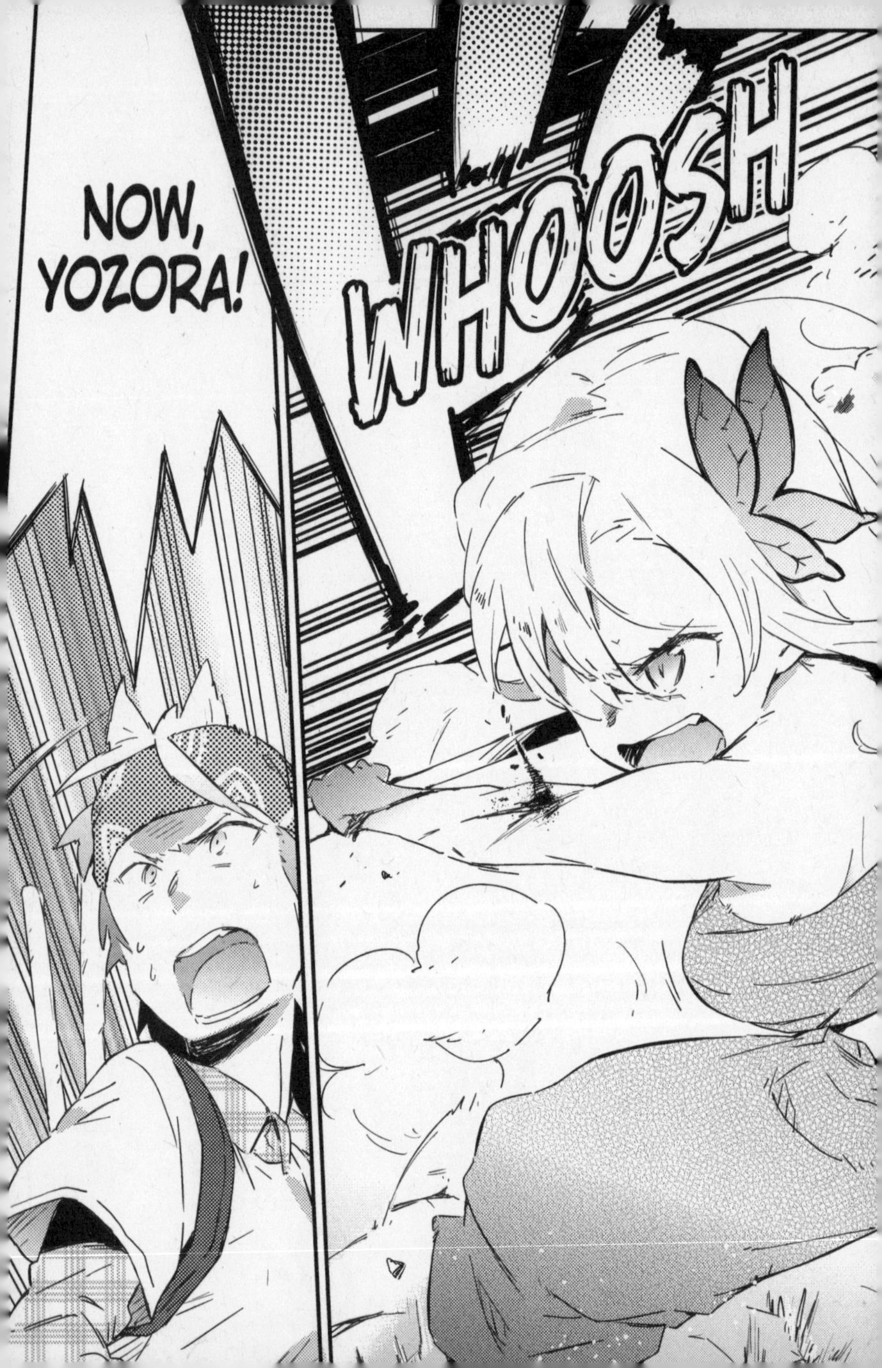
WHOOSH
NOW, YOZORA!

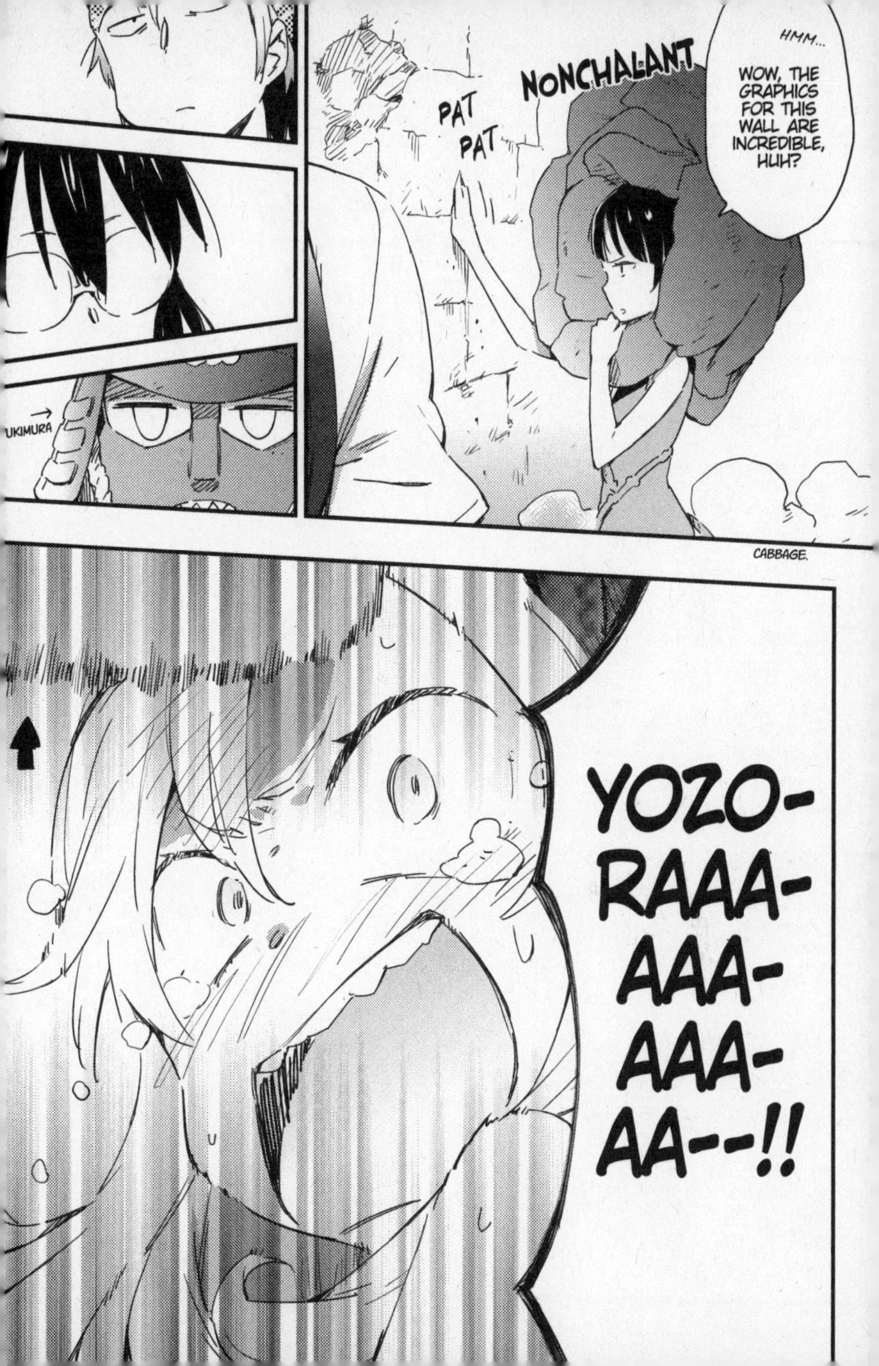
HMM...
WOW, THE GRAPHICS FOR THIS WALL ARE INCREDIBLE, HUH?
NONCHALANT
PAT PAT
CABBAGE.
UKIMURA
YOZO-RAAA-AAA-AAA-AA--!!

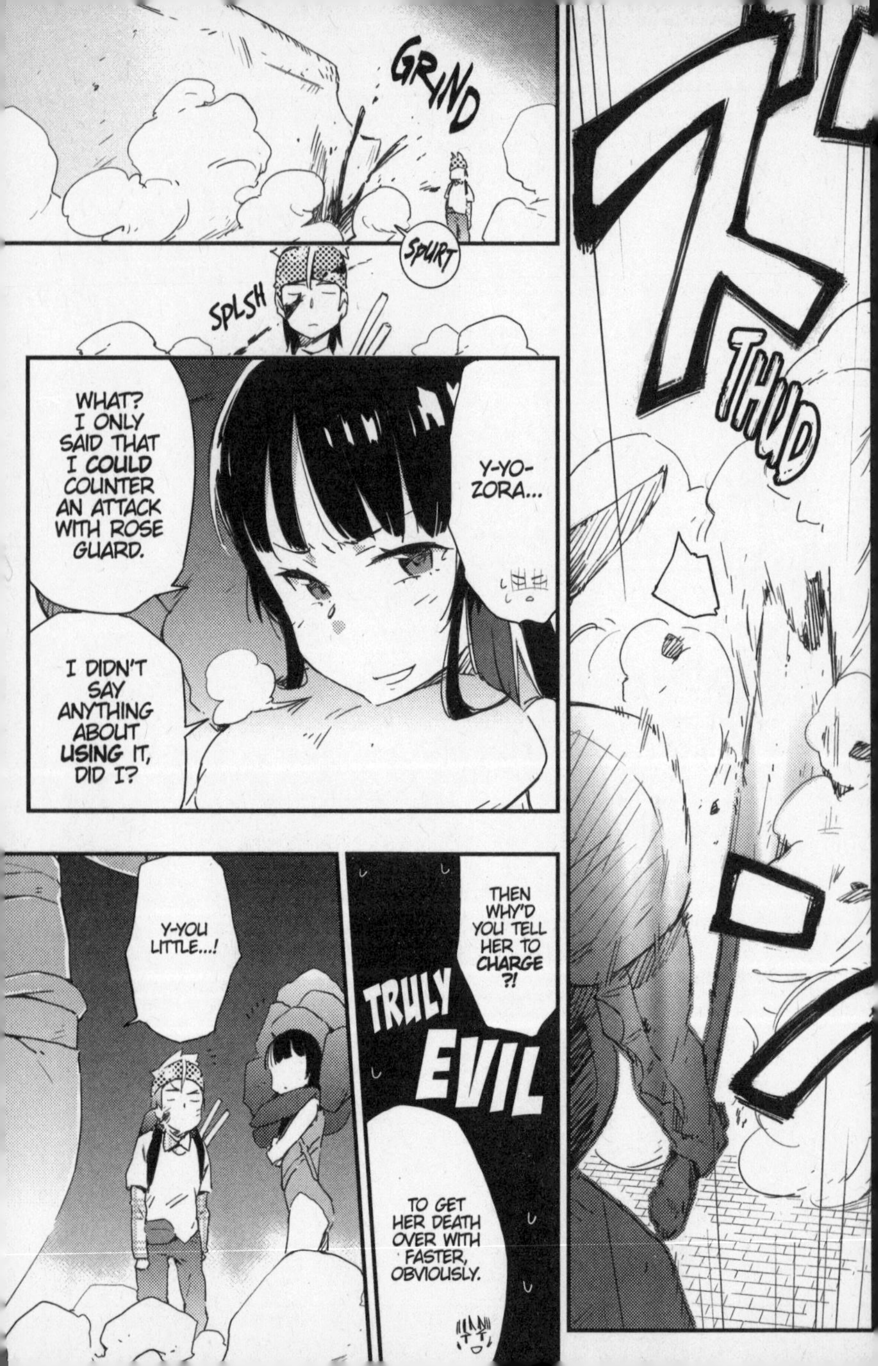
THUD
GRIND
SPURT
SPLSH
Y-YO-
ZORA...
WHAT? I ONLY SAID THAT I COULD COUNTER AN ATTACK WITH ROSE GUARD.
I DIDN'T SAY ANYTHING ABOUT USING IT, DID I?
THEN WHY'D YOU TELL HER TO CHARGE ?!
TRULY EVIL
TO GET HER DEATH OVER WITH FASTER, OBVIOUSLY.
Y-YOU LITTLE...!

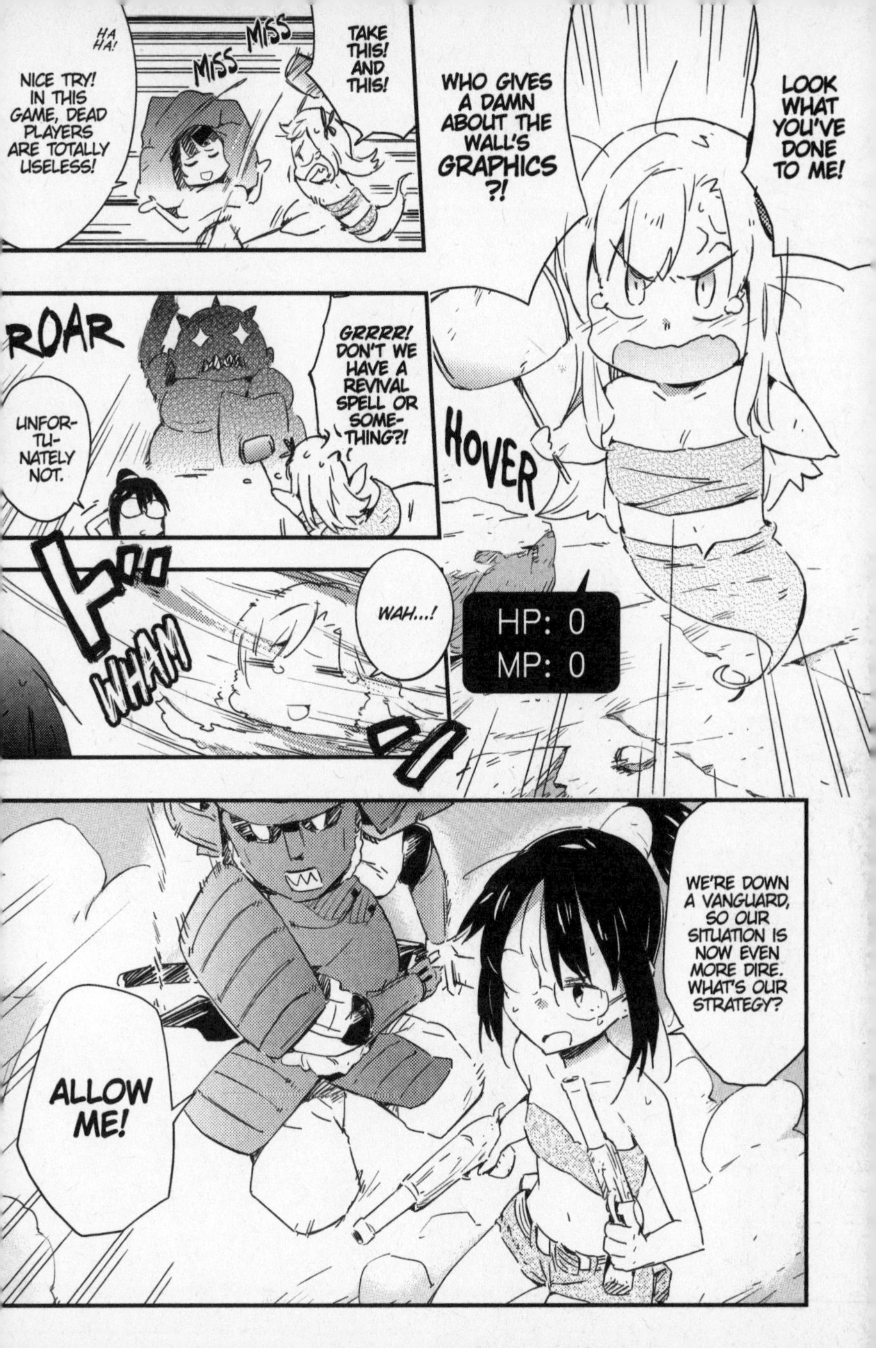
LOOK WHAT YOU'VE DONE TO ME!
WHO GIVES A DAMN ABOUT THE WALL'S GRAPHICS ?!
HOVER
TAKE THIS! AND THIS!
MISS
MISS
HA HA!
NICE TRY! IN THIS GAME, DEAD PLAYERS ARE TOTALLY USELESS!
GRRRR! DON'T WE HAVE A REVIVAL SPELL OR SOME-THING?!
ROAR
UNFOR-TU-NATELY NOT.
HP: 0
MP: 0
WAH...!
WHAM
WE'RE DOWN A VANGUARD, SO OUR SITUATION IS NOW EVEN MORE DIRE. WHAT'S OUR STRATEGY?
ALLOW ME!

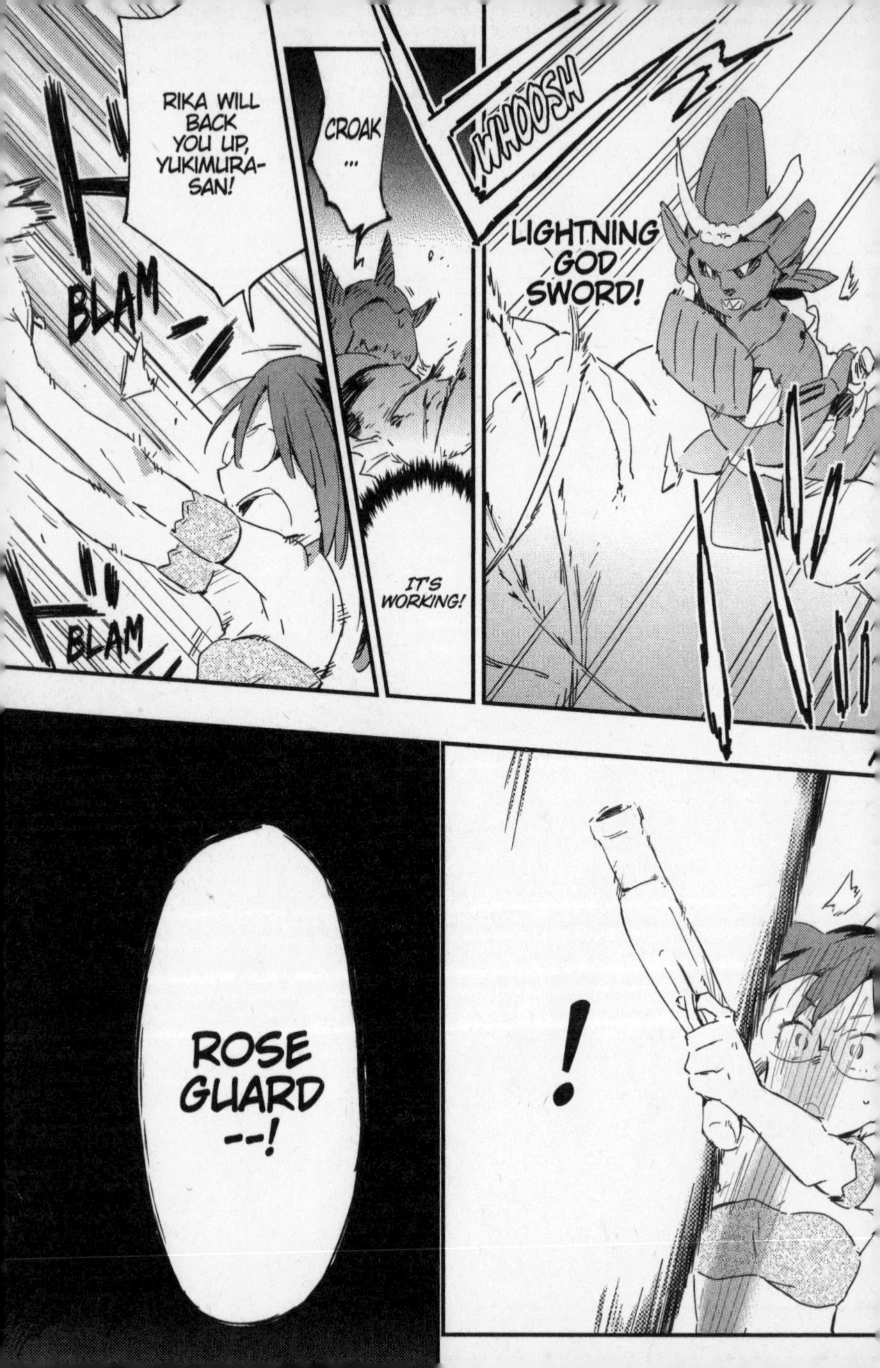
WHOOSH
LIGHTNING GOD SWORD!
CROAK ...
IT'S WORKING!
RIKA WILL BACK YOU UP, YUKIMURA-SAN!
BLAM
BLAM
!
ROSE GUARD --!

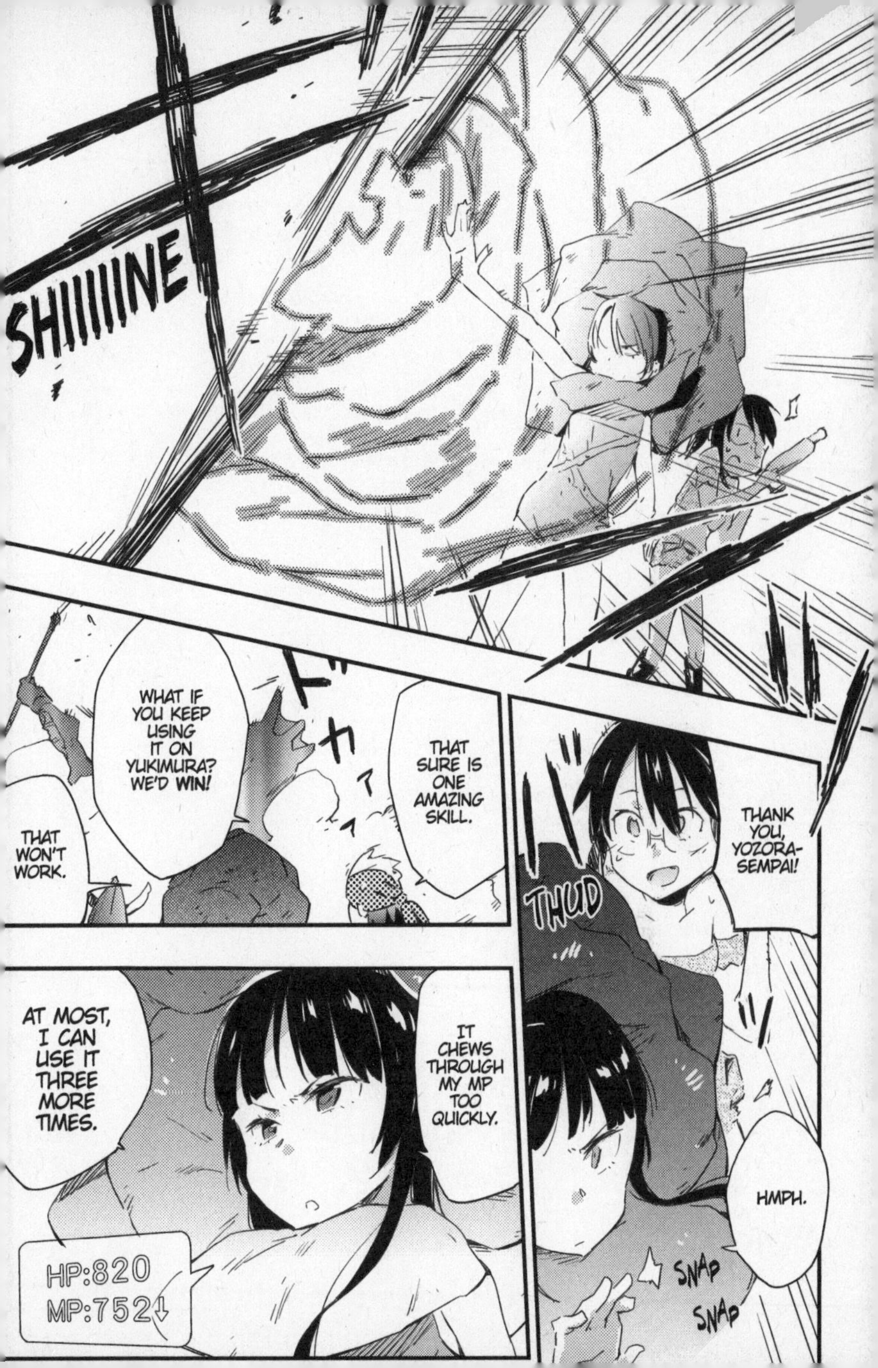
SHIIIINE
THUD
THANK YOU, YOZORA-SEMPAI!
HMPH.
SNAP
SNAP
THAT SURE IS ONE AMAZING SKILL.
WHAT IF YOU KEEP USING IT ON YUKIMURA? WE'D WIN!
THAT WON'T WORK.
IT CHEWS THROUGH MY MP TOO QUICKLY.
AT MOST, I CAN USE IT THREE MORE TIMES.
HP:820
MP:752↓

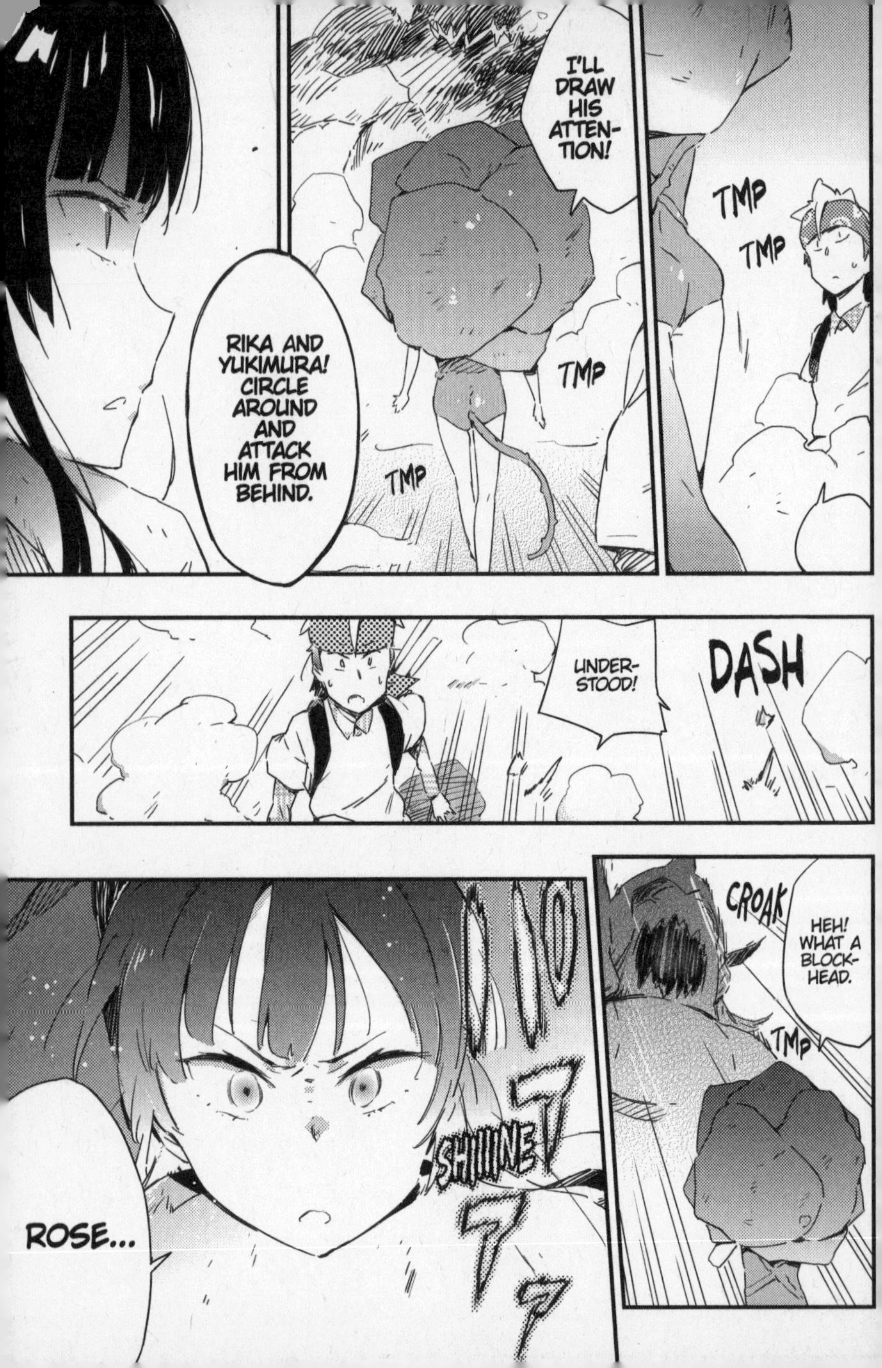
TMP
TMP
I'LL DRAW HIS ATTEN-TION!
TMP
TMP
RIKA AND YUKIMURA! CIRCLE AROUND AND ATTACK HIM FROM BEHIND.
DASH
UNDER-STOOD!
CROAK
HEH! WHAT A BLOCK-HEAD.
TMP
SHIIINE
ROSE...

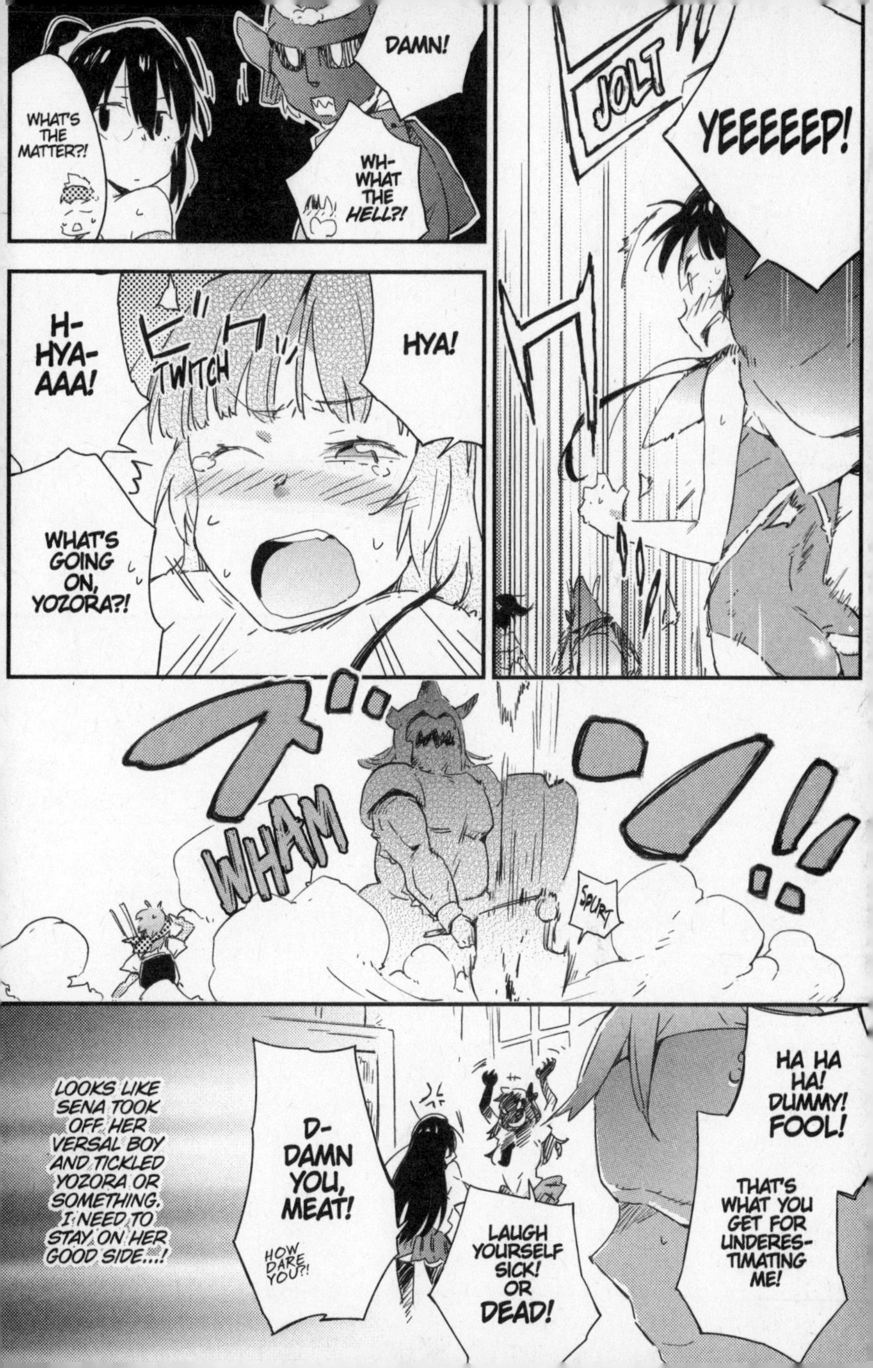
JOLT
YEEEEEP!
DAMN!
WH-WHAT THE HELL?!
WHAT'S THE MATTER?!
HYA!
TWITCH
H-HYA-AAA!
WHAT'S GOING ON, YOZORA?!
WHAM
SPURT
HA HA HA! DUMMY! FOOL!
THAT'S WHAT YOU GET FOR UNDERES-TIMATING ME!
D-DAMN YOU, MEAT!
LAUGH YOURSELF SICK! OR DEAD!
HOW DARE YOU?!
LOOKS LIKE SENA TOOK OFF HER VERSAL BOY AND TICKLED YOZORA OR SOMETHING. I NEED TO STAY ON HER GOOD SIDE...!

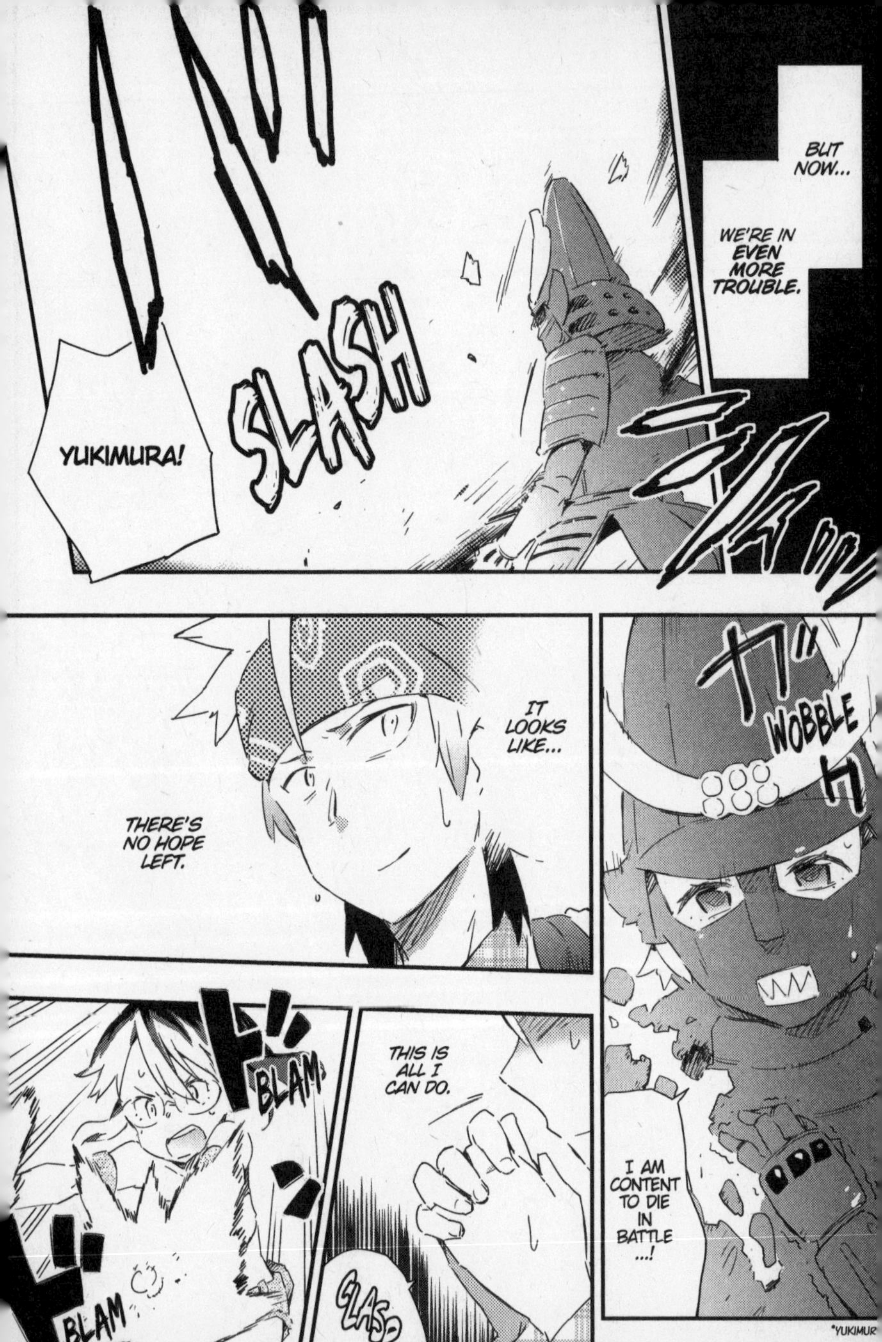
BUT NOW...
WE'RE IN EVEN MORE TROUBLE.
SLASH
YUKIMURA!
WOBBLE
I AM CONTENT TO DIE IN BATTLE ...!
IT LOOKS LIKE...
THERE'S NO HOPE LEFT.
THIS IS ALL I CAN DO.
CLASP
BLAM
BLAM

*YUKIMUR

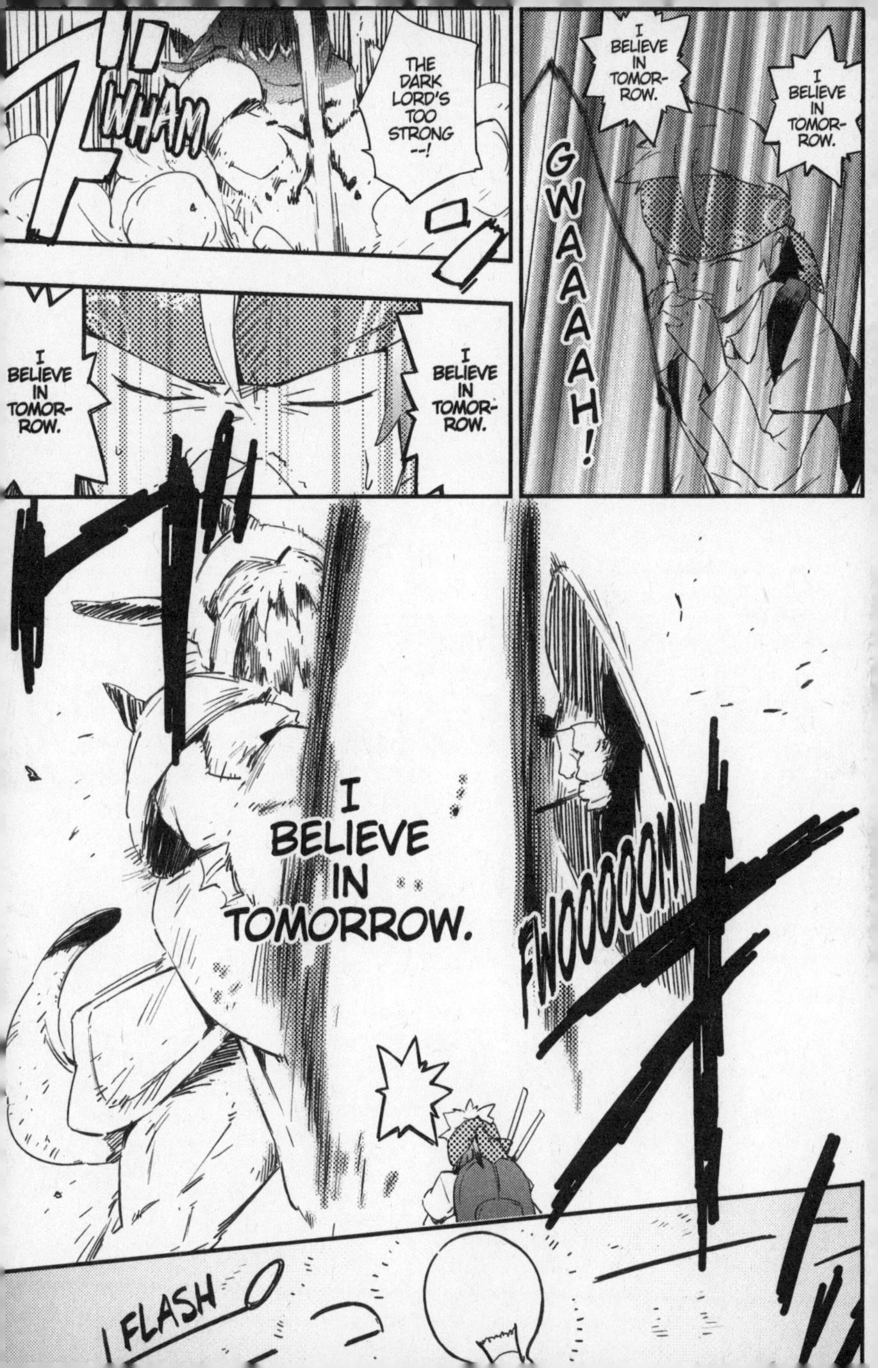
I BELIEVE IN TOMORROW.
I BELIEVE IN TOMORROW.
GWAAAAAH!
WHAM
THE DARK LORD'S TOO STRONG--!
I BELIEVE IN TOMORROW.
I BELIEVE IN TOMORROW.
FWOOOOOM
I BELIEVE IN TOMORROW.
FLASH

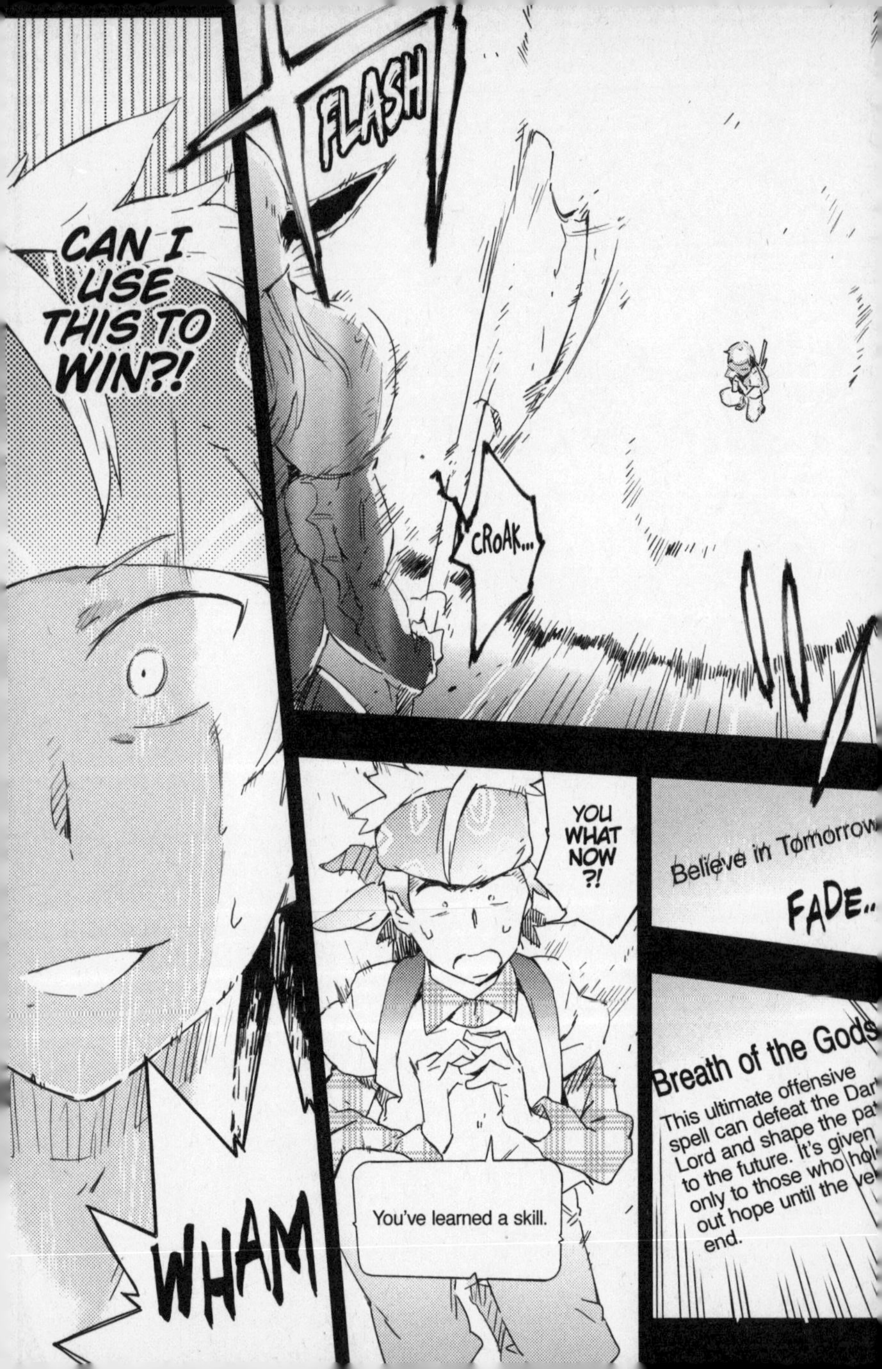
FLASH
CROAK...
Believe in Tomorrow
FADE..
Breath of the Gods
This ultimate offensive spell can defeat the Dar Lord and shape the pat to the future. It's given only to those who hol out hope until the ve end.
YOU WHAT NOW?!
You've learned a skill.
CAN I USE THIS TO WIN?!
WHAM

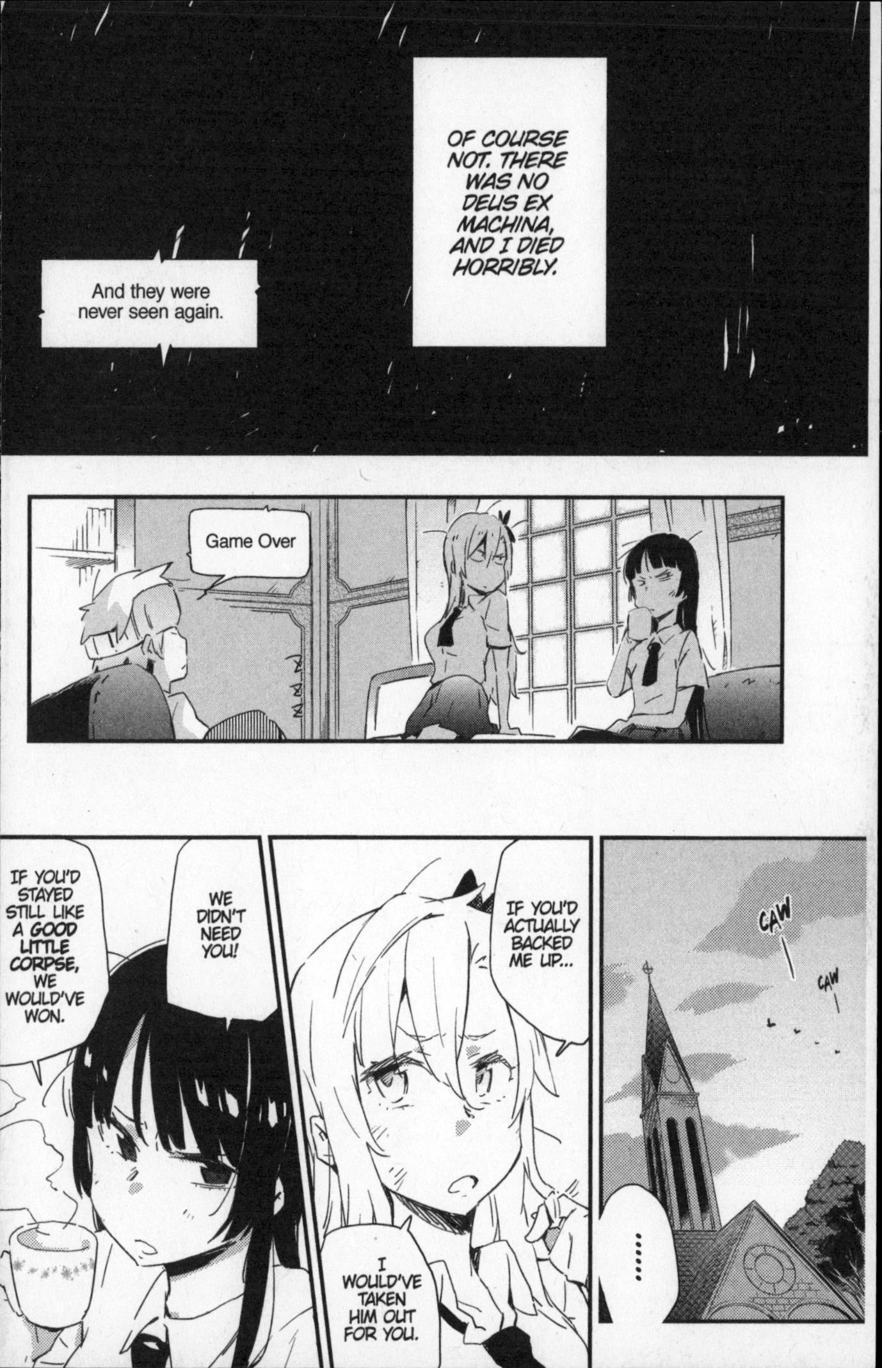
OF COURSE NOT. THERE WAS NO DEUS EX MACHINA, AND I DIED HORRIBLY.
And they were never seen again.
Game Over
CAW
CAW
......
IF YOU'D ACTUALLY BACKED ME UP...
I WOULD'VE TAKEN HIM OUT FOR YOU.
WE DIDN'T NEED YOU!
IF YOU'D STAYED STILL LIKE A GOOD LITTLE CORPSE, WE WOULD'VE WON.

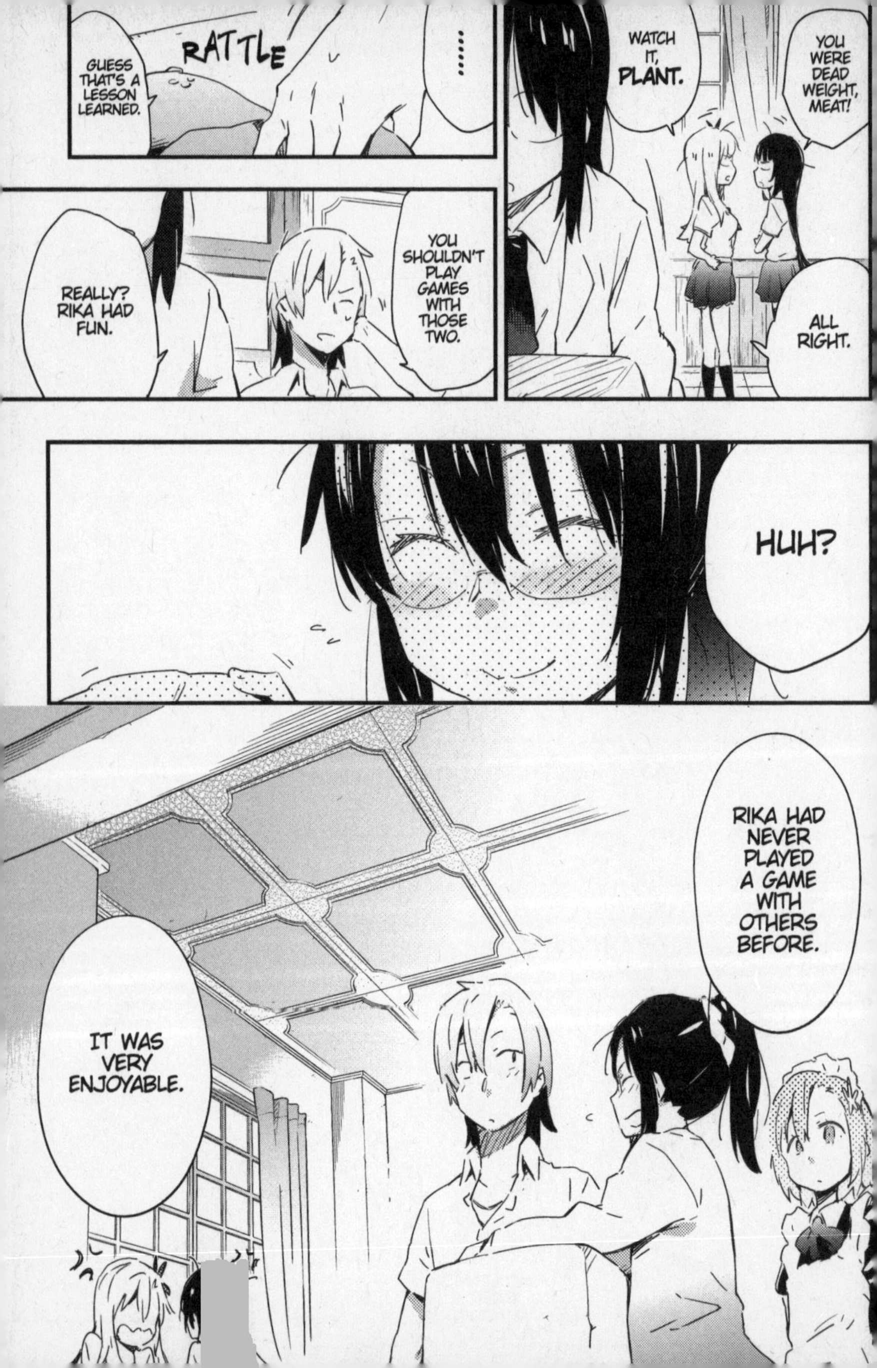
YOU WERE DEAD WEIGHT, MEAT!
WATCH IT, PLANT.
ALL RIGHT.
......
RATTLE
GUESS THAT'S A LESSON LEARNED.
YOU SHOULDN'T PLAY GAMES WITH THOSE TWO.
REALLY? RIKA HAD FUN.
HUH?
RIKA HAD NEVER PLAYED A GAME WITH OTHERS BEFORE.
IT WAS VERY ENJOYABLE.

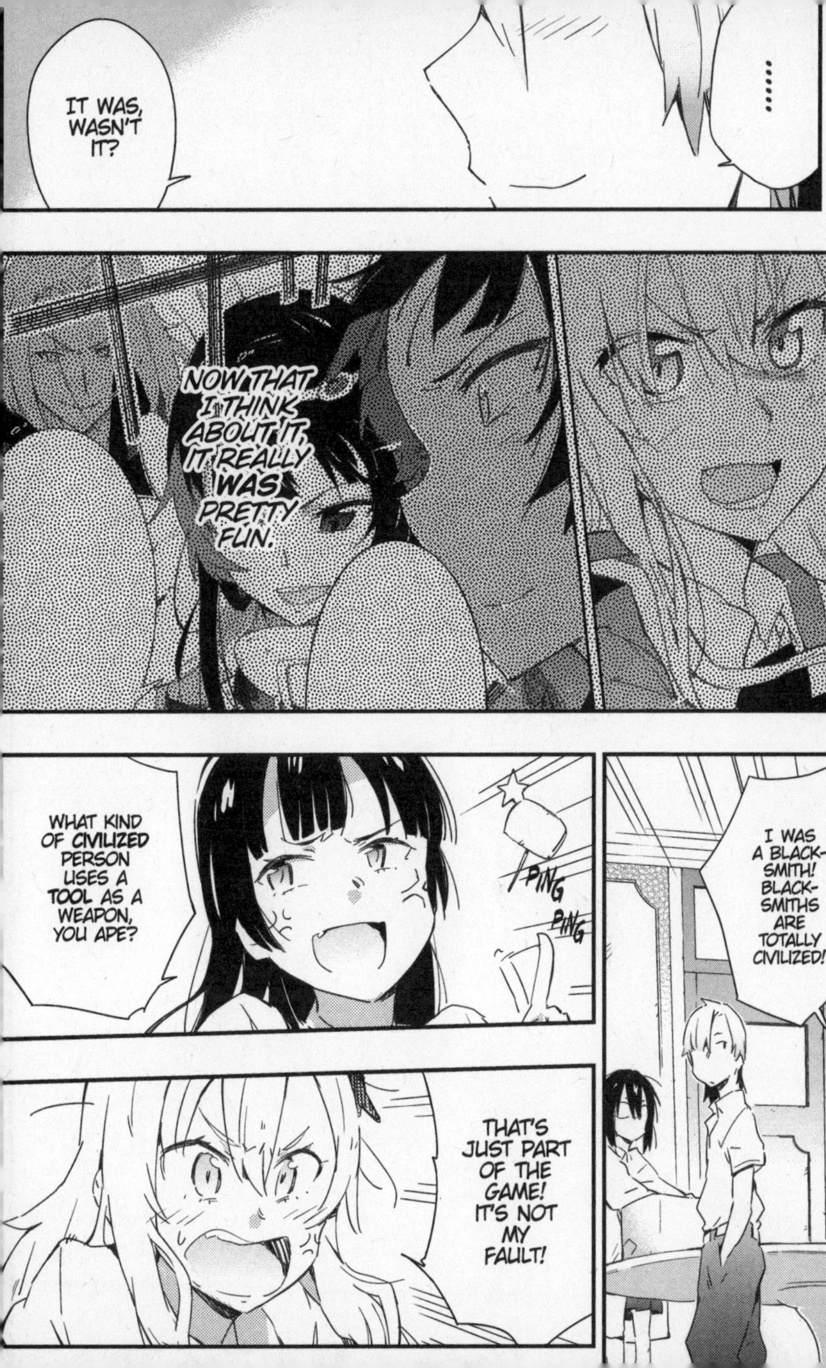
......
IT WAS, WASN'T IT?
NOW THAT I THINK ABOUT IT, IT REALLY WAS PRETTY FUN.
I WAS A BLACKSMITH! BLACKSMITHS ARE TOTALLY CIVILIZED!
PING
PING
WHAT KIND OF CIVILIZED PERSON USES A TOOL AS A WEAPON, YOU APE?
THAT'S JUST PART OF THE GAME! IT'S NOT MY FAULT!

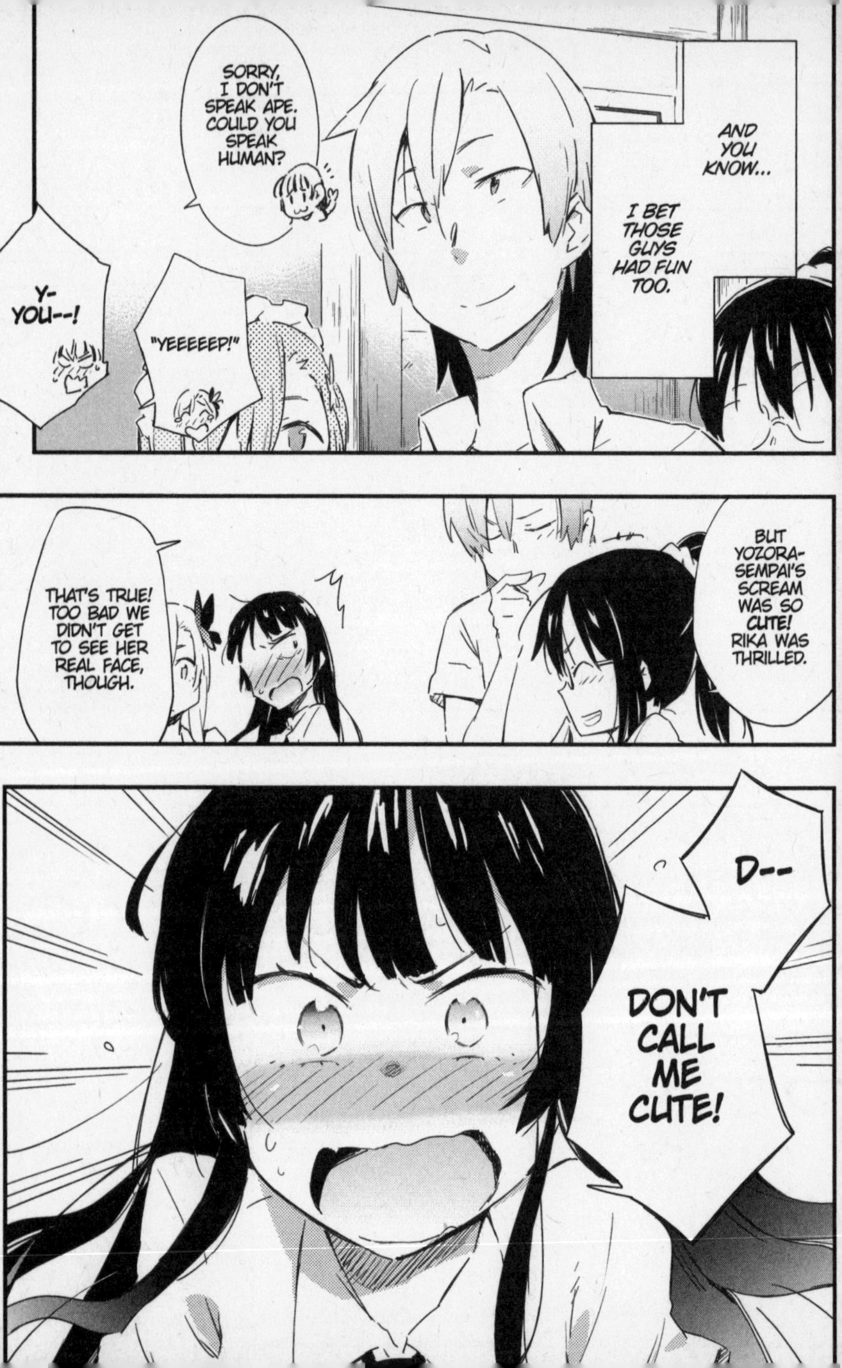
AND YOU KNOW...
I BET THOSE GUYS HAD FUN TOO.
SORRY, I DON'T SPEAK APE. COULD YOU SPEAK HUMAN?
"YEEEEEP!"
Y-YOU--!
BUT YOZORA-SEMPAI'S SCREAM WAS SO CUTE! RIKA WAS THRILLED.
THAT'S TRUE! TOO BAD WE DIDN'T GET TO SEE HER REAL FACE, THOUGH.
D--
DON'T CALL ME CUTE!

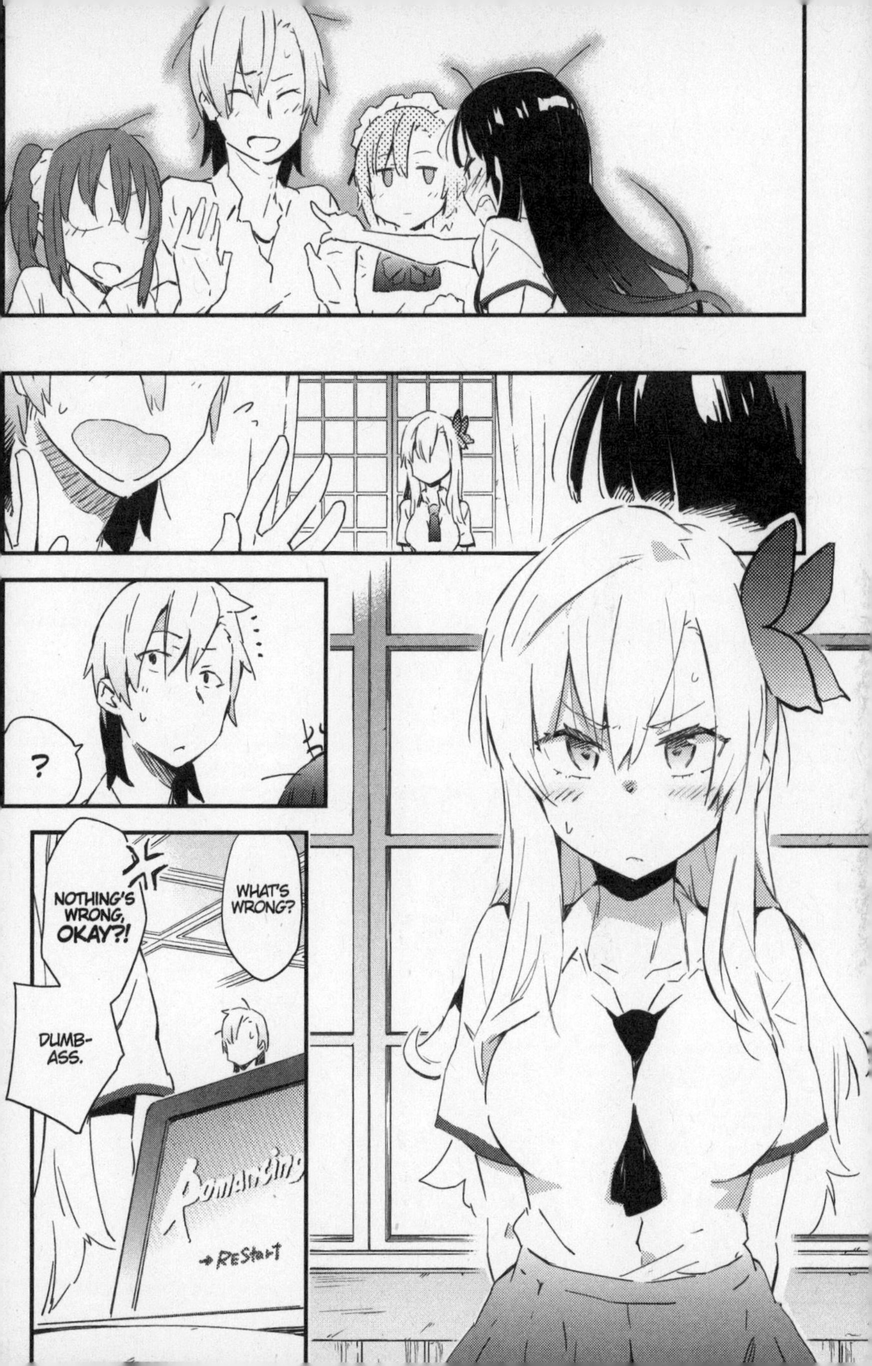
?
WHAT'S WRONG?
NOTHING'S WRONG, OKAY?!
DUMB-ASS.
Romancing
→ReStart

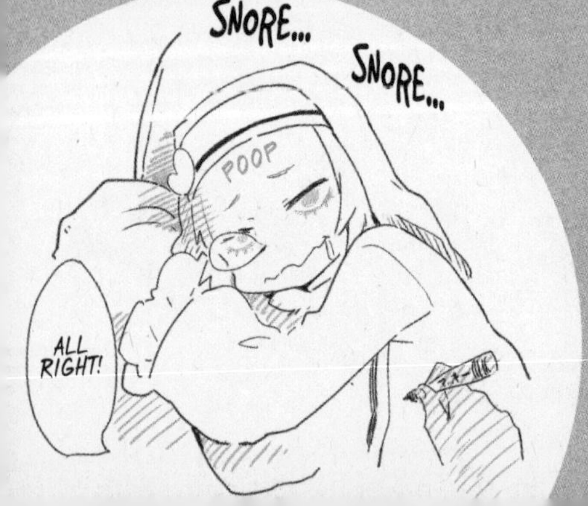
SNORE...
SNORE...
POOP
ALL RIGHT!

Haganai

I don't have many friends

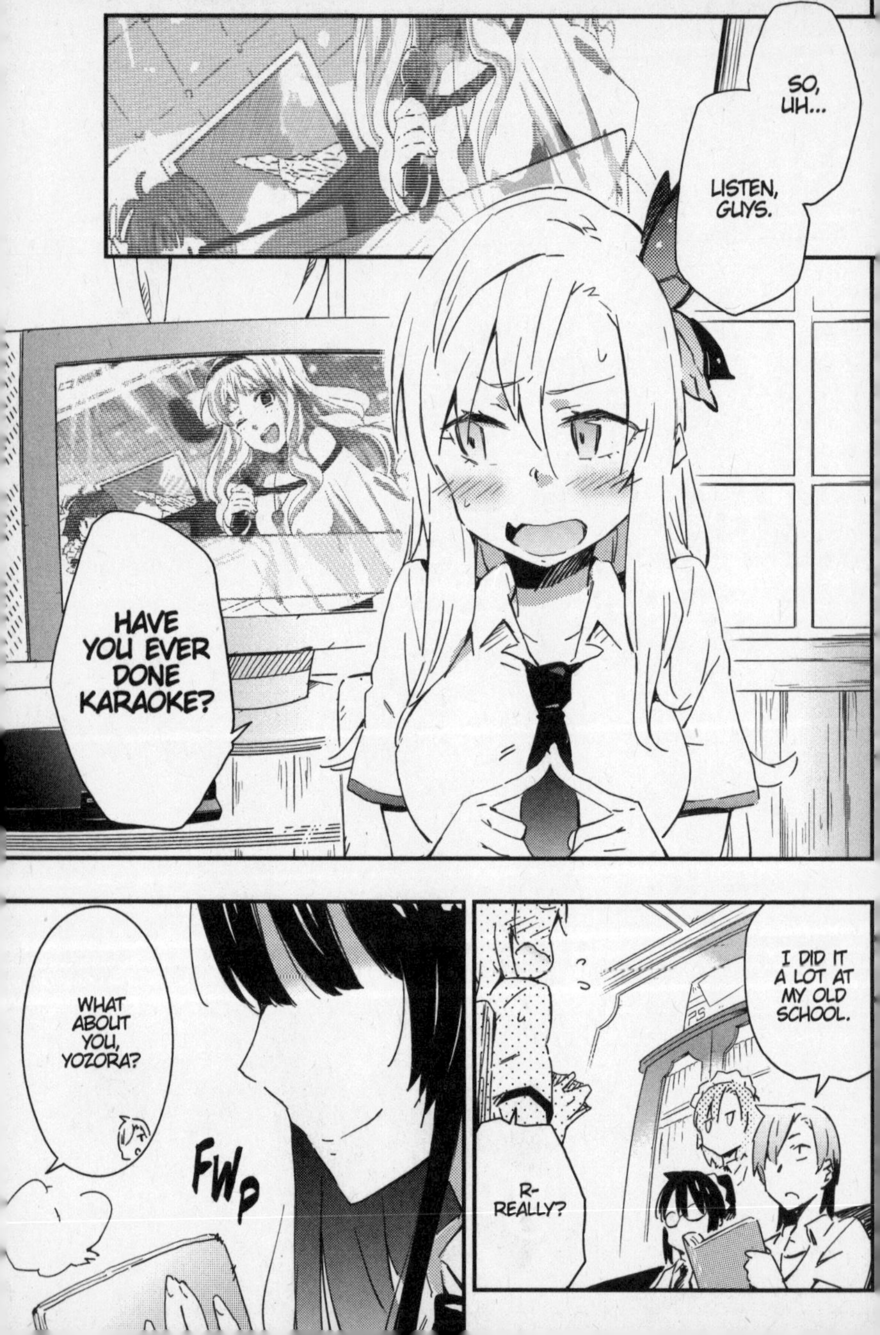
SO, UH...
LISTEN, GUYS.
HAVE YOU EVER DONE KARAOKE?
I DID IT A LOT AT MY OLD SCHOOL.
R-REALLY?
WHAT ABOUT YOU, YOZORA?
FWP

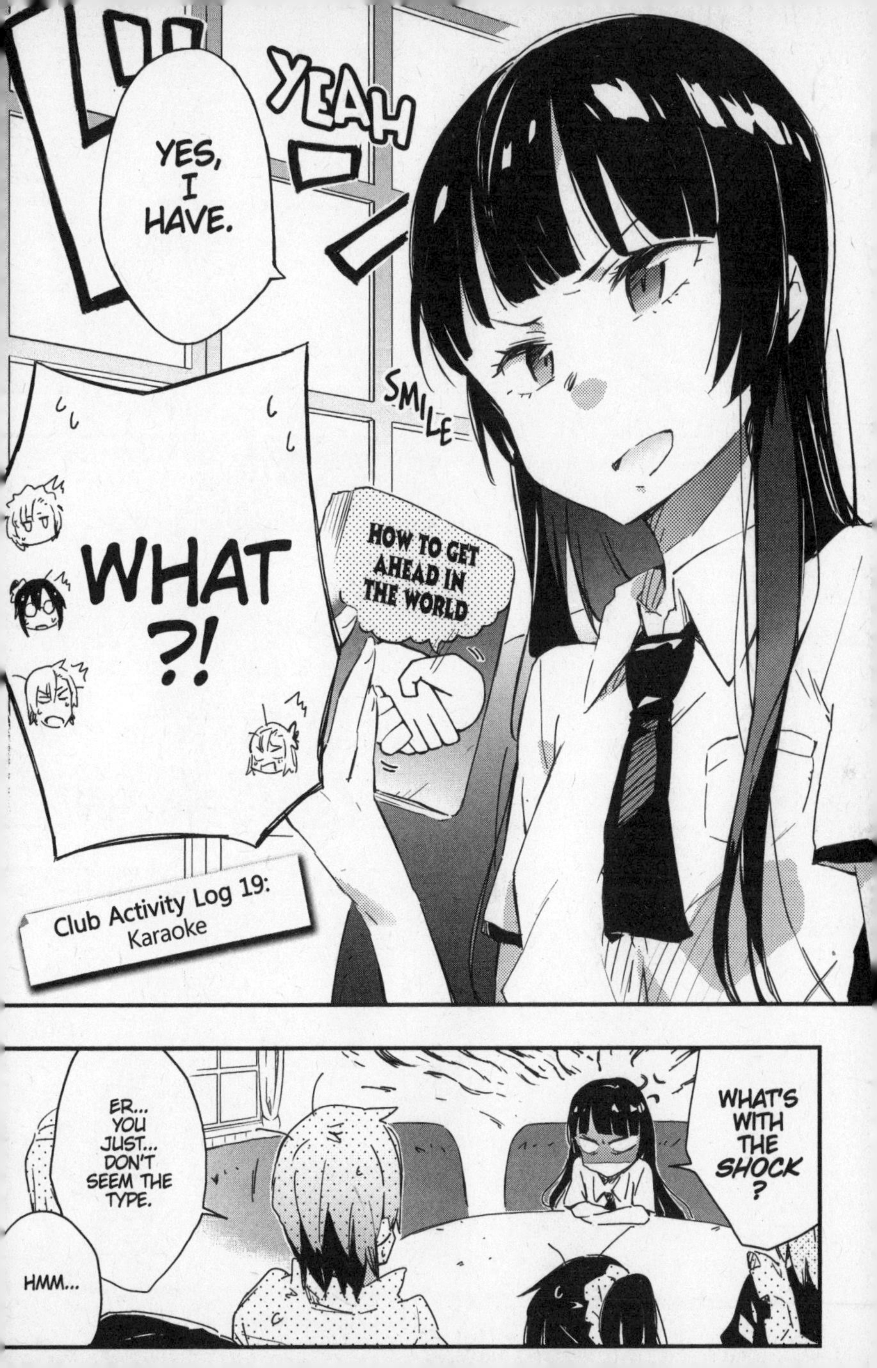
YEAH
YES, I HAVE.
SMILE
HOW TO GET AHEAD IN THE WORLD
WHAT?!
Club Activity Log 19:
Karaoke
WHAT'S WITH THE SHOCK?
ER... YOU JUST... DON'T SEEM THE TYPE.
HMM...

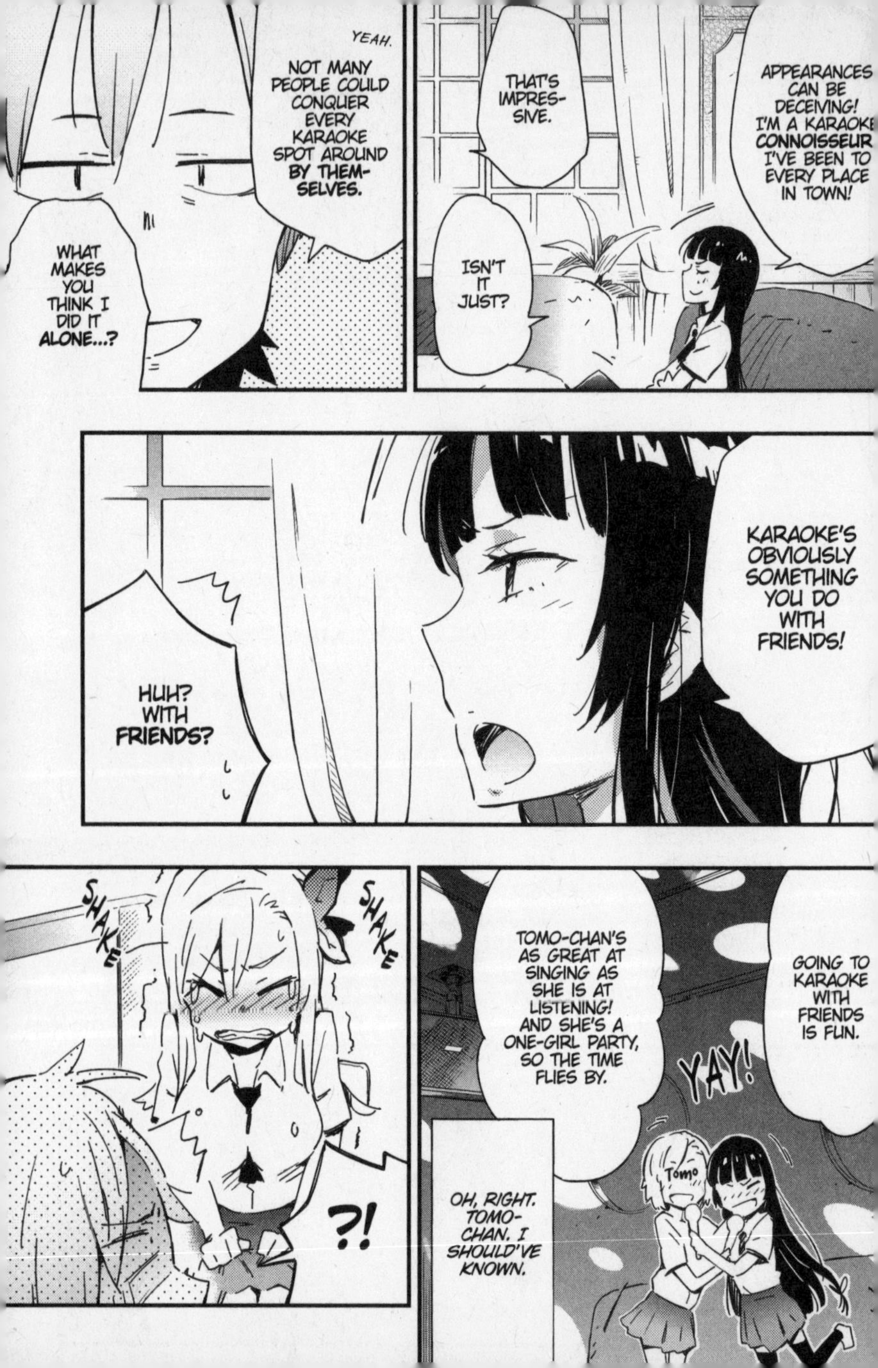
APPEARANCES CAN BE DECEIVING! I'M A KARAOKE CONNOISSEUR! I'VE BEEN TO EVERY PLACE IN TOWN!
THAT'S IMPRESSIVE.
ISN'T IT JUST?
YEAH.
NOT MANY PEOPLE COULD CONQUER EVERY KARAOKE SPOT AROUND BY THEMSELVES.
WHAT MAKES YOU THINK I DID IT ALONE...?
KARAOKE'S OBVIOUSLY SOMETHING YOU DO WITH FRIENDS!
HUH? WITH FRIENDS?
GOING TO KARAOKE WITH FRIENDS IS FUN.
TOMO-CHAN'S AS GREAT AT SINGING AS SHE IS AT LISTENING! AND SHE'S A ONE-GIRL PARTY, SO THE TIME FLIES BY.
YAY!
Tomo
OH, RIGHT. TOMO-CHAN. I SHOULD'VE KNOWN.
SHAKE
SHAKE
?!

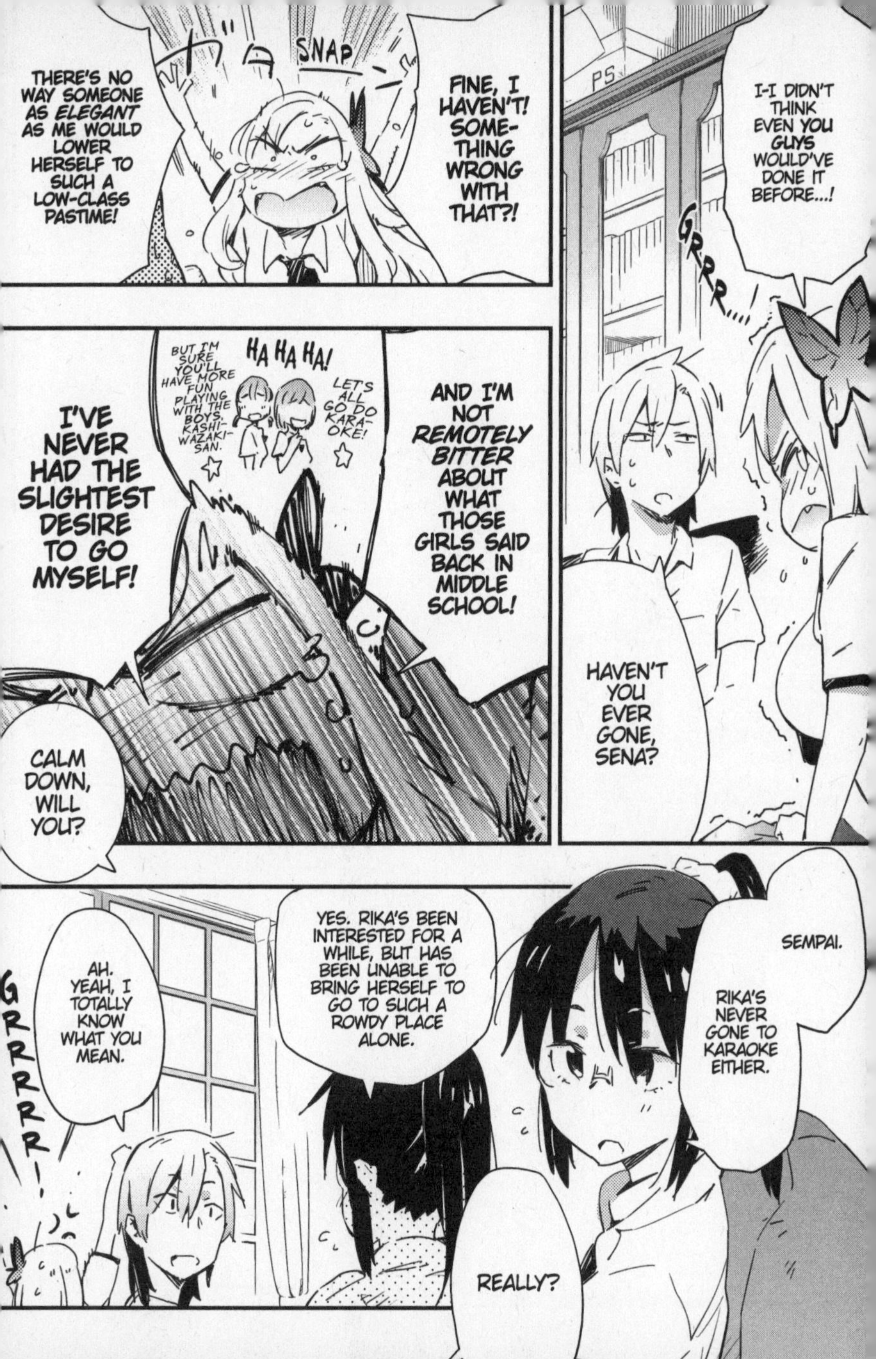
I-I DIDN'T THINK EVEN YOU GUYS WOULD'VE DONE IT BEFORE...!
GRRR...!
HAVEN'T YOU EVER GONE, SENA?
SNAP
FINE, I HAVEN'T! SOMETHING WRONG WITH THAT?!
THERE'S NO WAY SOMEONE AS *ELEGANT* AS ME WOULD LOWER HERSELF TO SUCH A LOW-CLASS PASTIME!
AND I'M NOT *REMOTELY BITTER* ABOUT WHAT THOSE GIRLS SAID BACK IN MIDDLE SCHOOL!
LET'S ALL GO DO KARAOKE!
HA HA HA!
BUT I'M SURE YOU'LL HAVE MORE FUN PLAYING WITH THE BOYS, KASHIWAZAKI-SAN.
I'VE NEVER HAD THE SLIGHTEST DESIRE TO GO MYSELF!
CALM DOWN, WILL YOU?
SEMPAI.
RIKA'S NEVER GONE TO KARAOKE EITHER.
REALLY?
YES. RIKA'S BEEN INTERESTED FOR A WHILE, BUT HAS BEEN UNABLE TO BRING HERSELF TO GO TO SUCH A ROWDY PLACE ALONE.
AH. YEAH, I TOTALLY KNOW WHAT YOU MEAN.
GRRRRRR!

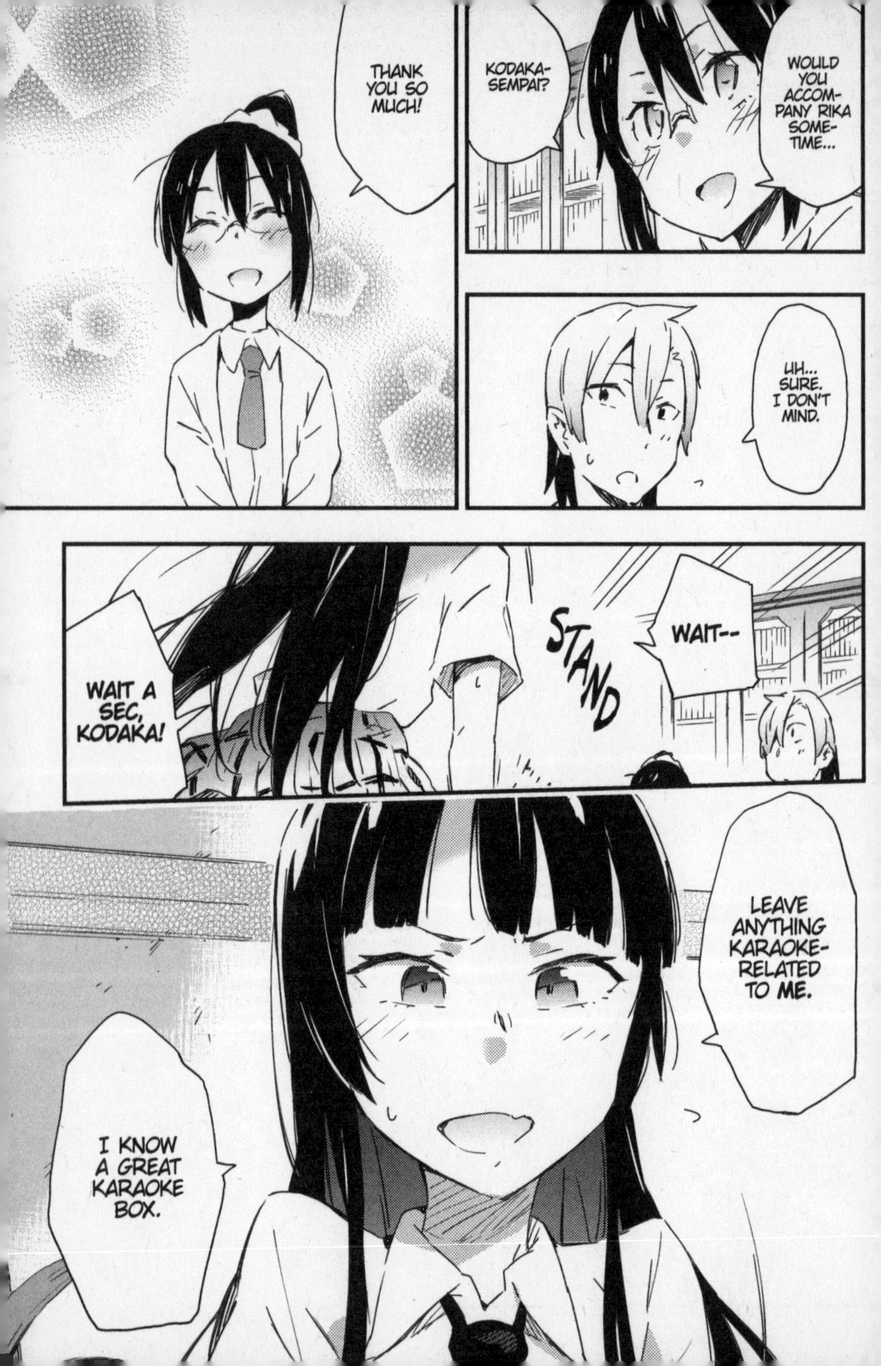
WOULD YOU ACCOMPANY RIKA SOMETIME...
KODAKA-SEMPAI?
UH... SURE. I DON'T MIND.
THANK YOU SO MUCH!
WAIT--
STAND
WAIT A SEC, KODAKA!
LEAVE ANYTHING KARAOKE-RELATED TO ME.
I KNOW A GREAT KARAOKE BOX.

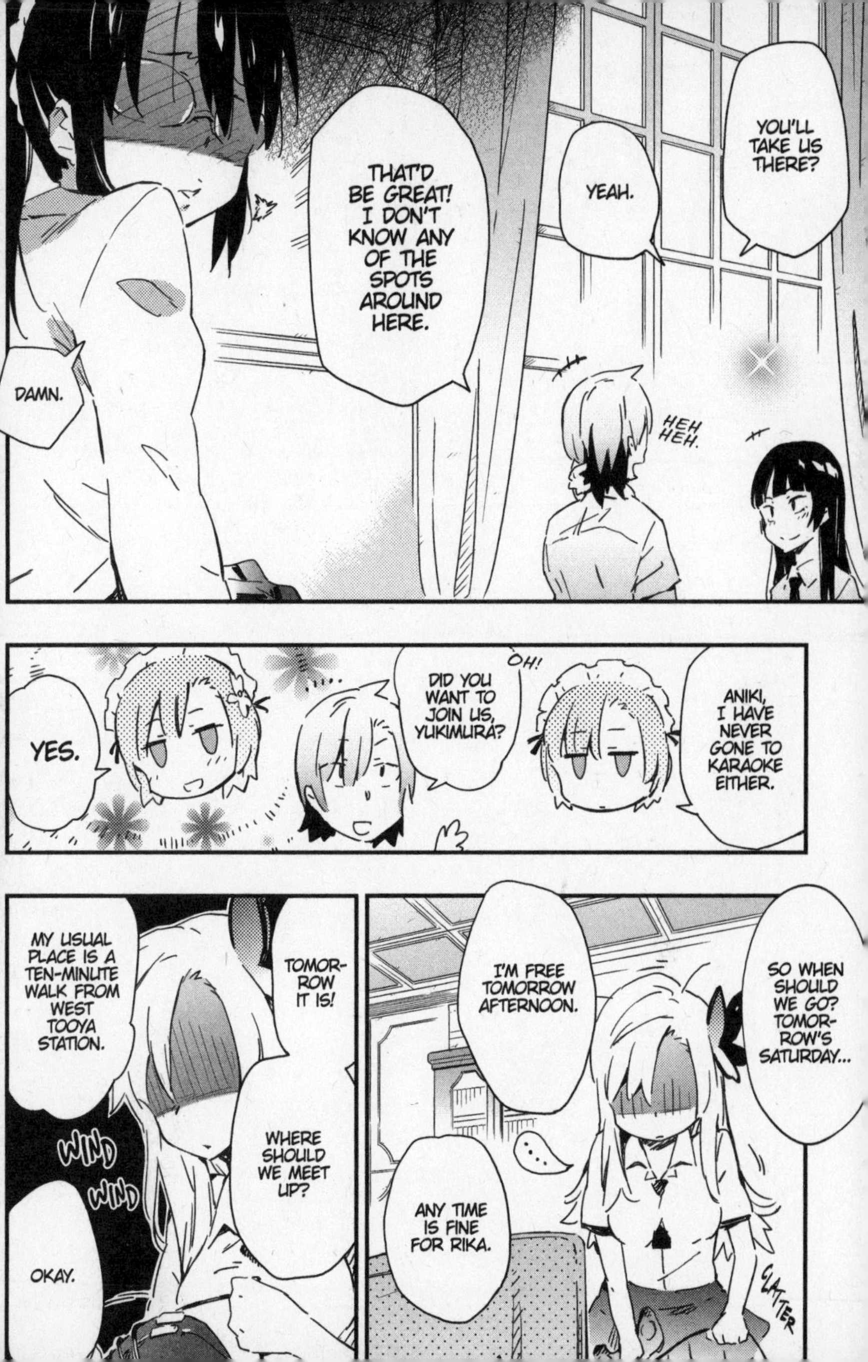

YOU'LL TAKE US THERE?
YEAH.
HEH HEH.
THAT'D BE GREAT! I DON'T KNOW ANY OF THE SPOTS AROUND HERE.
DAMN.
ANIKI, I HAVE NEVER GONE TO KARAOKE EITHER.
OH!
DID YOU WANT TO JOIN US, YUKIMURA?
YES.
SO WHEN SHOULD WE GO? TOMOR-ROW'S SATURDAY...
I'M FREE TOMORROW AFTERNOON.
...
ANY TIME IS FINE FOR RIKA.
CLATTER
TOMOR-ROW IT IS!
WHERE SHOULD WE MEET UP?
MY USUAL PLACE IS A TEN-MINUTE WALK FROM WEST TOOYA STATION.
WIND
WIND
OKAY.

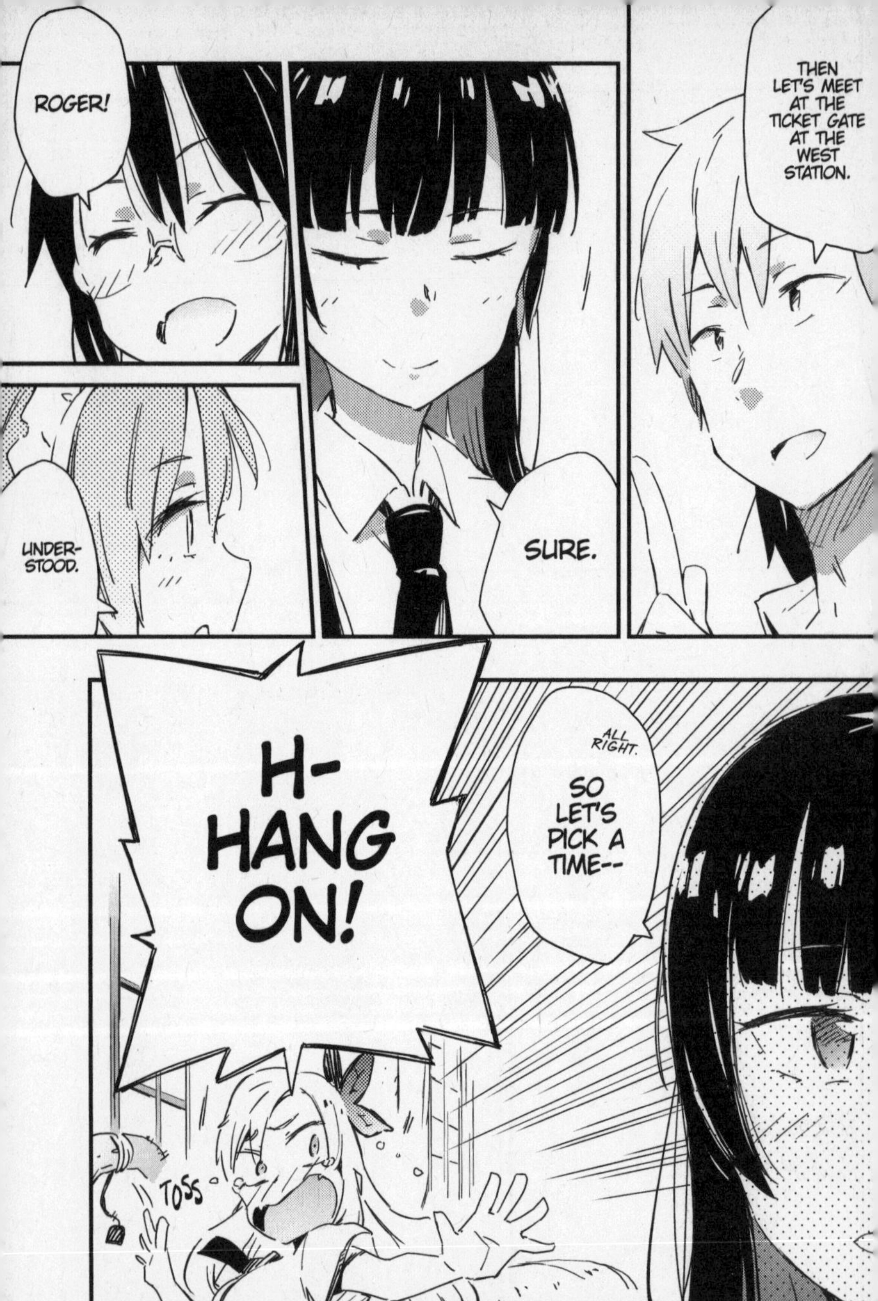
THEN LET'S MEET AT THE TICKET GATE AT THE WEST STATION.
SURE.
ROGER!
UNDER-STOOD.
ALL RIGHT.
SO LET'S PICK A TIME--
H-HANG ON!
TOSS

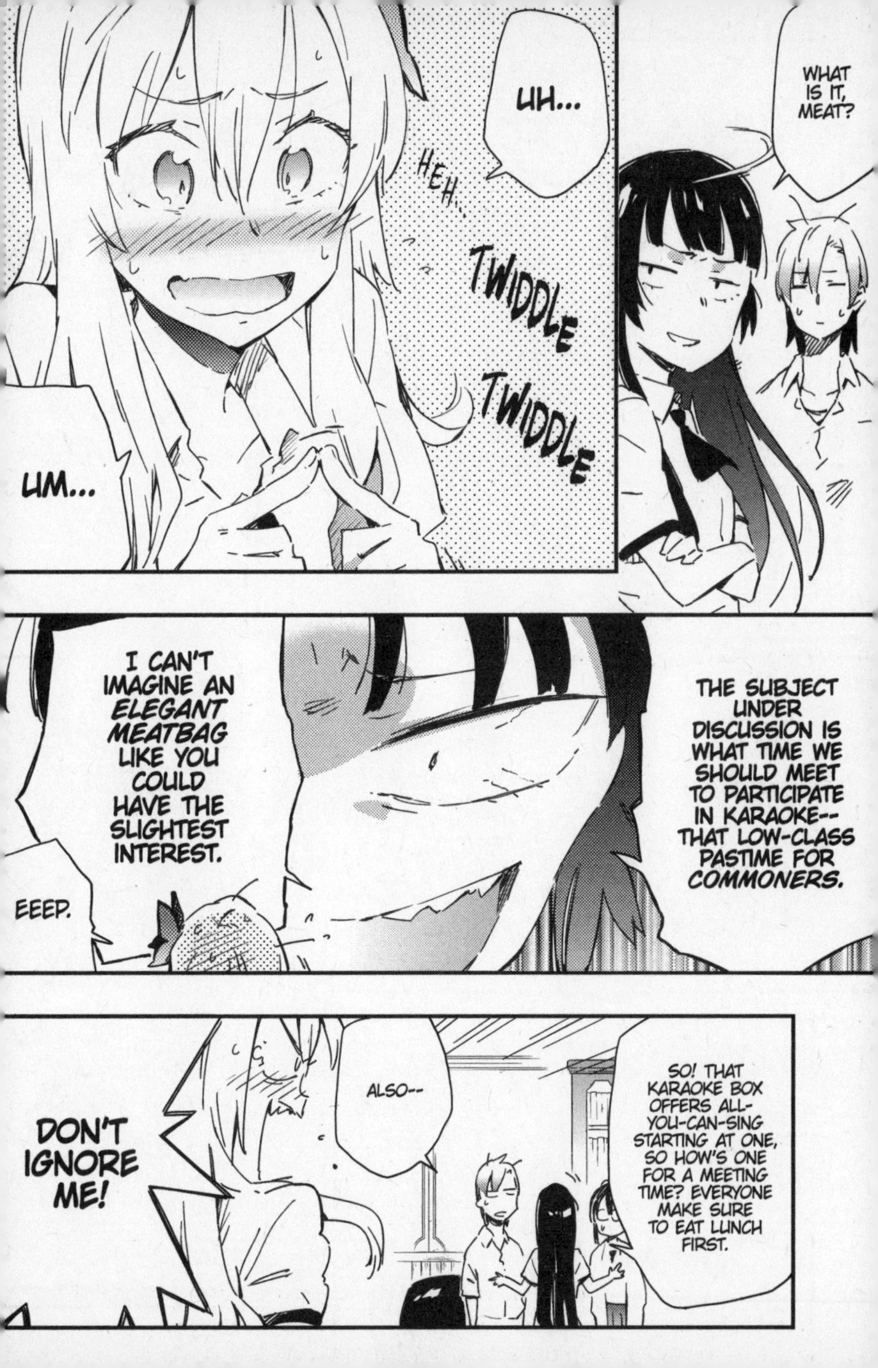
WHAT IS IT, MEAT?
UH...
HEH...
TWIDDLE TWIDDLE
UM...
THE SUBJECT UNDER DISCUSSION IS WHAT TIME WE SHOULD MEET TO PARTICIPATE IN KARAOKE--THAT LOW-CLASS PASTIME FOR COMMONERS.
I CAN'T IMAGINE AN ELEGANT MEATBAG LIKE YOU COULD HAVE THE SLIGHTEST INTEREST.
EEEP.
SO! THAT KARAOKE BOX OFFERS ALL-YOU-CAN-SING STARTING AT ONE, SO HOW'S ONE FOR A MEETING TIME? EVERYONE MAKE SURE TO EAT LUNCH FIRST.
ALSO--
DON'T IGNORE ME!

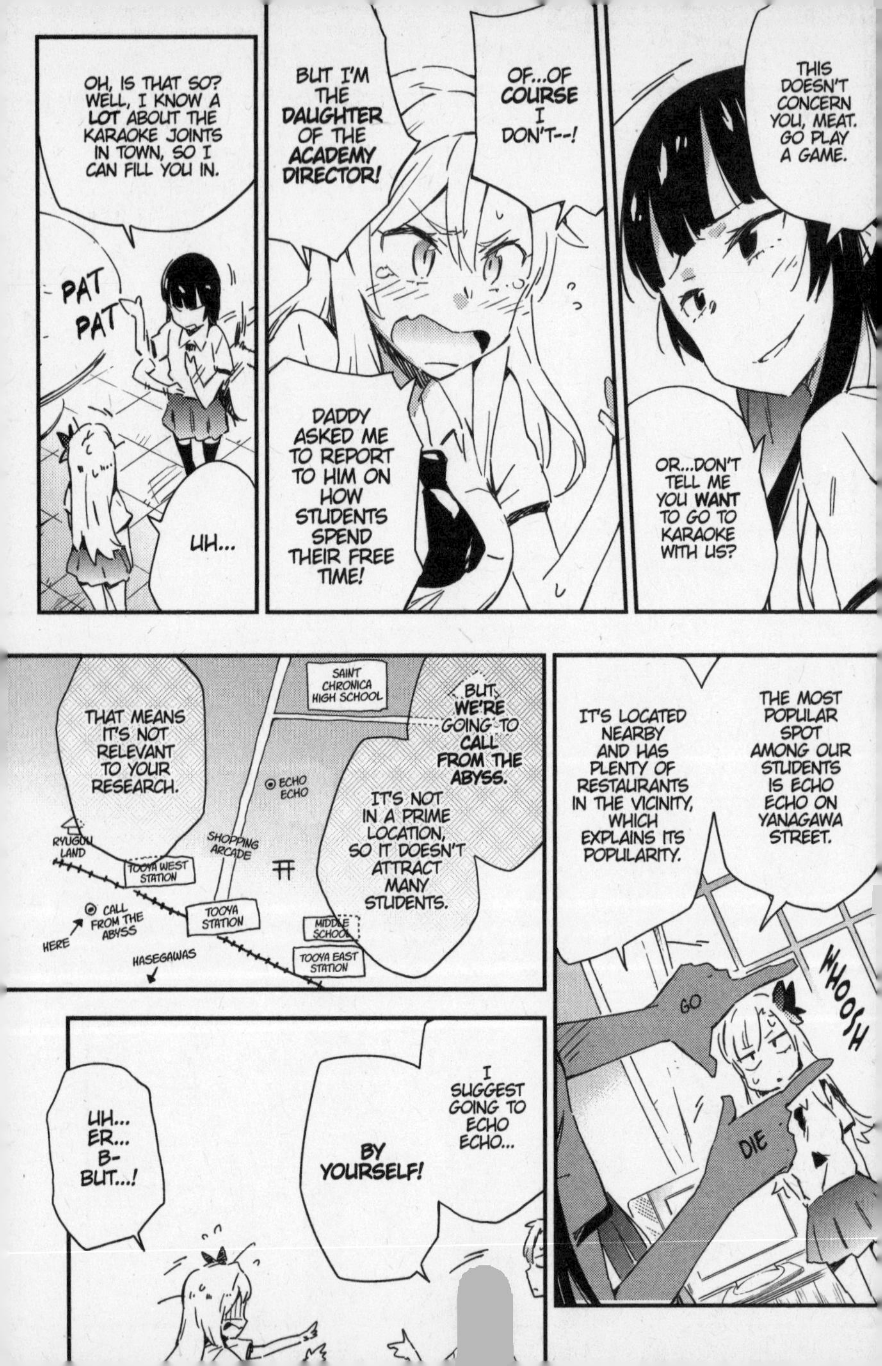
THIS DOESN'T CONCERN YOU, MEAT. GO PLAY A GAME.
OR...DON'T TELL ME YOU WANT TO GO TO KARAOKE WITH US?
OF...OF COURSE I DON'T--!
BUT I'M THE DAUGHTER OF THE ACADEMY DIRECTOR!
DADDY ASKED ME TO REPORT TO HIM ON HOW STUDENTS SPEND THEIR FREE TIME!
OH, IS THAT SO? WELL, I KNOW A LOT ABOUT THE KARAOKE JOINTS IN TOWN, SO I CAN FILL YOU IN.
PAT PAT
UH...
THE MOST POPULAR SPOT AMONG OUR STUDENTS IS ECHO ECHO ON YANAGAWA STREET.
IT'S LOCATED NEARBY AND HAS PLENTY OF RESTAURANTS IN THE VICINITY, WHICH EXPLAINS ITS POPULARITY.
WHOOSH
GO
DIE
BUT, WE'RE GOING TO CALL FROM THE ABYSS.
IT'S NOT IN A PRIME LOCATION, SO IT DOESN'T ATTRACT MANY STUDENTS.
THAT MEANS IT'S NOT RELEVANT TO YOUR RESEARCH.
SAINT CHRONICA HIGH SCHOOL
ECHO ECHO
SHOPPING ARCADE
RYUGOU LAND
TOOYA WEST STATION
TOOYA STATION
CALL FROM THE ABYSS
HERE
HASEGAWAS
MIDDLE SCHOOL
TOOYA EAST STATION
I SUGGEST GOING TO ECHO ECHO...
BY YOURSELF!
UH... ER... B-BUT...!

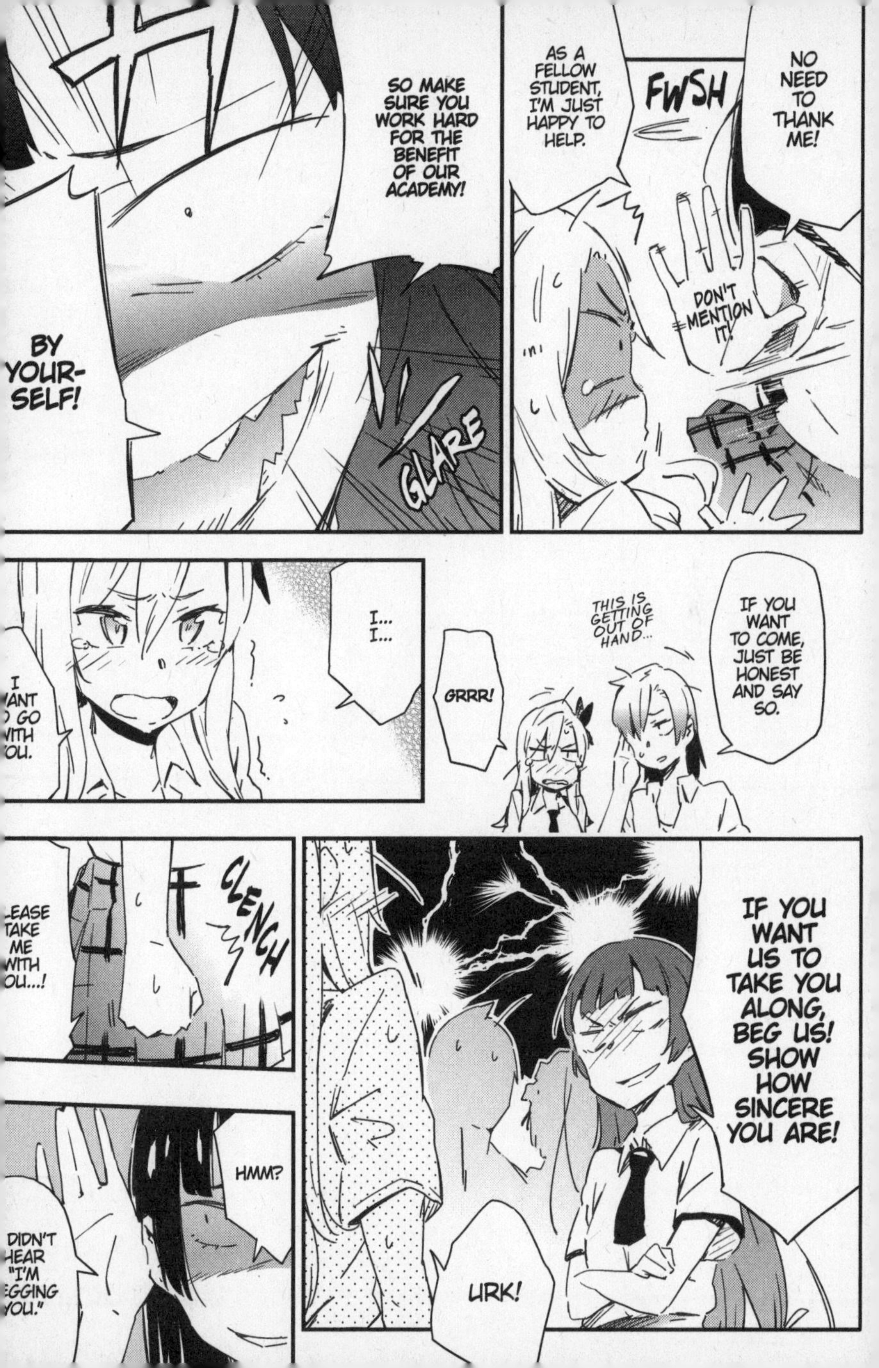
NO NEED TO THANK ME!
FWSH
AS A FELLOW STUDENT, I'M JUST HAPPY TO HELP.
DON'T MENTION IT!
SO MAKE SURE YOU WORK HARD FOR THE BENEFIT OF OUR ACADEMY!
GLARE
BY YOUR-SELF!
IF YOU WANT TO COME, JUST BE HONEST AND SAY SO.
THIS IS GETTING OUT OF HAND...
GRRR!
I... I...
I ANT O GO WITH OU.
IF YOU WANT US TO TAKE YOU ALONG, BEG US! SHOW HOW SINCERE YOU ARE!
URK!
CLENCH
LEASE TAKE ME WITH OU...!
HMM?
DIDN'T HEAR "I'M EGGING YOU."

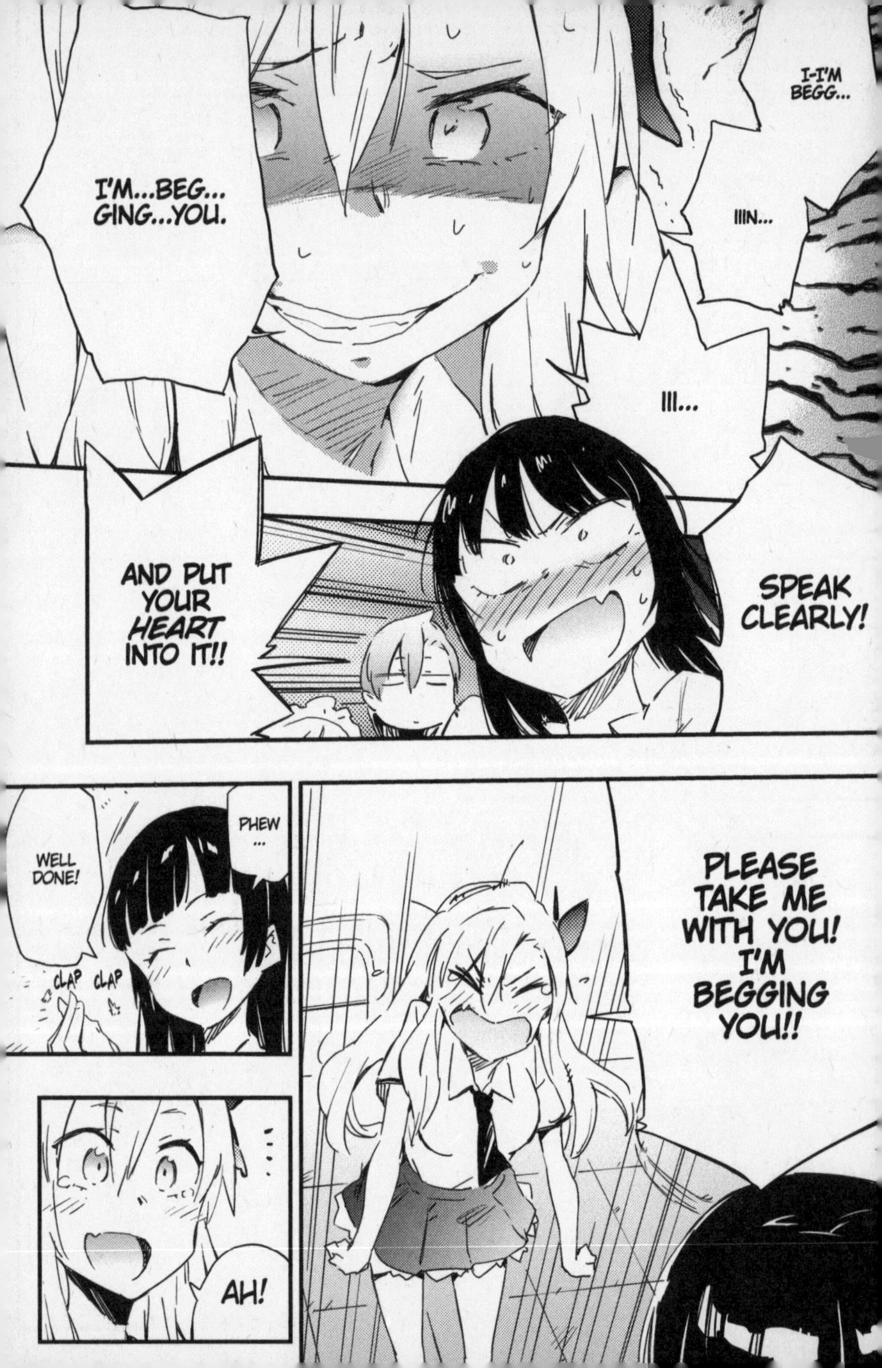

I-I'M BEGG...
IIIN...
III...
I'M...BEG... GING...YOU.
SPEAK CLEARLY!
AND PUT YOUR HEART INTO IT!!
PLEASE TAKE ME WITH YOU! I'M BEGGING YOU!!
PHEW...
WELL DONE!
CLAP CLAP
...
AH!

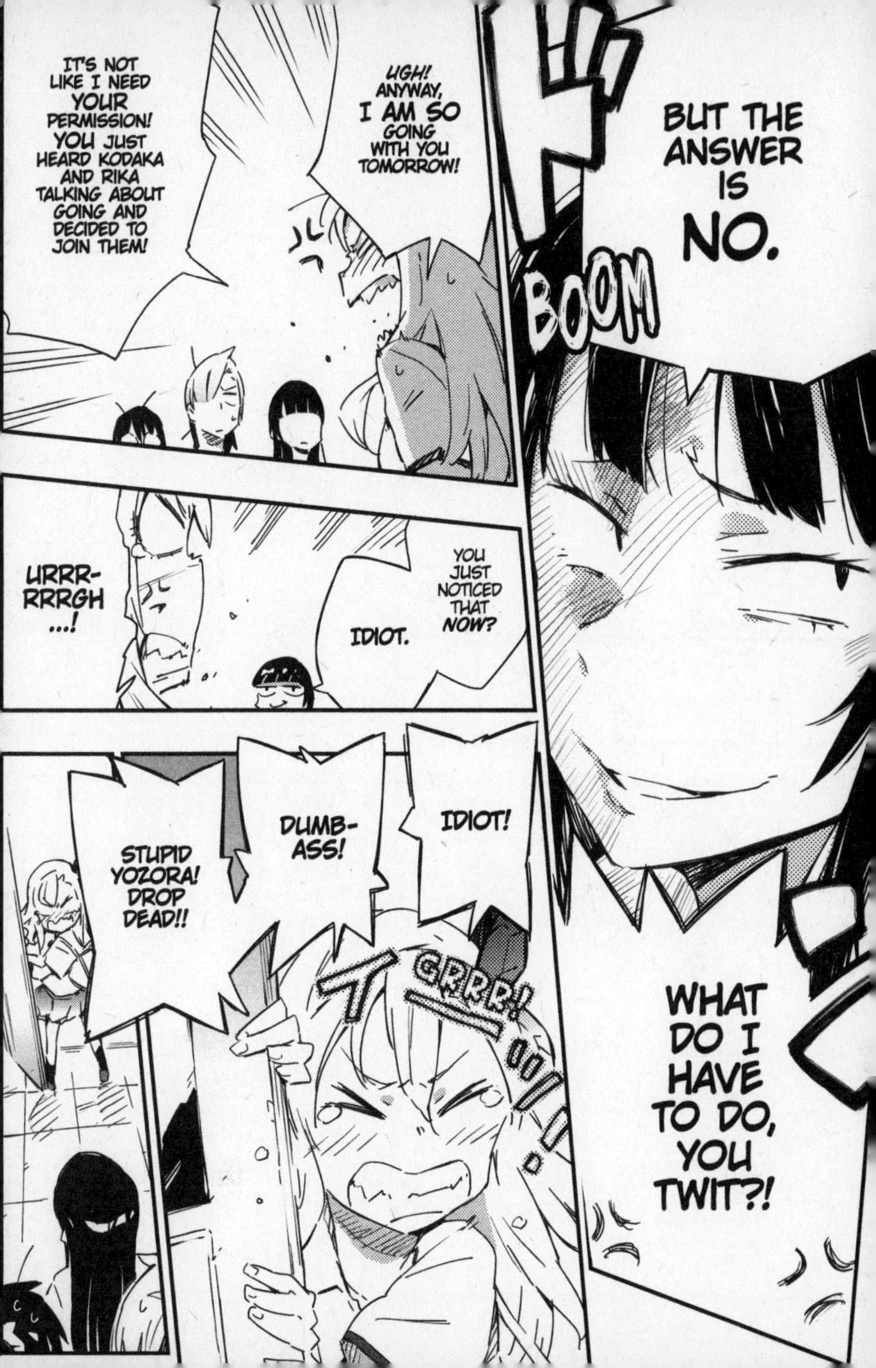
BUT THE ANSWER IS NO.
BOOM
WHAT DO I HAVE TO DO, YOU TWIT?!
UGH! ANYWAY, I AM SO GOING WITH YOU TOMORROW!
IT'S NOT LIKE I NEED YOUR PERMISSION! YOU JUST HEARD KODAKA AND RIKA TALKING ABOUT GOING AND DECIDED TO JOIN THEM!
YOU JUST NOTICED THAT NOW?
IDIOT.
URRR-RRRGH ...!
IDIOT!
DUMB-ASS!
STUPID YOZORA! DROP DEAD!!
GRRR!

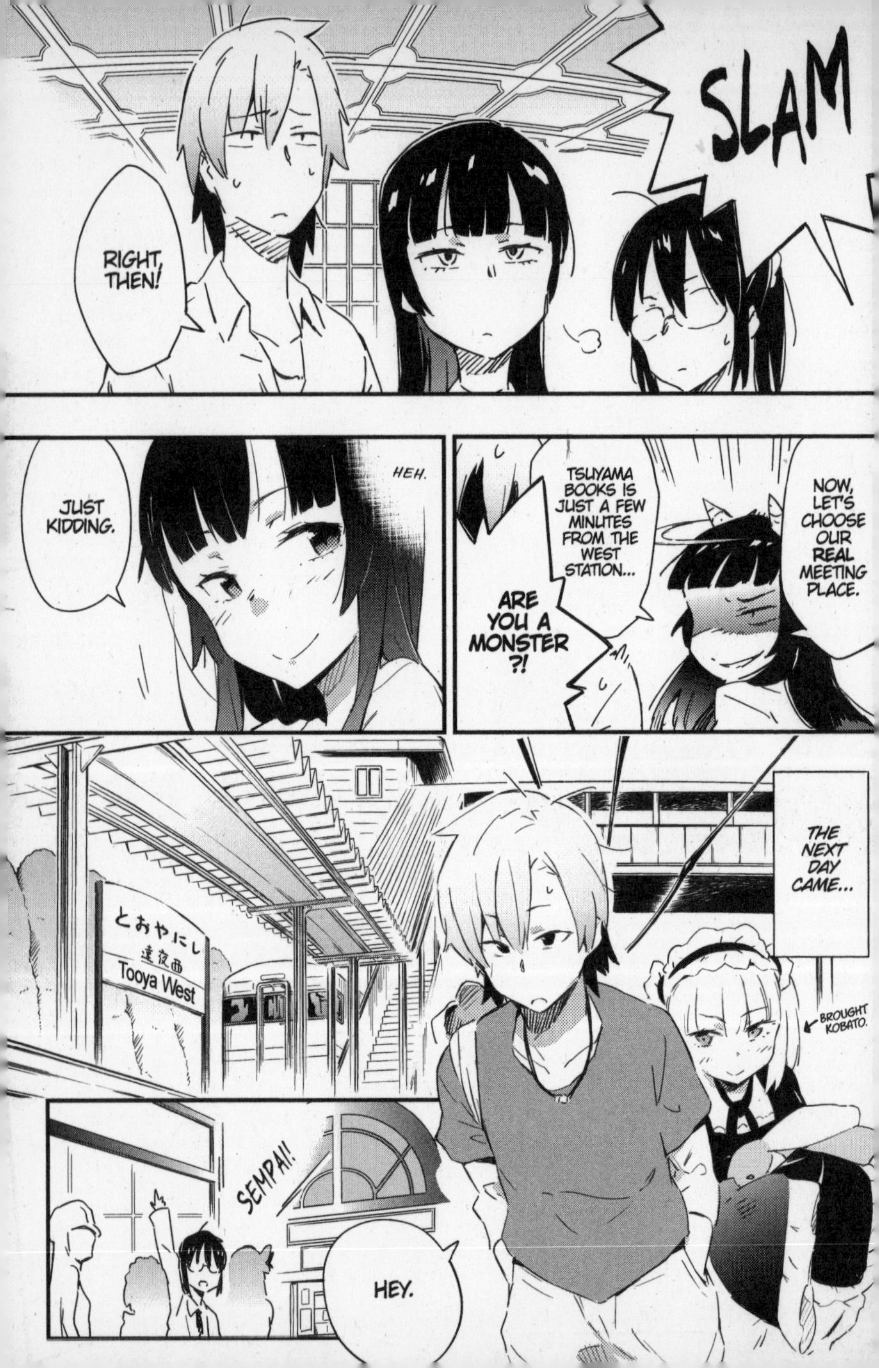
SLAM
RIGHT, THEN!
NOW, LET'S CHOOSE OUR REAL MEETING PLACE.
TSUYAMA BOOKS IS JUST A FEW MINUTES FROM THE WEST STATION...
ARE YOU A MONSTER?!
HEH.
JUST KIDDING.
THE NEXT DAY CAME...
BROUGHT KOBATO.
とおやにし
遠夜西
Tooya West
SEMPAI!!
HEY.

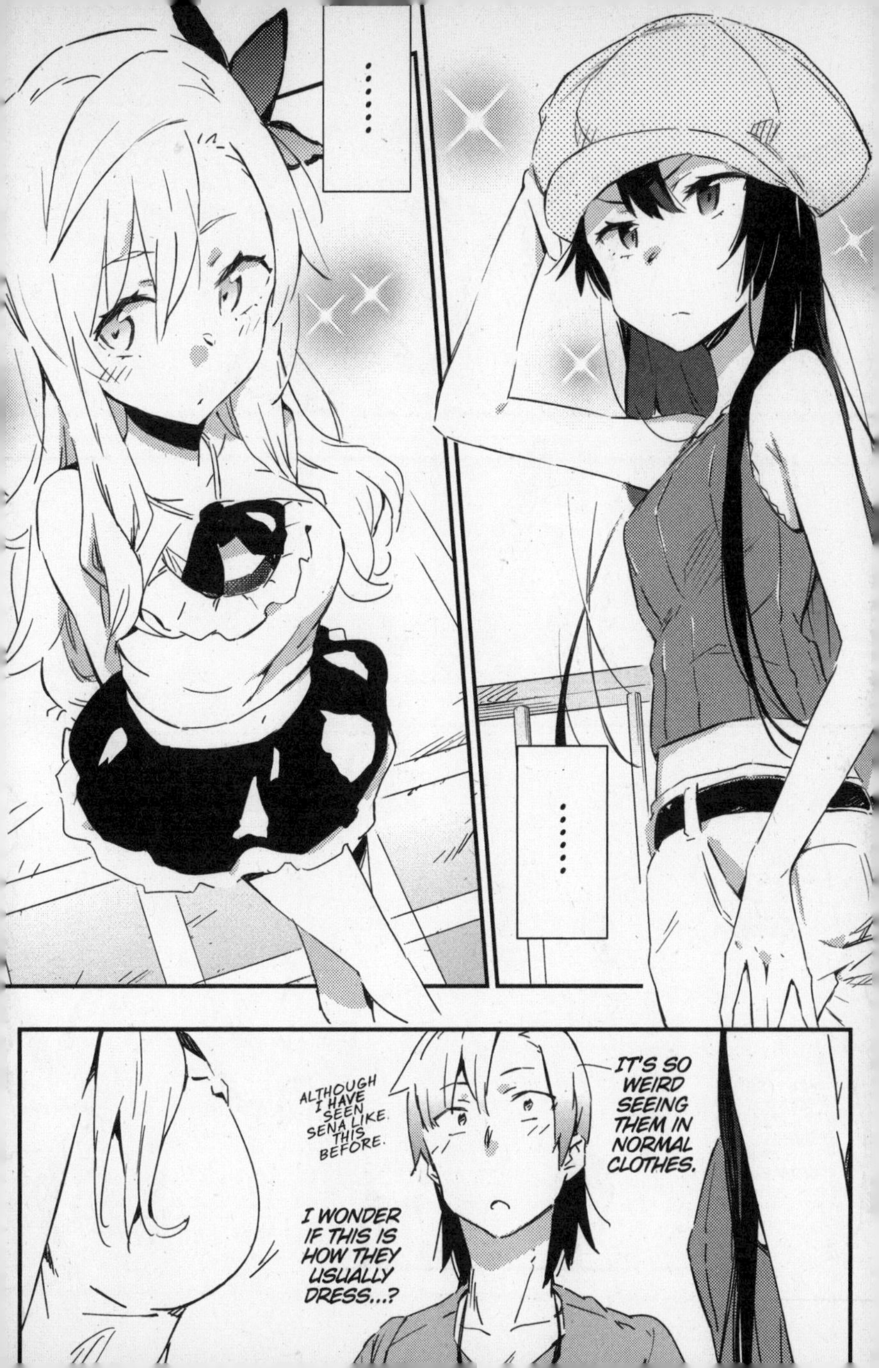
……
……
IT'S SO WEIRD SEEING THEM IN NORMAL CLOTHES.
ALTHOUGH I HAVE SEEN SENA LIKE THIS BEFORE.
I WONDER IF THIS IS HOW THEY USUALLY DRESS...?

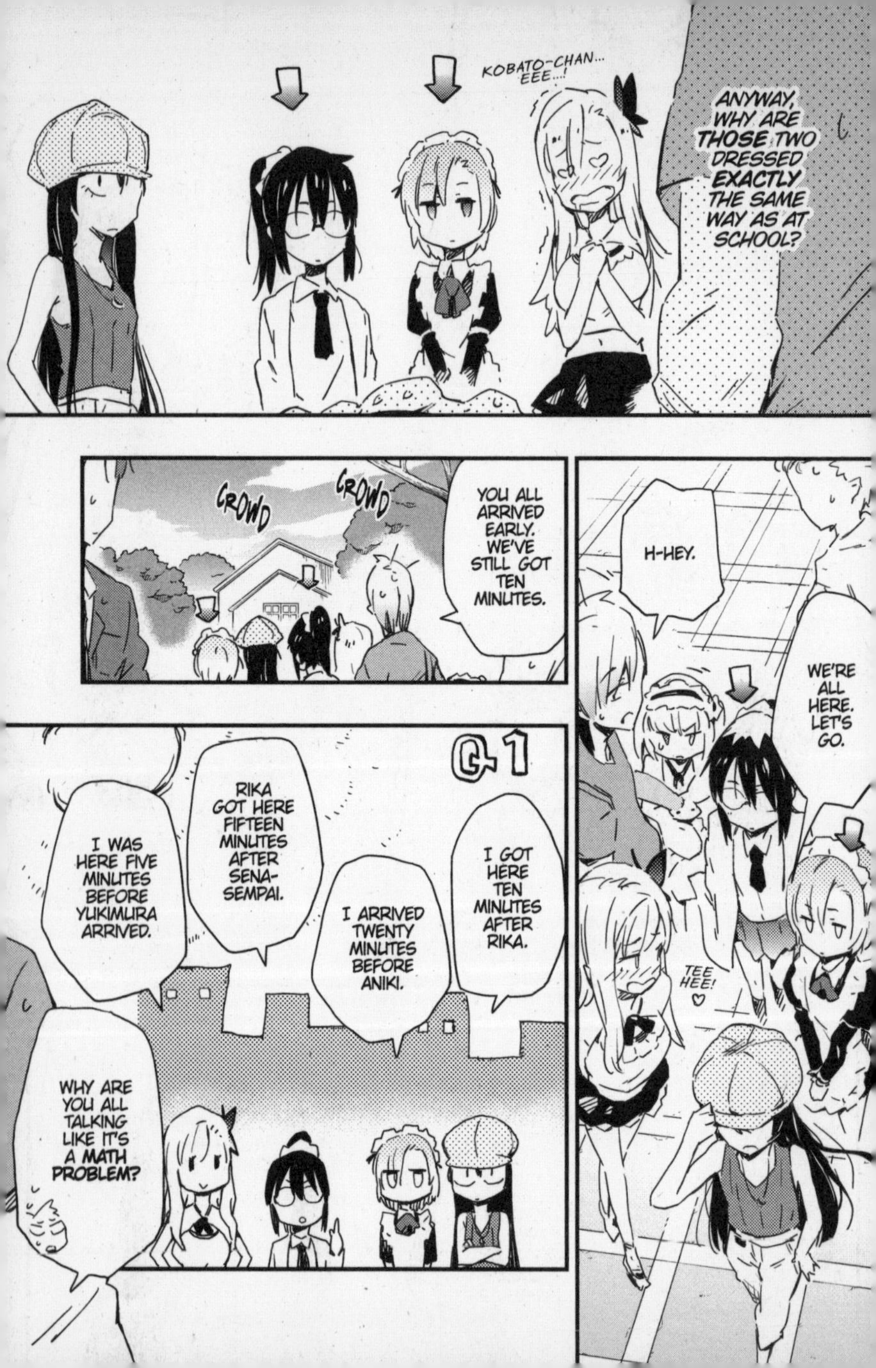
ANYWAY, WHY ARE THOSE TWO DRESSED EXACTLY THE SAME WAY AS AT SCHOOL?
KOBATO-CHAN... EEE...!
H-HEY.
WE'RE ALL HERE. LET'S GO.
TEE HEE! ♡
YOU ALL ARRIVED EARLY. WE'VE STILL GOT TEN MINUTES.
CROWD
CROWD
Q1
I GOT HERE TEN MINUTES AFTER RIKA.
I ARRIVED TWENTY MINUTES BEFORE ANIKI.
RIKA GOT HERE FIFTEEN MINUTES AFTER SENA-SEMPAI.
I WAS HERE FIVE MINUTES BEFORE YUKIMURA ARRIVED.
WHY ARE YOU ALL TALKING LIKE IT'S A MATH PROBLEM?

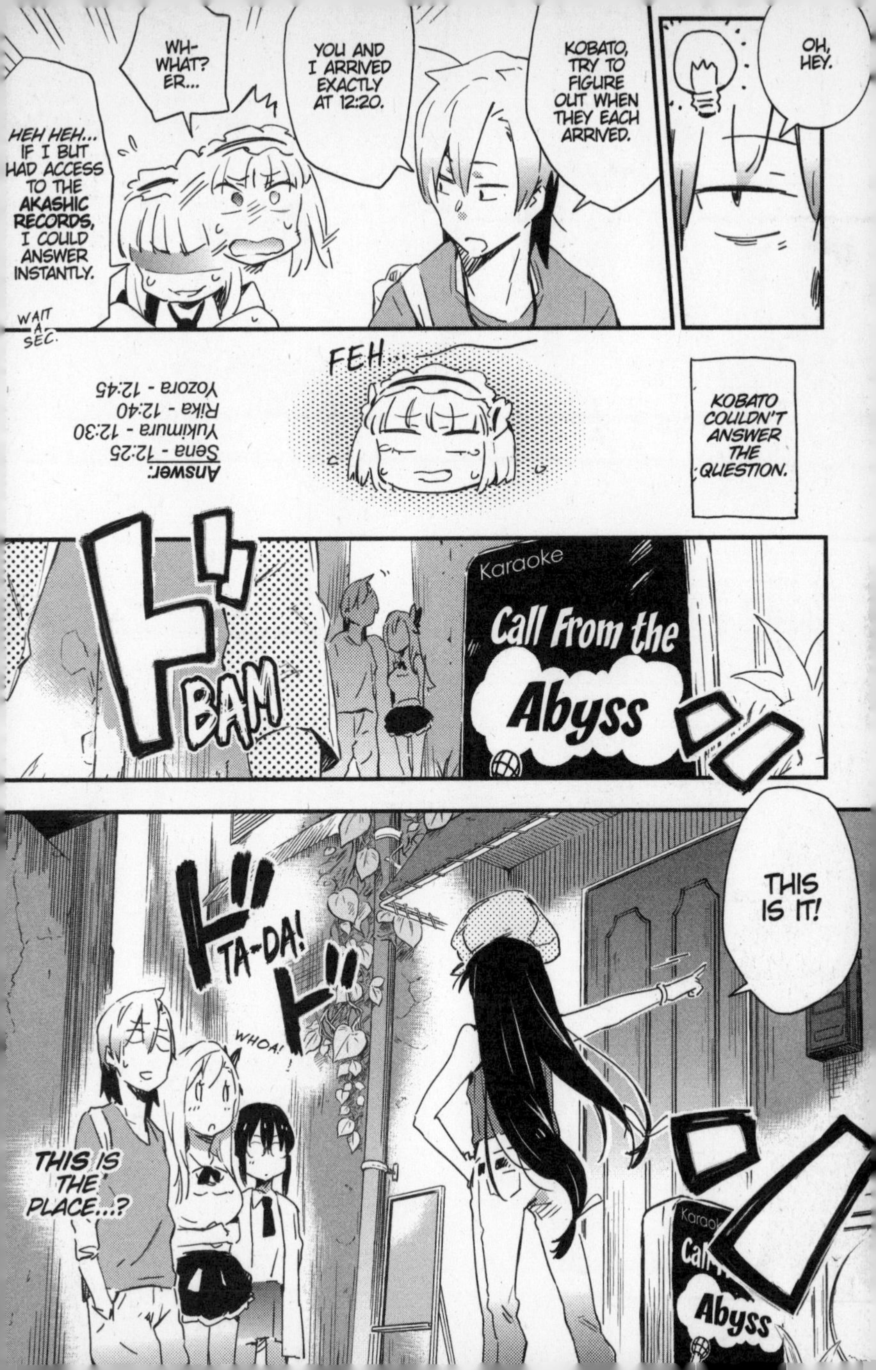
OH, HEY.
KOBATO, TRY TO FIGURE OUT WHEN THEY EACH ARRIVED.
YOU AND I ARRIVED EXACTLY AT 12:20.
WH-WHAT? ER...
HEH HEH... IF I BUT HAD ACCESS TO THE AKASHIC RECORDS, I COULD ANSWER INSTANTLY.
WAIT A SEC.
KOBATO COULDN'T ANSWER THE QUESTION.
FEH...
Answer:
Sena - 12:25
Yukimura - 12:30
Rika - 12:40
Yozora - 12:45
Karaoke
Call From the Abyss
BAM
THIS IS IT!
TA-DA!
WHOA!
THIS IS THE PLACE...?

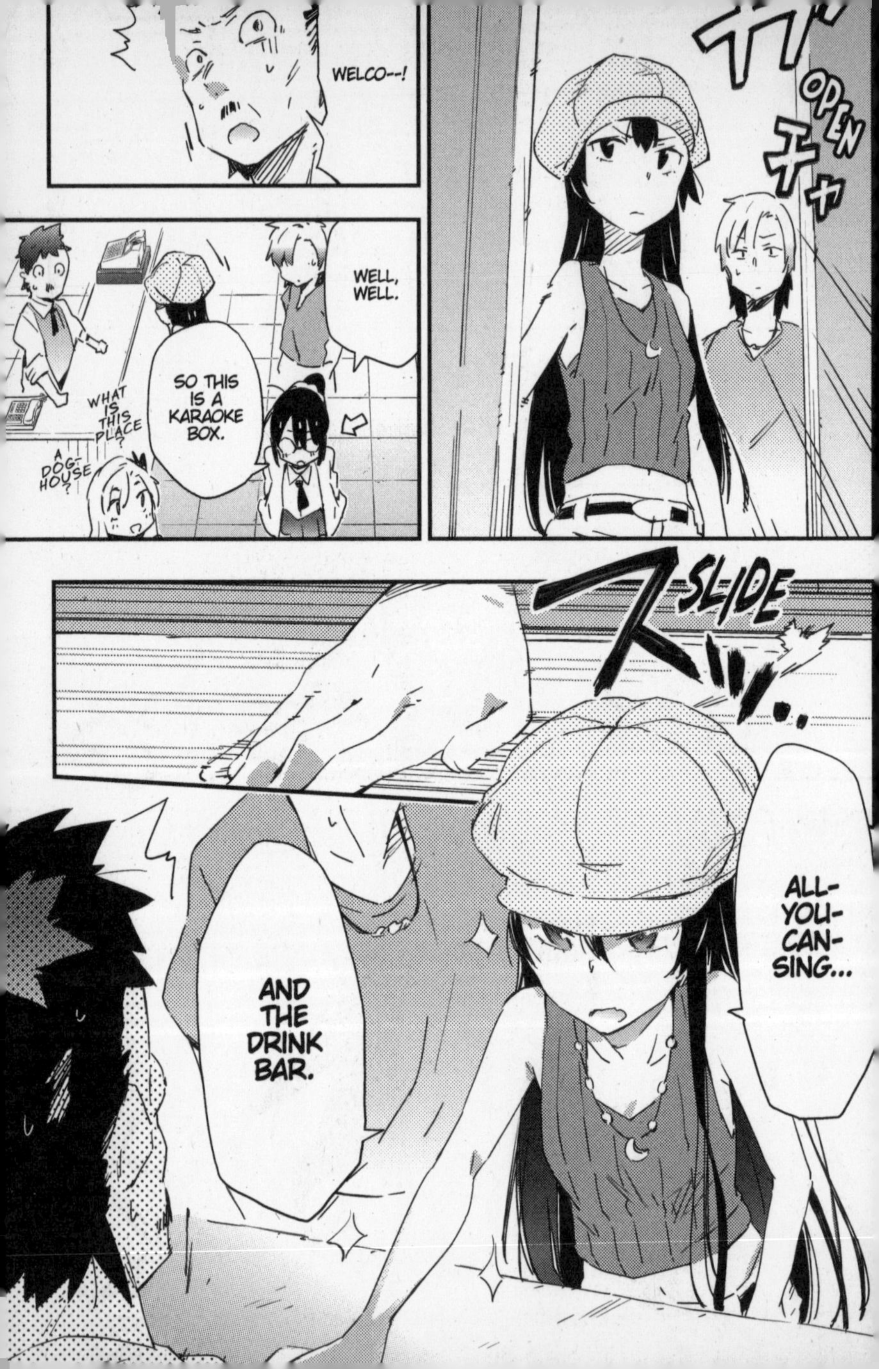
OPEN
WELCO--!
WELL, WELL.
SO THIS IS A KARAOKE BOX.
WHAT IS THIS PLACE?
A DOG-HOUSE?
SLIDE
ALL-YOU-CAN-SING...
AND THE DRINK BAR.

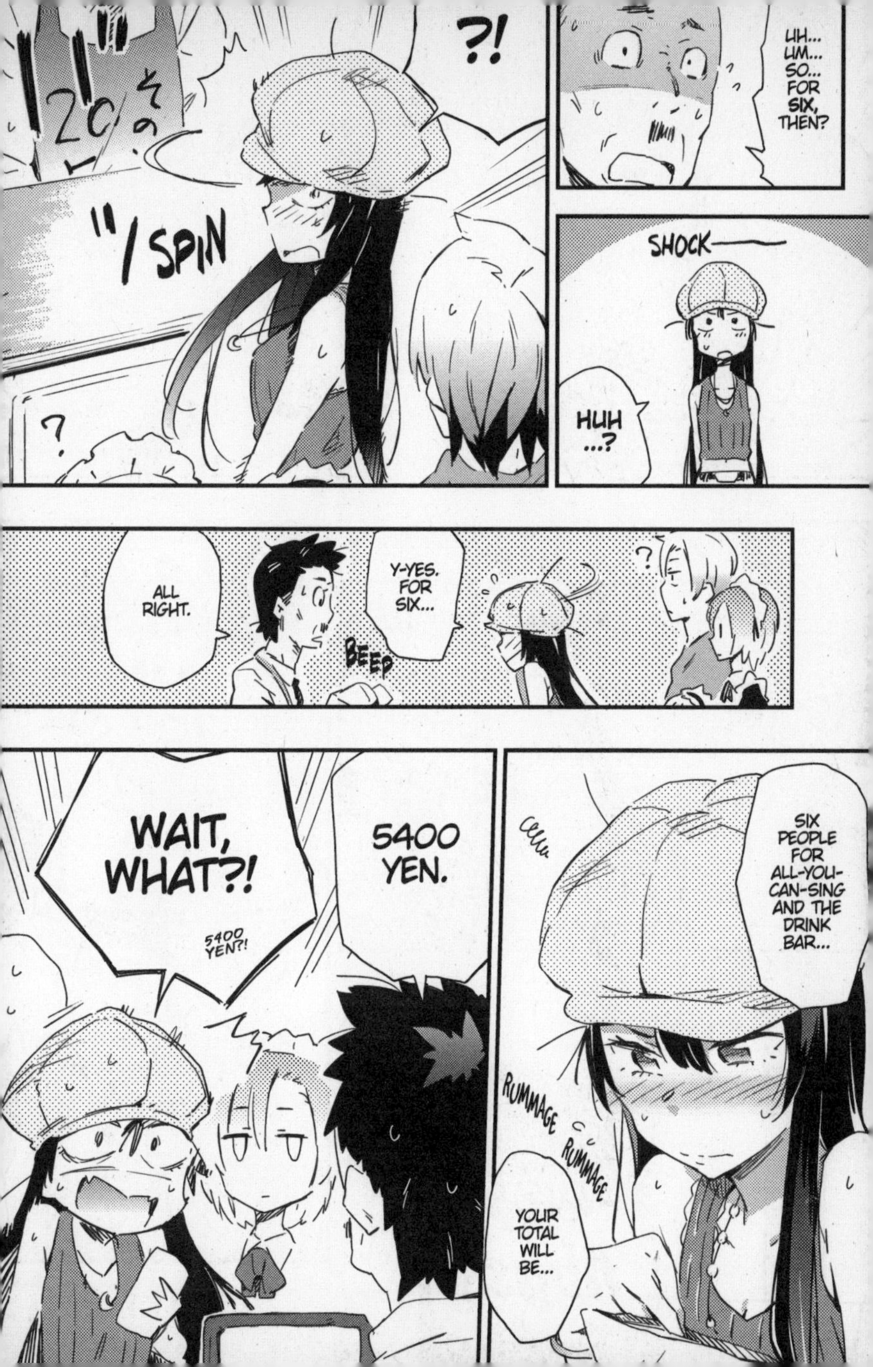
UH... UM... SO... FOR SIX, THEN?
SHOCK———
HUH ...?
?!
SPIN
?
Y-YES. FOR SIX...
BEEP
ALL RIGHT.
SIX PEOPLE FOR ALL-YOU-CAN-SING AND THE DRINK BAR...
RUMMAGE RUMMAGE
YOUR TOTAL WILL BE...
5400 YEN.
WAIT, WHAT?!
5400 YEN?!

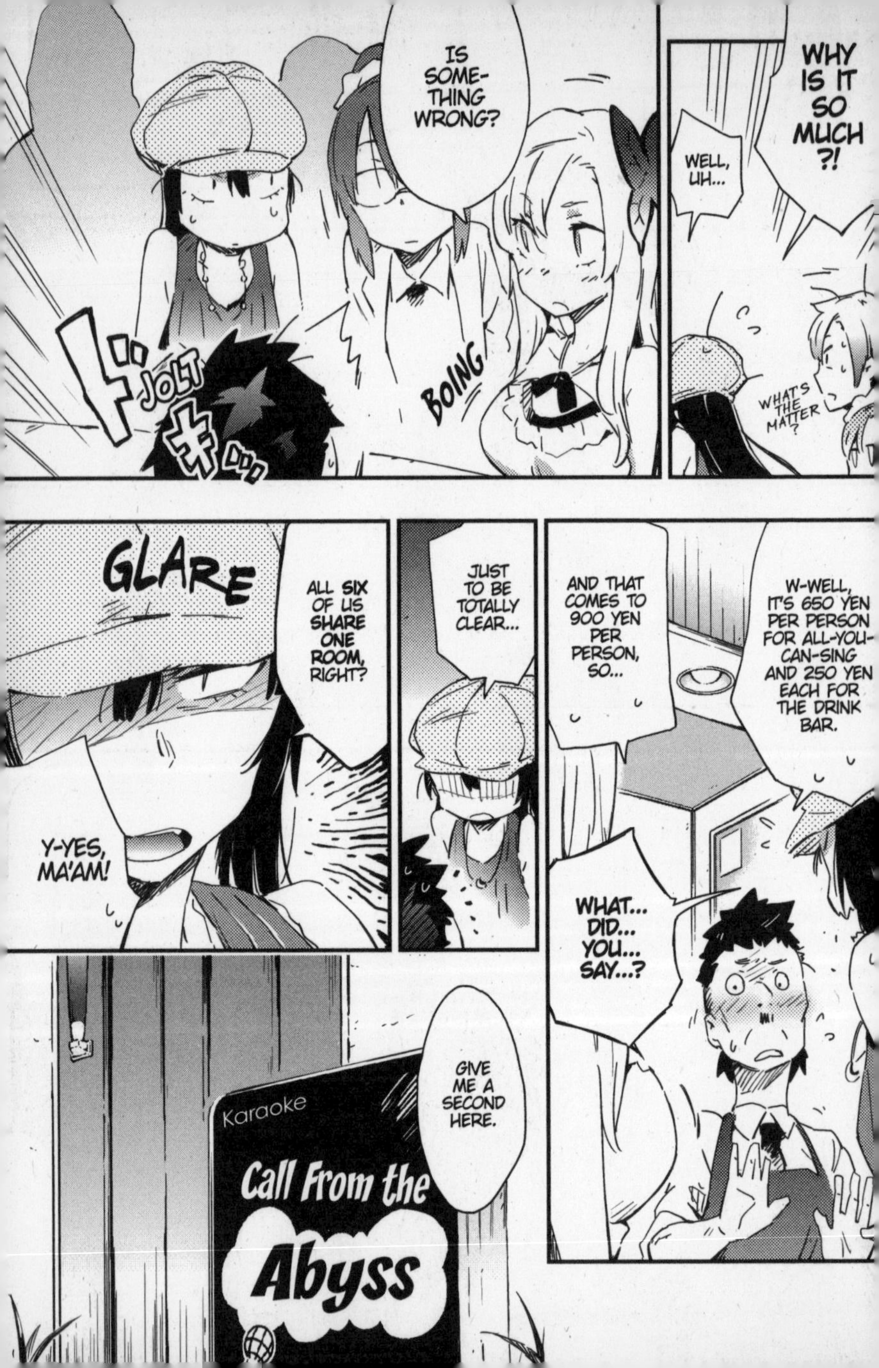
WHY IS IT SO MUCH?!
WELL, UH...
WHAT'S THE MATTER?
IS SOME-THING WRONG?
JOLT
BOING
W-WELL, IT'S 650 YEN PER PERSON FOR ALL-YOU-CAN-SING AND 250 YEN EACH FOR THE DRINK BAR.
AND THAT COMES TO 900 YEN PER PERSON, SO...
WHAT... DID... YOU... SAY...?
JUST TO BE TOTALLY CLEAR...
ALL SIX OF US SHARE ONE ROOM, RIGHT?
GLARE
Y-YES, MA'AM!
GIVE ME A SECOND HERE.
Karaoke
Call From the Abyss

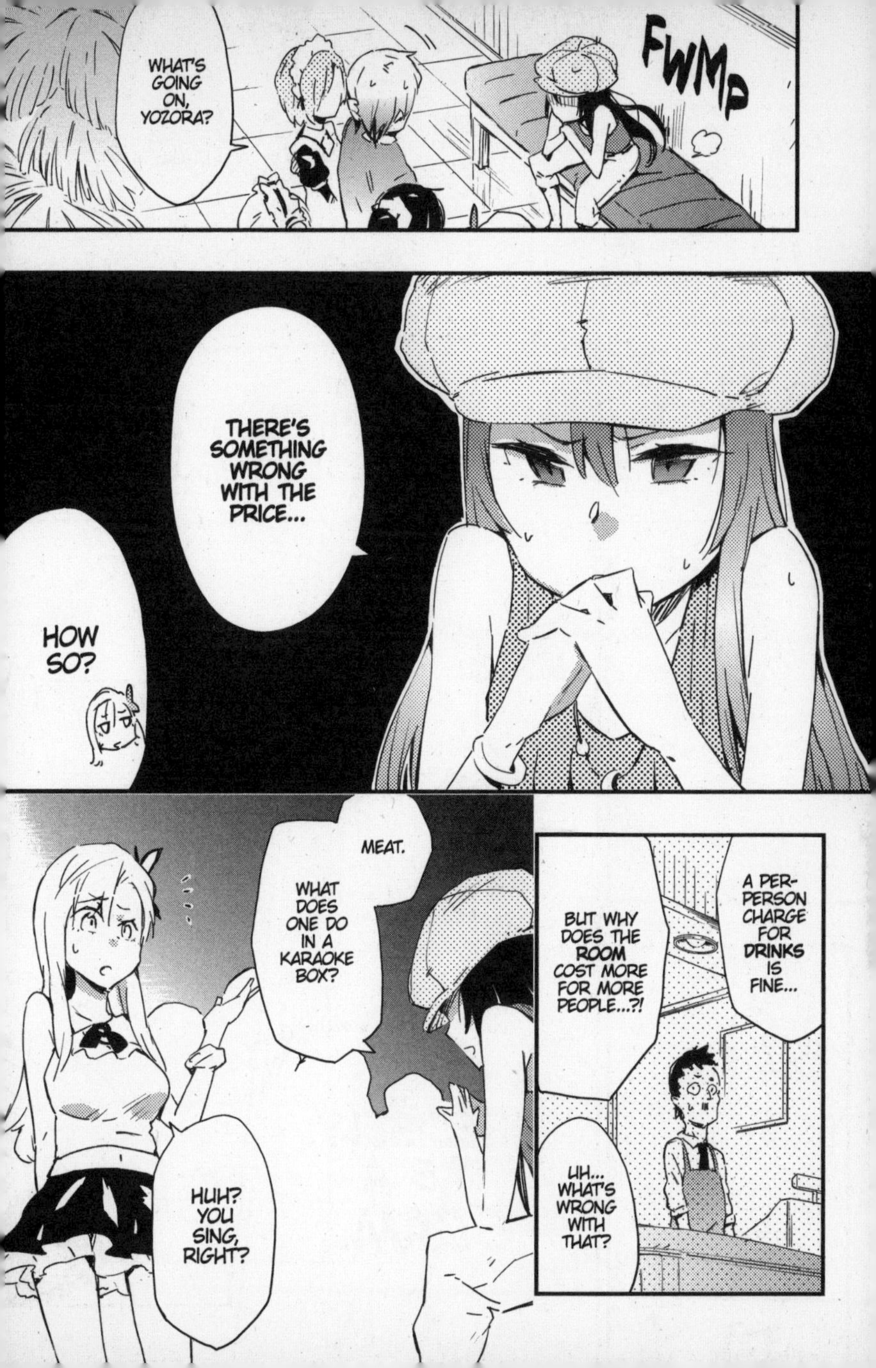
FWMP
WHAT'S GOING ON, YOZORA?
THERE'S SOMETHING WRONG WITH THE PRICE...
HOW SO?
A PER-PERSON CHARGE FOR DRINKS IS FINE...
BUT WHY DOES THE ROOM COST MORE FOR MORE PEOPLE...?!
UH... WHAT'S WRONG WITH THAT?
MEAT.
WHAT DOES ONE DO IN A KARAOKE BOX?
HUH? YOU SING, RIGHT?

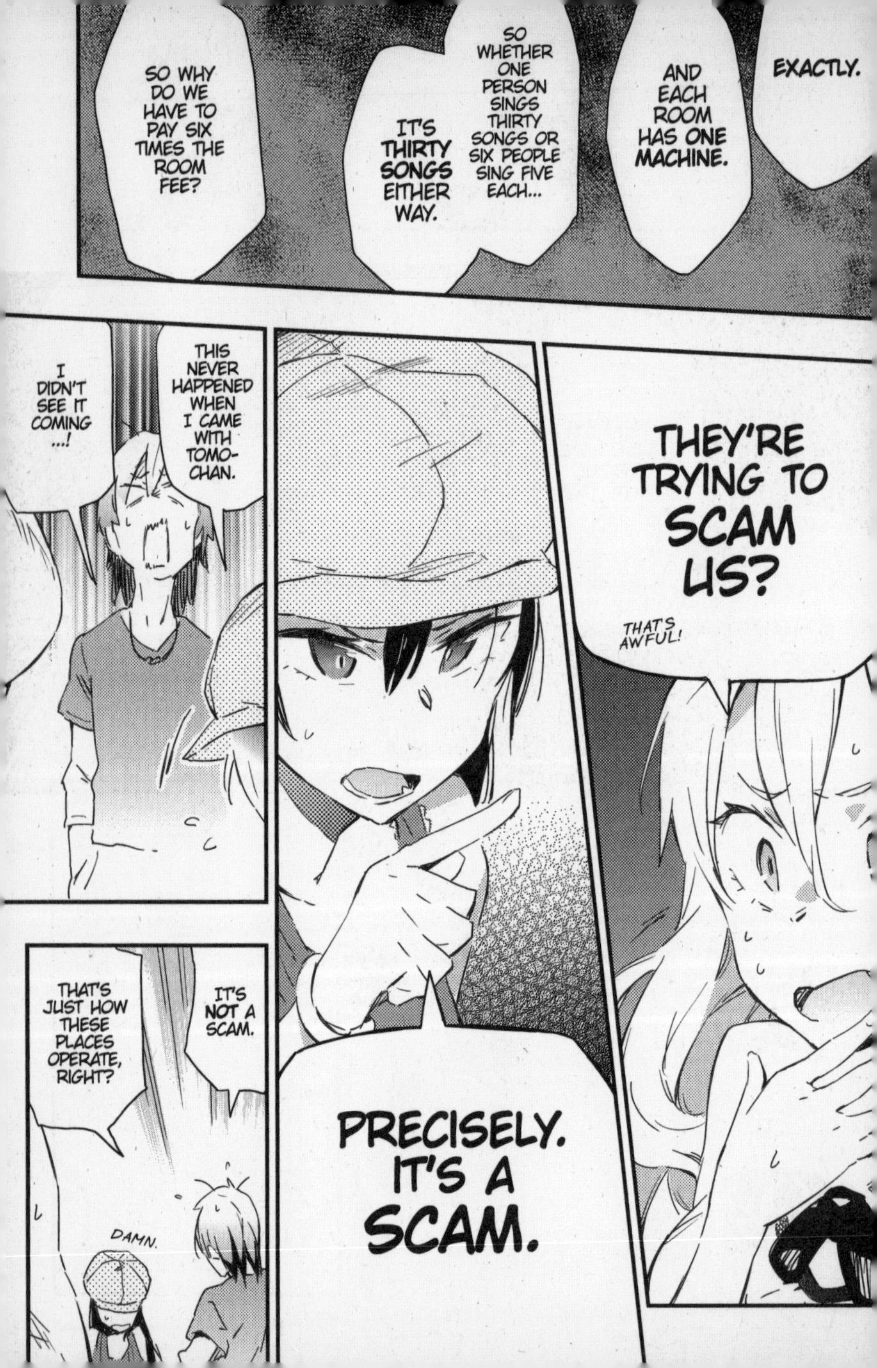
EXACTLY.
AND EACH ROOM HAS ONE MACHINE.
SO WHETHER ONE PERSON SINGS THIRTY SONGS OR SIX PEOPLE SING FIVE EACH...
IT'S THIRTY SONGS EITHER WAY.
SO WHY DO WE HAVE TO PAY SIX TIMES THE ROOM FEE?
THEY'RE TRYING TO SCAM US?
THAT'S AWFUL!
PRECISELY. IT'S A SCAM.
THIS NEVER HAPPENED WHEN I CAME WITH TOMO-CHAN.
I DIDN'T SEE IT COMING ...!
IT'S NOT A SCAM.
THAT'S JUST HOW THESE PLACES OPERATE, RIGHT?
DAMN.

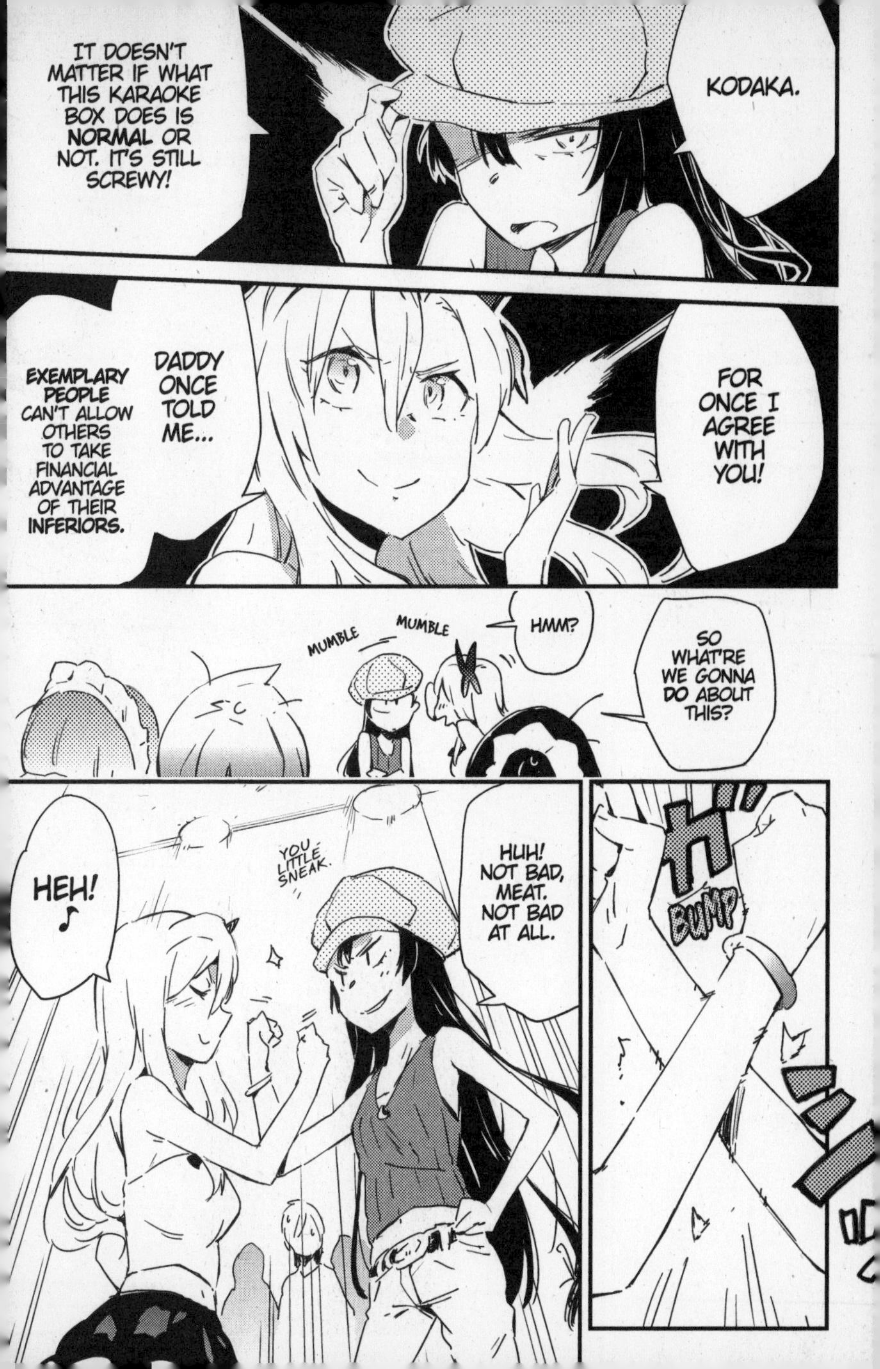
KODAKA.
IT DOESN'T MATTER IF WHAT THIS KARAOKE BOX DOES IS NORMAL OR NOT. IT'S STILL SCREWY!
FOR ONCE I AGREE WITH YOU!
DADDY ONCE TOLD ME...
EXEMPLARY PEOPLE CAN'T ALLOW OTHERS TO TAKE FINANCIAL ADVANTAGE OF THEIR INFERIORS.
SO WHAT'RE WE GONNA DO ABOUT THIS?
HMM?
MUMBLE
MUMBLE
BUMP
HUH! NOT BAD, MEAT. NOT BAD AT ALL.
YOU LITTLE SNEAK.
HEH! ♪

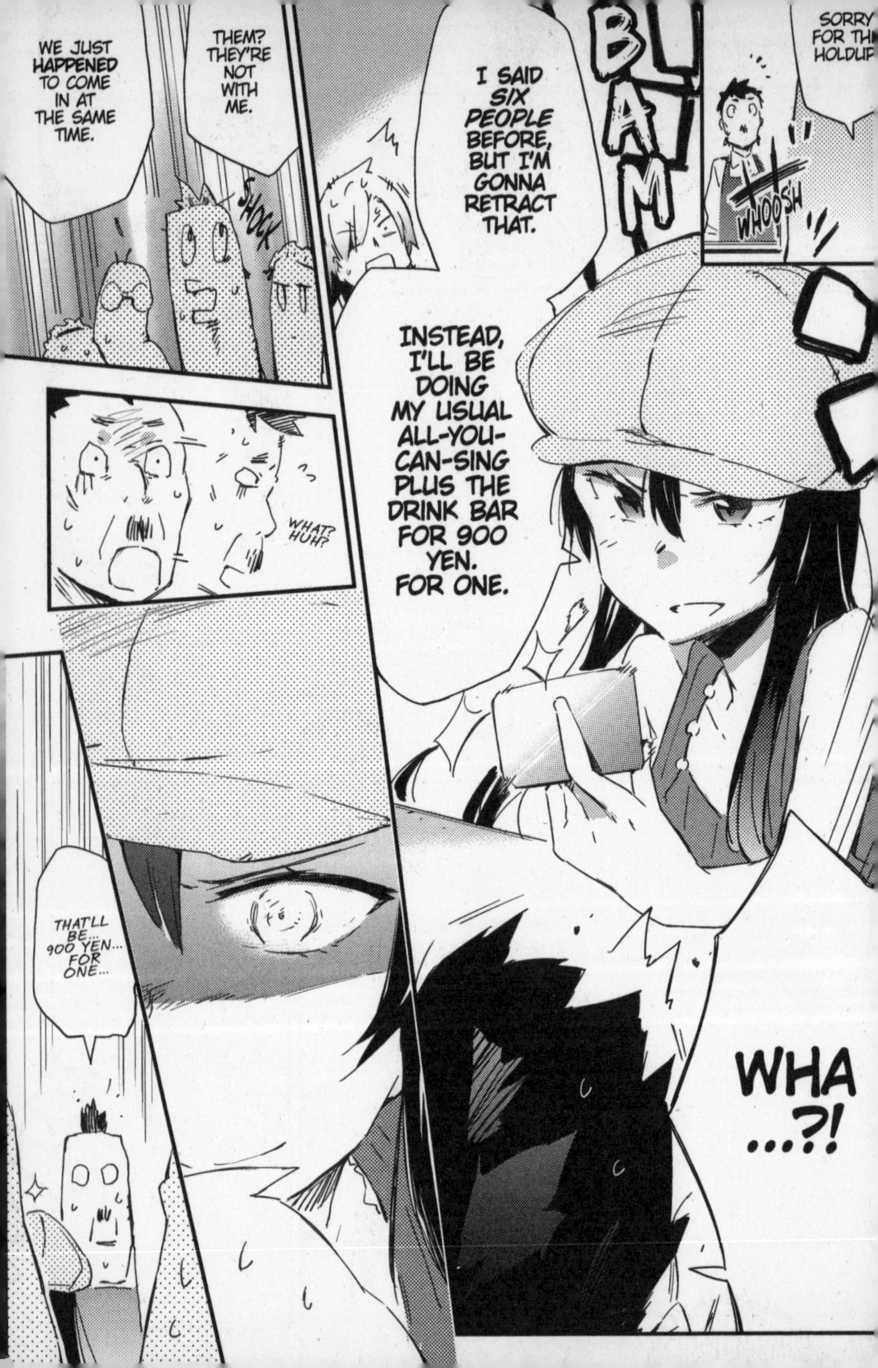
SORRY FOR TH HOLDUP
WHOOSH
BLAM
I SAID SIX PEOPLE BEFORE, BUT I'M GONNA RETRACT THAT.
INSTEAD, I'LL BE DOING MY USUAL ALL-YOU-CAN-SING PLUS THE DRINK BAR FOR 900 YEN. FOR ONE.
THEM? THEY'RE NOT WITH ME.
WE JUST HAPPENED TO COME IN AT THE SAME TIME.
SHOCK
WHAT? HUH?
WHA ...?!
THAT'LL BE... 900 YEN... FOR ONE...

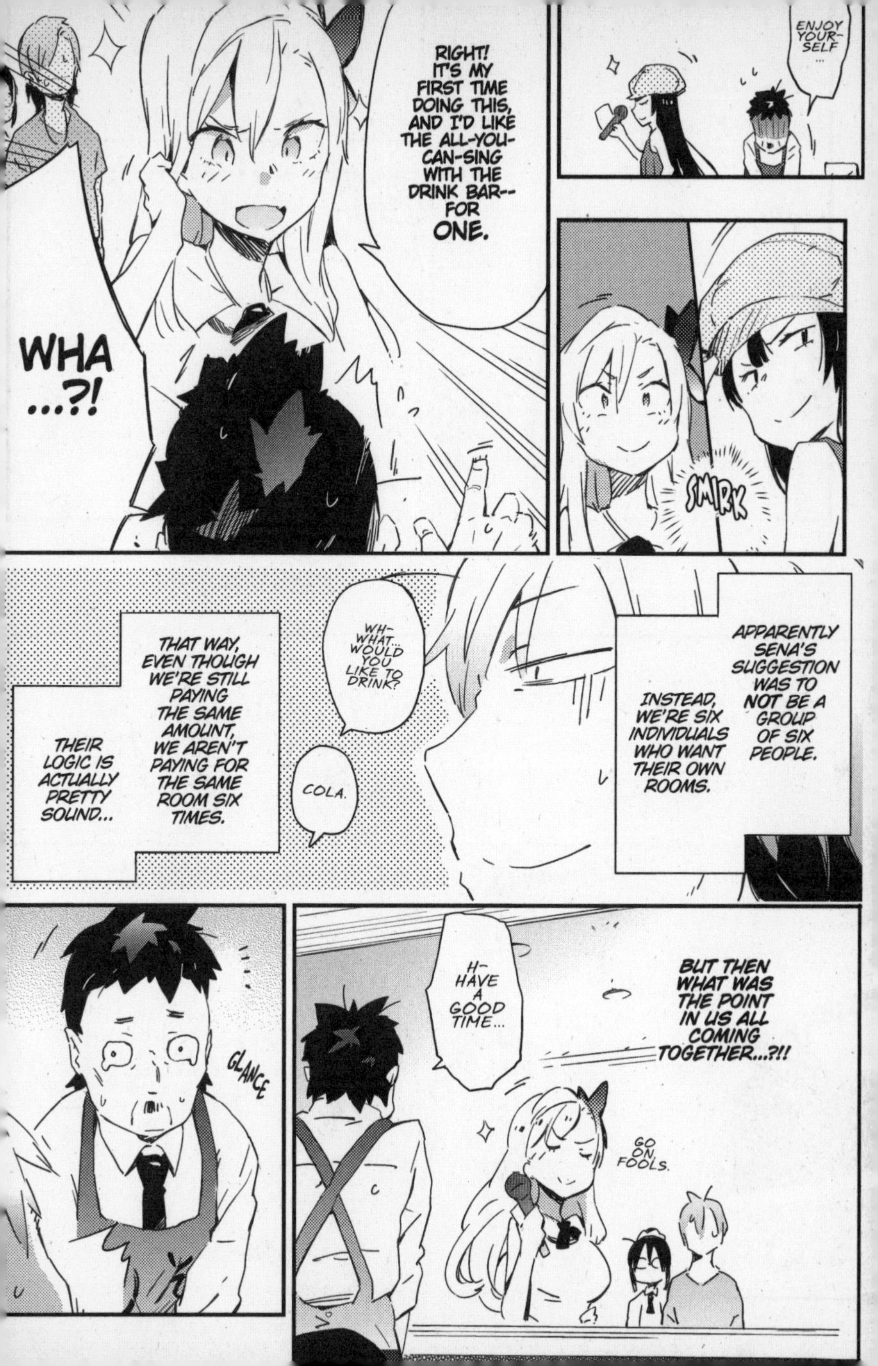

ENJOY YOURSELF...
SMIRK
RIGHT! IT'S MY FIRST TIME DOING THIS, AND I'D LIKE THE ALL-YOU-CAN-SING WITH THE DRINK BAR-- FOR ONE.
WHA...?!
APPARENTLY SENA'S SUGGESTION WAS TO NOT BE A GROUP OF SIX PEOPLE.
INSTEAD, WE'RE SIX INDIVIDUALS WHO WANT THEIR OWN ROOMS.
WH-WHAT... WOULD YOU LIKE TO DRINK?
COLA.
THAT WAY, EVEN THOUGH WE'RE STILL PAYING THE SAME AMOUNT, WE AREN'T PAYING FOR THE SAME ROOM SIX TIMES.
THEIR LOGIC IS ACTUALLY PRETTY SOUND...
BUT THEN WHAT WAS THE POINT IN US ALL COMING TOGETHER...?!!
H-HAVE A GOOD TIME...
GO ON, FOOLS.
GLANCE

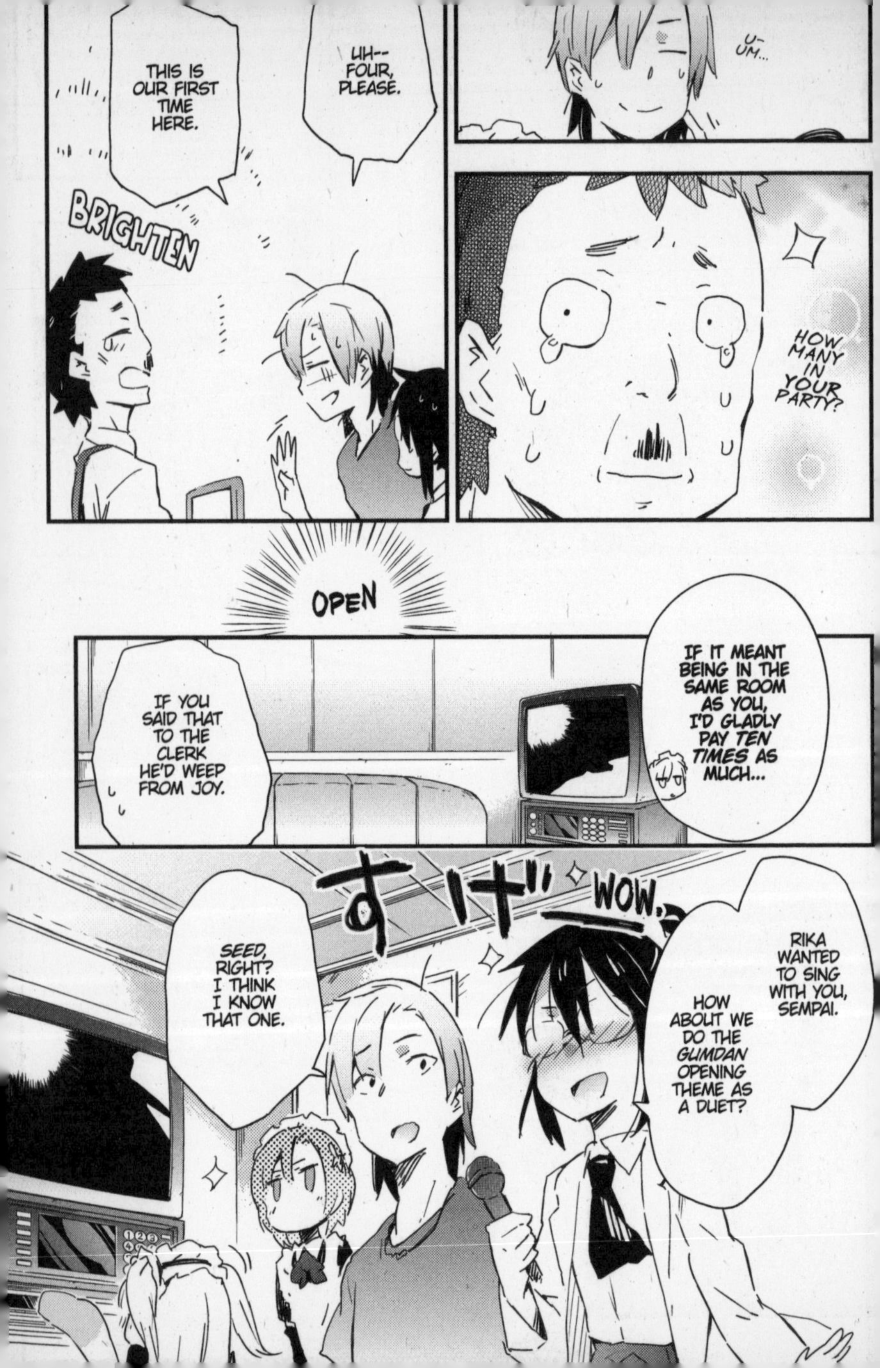
U-UM...
HOW MANY IN YOUR PARTY?
UH-- FOUR, PLEASE.
THIS IS OUR FIRST TIME HERE.
BRIGHTEN
OPEN
IF IT MEANT BEING IN THE SAME ROOM AS YOU, I'D GLADLY PAY *TEN TIMES* AS MUCH...
IF YOU SAID THAT TO THE CLERK HE'D WEEP FROM JOY.
RIKA WANTED TO SING WITH YOU, SEMPAI.
HOW ABOUT WE DO THE *GUMDAN* OPENING THEME AS A DUET?
WOW.
すげ
SEED, RIGHT? I THINK I KNOW THAT ONE.

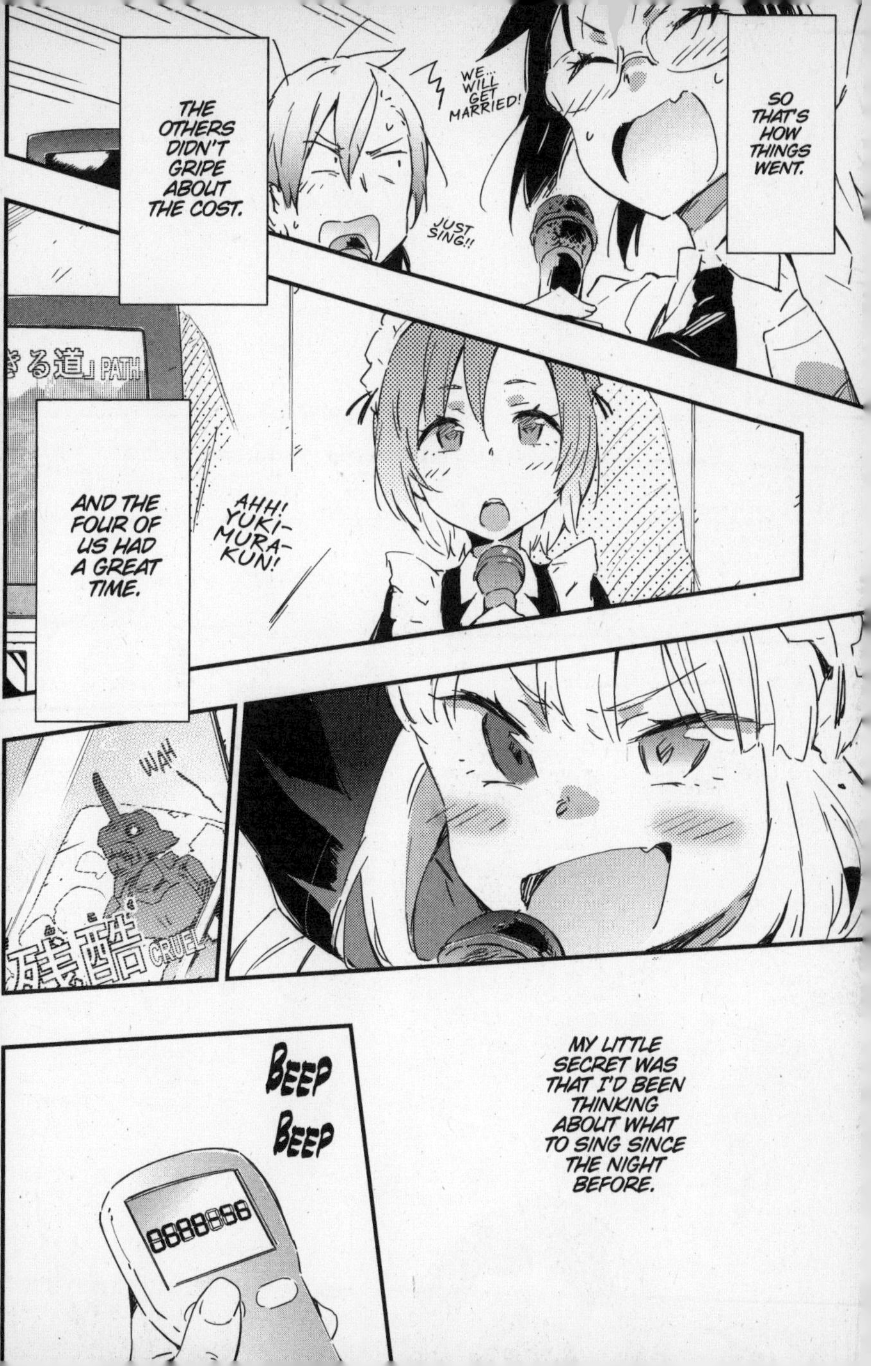
SO THAT'S HOW THINGS WENT.
WE... WILL GET MARRIED!
JUST SING!!
THE OTHERS DIDN'T GRIPE ABOUT THE COST.
AHH! YUKI-MURA-KUN!
きる道」PATH
AND THE FOUR OF US HAD A GREAT TIME.
WAH
残酷 CRUEL
MY LITTLE SECRET WAS THAT I'D BEEN THINKING ABOUT WHAT TO SING SINCE THE NIGHT BEFORE.
BEEP BEEP

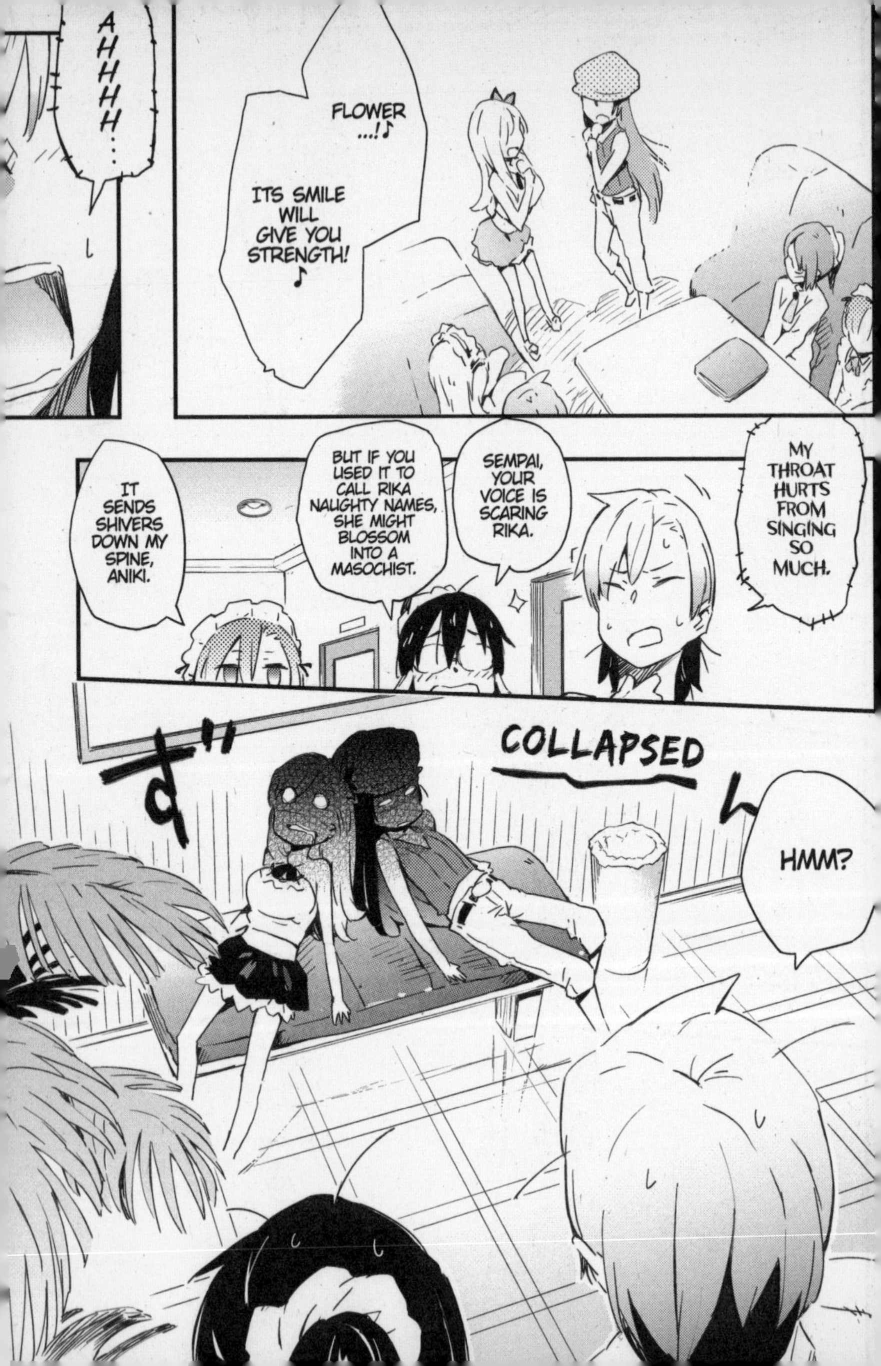
FLOWER ...!♪
ITS SMILE WILL GIVE YOU STRENGTH! ♪
AHHHHH...
MY THROAT HURTS FROM SINGING SO MUCH.
SEMPAI, YOUR VOICE IS SCARING RIKA.
BUT IF YOU USED IT TO CALL RIKA NAUGHTY NAMES, SHE MIGHT BLOSSOM INTO A MASOCHIST.
IT SENDS SHIVERS DOWN MY SPINE, ANIKI.
HMM?
COLLAPSED

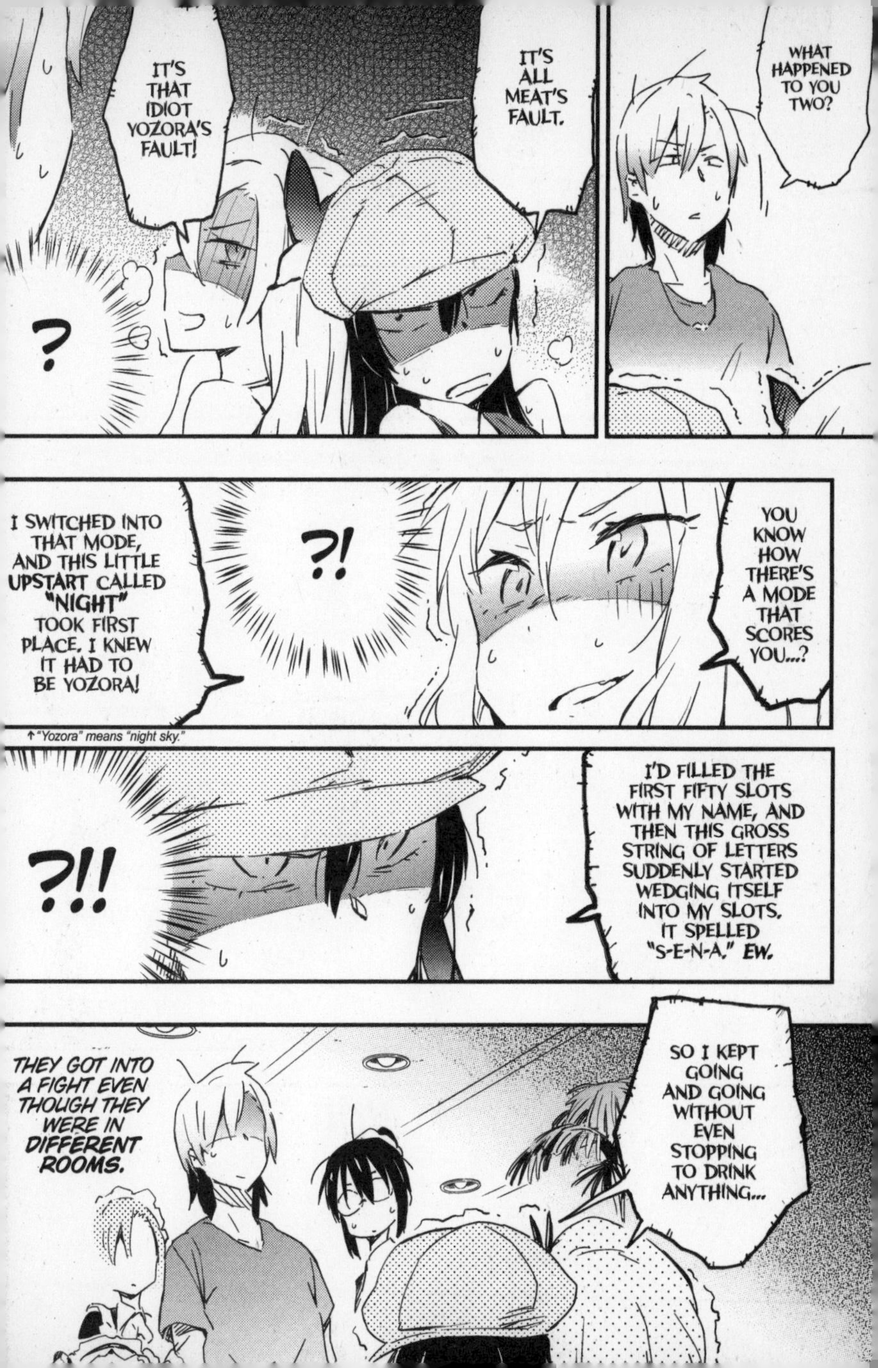

WHAT HAPPENED TO YOU TWO?
IT'S ALL MEAT'S FAULT.
IT'S THAT IDIOT YOZORA'S FAULT!
?
YOU KNOW HOW THERE'S A MODE THAT SCORES YOU...?
?!
I SWITCHED INTO THAT MODE, AND THIS LITTLE UPSTART CALLED "NIGHT" TOOK FIRST PLACE. I KNEW IT HAD TO BE YOZORA!
↑"Yozora" means "night sky."
I'D FILLED THE FIRST FIFTY SLOTS WITH MY NAME, AND THEN THIS GROSS STRING OF LETTERS SUDDENLY STARTED WEDGING ITSELF INTO MY SLOTS. IT SPELLED "S-E-N-A." EW.
?!!
SO I KEPT GOING AND GOING WITHOUT EVEN STOPPING TO DRINK ANYTHING...
THEY GOT INTO A FIGHT EVEN THOUGH THEY WERE IN DIFFERENT ROOMS.

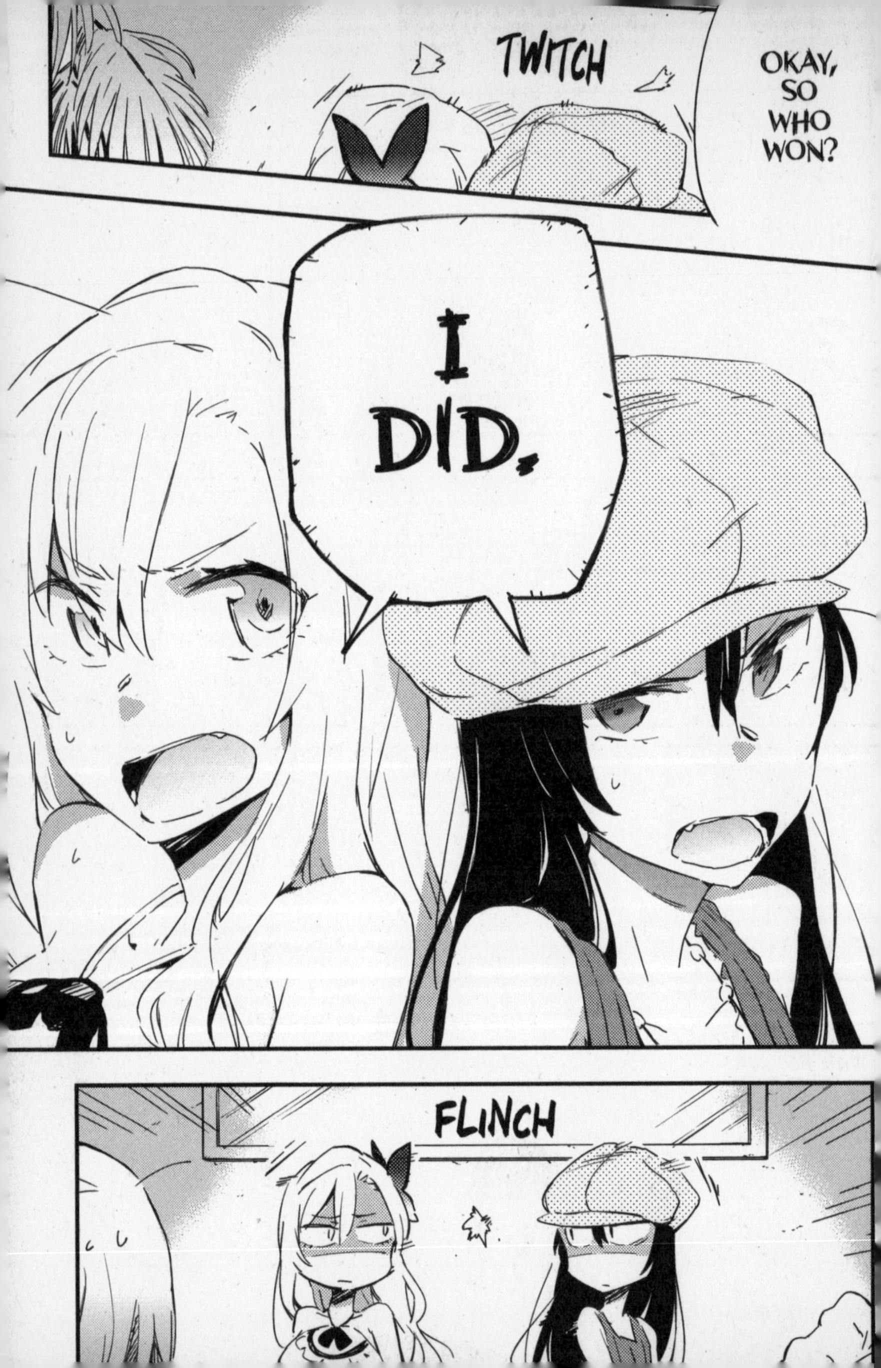
OKAY, SO WHO WON?
TWITCH
I DID.
FLINCH

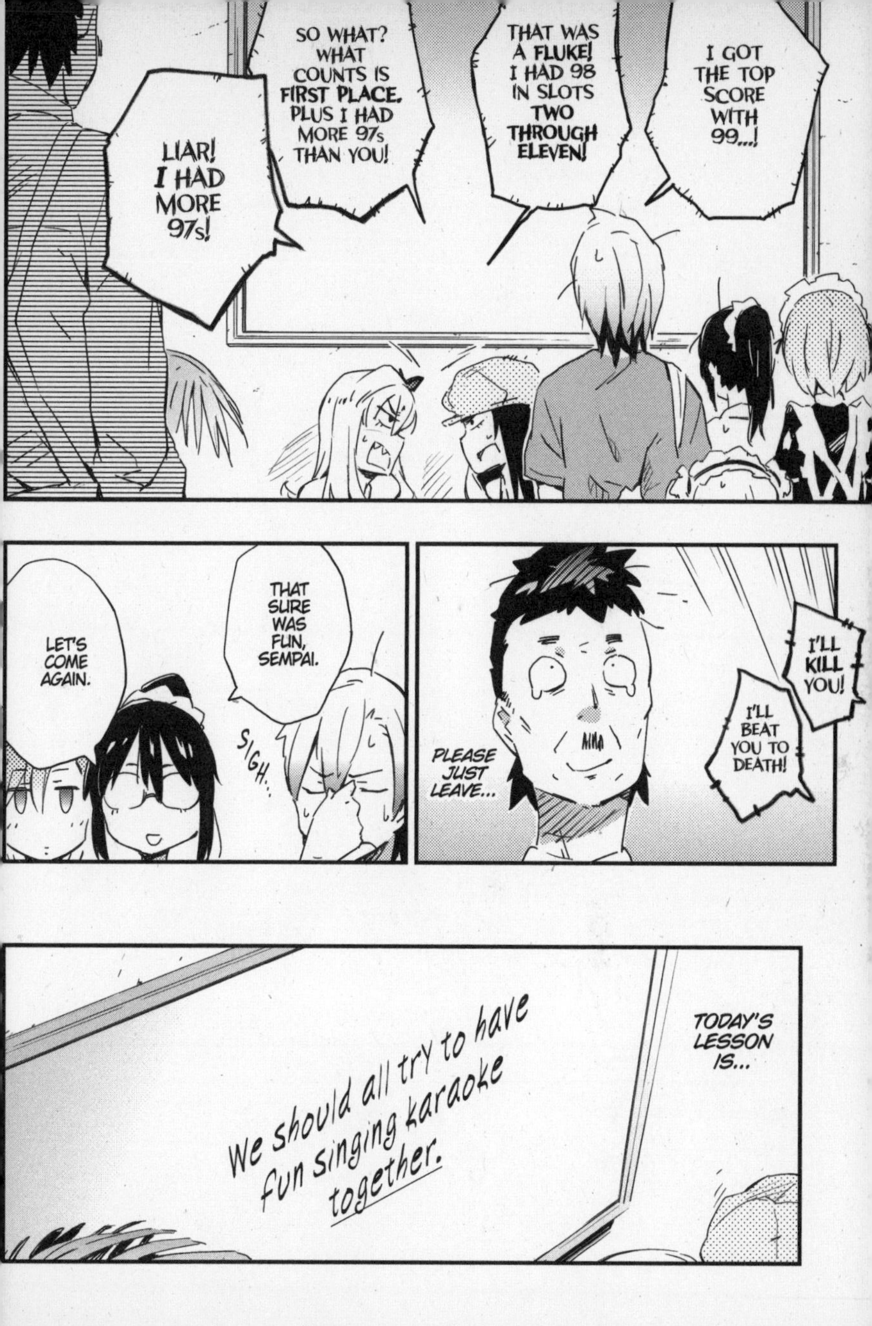
I GOT THE TOP SCORE WITH 99...!
THAT WAS A FLUKE! I HAD 98 IN SLOTS TWO THROUGH ELEVEN!
SO WHAT? WHAT COUNTS IS FIRST PLACE. PLUS I HAD MORE 97s THAN YOU!
LIAR! I HAD MORE 97s!
I'LL KILL YOU!
I'LL BEAT YOU TO DEATH!
PLEASE JUST LEAVE...
THAT SURE WAS FUN, SEMPAI.
SIGH...
LET'S COME AGAIN.
TODAY'S LESSON IS...
We should all try to have fun singing karaoke together.

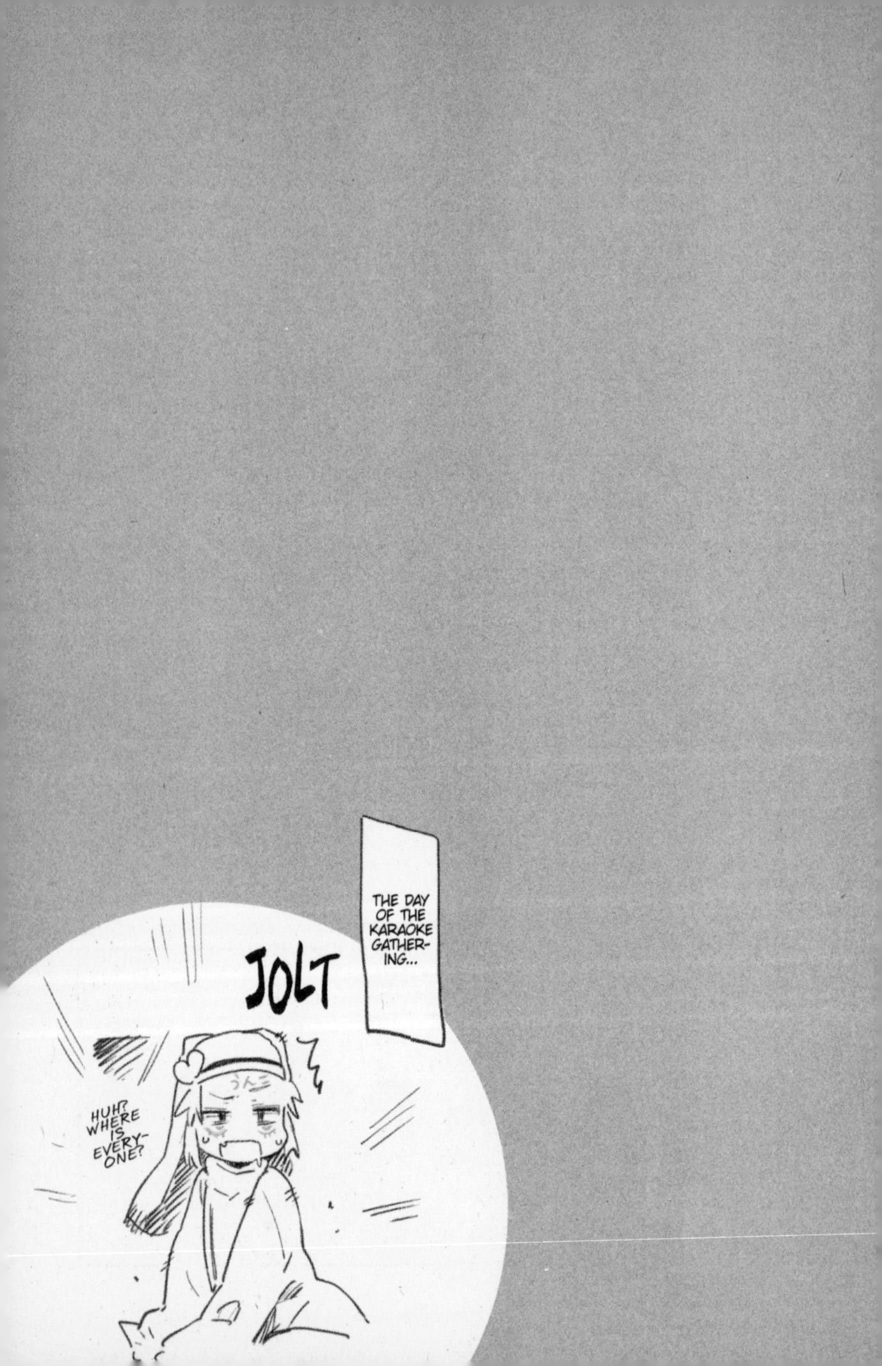
THE DAY OF THE KARAOKE GATHER-ING...
JOLT
HUH? WHERE IS EVERY-ONE?

Haganai

I don't have many friends

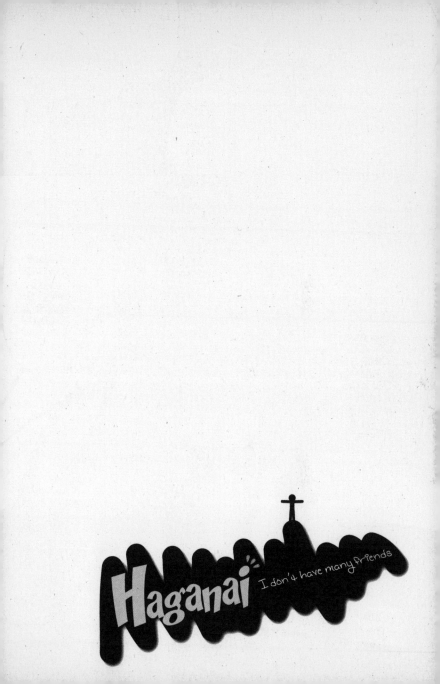

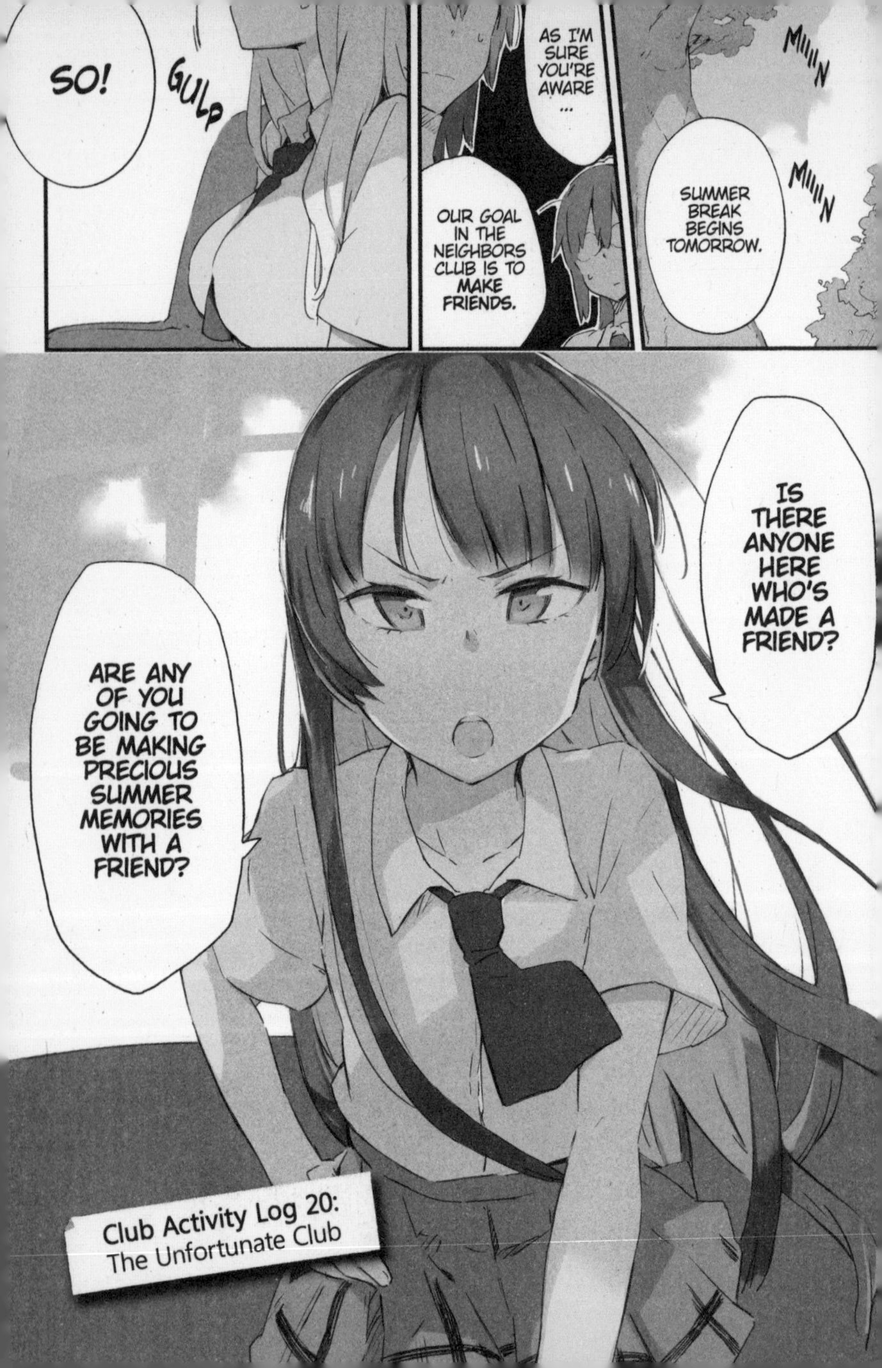
MIIIN
SUMMER BREAK BEGINS TOMORROW.
MIIIN
AS I'M SURE YOU'RE AWARE ...
OUR GOAL IN THE NEIGHBORS CLUB IS TO MAKE FRIENDS.
GULP
SO!
IS THERE ANYONE HERE WHO'S MADE A FRIEND?
ARE ANY OF YOU GOING TO BE MAKING PRECIOUS SUMMER MEMORIES WITH A FRIEND?
Club Activity Log 20:
The Unfortunate Club

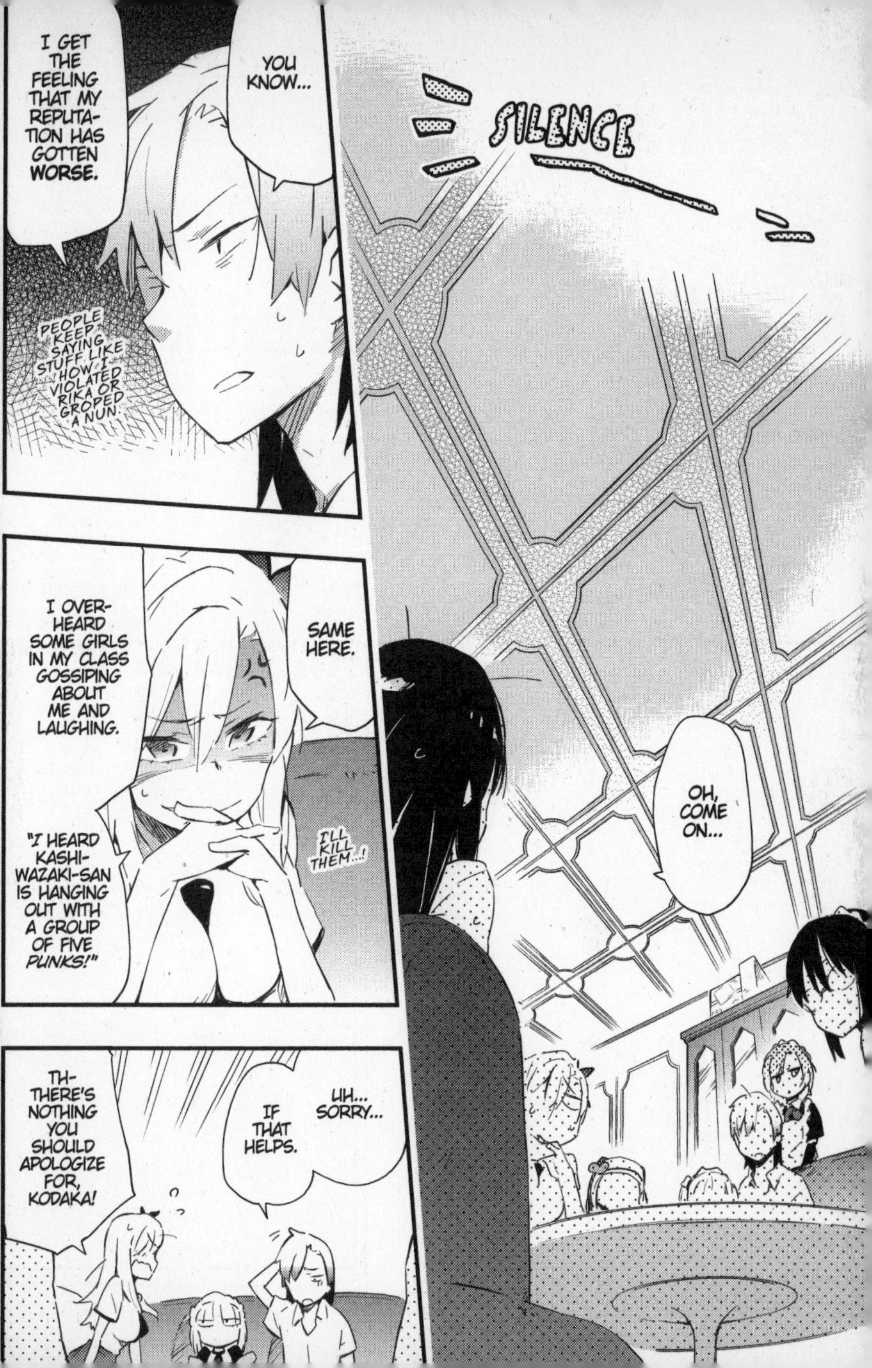
SILENCE
OH, COME ON...
YOU KNOW...
I GET THE FEELING THAT MY REPUTATION HAS GOTTEN WORSE.
PEOPLE KEEP SAYING STUFF LIKE HOW I VIOLATED RIKA OR GROPED A NUN.
SAME HERE.
I OVERHEARD SOME GIRLS IN MY CLASS GOSSIPING ABOUT ME AND LAUGHING.
"I HEARD KASHIWAZAKI-SAN IS HANGING OUT WITH A GROUP OF FIVE PUNKS!"
I'LL KILL THEM...!
UH... SORRY...
IF THAT HELPS.
TH-THERE'S NOTHING YOU SHOULD APOLOGIZE FOR, KODAKA!

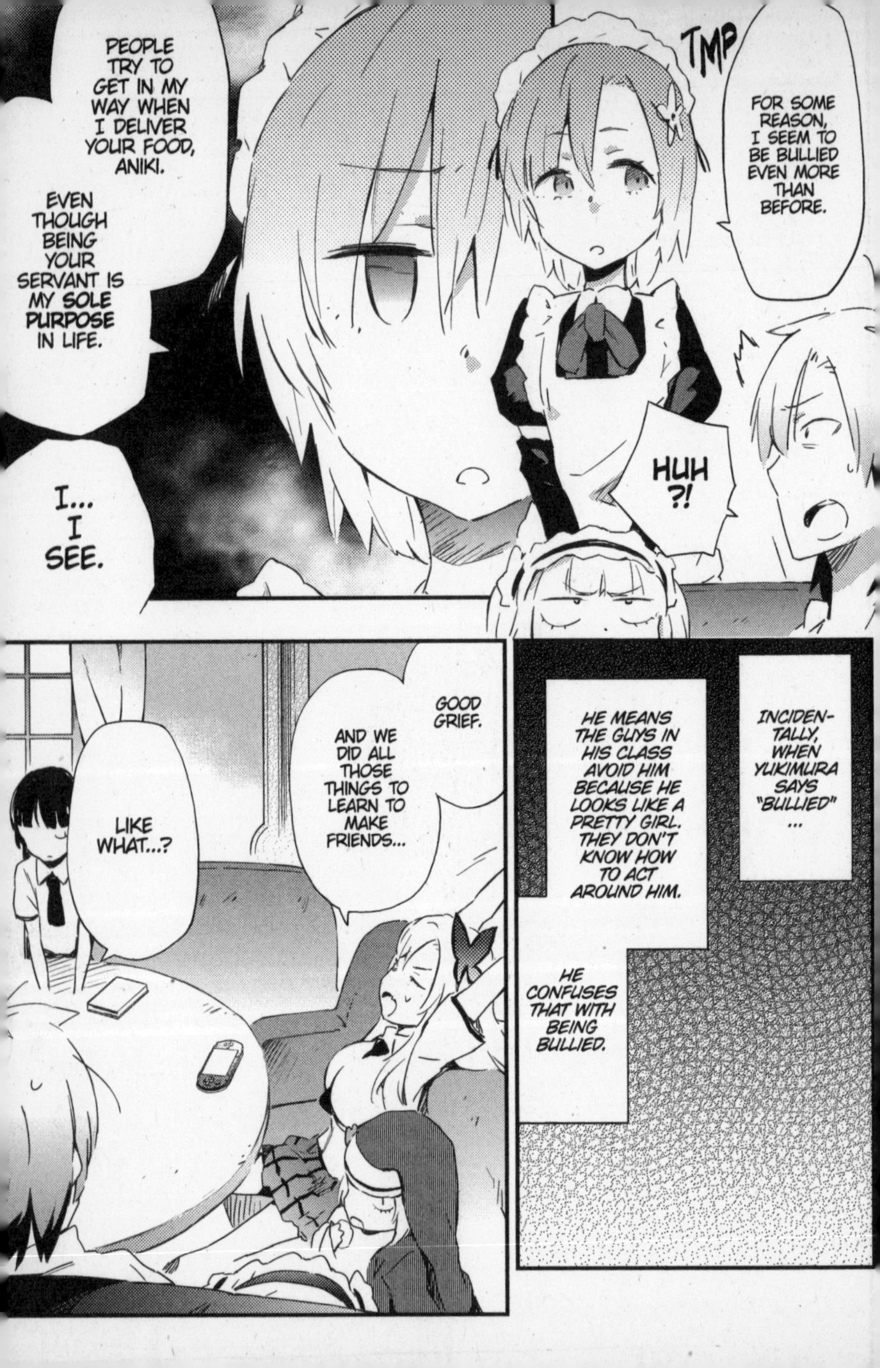
TMP
FOR SOME REASON, I SEEM TO BE BULLIED EVEN MORE THAN BEFORE.
PEOPLE TRY TO GET IN MY WAY WHEN I DELIVER YOUR FOOD, ANIKI.
EVEN THOUGH BEING YOUR SERVANT IS MY SOLE PURPOSE IN LIFE.
HUH ?!
I... I SEE.
INCIDENTALLY, WHEN YUKIMURA SAYS "BULLIED"...
HE MEANS THE GUYS IN HIS CLASS AVOID HIM BECAUSE HE LOOKS LIKE A PRETTY GIRL. THEY DON'T KNOW HOW TO ACT AROUND HIM.
HE CONFUSES THAT WITH BEING BULLIED.
GOOD GRIEF.
AND WE DID ALL THOSE THINGS TO LEARN TO MAKE FRIENDS...
LIKE WHAT...?

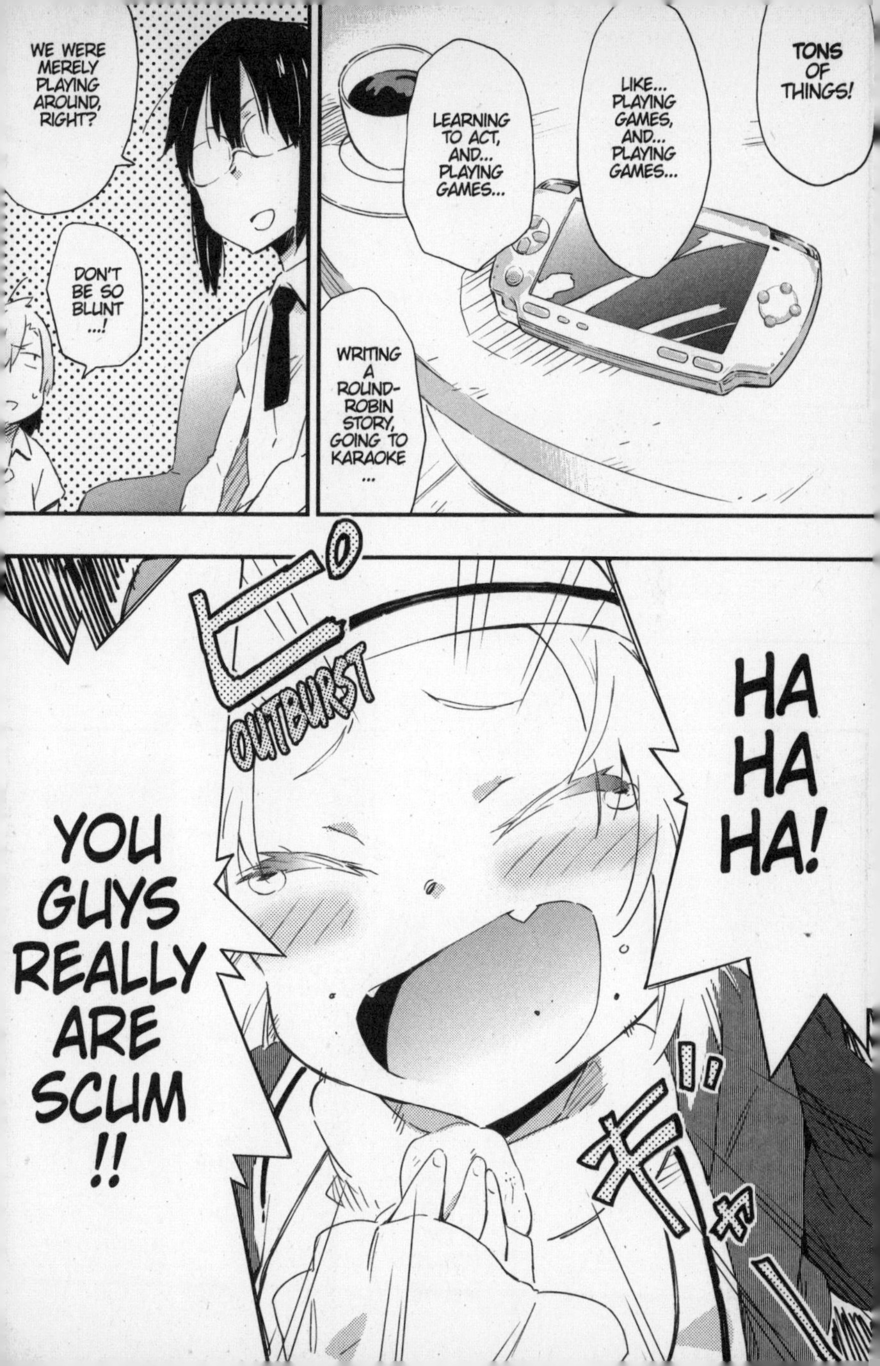
TONS OF THINGS!
LIKE... PLAYING GAMES, AND... PLAYING GAMES...
LEARNING TO ACT, AND... PLAYING GAMES...
WRITING A ROUND-ROBIN STORY, GOING TO KARAOKE ...
WE WERE MERELY PLAYING AROUND, RIGHT?
DON'T BE SO BLUNT ...!
HA HA HA!
OUTBURST
YOU GUYS REALLY ARE SCUM !!

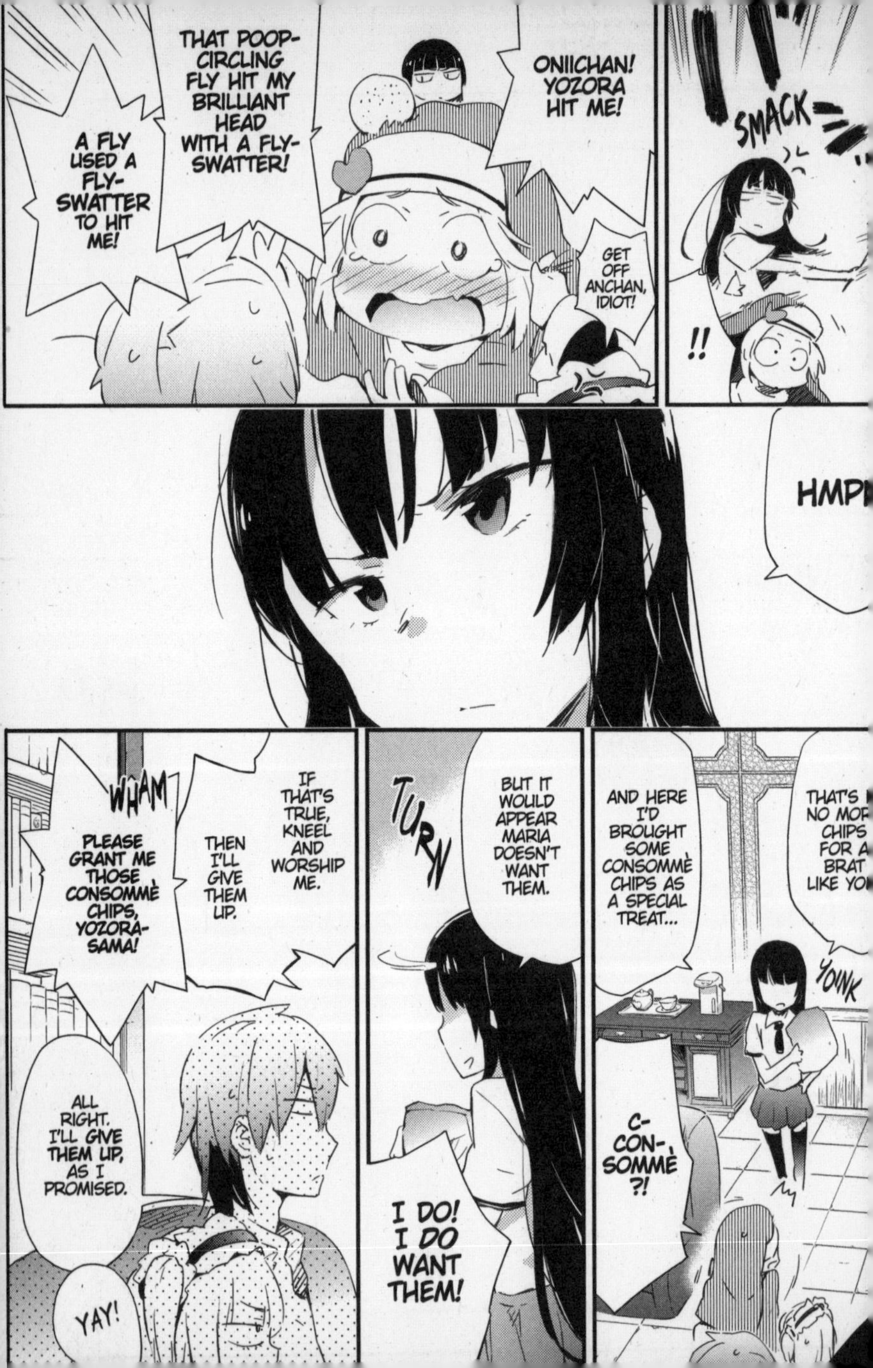
SMACK
!!
GET OFF ANCHAN, IDIOT!
ONIICHAN! YOZORA HIT ME!
THAT POOP-CIRCLING FLY HIT MY BRILLIANT HEAD WITH A FLY-SWATTER!
A FLY USED A FLY-SWATTER TO HIT ME!
HMP
THAT'S NO MOR CHIPS FOR A BRAT LIKE YO
AND HERE I'D BROUGHT SOME CONSOMMÈ CHIPS AS A SPECIAL TREAT...
YOINK
C-CON-, SOMMÈ?!
TURN
BUT IT WOULD APPEAR MARIA DOESN'T WANT THEM.
I DO! I DO WANT THEM!
IF THAT'S TRUE, KNEEL AND WORSHIP ME.
THEN I'LL GIVE THEM UP.
WHAM
PLEASE GRANT ME THOSE CONSOMMÈ CHIPS, YOZORA-SAMA!
ALL RIGHT. I'LL GIVE THEM UP, AS I PROMISED.
YAY!

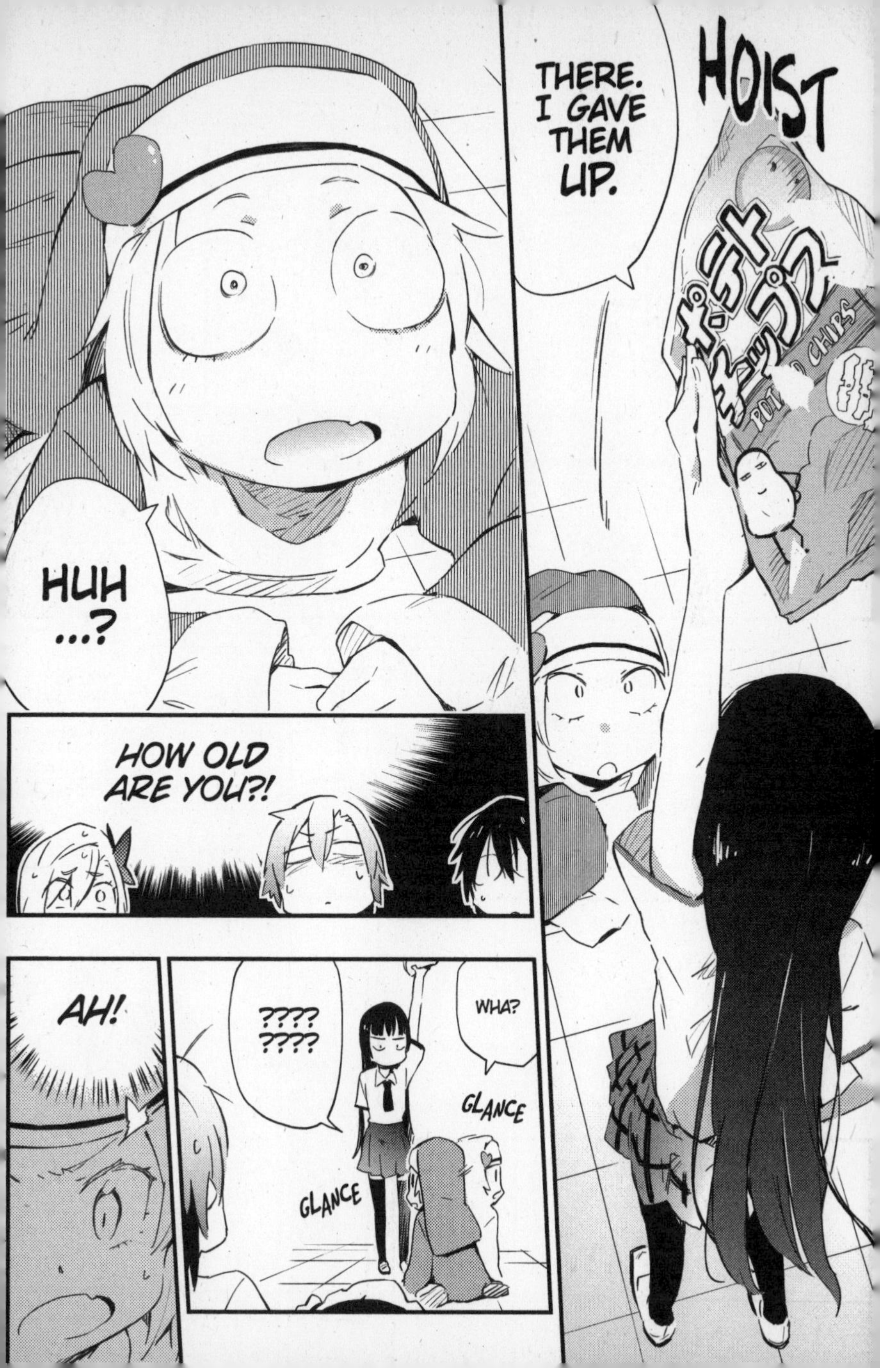
HOIST
THERE. I GAVE THEM UP.
HUH ...?
HOW OLD ARE YOU?!
WHA?
???? ????
GLANCE
GLANCE
AH!

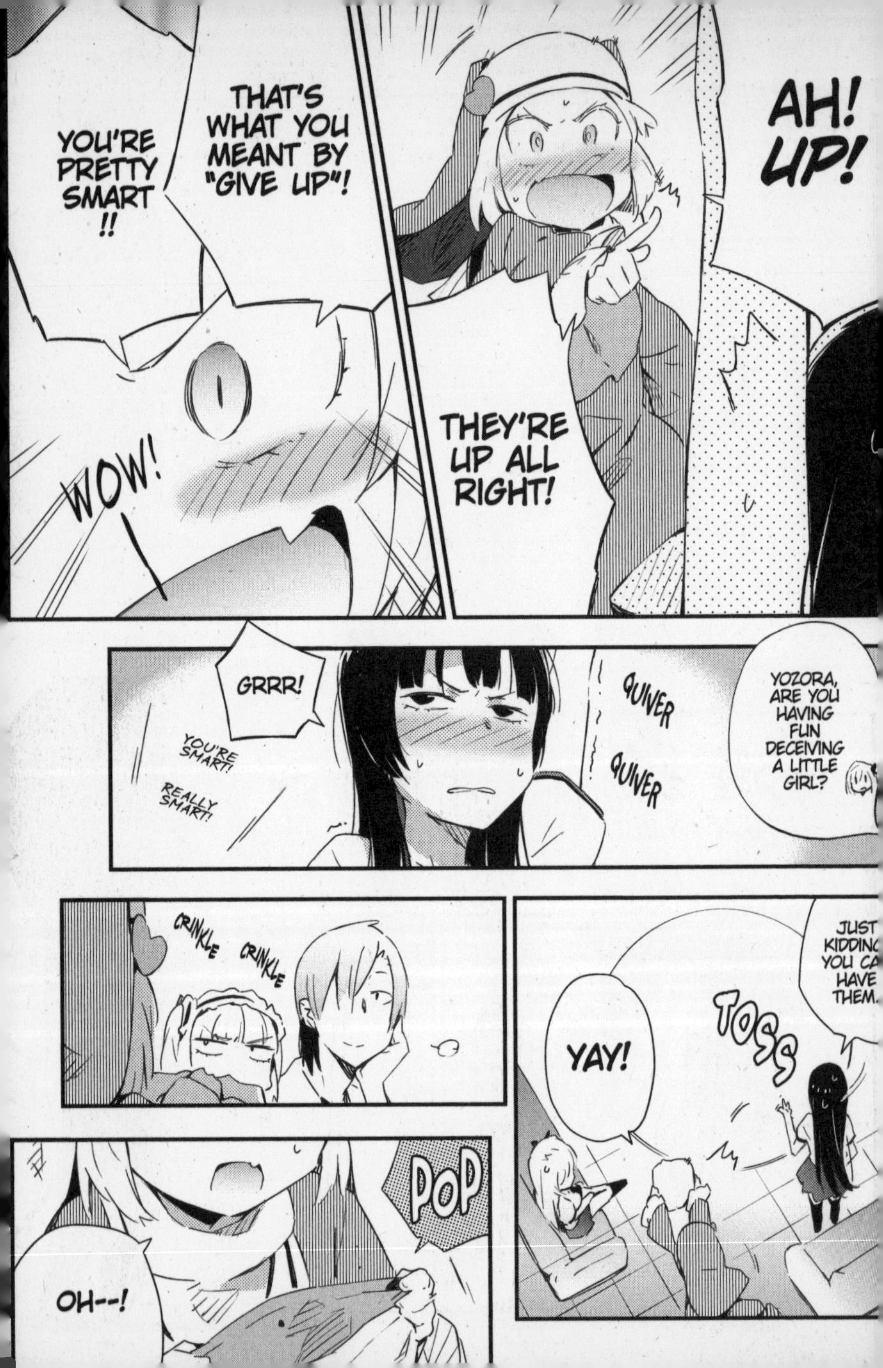
AH! UP!
THEY'RE UP ALL RIGHT!
THAT'S WHAT YOU MEANT BY "GIVE UP"!
YOU'RE PRETTY SMART !!
WOW!
YOZORA, ARE YOU HAVING FUN DECEIVING A LITTLE GIRL?
QUIVER
QUIVER
GRRR!
YOU'RE SMART!
REALLY SMART!
JUST KIDDIN YOU CA HAVE THEM.
TOSS
YAY!
CRINKLE
CRINKLE
POP
OH--!

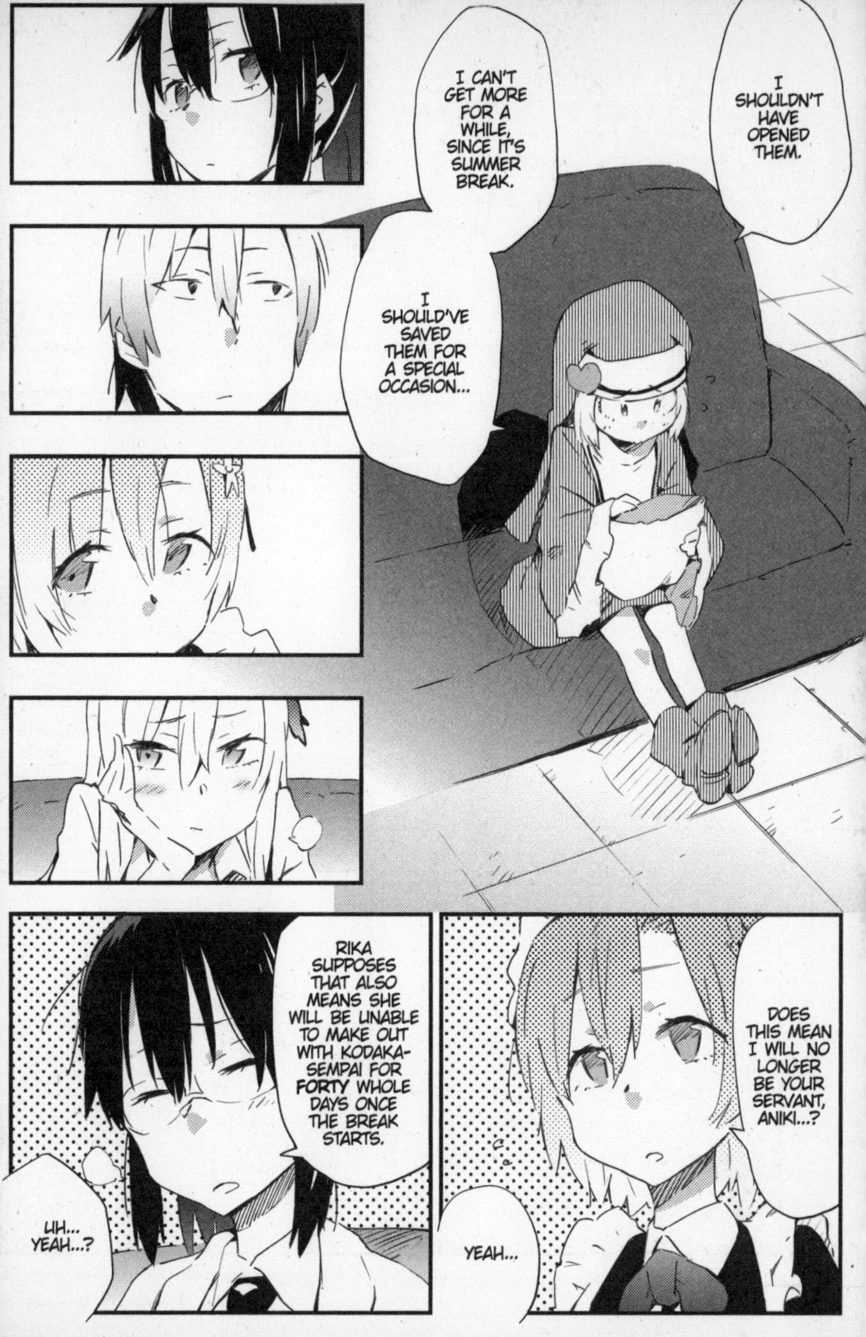
I SHOULDN'T HAVE OPENED THEM.
I CAN'T GET MORE FOR A WHILE, SINCE IT'S SUMMER BREAK.
I SHOULD'VE SAVED THEM FOR A SPECIAL OCCASION...
DOES THIS MEAN I WILL NO LONGER BE YOUR SERVANT, ANIKI...?
YEAH...
RIKA SUPPOSES THAT ALSO MEANS SHE WILL BE UNABLE TO MAKE OUT WITH KODAKA-SEMPAI FOR FORTY WHOLE DAYS ONCE THE BREAK STARTS.
UH... YEAH...?

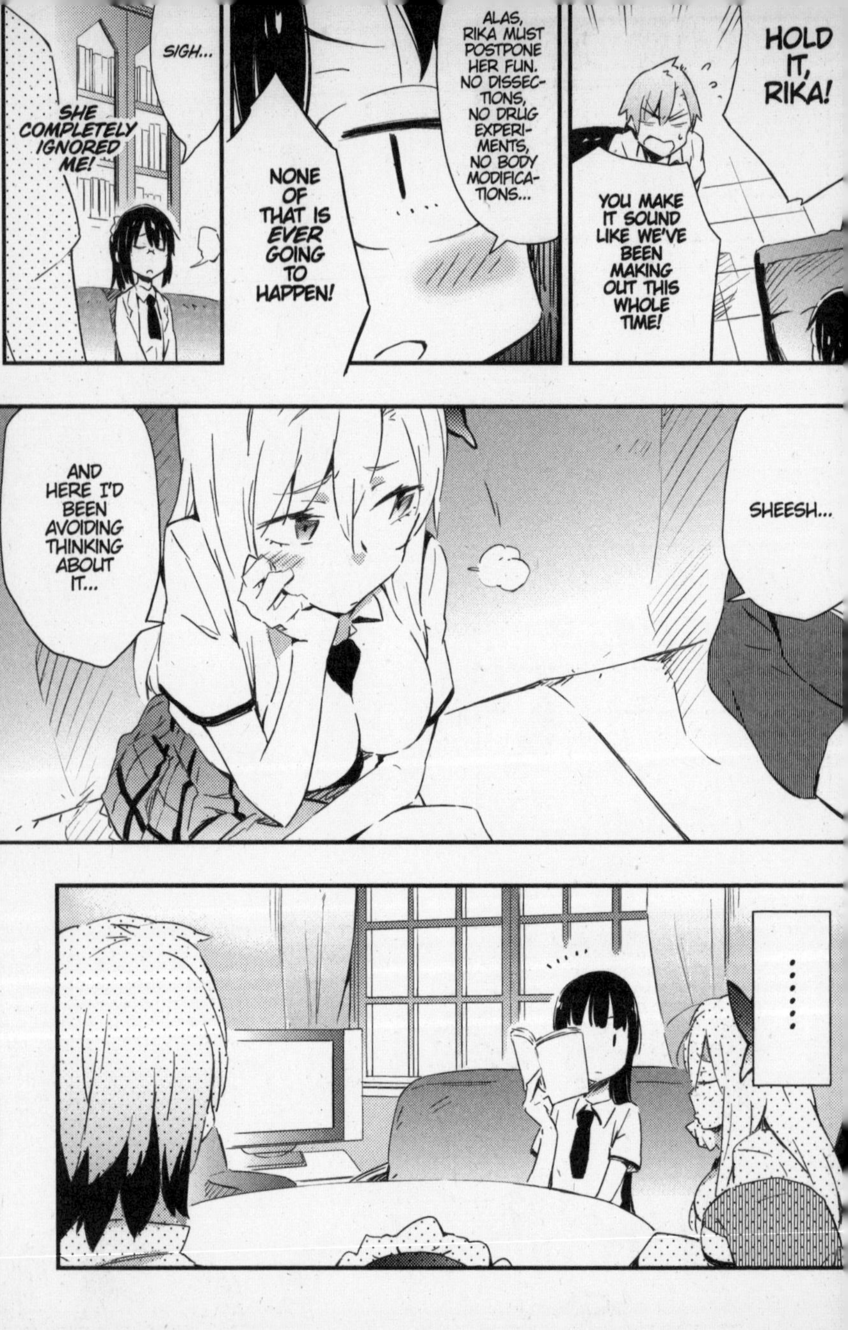
HOLD IT, RIKA!
YOU MAKE IT SOUND LIKE WE'VE BEEN MAKING OUT THIS WHOLE TIME!
ALAS, RIKA MUST POSTPONE HER FUN. NO DISSECTIONS, NO DRUG EXPERIMENTS, NO BODY MODIFICATIONS...
NONE OF THAT IS EVER GOING TO HAPPEN!
SIGH...
SHE COMPLETELY IGNORED ME!
SHEESH...
AND HERE I'D BEEN AVOIDING THINKING ABOUT IT...
......

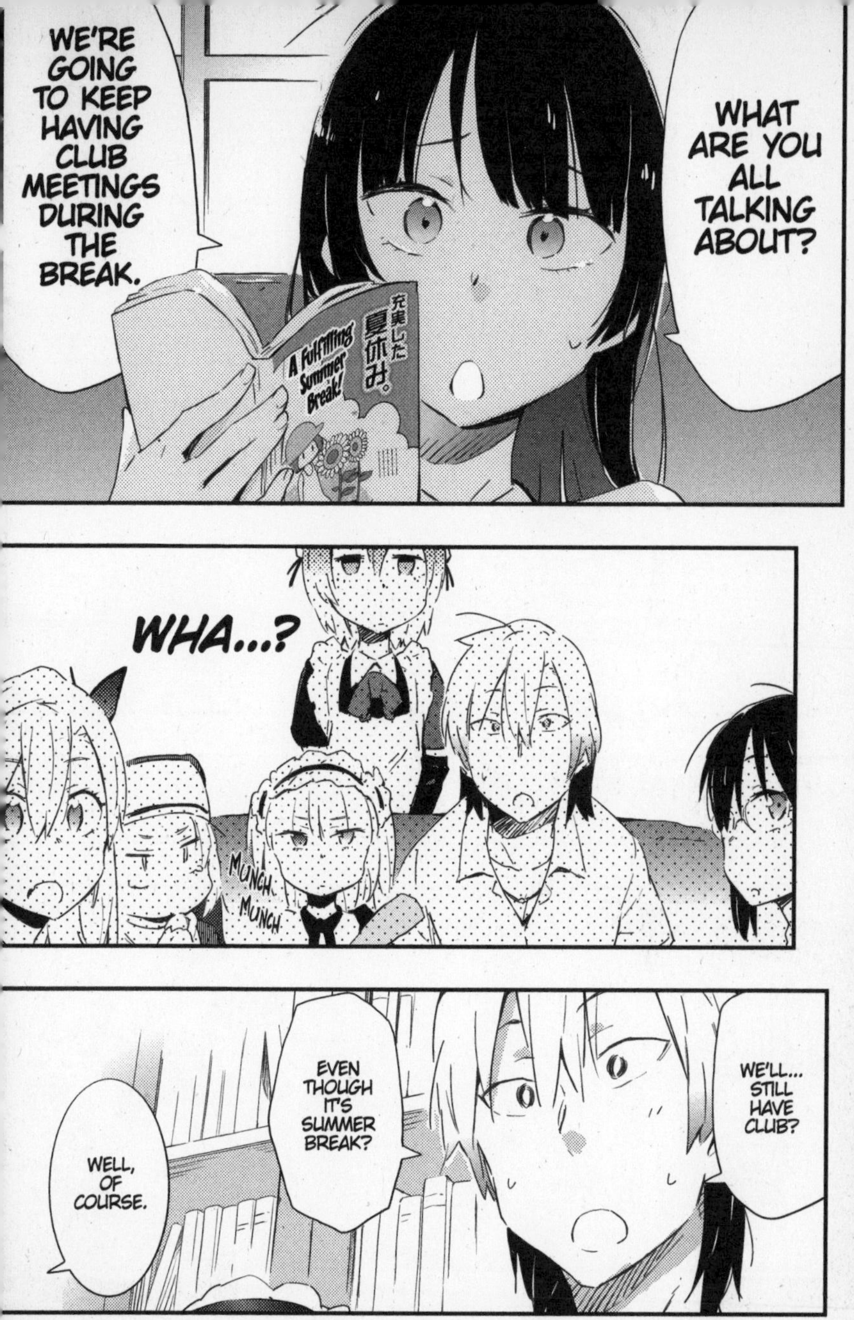
WHAT ARE YOU ALL TALKING ABOUT?
WE'RE GOING TO KEEP HAVING CLUB MEETINGS DURING THE BREAK.
充実した夏休み。
A Fulfilling Summer Break!
WHA...?
MUNCH MUNCH
WE'LL... STILL HAVE CLUB?
EVEN THOUGH IT'S SUMMER BREAK?
WELL, OF COURSE.

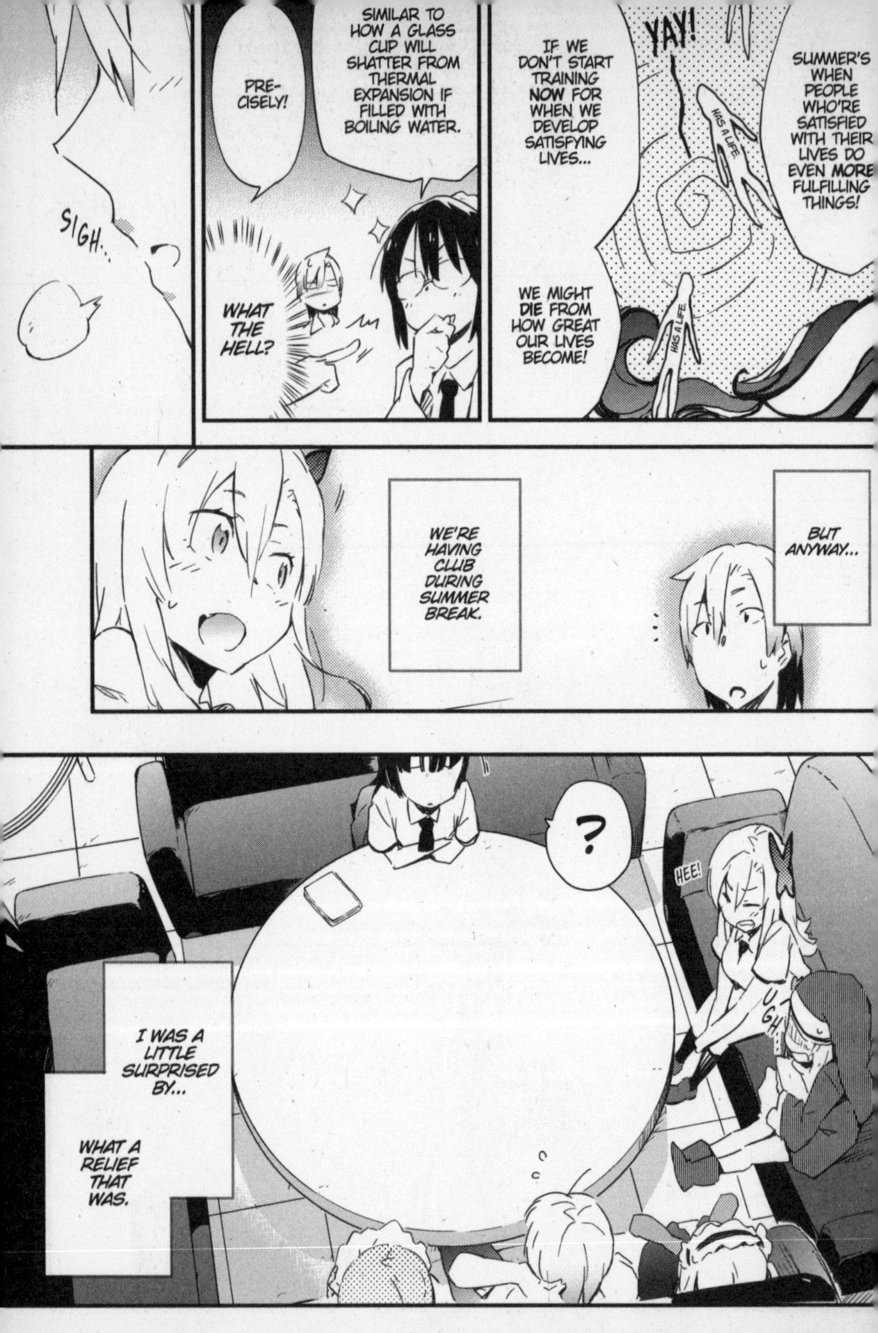
YAY!
SUMMER'S WHEN PEOPLE WHO'RE SATISFIED WITH THEIR LIVES DO EVEN MORE FULFILLING THINGS!
HAS A LIFE
HAS A LIFE
IF WE DON'T START TRAINING NOW FOR WHEN WE DEVELOP SATISFYING LIVES...
WE MIGHT DIE FROM HOW GREAT OUR LIVES BECOME!
SIMILAR TO HOW A GLASS CUP WILL SHATTER FROM THERMAL EXPANSION IF FILLED WITH BOILING WATER.
PRE-CISELY!
WHAT THE HELL?
SIGH...
BUT ANYWAY...
WE'RE HAVING CLUB DURING SUMMER BREAK.
?
HEE!
UGH
I WAS A LITTLE SURPRISED BY...
WHAT A RELIEF THAT WAS.

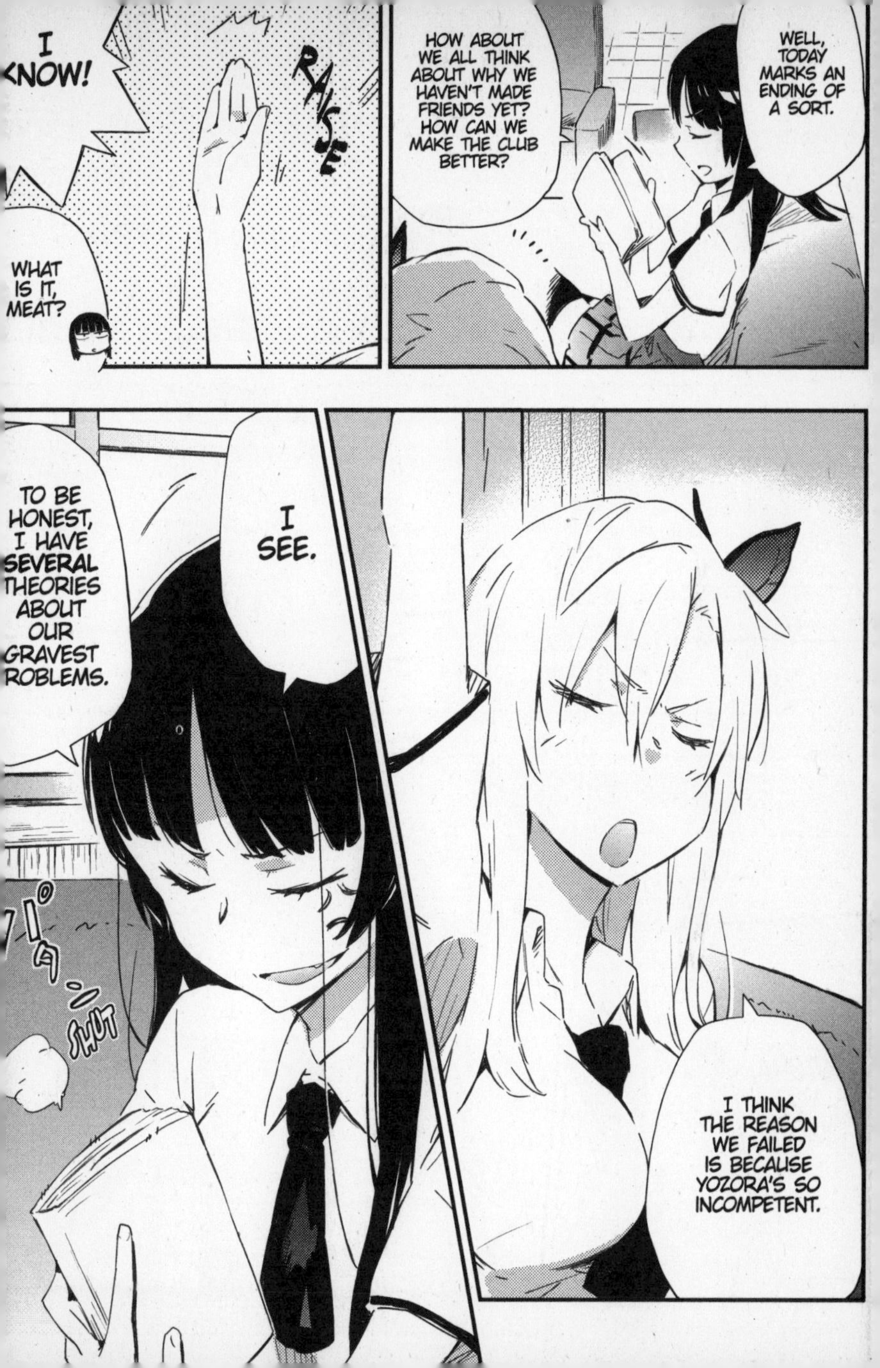
WELL, TODAY MARKS AN ENDING OF A SORT.
HOW ABOUT WE ALL THINK ABOUT WHY WE HAVEN'T MADE FRIENDS YET? HOW CAN WE MAKE THE CLUB BETTER?
I KNOW!
RAISE
WHAT IS IT, MEAT?
I THINK THE REASON WE FAILED IS BECAUSE YOZORA'S SO INCOMPETENT.
I SEE.
TO BE HONEST, I HAVE SEVERAL THEORIES ABOUT OUR GRAVEST ROBLEMS.
SHUT

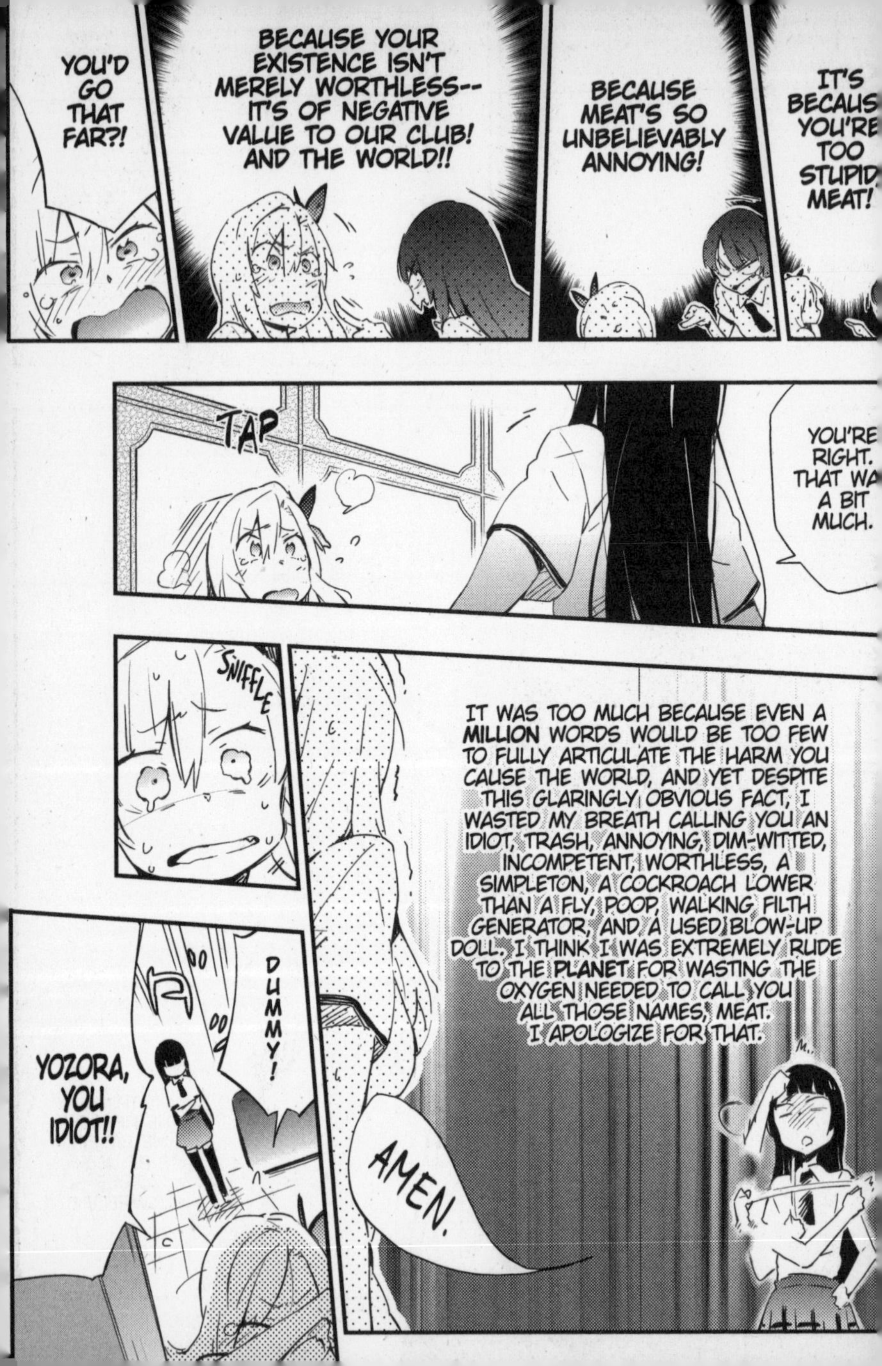
IT'S BECAUS YOU'RE TOO STUPID MEAT!
BECAUSE MEAT'S SO UNBELIEVABLY ANNOYING!
BECAUSE YOUR EXISTENCE ISN'T MERELY WORTHLESS-- IT'S OF NEGATIVE VALUE TO OUR CLUB! AND THE WORLD!!
YOU'D GO THAT FAR?!
YOU'RE RIGHT. THAT WA A BIT MUCH.
TAP
IT WAS TOO MUCH BECAUSE EVEN A MILLION WORDS WOULD BE TOO FEW TO FULLY ARTICULATE THE HARM YOU CAUSE THE WORLD, AND YET DESPITE THIS GLARINGLY OBVIOUS FACT, I WASTED MY BREATH CALLING YOU AN IDIOT, TRASH, ANNOYING, DIM-WITTED, INCOMPETENT, WORTHLESS, A SIMPLETON, A COCKROACH LOWER THAN A FLY, POOP, WALKING FILTH GENERATOR, AND A USED BLOW-UP DOLL. I THINK I WAS EXTREMELY RUDE TO THE PLANET FOR WASTING THE OXYGEN NEEDED TO CALL YOU ALL THOSE NAMES, MEAT. I APOLOGIZE FOR THAT.
AMEN.
SNIFFLE
DUMMY!
YOZORA, YOU IDIOT!!

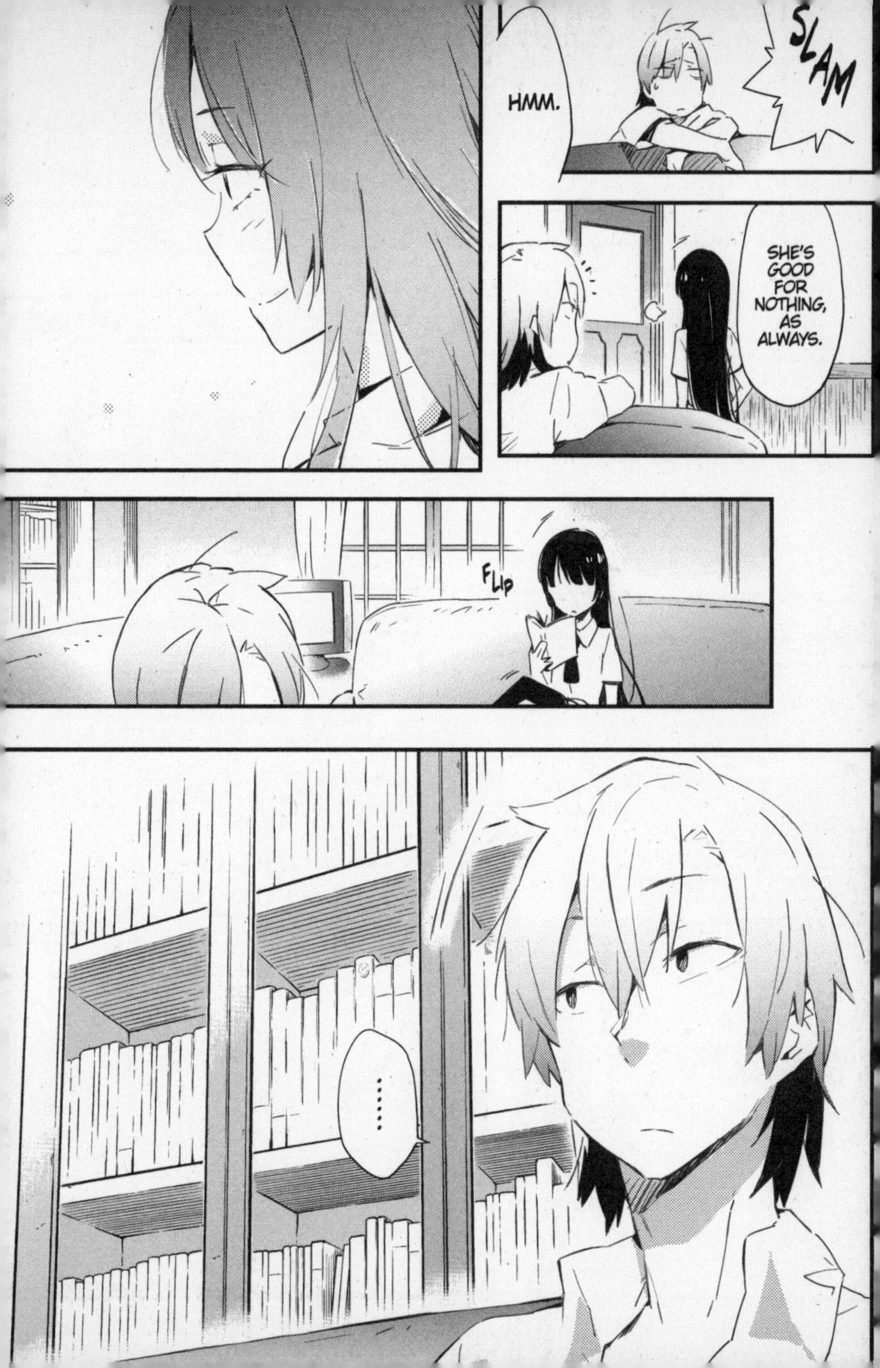
SLAM
HMM.
SHE'S GOOD FOR NOTHING, AS ALWAYS.
FLIP
......

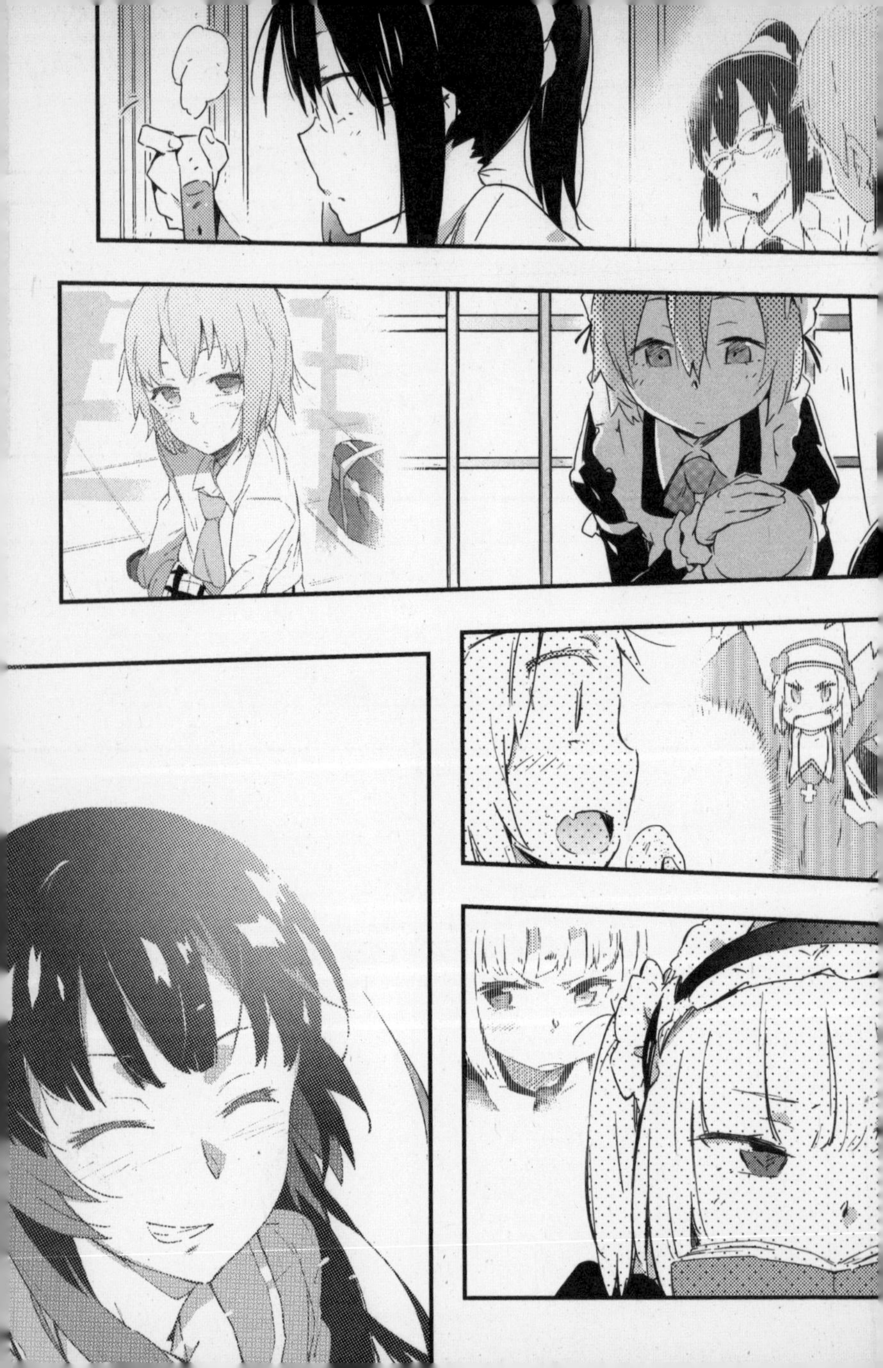

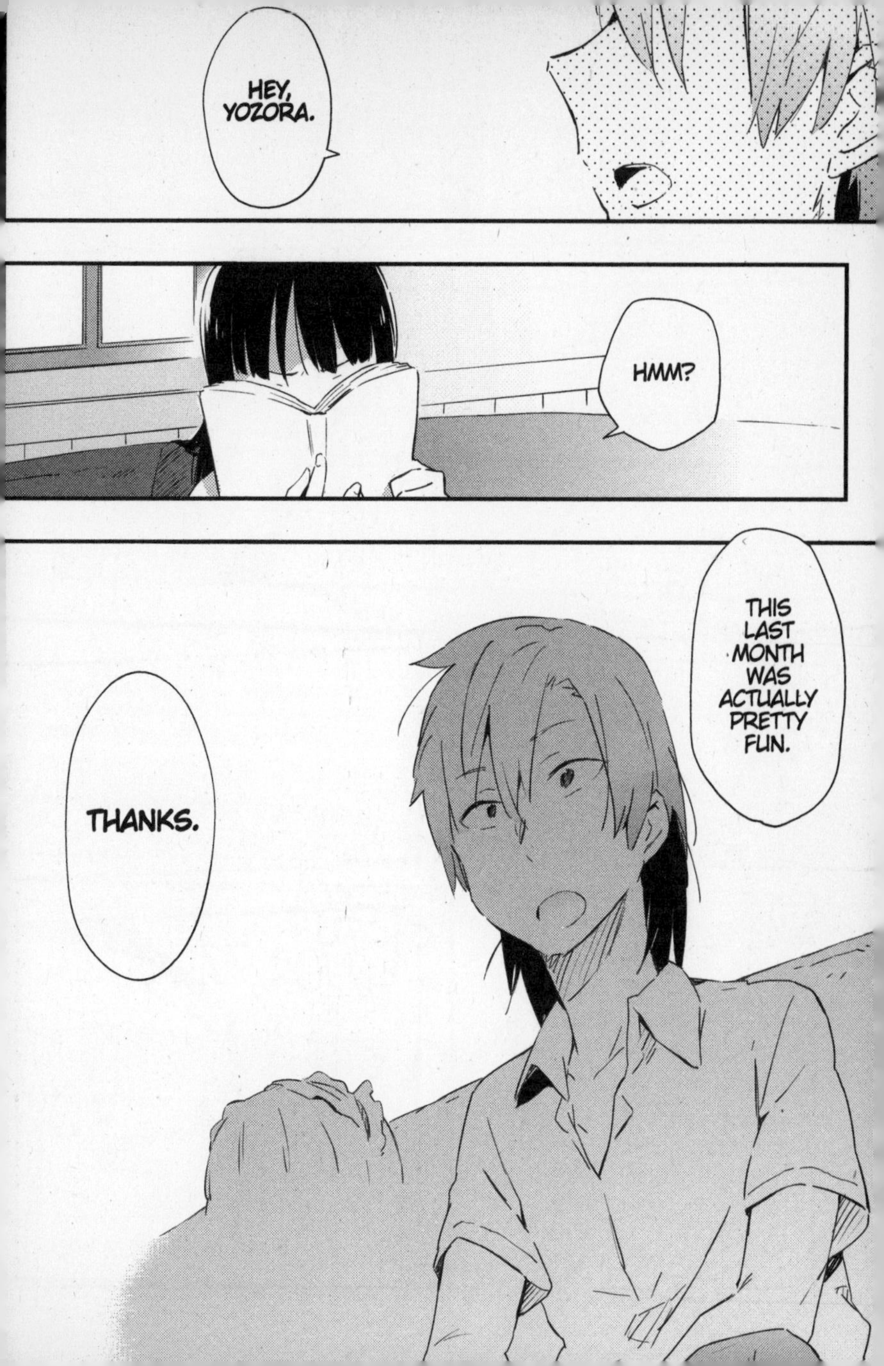
HEY, YOZORA.
HMM?
THIS LAST MONTH WAS ACTUALLY PRETTY FUN.
THANKS.

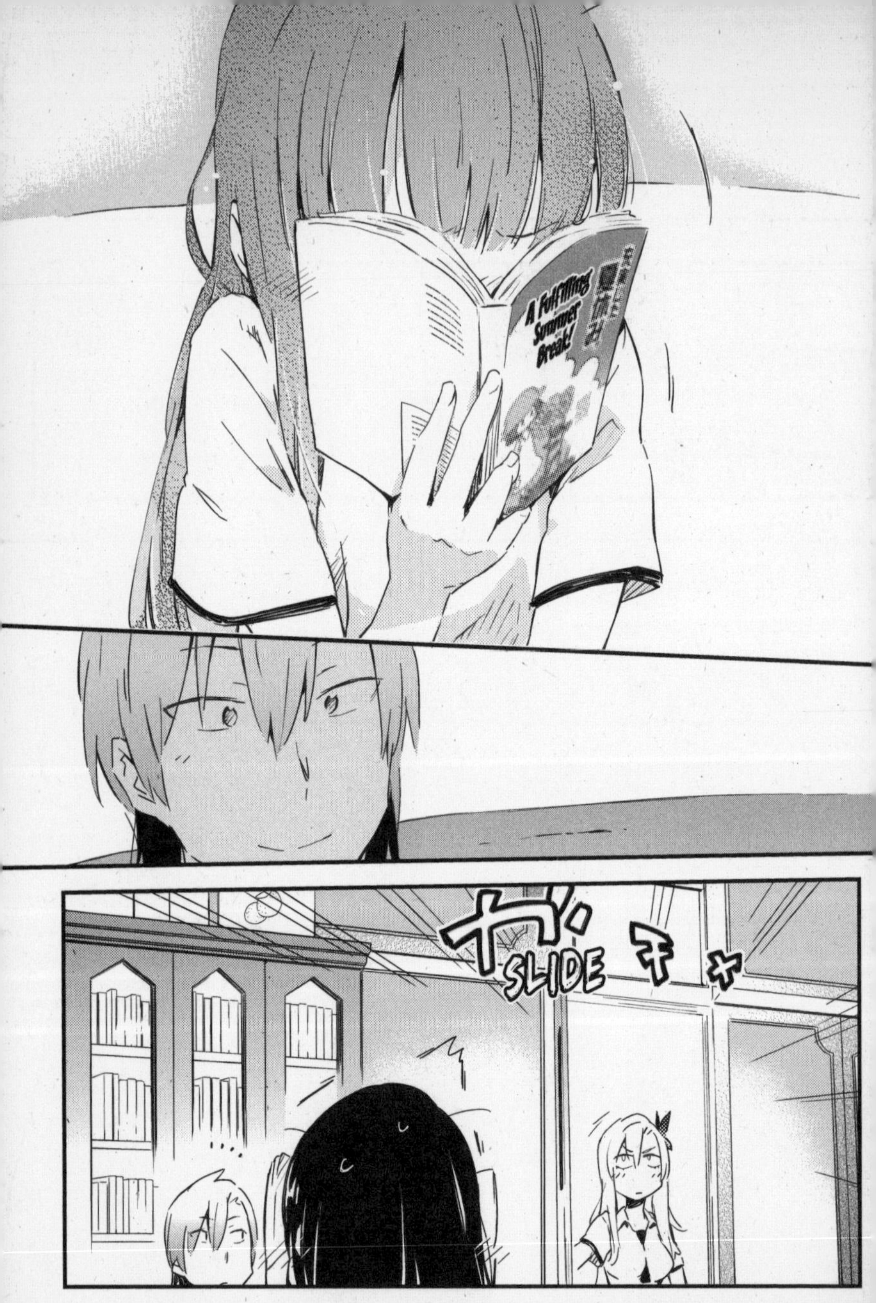
A Fulfilling Summer Break!
SLIDE

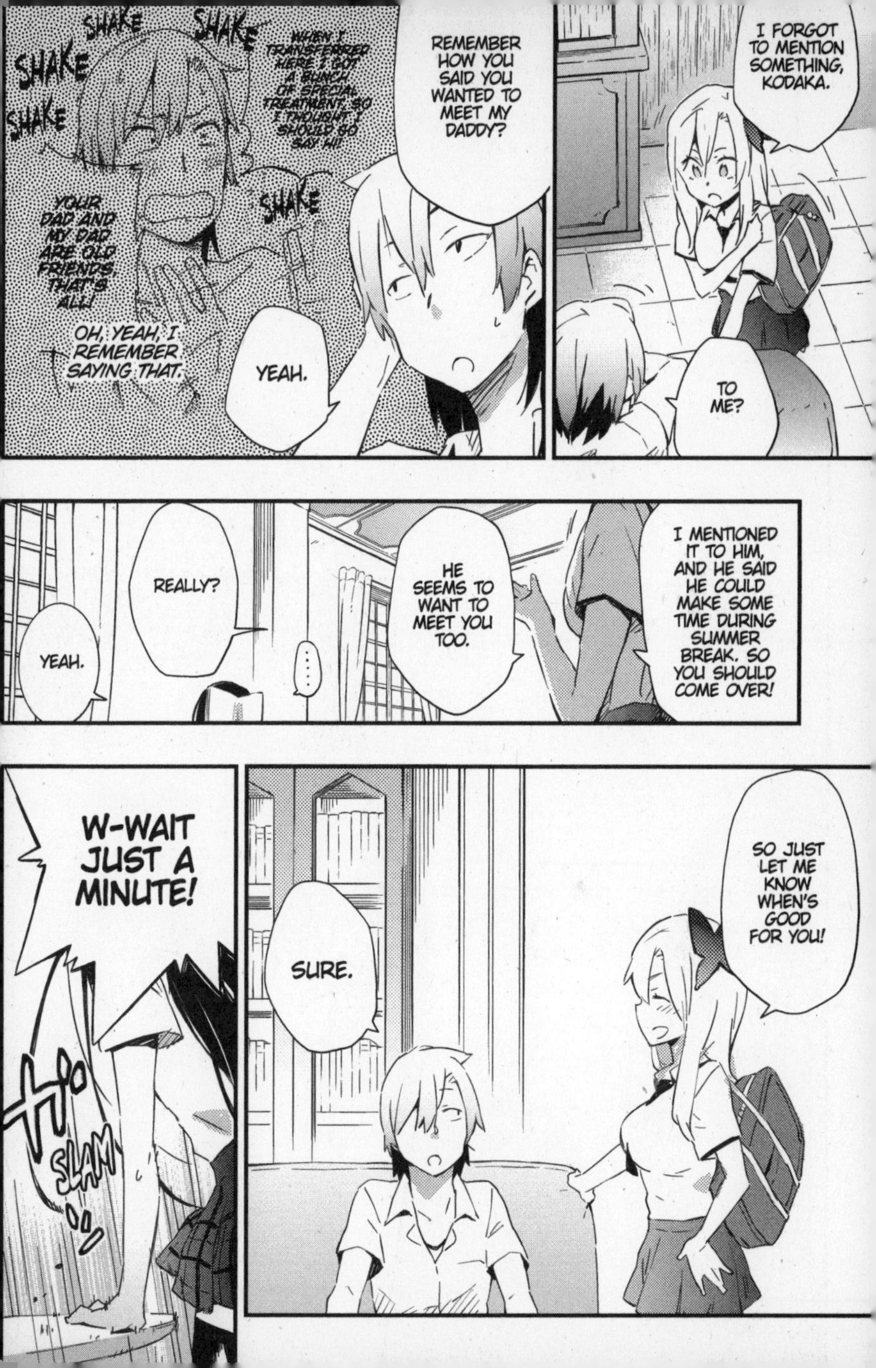
I FORGOT TO MENTION SOMETHING, KODAKA.
TO ME?
REMEMBER HOW YOU SAID YOU WANTED TO MEET MY DADDY?
YEAH.
SHAKE SHAKE SHAKE SHAKE SHAKE
WHEN I TRANSFERRED HERE I GOT A BUNCH OF SPECIAL TREATMENT, SO I THOUGHT I SHOULD GO SAY HI!
YOUR DAD AND MY DAD ARE OLD FRIENDS, THAT'S ALL!
OH, YEAH, I REMEMBER SAYING THAT.
I MENTIONED IT TO HIM, AND HE SAID HE COULD MAKE SOME TIME DURING SUMMER BREAK. SO YOU SHOULD COME OVER!
HE SEEMS TO WANT TO MEET YOU TOO.
......
REALLY?
YEAH.
SO JUST LET ME KNOW WHEN'S GOOD FOR YOU!
SURE.
W-WAIT JUST A MINUTE!
SLAM

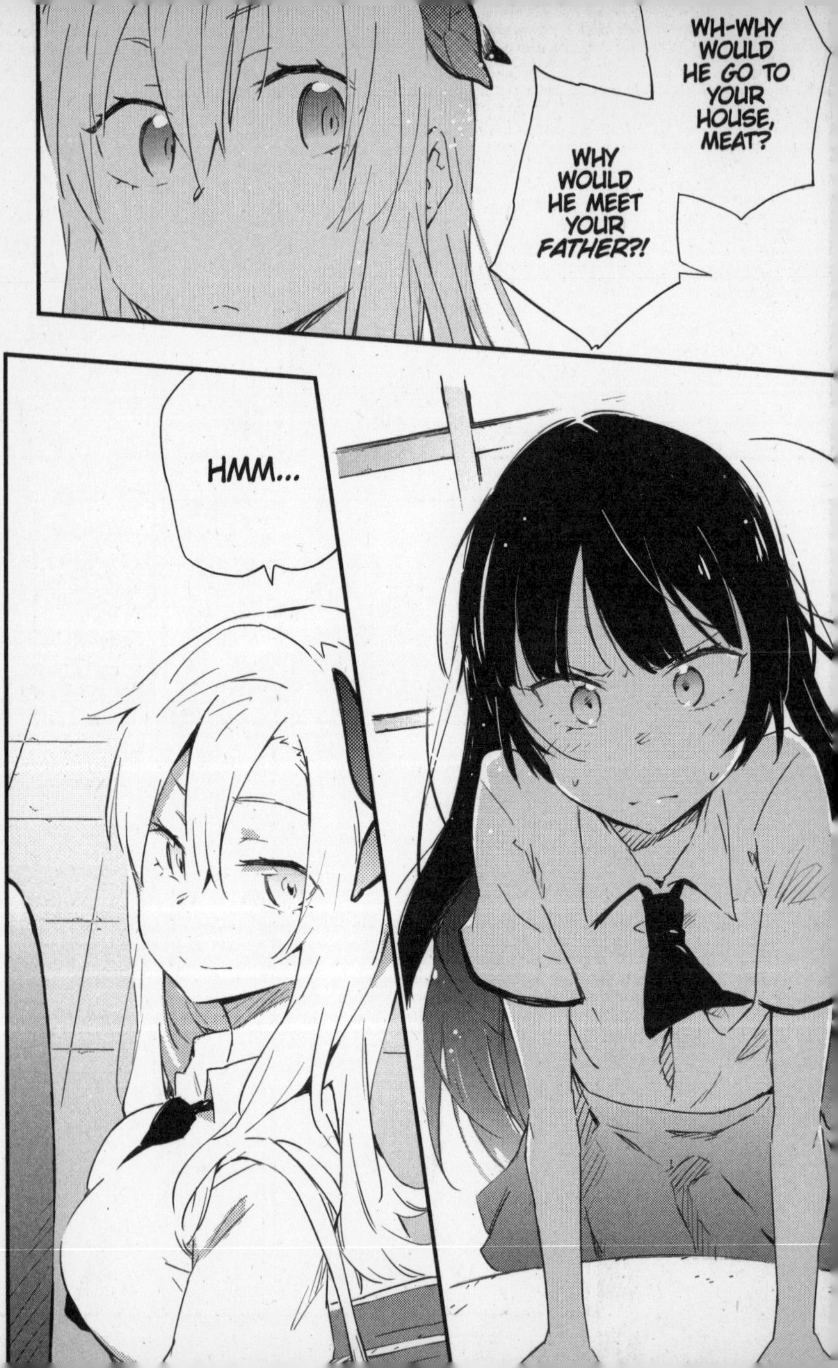
WH-WHY WOULD HE GO TO YOUR HOUSE, MEAT?
WHY WOULD HE MEET YOUR FATHER?!
HMM...

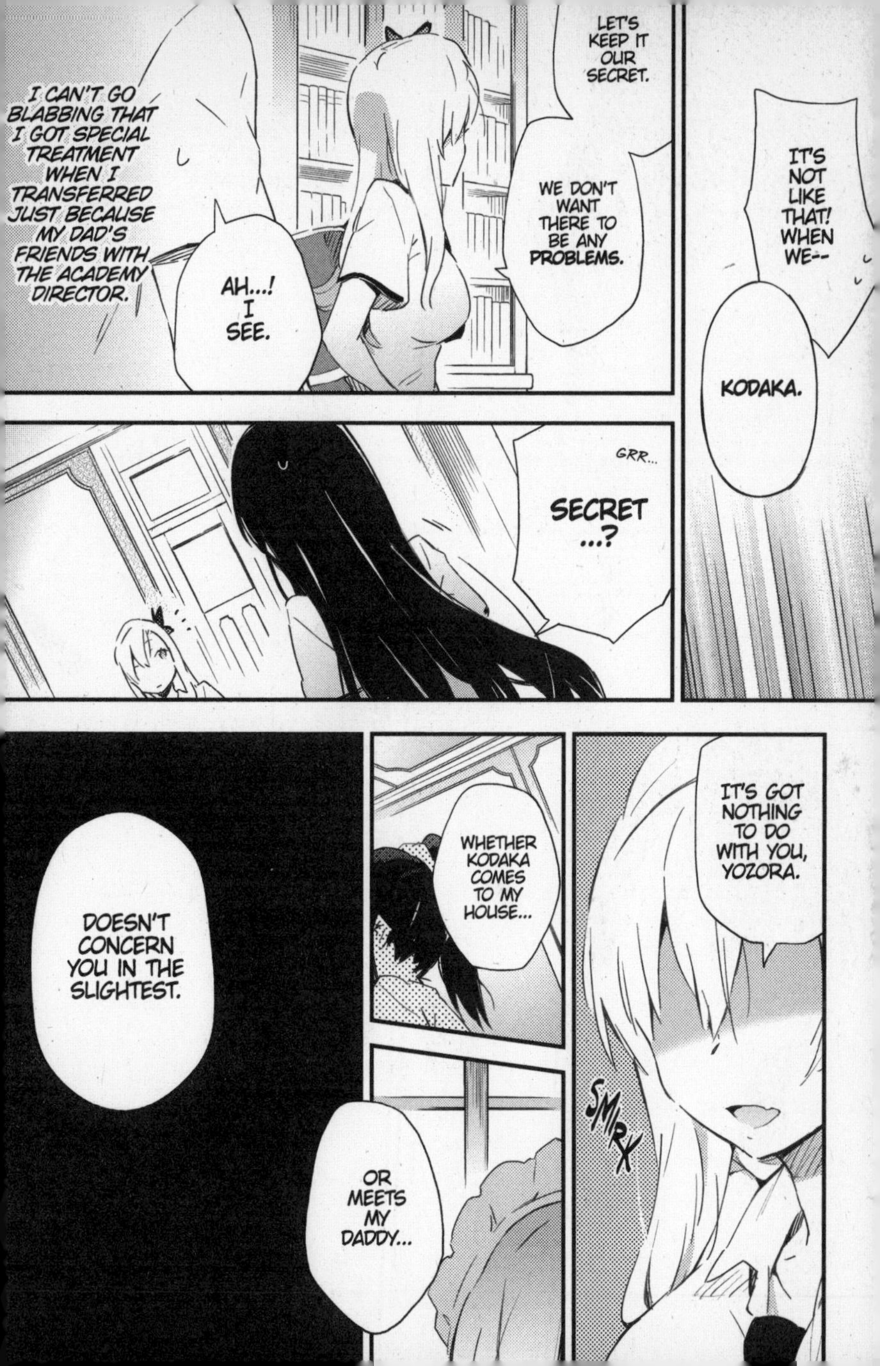
IT'S NOT LIKE THAT! WHEN WE--
KODAKA.
LET'S KEEP IT OUR SECRET.
WE DON'T WANT THERE TO BE ANY PROBLEMS.
AH...! I SEE.
I CAN'T GO BLABBING THAT I GOT SPECIAL TREATMENT WHEN I TRANSFERRED JUST BECAUSE MY DAD'S FRIENDS WITH THE ACADEMY DIRECTOR.
GRR...
SECRET ...?
IT'S GOT NOTHING TO DO WITH YOU, YOZORA.
SMIRK
WHETHER KODAKA COMES TO MY HOUSE...
OR MEETS MY DADDY...
DOESN'T CONCERN YOU IN THE SLIGHTEST.

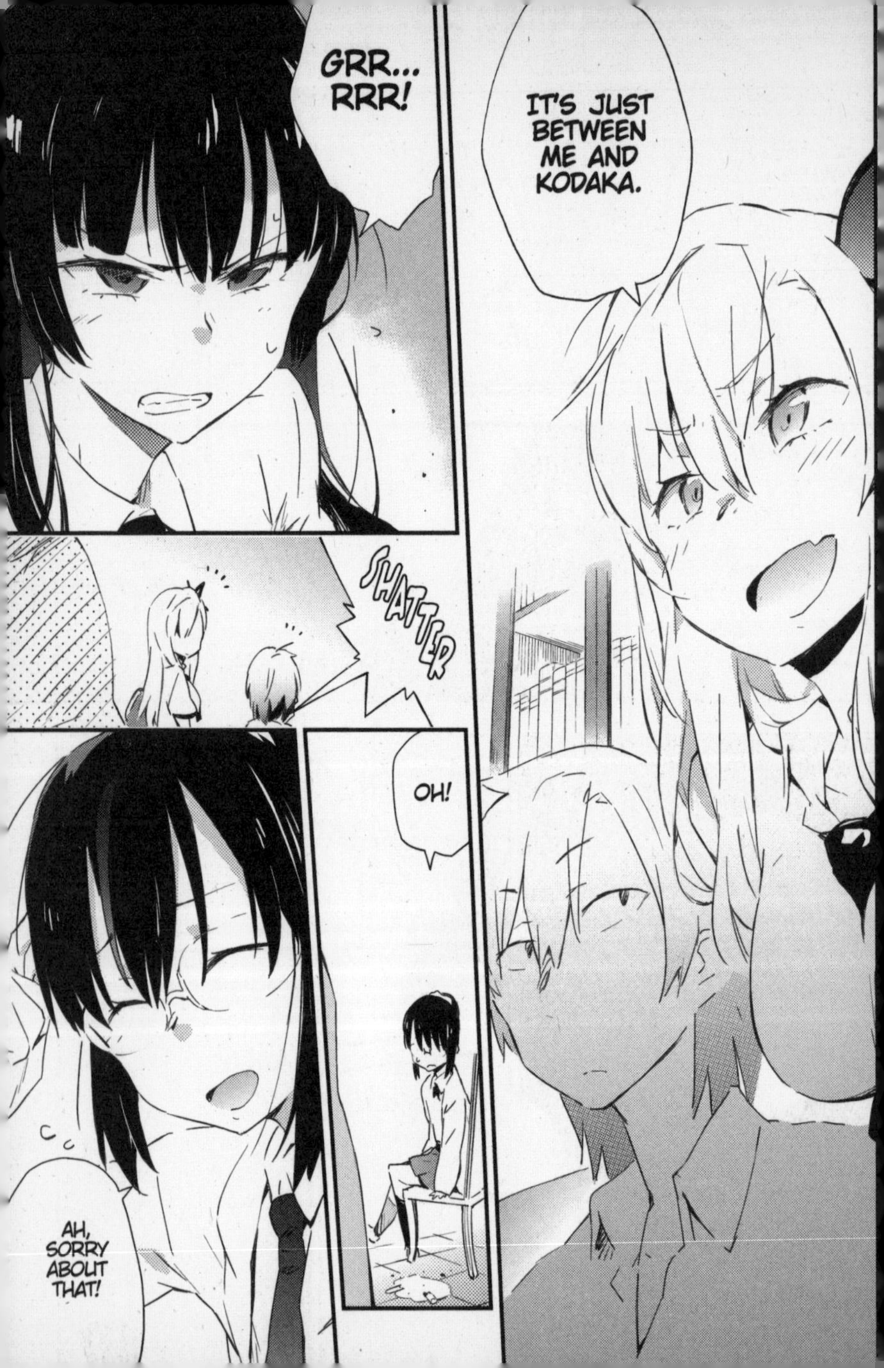
IT'S JUST BETWEEN ME AND KODAKA.
GRR... RRR!
SHATTER
OH!
AH, SORRY ABOUT THAT!

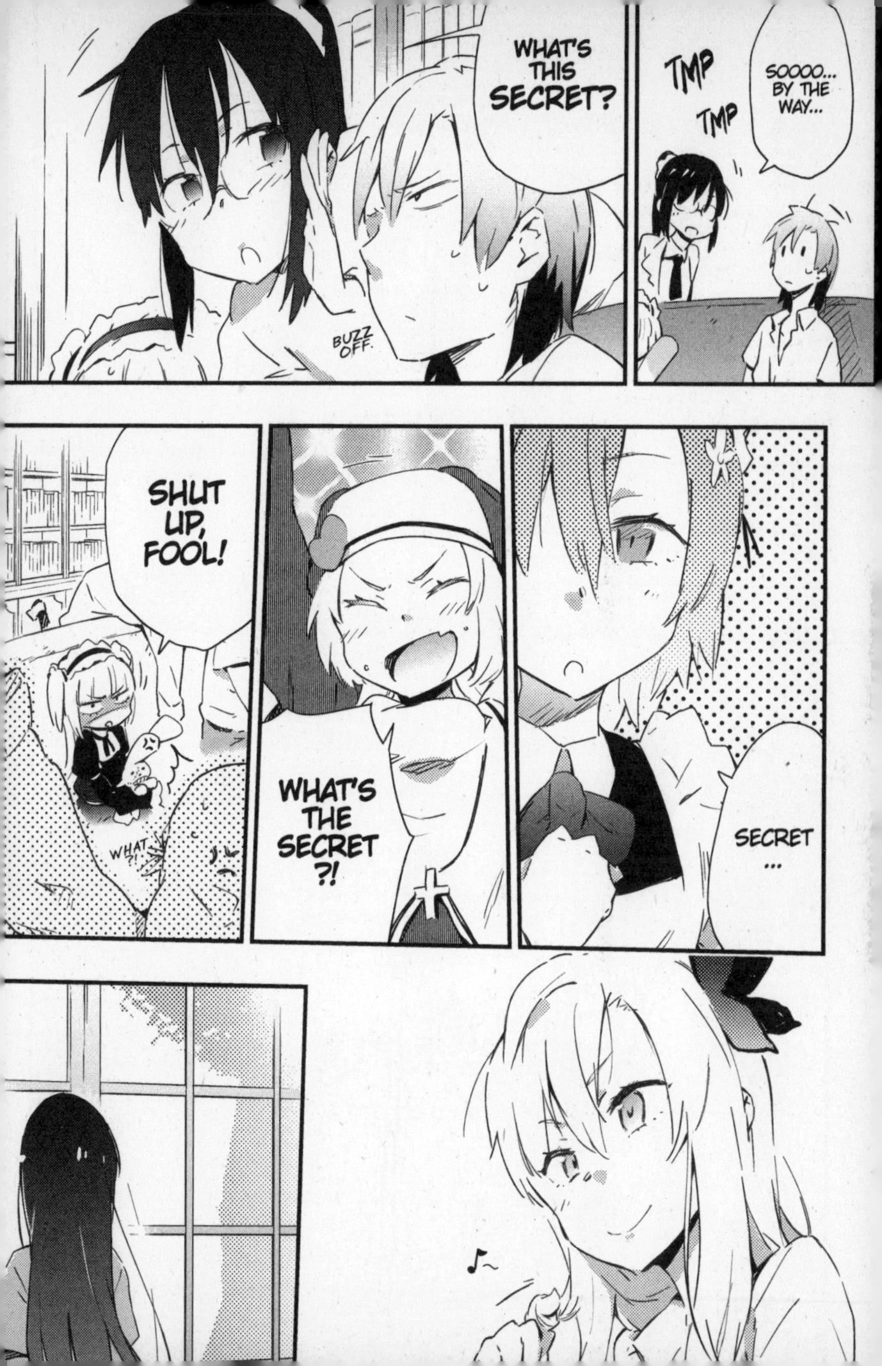
SOOOO... BY THE WAY...
TMP
TMP
WHAT'S THIS SECRET?
BUZZ OFF.
SECRET ...
WHAT'S THE SECRET ?!
SHUT UP, FOOL!
WHAT ?!
♪~

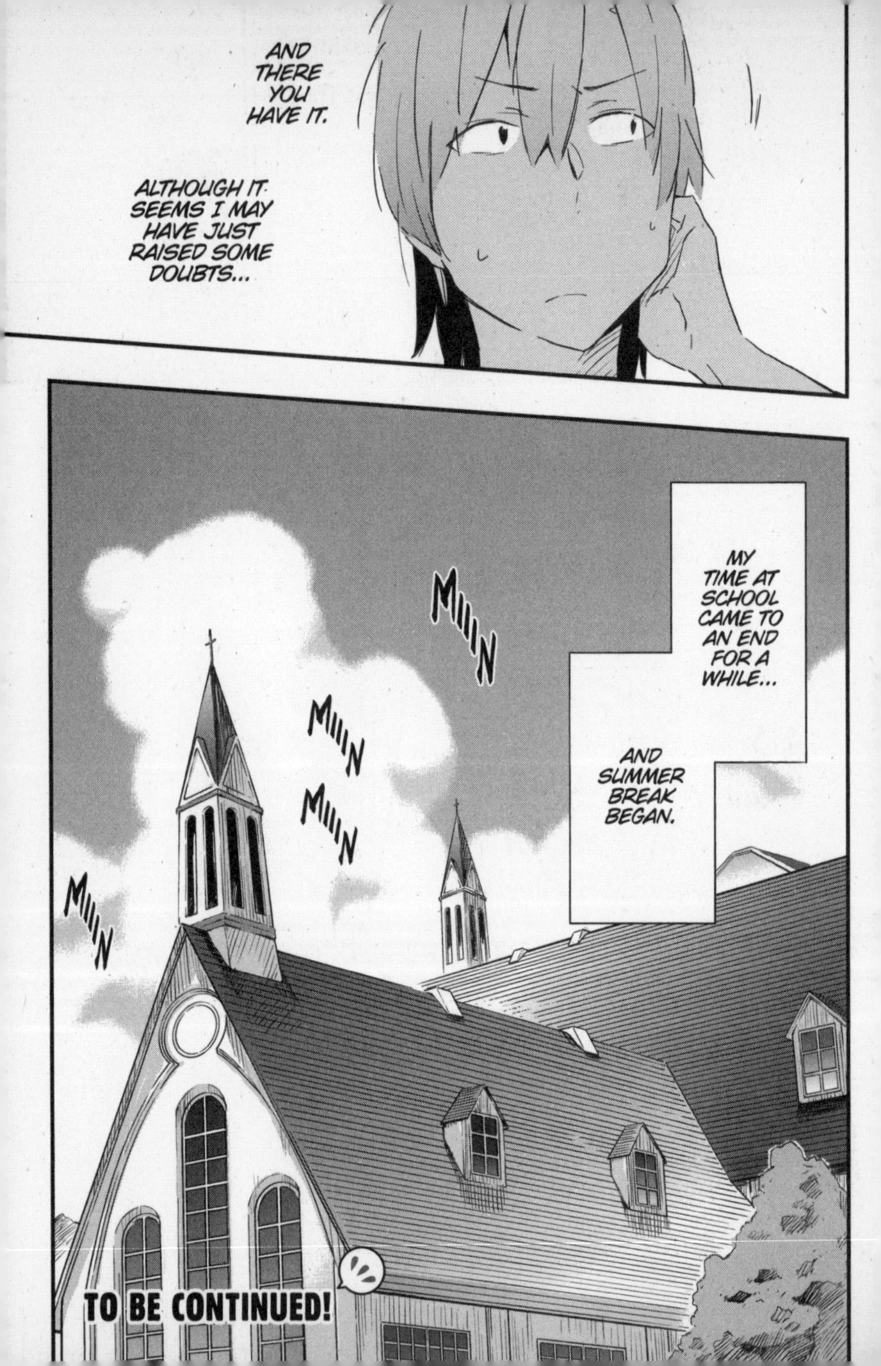
AND THERE YOU HAVE IT.
ALTHOUGH IT SEEMS I MAY HAVE JUST RAISED SOME DOUBTS...
MY TIME AT SCHOOL CAME TO AN END FOR A WHILE...
AND SUMMER BREAK BEGAN.
MIIIN
MIIIN
MIIIN
MIIIN
TO BE CONTINUED!

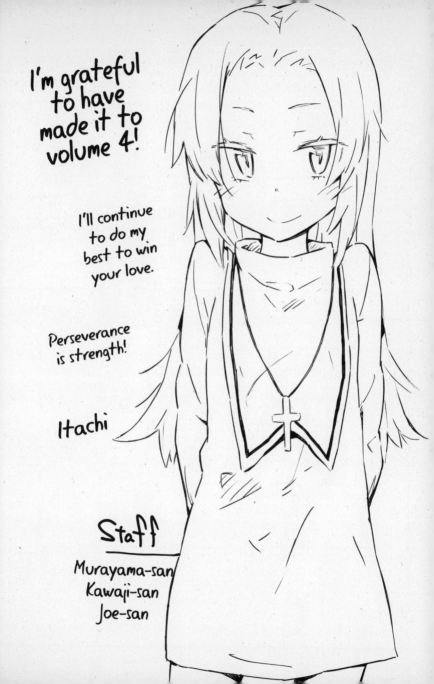

I'm grateful to have made it to volume 4!

I'll continue to do my best to win your love.

Perseverance is strength!

Itachi

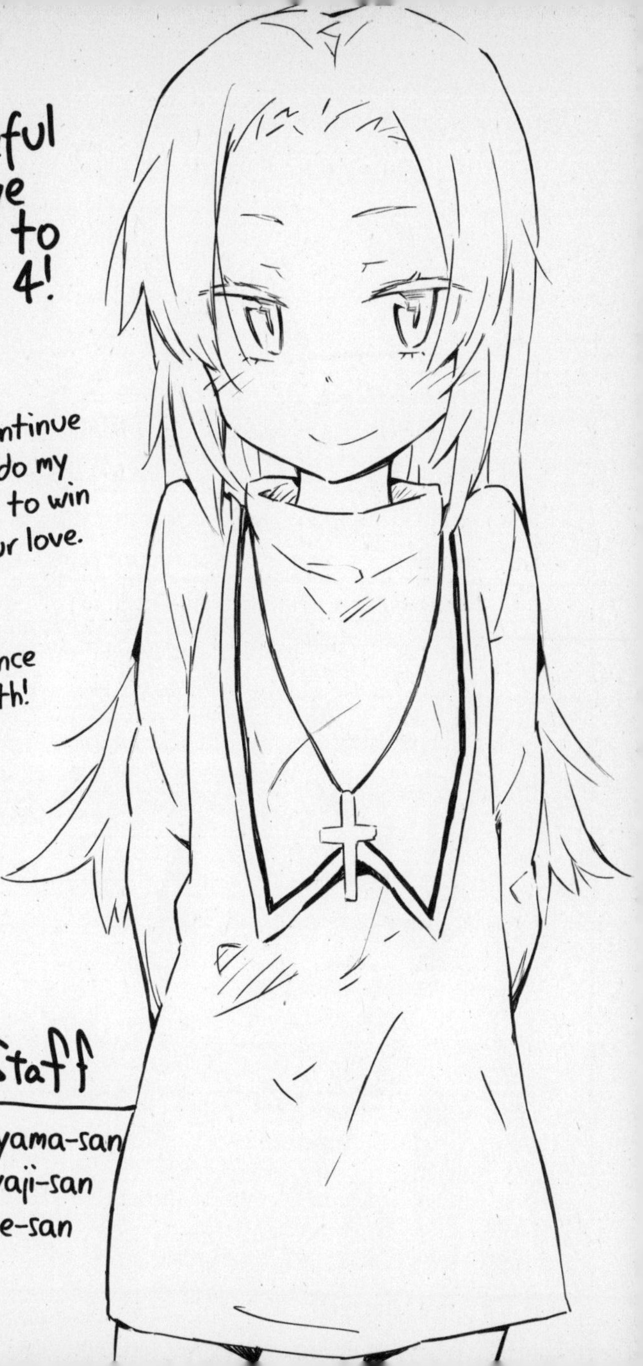

Staff

Murayama-san
Kawaji-san
Joe-san

This is Hirasaka, the original creator. Thank you for buying volume 4 of *Haganai: I Don't Have Many Friends!* This version perfectly replicates the feel and tempo, but in my mind the highlight of this volume was the round-robin story. To be honest, I didn't think that particular story would translate well into manga form, so I sincerely thank Itachi-san for making something that could surprise the original creator and make him laugh. Please continue to enjoy *Haganai!*

Yomi Hirasaka

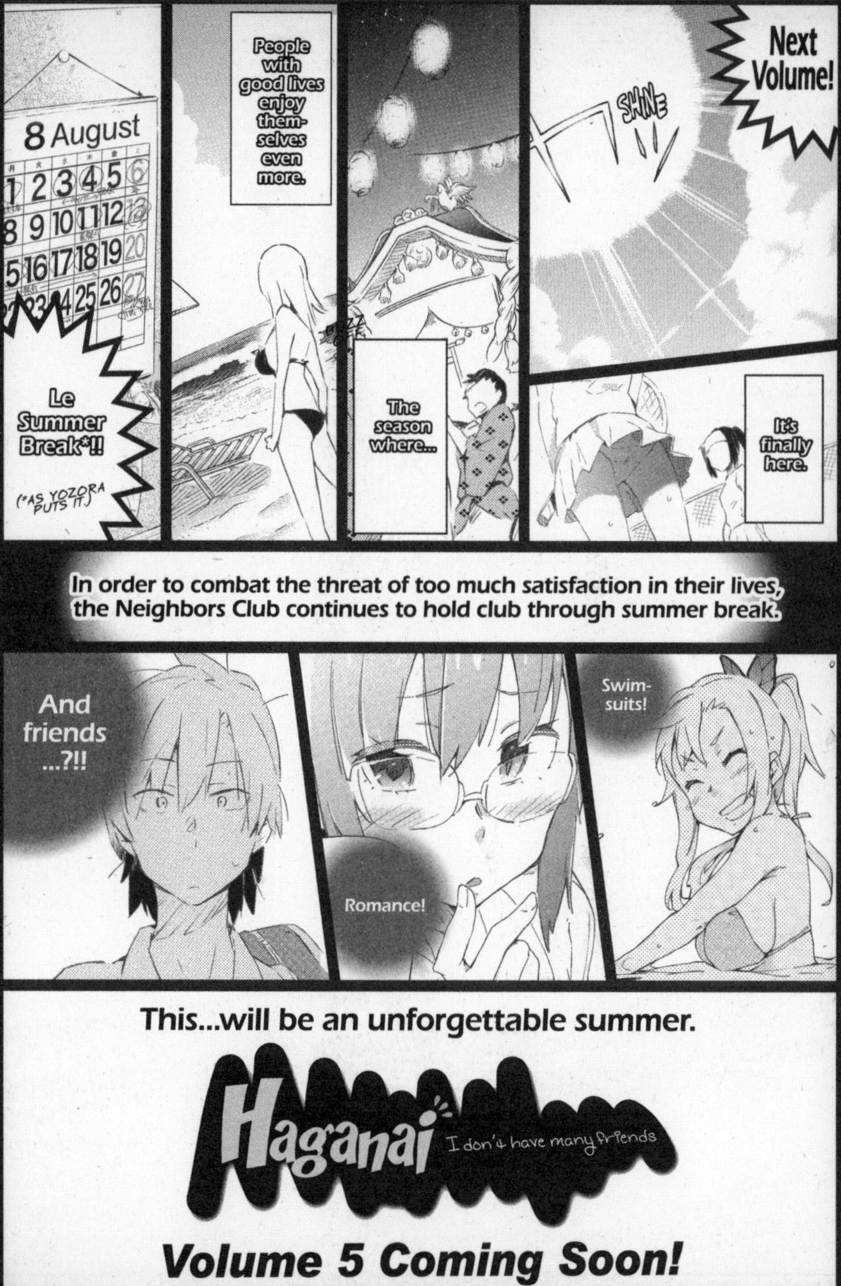
Next Volume!
SHINE
It's finally here.
The season where...
People with good lives enjoy them-selves even more.
8 August
Le Summer Break*!!
(*AS YOZORA PUTS IT.)
In order to combat the threat of too much satisfaction in their lives, the Neighbors Club continues to hold club through summer break.
Swim-suits!
Romance!
And friends ...?!!
This...will be an unforgettable summer.
Haganai
I don't have many friends
Volume 5 Coming Soon!

[Note: the images presented here are merely speculation. They may not actually reflect what is in the final product.]